Handbook of Behavior Therapy with Sexual Problems

Volume II — Approaches to Specific Problems

(pp. i-xxvi, 259-604)

PGPS-64

PERGAMON GENERAL PSYCHOLOGY SERIES

Editors: Arnold P. Goldstein, *Syracuse University*
Leonard Krasner, *SUNY, Stony Brook*

The terms of our inspection copy service apply to all the above books. A complete catalogue of all books in the Pergamon International Library is available on request.

The Publisher will be pleased to receive suggestions for revised editions and new titles.

Handbook of Behavior Therapy with Sexual Problems

Volume II
Approaches to Specific Problems

Joel Fischer, D.S.W.
and
Harvey L. Gochros, D.S.W.
University of Hawaii
Honolulu, Hawaii

PERGAMON PRESS
New York / Toronto / Oxford / Sydney / Frankfurt / Paris

Pergamon Press Offices:

U.S.A.   Pergamon Press Inc., Maxwell House, Fairview Park,
                  Elmsford, New York 10523, U.S.A.

U.K.   Pergamon Press Ltd., Headington Hill Hall, Oxford OX3,
                  OBW, England

CANADA   Pergamon of Canada, Ltd., 75 The East Mall,
                  Toronto, Ontario M8Z 5WR, Canada

AUSTRALIA   Pergamon Press (Aust) Pty. Ltd., 19a Boundary Street,
                  Rushcutters Bay, N.S.W. 2011, Australia

FRANCE   Pergamon Press SARL, 24 rue des Ecoles,
                  75240 Paris, Cedex 05, France

WEST GERMANY   Pergamon Press GmbH, 6242 Kronberg/Taunus,
                  Frankfurt-am-Main, West Germany

Library of Congress Cataloging in Publication Data

Main entry under title:

Handbook of behavior therapy with sexual problems.

(Pergamon general psychology series; 64)
Includes bibliographies and index.
1. Sexual disorders.   2. Sexual deviations.
3. Behavior therapy.   I. Fischer, Joel. II. Gochros;
Harvey L. (DNLM: 1. Sex deviation—Therapy.   2. Sexual
disorders—Therapy.   3. Behavior therapy. WM610 F529b
RC556.B37 1976   616.6   75-34411
ISBN 0-08-020373-6 Vol. I
ISBN 0-08-020374-4 Vol. II

Printed in the United States of America

This book is dedicated to the new breed of clinical scientists in the helping professions: the practitioner who is open to new ideas and practice methods, who carefully monitors his client's progress and evaluates outcome, and who takes the risk of critical analysis of his work by others through publication of his results in professional journals. All of our work—and the outcome for our clients—is enhanced by these efforts.

Contents

VOLUME I

VOLUME II

Preface

The main purpose of this Handbook is to provide a guide for practitioners who are attempting to alleviate the suffering associated with their clients' sexual problems. More specifically, we have attempted to provide descriptions of a range of behavioral techniques and the indications for their use with a wide range of sexual problems.

In order to accomplish this, we have divided this Handbook into two volumes. In Volume I, *General Procedures*, we presented a general Introduction in which we described the context for use of behavioral techniques, the role of behavior therapy in dealing with sexual problems, brief descriptions of most of the behavioral techniques, and some comments on the ethical implications of use of behavior therapy with sexual problems. The two parts of Volume I were devoted to general guidelines for use of behavior therapy with sexual problems and in-depth descriptions of the behavior therapy techniques that have been adapted or developed for use with sexual problems.

This volume — *Approaches to Specific Problems* — is organized in a manner congruent with Volume I, with Part 1 consisting of "Problems Involving Heterosexual Couple Relationships" and Part 2 dealing with "Problems Involving Undesired Sexual Object Choices." In distinction to Volume I which was focused on the techniques, per se, however, this volume is devoted largely to case studies illustrating the use of the variety of techniques as they are applied to specific sexual problems. Hence, several of the techniques—e.g., systematic desensitization or aversive conditioning—are illustrated in different contexts as they are used with different problems. The goal here is to provide for the reader concrete examples of technique utilization with a variety of problems. Thus, this material is intended to complement and extend through case illustrations the more general focus on techniques in Volume I.

Once again, we would like to express our deep appreciation to our colleagues for their work which is reprinted in these two volumes. We are also particularly grateful to Dr. Leonard P. Ullmann for writing the Foreword to this Handbook (the Foreword appears in Volume I). It is our hope that in some measure, this Handbook will have an impact on improving practitioners' skills as they work to enhance their clients' sexual functioning.

J.F.
H.L.G.
University of Hawaii
Honolulu, Hawaii

Acknowledgments—Volume II

The editors are grateful to the authors and publishers of the articles reprinted in this book for permission to reprint them. Following are the sources and publishers of the articles according to their Chapter in this volume, with the chapters in Volume II numbered sequentially to those in Volume I.

Chapter

25. "The Treatment of Impotence by Behavior Modification Techniques," *Journal of Sex Research,* 1973, **9**, 226-240.

26. "A Case of Impotence Successfully Treated with Desensitization Combined with *In Vivo* Operant Training and Thought Substitution," in Richard D. Rubin and Cyril M. Franks (eds.), *Advances in Behavior Therapy,* 1968. New York: Academic Press, 1969, Pp. 97-104.

3 "Treatment of Erectile Failure and Ejaculatory Incompetence of Homosexual Etiology," *Journal of Behavior Therapy and Experimental Psychiatry,* 1972, **3**, 233-236, Copyright 1972 by Pergamon Press.

28. "Two Case Reports on the Modification of the Ejaculatory Response with the Squeeze Technique," *Psychotherapy: Theory, Research and Practice,* 1973, **10**, 297-300, Copyright 1973.

29. "Ejaculatory Incompetence Treated by Deconditioning Anxiety," *Journal of Behavior Therapy and Experimental Psychiatry,* 1972, **3**, 65-67, Copyright 1973 by Pergamon Press.

30. "Group Treatment of Premature Ejaculation," *Archives of Sexual Behavior,* 1974, **3**, 443-452, Copyright 1974 by Plenum Publishing Co.

31. "Correcting Misconceptions in a Case of Frigidity: A Transcript," *Journal of Behavior Therapy and Experimental Psychiatry,* 1971, **2**, 251-258, Copyright 1971 by Pergamon Press.

32. "Case Conference: Conflict in a Case of Frigidity," *Journal of Behavior Therapy and Experimental Psychiatry,* 1971, **2**, 51-53, Copyright 1971 by Pergamon Press.

Pp. 239-242, Copyright 1965 by Holt, Rinehart and Winston. Reprinted by permission.

51. "Avoidance Therapy: Its Use in Two Cases of Underwear Fetishism," *Canadian Medical Association Journal,* 1967, **96**, 1160-1162.

52. " 'Aversive Imagery' Treatment in Adolescents," *Behaviour Research and Therapy,* 1967, **5**, 245-248, Copyright 1967 by Pergamon Press.

53. "Case Conference: A Transvestite Fantasy Treated by Thought-Stopping, Covert Sensitization and Aversive Shock," *Journal of Behavior Therapy and Experimental Psychiatry,* 1970, **1**, 153-161, Copyright 1970 by Pergamon Press.

54. "Treatment of Transvestism and Subsequent Coital Problems," *Journal of Behavior Therapy and Experimental Psychiatry,* 1974, **5**, 101, 102, Copyright 1974 by Pergamon Press.

55. "The Application of Learning Theory to the Treatment of a Case of Sexual Exhibitionism," *Psychotherapy: Theory, Research and Practice,* 1968, **5**, 108-112, Copyright 1968.

56. "Behavioral Treatment of An Exhibitionist," *Journal of Behavior Therapy and Experimental Psychiatry,* 1971, **2**, 61-66, Copyright 1971 by Pergamon Press.

57. "The Successful Application of Aversion Therapy to an Adolescent Exhibitionist," *Journal of Behavior Therapy and Experimental Psychiatry,* 1971, **2**, 61-66, Copyright 1971 by Pergamon Press.

58. "Reinforcement Control of Exhibitionism in a Profoundly Retarded Adult," *Proceedings, 81st Annual Convention,* A.P.A., 1973, Pp. 925, 926, Copyright 1973 by the American Psychological Association.

59. "Classical Conditioning of a Sexual Deviation: A Preliminary Note," *Behavior Therapy,* 1971, **2**, 400-402, Copyright 1971 by Academic Press.

60. "Case Conference: Assertive Training in a Case of Homosexual Pedophilia," *Journal of Behavior Therapy and Experimental Psychiatry,* 1972, **3**, 55-59, Copyright 1972 by Pergamon Press.

61. "Response-Contingent versus Fixed Punishment in Aversion Conditioning of Pedophilia: A Case Study," *Journal of Nervous and Mental Disease,* 1973, **156**, 440-443, Copyright 1973 by the Williams and Wilkins Co. Reproduced by permission.

62. "An Automated Fading Procedure to Alter Sexual Responsiveness in Pedophiles," *Journal of Homosexuality,* 1974/75, **1**, 149-163, Copyright 1974 by Haworth Press.

63. "Sadistic Fantasies Modified by Aversive Conditioning and Substitution: A Case Study," *Behaviour Research and Therapy,* 1966, **4**, 317-320, Copyright 1966 by Pergamon Press.

64. "Elimination of a Sadistic Fantasy by a Client-Controlled Counterconditioning Technique: A Case Study," *Journal of Abnormal Psychology,* 1968, **73**, 84-90, Copyright 1968 by the American Psychological Association.

65. "A Case of Voyeurism Treated by Counterconditioning," *Behaviour Research and Therapy,* 1969, **7**, 133, 134, Copyright 1969 by Pergamon Press.

66. "The Use of Aversion-Relief Procedures in the Treatment of a Case of Voyeurism," *Behavior Therapy*, 1971, **2**, 585-588. Copyright 1971 by Academic Press.
67. "A Case of Public Masturbation Treated by Operant Conditioning," *Journal of Child Psychology and Psychiatry*, 1968, **9**, 61-65, Copyright 1968 by Pergamon Press.
68. "The Treatment of a Sexually Inadequate Man," in Leonard P. Ullman and Leonard Krasner (eds.) *Case Studies in Behavior Modification.* New York: Holt, Rinehart and Winston, 1965. Pp. 243-245, Copyright 1965 by Holt, Rinehart and Winston. Reprinted by permission.
69. "Verbal Aversion Therapy with a Promiscuous Girl: Case Report," *Psychological Reports*, 1968, **22**, 795-796.
70. "Desensitization, Re-sensitization and Desensitization Again: A Preliminary Study," *Journal of Behavior Therapy and Experimental Psychiatry*, 1970, **1**, 257-262, Copyright 1970 by Pergamon Press.
71. "A Case of Pseudonecrophilia Treated by Behavior Therapy," *Journal of Clinical Psychology*, 1968, **24**, Pp. 113-115.
72. "Treatment of the Housebound Housewife Syndrome," *Psychotherapy and Psychosomatics*, 1967, **15**, 446-453, Copyright 1967 by Karger, Basel.
73. "Reducing Masturbatory Guilt," *Journal of Behavior Therapy and Experimental Psychiatry*, 1975, **6**, 260-261, Copyright 1975 by Pergamon Press.
74. "Behavior Therapy In a Case of Multiple Sexual Disorders," *Journal of Behavior Therapy and Experimental Psychiatry*, 1975, **5**, 171-174, Copyright 1974 by Pergamon Press.
75. "Conditioning Appropriate Heterosexual Behavior in Mentally and Socially Handicapped Populations," *Training School Bulletin*, 1970, **66**, 172-177.

Contributors — Volume II

AGRAS, W. STEWART, M.D., Department of Psychiatry and Behavioral Sciences, Stanford University Medical School, Stanford, California.

ANANT, SANTOKH S., Ph.D., Department of Psychology, University of Lethbridge, Lethbridge, Alberta, Canada.

BARLOW, DAVID H., Ph.D., Professor of Psychiatry, Brown University and Butler Hospital, Providence, Rhode Island.

BEECH, H.R., Ph.D., Consultant Psychologist, Withington Hospital, Manchester, U.K.

BELLACK, ALAN S., Ph.D., Department of Psychology, University of Pittsburgh, Pittsburgh, Pennsylvania.

BIRTLES, C.J., University of Birmingham, Birmingham, U.K.

BLITCH, JOSEPH W., Ph.D., Psychological and Psychiatric Services Center, Charleston, South Carolina.

BOND, I.K., L.R.C.P., L.R.C.S., L.F.P.S., F.R.C.P., Medical Director, Lakeshore Psychiatric Hospital, Toronto, Ontario, Canada.

CARR, JOHN E., Ph.D., Professor of Psychiatry and Behavioral Sciences, and Psychology, University of Washington, Seattle, Washington.

COOPER, ALAN J., M.D., Senior Lecturer in Psychiatry, St. Mary's Hospital Medical School, London, U.K.

CURTIS, R.H., M.A., Dip. Psych., Senior Clinical Psychologist, Department of Clinical Psychology, Birch Hill Hospital, Rochdale, Lancs, England.

DAVISON, GERALD C., Ph.D., Professor of Psychology and Psychiatry, State University of New York at Stony Brook, Stony Brook, New York.

DICHTER, MARVIN, Ph.D., Eagleville Hospital and Rehabilitation Center, Eagleville, Pennsylvania.

DUEHN, WAYNE D., Ph.D., Professor of Social Work, University of Texas, Arlington, Texas.

EDWARDS, NEIL B., M.D., Department of Psychiatry, Temple University, Philadelphia, Pennsylvania.

EVANS, D.R., Lakeshore Psychiatric Hospital, Toronto, Ontario, Canada.

FELDMAN, M.P., Ph.D., Reader in Clinical Psychology, University of Birmingham, U.K.

FREEMAN, WILLIAM, Ph.D., Kentucky Reception Center, Louisville, Kentucky.

GARFIELD, ZALMON H., Ph.D., Licensed Psychologist, San Francisco, California.

GAUPP, LARRY A., Ph.D., Chief, Psychology Service, Brooke Army Medical Center, Ft. Sam Houston, Texas.

GEORGE, FREDERICK S., Ph.D., Private Practice, Enterprise, Alabama.

GERSHMAN, LOUIS, Ph.D., Professor of Psychology, Villanova University, Villanova, Pennsylvania.

GOLDSTEIN, ALAN, Ph.D., Associate Professor and Director of Sex Therapy and Research Center, Department of Psychiatry, Temple University Medical School, Philadelphia, Pennsylvania.

HASLAM, M.T., M.A., M.D., M.T.C.P., M.R.C. Psych., Consultant in Psychological Medicine, York, U.K.

HAYNES, STEPHEN N., Ph.D., Department of Psychology, University of South Carolina, Columbia, South Carolina.

HERMAN, STEVEN H., Ph.D., Psychology Service, Miami Veterans Administration Hospital, Miami, Florida.

HOGAN, BARBARA, M.A., Research Assistant in Psychiatry, Cornell University Medical College, New York, New York.

HUFF, FREDERICK W., Ph.D., Clinical Psychologist, Center for Interpersonal Studies, P.A., Smyro, Georgia.

JACKSON, B.T., Ontario Hospital, Whitby, Ontario, Canada.

KAPLAN, HELEN S., M.D., Ph.D., Clinical Associate Professor of Psychiatry, Cornell University Medical College; Head, Sex Therapy and Education Program, Payne Whitney Psychiatric Clinic of the New York Hospital, New York, New York.

KEIL, WILLIAM E., Ph.D., Victoria Hospital, Ontario, Canada.

KOHL, RICHARD N., M.D., Professor of Psychiatry, Cornell University Medical College; Medical Director, Payne Whitney Psychiatric Clinic of the New York Hospital, New York, New York.

KOHLENBERG, ROBERT J., Ph.D., Department of Psychology, University of Washington, Seattle, Washington.

KOLVIN, ISRAEL, M.D., F.R.C. Psych., Dip. Psych., Reader in Child Psychiatry, University of Newcastle, Director, Human Development Unit, Newcastle, U.K.

KRAFT, TOM, M.B., M.R.C. Psych., D.P.M., Private Practice, London, U.K.

KUSHNER, MALCOLM, Ph.D., Private Practice, Miami, Florida.

LAMBLEY, PETER, Ph.D., Psychological Research Associates, Capetown, South America.

LAWS, D.R., Ph.D., Director, Sexual Behavior Laboratory, Atascadero State Hospital, Atascadero, California.

LAZARUS, ARNOLD, A., Ph.D., Professor, Graduate School of Applied and Professional Psychology, Rutgers University, New Brunswick, New Jersey.

LOPICCOLO, JOSEPH, Ph.D., Associate Professor of Psychiatry, School of Medicine, State University of New York, Stony Brook, New York.

LOPICCOLO, LESLIE, M.S., Department of Psychiatry and Behavioral Science, State University of New York, Stony Brook, New York.

LUTZKER, JOHN R., Ph.D., Department of Psychology, University of the Pacific, Stockton, California.

MacCULLOCH, M.J., M.D., Principal Medical Officer (Psychiatry) Department of Health and Social Security, London, U.K.

MADSEN, CHARLES H., JR., Ph.D., Department of Psychology, Florida State University, Tallahassee, Florida.

MALETZKY, BARRY M., M.D., Director of Research, Woodland Park Mental Health Center, Portland, Oregon, and Assistant Clinical Professor, University of Oregon Medical School.

MARSHALL, W.L., Ph.D., Queen's University, Kingston, Ontario, Canada.

MAYADAS, NAZNEEN S., D.S.W., Professor of Social Work, University of Texas, Arlington, Texas.

McBREARTY, JOHN F., Ph.D., Professor of Psychology, Temple University, Philadelphia, Pennsylvania.

MEES, HAYDEN L., Ph.D., Department of Psychology, Western Washington State College, Bellingham, Washington.

MEYER, ROBERT G., Ph.D., Department of Psychology, University of Louisville, Louisville, Kentucky.

OFFIT, AVODAH K., M.D., Clinical Instructor in Psychiatry, Cornell University Medical College, New York, New York.

PAWLOWSKI, A.V., Universal Engineered Systems, Pleasanton, California.

POMEROY, WARDELL B., Ph.D., Clinical Associate Professor of Psychology in Psychiatry, Cornell University Medical College, New York, New York.

POOLE, A. DESMOND, Trinity College, Dublin, Ireland.

PRESLY, ALLAN S., M.A., Ph.D., Dip. Psych., Principal Psychologist, Dundee Liff Hospital, Scotland.

RATLIFF, RICHARD G., Ph.D., Department of Psychology, University of Colorado, Boulder, Colorado.

RAZANI, JAVAD, Department of Psychiatry, Temple University Health Sciences Center, Philadelphia, Pennsylvania.

REHM, LYNN P., Ph.D., Department of Psychology, University of Pittsburgh, Pittsburgh, Pennsylvania.

REITZ, WILLARD E., Ph.D., Mayview State Hospital, Bridgeville, Pennsylvania.

ROSEN, MARVIN, Ph.D., Director of Psychology, Elwyn Institute, Media, Pennsylvania.

ROSENTHAL, TED L., Ph.D., Memphis State University, Memphis, Tennessee.

ROZENSKY, RONALD H., Ph.D., Department of Psychology, University of Pittsburgh, Pittsburgh, Pennsylvania.

SHUSTERMAN, LISA ROSEMAN, Ph.D., Department of Psychology, Northwestern University, Evanston, Illinois.

SNYDER, ARDEN L., Ph.D., Private Practice, George Kjaer, M.D.P.C., Eugene, Oregon.

STERN, ROBERT M., Ph.D., Psychology Department, Pennsylvania State University, University Park, Pennsylvania.

STEWART, RITA, Ph.D., University of Oregon, Eugene, Oregon.

TANNER, BARRY A., Ph.D., Northeast Guidance Center, Detroit, Michigan.

ULLMANN, LEONARD P., Ph.D., Professor, Department of Psychology, University of Hawaii, Honolulu, Hawaii.

WAGNER, MERVYN L., Ph.D., Department of Psychology, University of South Carolina, Columbia, South Carolina.

WATKINS, BRUCE, Ph.D., Psychology Clinic, University of Oregon, Eugene, Oregon.

WATTS, FRASER, Ph.D., Psychology Department, Institute of Psychiatry, University of London, London, U.K.

WICKRAMASEKERA, IAN, Ph.D., Assistant Professor of Psychiatry, University of Illinois, College of Medicine, Peoria, Illinois.

WILLIAMS, C., University of Birmingham, Birmingham, U.K.

WILSON, G. TERENCE, Ph.D., Associate Professor, Graduate School of Applied and Professional Psychology, Rutgers University, New Brunswick, New Jersey.

WOLPE, JOSEPH, M.D., Professor of Psychiatry, Temple University, School of Medicine and Eastern Pennsylvania Psychiatric Institute, Philadelphia, Pennsylvania.

Introduction

The articles in this volume are organized according to a variety of types of sexual problems. Most of the articles are case studies illustrating successful treatment approaches to these problems. All of the articles in this volume are intended to illustrate and complement the material in Volume I which was focused on general assessment and treatment guidelines, and the treatment programs and techniques, per se, that form the basis for the behavior therapy approach to dysfunctional sexual behavior.

Part I illustrates approaches to the problems often encountered by men and women in heterosexual intercourse. For men, the two major areas included are problems with achieving or maintaining erections during sexual activities and problems associated with ejaculation. The problem areas covered for women are problems in orgasmic functioning and problems of painful or difficult intercourse.

All the problems in these sections focus on problems experienced in the context of genital intercourse. It could be argued that such an emphasis on physical responses to genital intercourse, such as orgasm and erection, reinforces a "performance" orientation to sexual activities. That is, couples who are preoccupied with such matters lose sight not only of emotional aspects of sexual relations, but also the wide range of tactile and other sensual components of sexual relations not directly related to coitus. Undue emphasis on the "plumbing" aspects of sexual relationships may, indeed, prevent enjoyment of sexual activities. The effective therapist of these sexual problems, therefore, must assess and work with all important aspects of the relationship of the couple.

However, it is not the intent of most behaviorists to ignore the interpersonal gestalt of sexual relationships, nor the importance of the expression of individuality and spontaneity. What therapists recognize, however, is that the common vicious circle of anxiety leading to lack of enjoyment in sexual activities leading to orgasmic or erectile problems and sometimes pain, and, subsequently, more anxiety, must be broken somewhere. Once enjoyable physical functioning is restored, then the individual or the couple can better relax and learn together to more fully enjoy their sexual relationship.

The second major area of sexual problems described in Part 2 of this volume is that associated with undesired sexual object choices, i.e., sexual object choices which the client has identified as undesired and that he or she wishes to change. Included in this part are sections dealing with homosexual, fetishistic, cross-dressing, exhibitionistic, pedophiliac, sadomasochistic, voyeuristic and miscellaneous behaviors. Such behaviors generally are perceived as problems either because the individual engaging in these behaviors (such as fetishistic, cross-dressing, or homosexual behaviors) finds them incompatible with achieving other life goals, or the object of the individual's behavior (such as in situations of voyeuristic, exhibitionistic, or pedophiliac behaviors) objects or is endangered by the behavior.

In some instances, those who exhibit these behaviors are violating state and local laws as well as social, medical and religious mores. However, there are many individuals who live satisfying and productive lives who engage in some of these behaviors—in which there are no victims—with little or no problems except, perhaps, those imposed upon them by hostile elements in their environment. Further, over recent years, diverse sexual expressions have become more tolerated, if not fully accepted, by American society. Over a dozen states have removed legal penalties against any form of sexual activities between consenting adults. As another example of changing attitudes toward diverse forms of sexual expression, the American Psychiatric Association in December, 1973, by a vote of its members, removed "homosexuality" as a type of disease classified in its Diagnostic and Statistical Manual. According to the APA, those who engage in homosexual behavior now have a "condition," not a "disease."

Certainly there is a risk in inferring "problems" for those involved in atypical (and often not so atypical) sexual life styles. The effective therapist evaluates the total life situation of individuals exhibiting these behaviors in the context of their social environment before rushing into a behavioral change program.

Such an approach, of course, depends to a great degree on the therapist's own perception of atypical or different or dysfunctional sexual behavior patterns. There are still many therapists who perceive such patterns as forms of "pathology" or "diseases" to be "cured." Such attitudes are often revealed by the use of such traditional disease classifications and labels as "homosexual," or "deviant" or "impotent" or "frigid." Such terms do not allow for or reflect the wide diversity of behavioral patterns subsumed under the labels applied to the people engaging in these behaviors, and infer an inner disease process.

In this book, behaviorally-specific terms were used to delineate the several sections rather than labels describing disease entities. Unfortunately, many of the authors of the chapters did not elect to be behaviorally specific, and one wonders whether this perception of the problem behaviors encountered may in any way have affected their own therapeutic perceptions and behaviors. Thus, it appears that in many instances, behaviorists themselves have "deviated" from the behavioral perspective of use of behaviorally specific terms rather than labels. The labels "fetishist" or "exhibitionist" which imply that more is involved than engaging in certain sexual behaviors, tend to be demeaning and vague, and certainly not adequately descriptive of a total person in the context of his or her environment.

Each of the sections in this volume describes a particular potential problem area, such as cross-dressing behavior or ejaculatory problems. However, the separation of these sections does not imply that these problems (and other problems, both sexual or non-sexual) are mutually exclusive. It is conceivable to encounter a man who has problems with erection in his marriage, but also engages in exhibitionistic and pedophiliac behavior. In such cases, more than a single behavior may be the target of intervention. The assessment skills of the therapist along with the wishes and environmental contingencies of the client will then in such cases determine the sequence and emphasis of intervention.

As behavior therapy with sexual problems has evolved over the past fifteen years, it can be seen that an increasingly wider variety of techniques is being used to change undesired or problematic sexual behavior. For example, although use of physically aversive methods is fairly widespread, with some degree of success especially with problems highly refractory to other methods of change, experimentation has begun in the use of non-aversive methods with similar problems (e.g., the substitution of covert sensitization for electric shock). However, because of the range of sexual problems encountered by behaviorists, all techniques have not been applied to all problems. There does appear to be some justification for experimentation with a range of techniques, or for attempting to use a technique that has achieved success with one problem with other similar problems. Thus if covert sensitization can be demonstrated to be successfully applied in decreasing homosexual behavior in one or more instances, it would be logical to attempt to use this technique to decrease another form of undesired sexual behavior, say, exhibitionistic behavior. Thus, it is hoped that providing guidelines for a variety of techniques in this and Volume I also will lead to their experimental use with other problems.

Of course, as in all instances, appropriate use of any technique should be a product of a complete assessment by the clinician and logical selection of a technique that is designed to do a particular job (e.g., a technique designed to decrease behavior may be logically used to decrease a variety of undesired sexual behaviors, even if the evidence of its success is available with only one behavior).

Similarly, as mentioned in Volume I, many of the articles reveal a rather complicated use of instrumentation, e.g., shock devices or equipment to measure changes in penile responding as an objective indicator of sexual arousal. Again, it is likely that the future will see some diminishing in this use of equipment as a broader range of techniques becomes available, as data increase about alternative methods of intervention with equivalent effectiveness, and as indicators of success such as paper and pencil measures, subjective reports, and so on, that are cross validated against the more esoteric instrumentation, become more available. In both this and Volume I, however, the purpose is to present a broad cross-section of the procedures and instruments that behaviorally-oriented clinicians are using. It is hoped that this information will help the reader make intelligent selections from among the wide array of procedures available based on his own resources in interaction with the criteria of efficiency and effectiveness in helping clients resolve their sexual problems.

Part 1
Problems Involving Heterosexual Couple Relationships

Problems in Achieving or Maintaining Erection

Erection is a complicated and delicate physiological process. As such, it is easily interfered with by both physical and emotional stress. Failure to achieve erection, commonly called "impotence," can occur in a range of patterns: from individuals who never achieve erections under any circumstances ("primary impotence") to those men who from time to time do not achieve erection under particular situations, for example, when tired or angry with their wives ("secondary impotence"). In addition to varying in frequency, problems with erection may be a matter of degree or timing. For example, a man may achieve a firm erection but find that it loses some firmness just prior to intromission.

Since a problem in achieving or maintaining an erection is a very subjective condition, it is difficult to accurately estimate its incidence. Occasional inability to achieve or maintain an erection, however, is a very common situation occurring with the majority of men at some time or other, although in most cases, the problem is temporary and generally straightens itself out without the need for professional intervention. Yet its occurrence can create considerable anxiety. Since anxiety may be stronger than and, hence, overcome sexual arousal, the fear of having problems in achieving or maintaining an erection may tend to maintain the difficulty. The problem then resembles nothing so much as a vicious circle.

The label given to men experiencing difficulties associated with erection is "impotence." Being labeled "impotent" can be a humiliating and frightening experience since a wide variety of behaviors as described above have been subsumed under this rubric. It is at best, unclear, and at worst, a useless and potentially harmful label, hence, the behaviorally specific description in this book of what is typically called impotence, as, simply "problems in achieving or maintaining erections." Although up to 90% of erectile problems are related to psychological conditions such as performance anxiety, the fact that physical factors can play a role in a small percentage of these problems

261

suggests that examination by a physician prior to the beginning of behavioral intervention would not be unwarranted. Indeed, with all of the problems discussed in this book, a preliminary examination by a physician would be a sound guideline to follow before beginning behavioral intervention.

The first article, "The Treatment of Impotence by Behavior Modification Techniques," by Shusterman, could probably have been placed in either this, or the next, category (problems associated with ejaculation). However, since "impotence" typically is taken to refer to erectile problems, and since such problems constitute, as Shusterman notes, the vast majority of "impotence" cases, the article was included in the category dealing with erectile problems.

The article reviews the literature describing the range of problems considered to fall under the rubric "impotence," and presents a learning theory analysis of the causes of such problems. The article then reviews the behavior therapy procedures generally used to treat these dysfunctions. Most of these methods involve the attempt to desensitize the anxiety associated with the sexual act. Shusterman organizes her review around the following procedures: individual systematic desensitization with (self-induced) relaxation and assertive training in sexual behavior, individual desensitization with drugs, group desensitization with relaxation, the Masters and Johnson techniques, and miscellaneous techniques. Shusterman also notes that these techniques are often combined with others such as re-education, encouragement and so on, and the contribution of each of these to over-all success should be assessed through future research.

The next article, by Garfield, McBrearty and Dichter, describes "A Case of Impotence Successfully Treated with Desensitization Combined with *In Vivo* Operant Training and Thought Substitution." This detailed case study uses a "broad spectrum" approach combining respondent and operant procedures. The authors describe the novel use of desensitization to monitor and control overly rapid and premature efforts to complete the sexual act, as well as to reduce the anxiety related to inability to achieve satisfactory intercourse. The authors also utilize training in sexual assertiveness, and as an additional and innovative step, trained the client in thought-stopping and thought substitution with regard to an inhibiting preoccupation with his partner's orgasm.

The last article by LoPiccolo, Stewart and Watkins describes the "Treatment of Erectile Failure and Ejaculatory Incompetence of Homosexual Etiology." In this interesting case study, the clients' request was not to eliminate homosexual behavior, but to increase heterosexual arousal and functioning. The authors do this by utilizing a combination of procedures. *In vivo* desensitization was used to reduce performance anxiety. In addition to this, an arousal reconditioning procedure was used in which heterosexual stimuli were introduced at chosen times in the arousal induced by homosexual fantasies during masturbation and also during heterosexual activity. The homosexual arousal was later phased out of treatment. This case illustrates a flexible use of behavioral principles to fit individual situations. Interestingly, at the close of treatment, and at a six-month follow-up, the client rated himself as being substantially more satisfied than at the beginning of treatment with his sexual relationships to both women *and* men.

25
The Treatment of Impotence by Behavior Modification Techniques

LISA ROSEMAN SHUSTERMAN

Specific forms of sexual behavior, like most other behavior, are learned. In operant behavioristic terms, the learning process involves the rewards and punishments which follow performance of the behavior; those behaviors which are rewarded tend to occur more often, whereas those behaviors which are not rewarded tend to occur less often. Adequate sexual performance is intrinsically rewarding to an individual; he feels physical pleasure and receives approval from others. Due to our society's great emphasis on successful sexual behavior, and due to the perceived unpleasant bodily sensations of unsuccessful behavior, inadequate sexual performance is quite unpleasant to the suffering male. In many cases because the impotent male has experienced unpleasant consequences for his sexual behavior, he anxiously tries to perform adequately on subsequent occasions. Since the anxiety he feels may actually prevent further adequate sexual performance, the impotent man may not learn successful behavior.

In this review, male impotence is described briefly, the causes of male impotence are analyzed within a learning theory framework, and the techniques used to treat male impotence are presented. Male sexual impotence has been a successful candidate for treatment by behavior modification, specifically systematic desensitization, relaxation training and training in progressively intimate sexual behavior.

DESCRIPTION

A number of different sexual disorders typically are classified as impotence. In order to understand why they are considered inadequacies, it is necessary to see how they deviate from healthy male sexual performance. Masters and Johnson (1970) describe four stages of physiological changes during the male sexual response cycle: excitement, plateau, orgasm, and resolution. Impotence, then, is unsatisfactory performances in any of the first three stages of the response cycle. Such inadequacies include inability to attain an erection, semi-erection, unreasonably delayed erection, inability to sustain an erection following penetration of the female, failure to ejaculate, premature ejaculation, and general sexual apathy. Ejaculatory incompetence is very rare and erectile problems constitute the majority of impotence cases (Kinsey, 1948).

CAUSES OF IMPOTENCE

In most cases, individuals desiring therapy for impotence first seek medical advice from a physician. Although 95-99 percent of all impotence is caused by psychological rather than organic problems (Mirowitz, 1966), men who do not behave according to the cultural and/or self-ideal of the forever potent male typically do not want to accept that their problem is psychologically caused.

Physically caused impotence can be a result of anatomic abnormalities, neurologic diseases, systemic diseases, physical trauma, hormone deficiency or chemical imbalance (Roen, 1965). Treatment of these physical problems follows normal medical procedures. Often, however, medical treatments may be administered to men who have no organically based problem. Roen (1965) and Mirowitz (1966) found that injections of testosterone, prostatic massage and application of anaesthetic ointment, all commonly used "medical" treatments intended to increase potency and sexual drive, actually have no physical effect on sexual performance. Thus, impotent men with psychological disorders, i.e., the majority of men, who do improve as a result of such treatments may be demonstrating the powerful placebo effects of the procedures.

Within a learning theory framework, psychologically caused impotence can be seen as a result of early experiences of sexual inadequacy. For many impotent men, the first attempt at sexual intercourse was a failure in some way. Since failure is an unpleasant consequence of the attempted sexual behavior, the behavior itself acquires negative and unpleasant values to the individual. It may be that a man who has experienced an early sexual failure thereafter becomes extremely anxious to perform successfully, to "prove" himself. The anxiety he feels, then interrupts the bodily performance of the normal sexual response cycle on subsequent occasions. Due to the numerous repetitions of unsuccessful sexual behavior, a male can learn inadequate responses. The above is an operant explanation of the manner in which impotent behaviors are learned.

Ejaculatory Problems

An initial ejaculatory failure can be caused by a number of different factors. Caprio (1952), for example, stated that failure can occur from the interruption of the sexual act by a telephone ring, a knock on the door, fatigue or illness. In cases of premature ejaculation, Masters and Johnson (1970) found that for many impotent men the first sexual experience took place in a house of prostitution where the happiness of the male's partner was a function of the rapidity with which he ejaculated. For other men, fast ejaculation was necessary because the first (or first few) sexual experiences occured in semi-private places, like the back seat of a parked car or in a room where others were likely to enter. Sexually inadequate behavior can also result from alcoholic intoxication. Thus, a male might acquire premature ejaculation in common social situations, such as attempting sexual relations after a night of drinking.

Ejaculatory failure can result from fears associated with the sex act. The fears provide potential negative consequences for the act and may produce anxiety which interferes with adequate performance. Many men who are unable to ejaculate at all have histories of strict religious training that makes them anxious about sex. For example, Masters and Johnson (1970) report a case of a Catholic man who, at age thirteen, was caught masturbating by his mother and was sent to confession to receive pardon for his act. His priest told him that masturbation was a sin that could lead to mental illness and marital unhappiness. When he came for treatment, the man had been incapable of ejaculation for twenty-three years.

Fear of one's partner's pregnancy can also prevent ejaculation. When the fear of impregnation leads to a repeated practice of prolonging the plateau phase of the sexual response cycle for a long period of time, this too, may, as Apter (1965) found, lead to ejaculatory impotence.

Erectile Problems

Men with erectile problems often have had successful intercourse many times before they failed on an occasion that they highly valued. The failure to get an erection could come from fatigue, anxiety or illness. Subsequently, such men were unable to attain or maintain an erection in either all sexual situations or in situations that became associated with the failure experience.

The typical history of men with erectile problems is somewhat different from the history of those with ejaculatory problems. Masters and Johnson (1970) report cases of early mother-son manipulation to ejaculation, of severe sexual restrictions placed on a male adolescent by his parents, or sexual abstinence due to strict religious upbringing, and of teenage homosexual experience. However, Masters and Johnson also state that "we really have no concept of the specific psychodynamic factors that render the young man failing in his first coital connection susceptible to continuing failure at sexual performance."

TREATMENT OF IMPOTENCE

The treatment of male impotence by behavior modification has involved a small number of techniques. Most of the methods employ some kind of desensitization to the anxieties associated with the sexual act, relaxation during sex, and/or training in assertive sexual responses.

Individual Desensitization with Relaxation

Wolpe (1958) was one of the first therapists to use behavior modification methods for the treatment of impotence. His treatment, systematic desensitization, is based on the principle of counterconditioning. It is theorized that the avoidance behavior is mediated by anxiety one feels to a stimulus. In the process of the treatment, the patient is taught to make a response occur that is "antagonistic to anxiety ... in the presence of anxiety-evoking stimuli so that (the response) is accompanied by a complete or partial suppression of anxiety responses, (and) the bond between the stimuli and anxiety responses (is) weakened" (Wolpe, 1958, p. 71). Since anxiety can affect the body on a physiological level, it seems probable that it could interfere with performance of a healthy sexual response cycle which involves complex bodily changes.

Briefly, in Wolpe's method, the therapist first collects a general history of the patient's difficulties. He explains principles of learning theory to the patient in terms of how it might relate to the patient's problem, and he also trains the patient to relax himself by the Jacobson relaxation method. The therapist then tries to identify a theme common to all (or a group) of stimuli that evoke anxiety in the patient. The patient ranks these stimuli in order of the increasing amount of anxiety-producing property in each stimulus. In a number of sessions, the therapist instructs the patient to imagine these stimuli while at the same time he relaxes his body. According to Wolpe's theory, relaxation will eventually inhibit the anxiety. (Recently, others have suggested cognitive and social factors, as opposed to or in addition to the counterconditioning factor, as the effective components of systematic desensitization (Leitenberg et al., 1969; Oliveau et al., 1969; Murray & Jacobson, 1971; Wilkins, 1971).

Of the three cases of male impotence that Wolpe (1958) described, it was necessary to use the complete systematic desensitization process (i.e., relaxation to imagined stimuli) with only one patient. The patient had experienced typical sexual encounters as a teenager until he was nineteen years old. At this age he dated a girl to whom he felt strong sexual attraction, but she refused to have intercourse with him for a long period of time. The first occasion when she agreed, he was unable to maintain an erection. The relationship ended unpleasantly but erectile impotence continued. The patient also disclosed that, when he was twelve years old, he heard his parents have sexual intercourse. Hearing his mother scream led him to believe that coitus was painful. Fear of pain was the theme common to situations in which he felt anxiety.

Wolpe (1958) and the patient constructed three hierarchies of threatening stimuli to which the patient was to desensitize himself. They were: 1) "vocal violence," ranging from a "child being shouted at" to a "quarrel in his family," 2) "vocalization of suffering," ranging from "a kicked dog howling" to "an unseen hospital patient groaning" and 3) "injury and suffering," ranging from "a schoolboy being caned" to the "idea of the uterus being scraped" (Wolpe, 1958, p. 155-156). According to the self-report of the patient, as he was able to suppress his anxiety to the imagined scenes, he felt less anxious in concommitant life situations. His sexual performance improved. Although there may be some reason to question the accuracy of a self-report, there are few other ways that the outcome of treatment can be evaluated when impotence is the problem.

In the other two cases that Wolpe (1958) reported, the treatment consisted primarily of inhibiting anxiety by relaxation and training in assertive sexual responses during sex play. Systematic desensitization to imagined scenes was not necessary. In one of these cases, failure to maintain an erection and occasions of premature ejaculation was the problem. A physician previously had been unsuccessful in treating the impotence by testosterone injections and other procedures. The patient said that he felt anxious in sexual situations because he feared he would not achieve an erection. Wolpe did not provide a detailed history of the patient nor any theme of anxiety that would have caused him to develop the fear of failure.

Wolpe treated the fear of failure directly. First, he discussed with the patient the physiological processes involved in sexual behavior, and the effect that anxiety might have on inhibiting erection or causing premature ejaculation. (Others, including Masters & Johnson, 1970, and Kinsey, 1948, have also reported that impotent men often hold a variety of myths about the physical processes of sexual behavior.) The treatment for Wolpe's patient included instructions to relax while lying nude in bed with his wife, to engage in foreplay and stimulation of the body, and to attempt coitus only if the patient felt an "unequivocal positive impulse" to do so. The patient was having successful intercourse within a week and reported being "satisfied" in a six-month follow-up.

Wolpe's (1958) other case was treated similarly. The patient had a problem of premature ejaculation. He also was taught to relax himself, and was told to engage in mild caressing until he felt impelled to engage in heavy petting. He was to try to have intercourse only when he was absolutely certain that he wanted to. Within a short time, he, too, recovered.

In contrast to the above two cases, most of the other studies that utilize the systematic desensitization technique do include the hierarchy of anxiety-evoking stimuli, not relaxation alone. Lazarus (1965), for example, reported the successful treatment of a 33-year-old engineer by the traditional desensitization method. As a growing child, the patient's mother constantly had preached to him the virtues of chastity and the evils of promiscuity. She had told him that masturbation led to insanity. Also, as a student in boarding school, the patient had "taught himself to masturbate without an erection" so that he would not be teased by his schoolmates if he were discovered. At age 33, he was impotent and felt very haughty and superior toward women.

Lazarus's therapy for the patient took the form of systematic desensitization to anxiety-evoking stimuli by relaxation, and assertive training in the sexual situation. His anxiety clustered around four themes for which the following hierarchies were established: "1) a sexual situation requiring increasing initiative, that is, embracing, kissing, fondling, undressing . . .; 2) expressing disapproval a) to a strange woman, b) to his sisters, c) to his mother, and refusing to accede to an unreasonable demand made by a) his sisters, b) his mother, and actually shouting at a) his sisters, . . .; 3) physical violence: a mild wrestling match between two young boys, to newspaper headlines dealing with violent riots in a foreign country . . .; and 4) rejection: overhearing a mildly uncomplementary remark passed about him, to being called neurotic." (Lazarus, 1965, p. 245). Lazarus also encouraged the patient to attempt to masturbate to ejaculation only when he felt an undeniable urge to do so. By the end of eight months of 57 desensitization sessions, the man was no longer impotent.

Individual Desensitization with Drugs

Friedman (1966) used a variation of the systematic desensitization technique to treat phobias. He felt that one of the difficulties with Wolpe's (1958) procedure was that some people could not achieve the necessary state of deep relaxation by the Jacobson method, nor could they be hypnotized to a state of relaxation. Also, Friedman believed that when self-induced relaxation was the inhibiting behavior, too many sessions were required to overcome anxiety. To be certain that all his patients reached maximal relaxation, Friedman (1966) injected intravenously barbituate methohexitone sodium (Brietal sodium) in them. Because the drug was effective in producing relaxation for a very short time, it was administered continuously throughout the entire session. He reported that there were no side-effects that interfered with the desensitization process. All cases of phobia treated in Friedman's initial research responded well to his Brietal treatment.

In 1968, Friedman applied the Brietal technique to 18 impotent men with the assumption that learned anxiety was the mediating factor causing the impotence. For each male, a hierarchy of imagined scenes of love-making was established, typically ranging from hand holding to ten-minute intravaginal erection before ejaculation. As before, an intravenous injection of methohexitone sodium was introduced for relaxation.

In six- and twelve-month follow-ups, cure was evaluated as coitus satisfying to the male and his female partner. Each male patient was rated as cured, much improved, slightly improved, or same at the end of treatment. The results were: eight out of ten men with erectile problems were cured at the end of treatment and in the follow-ups, and three of six men with ejaculatory problems were much improved at the end of treatment and in the follow-ups. Of the failures, some did not attend treatment regularly, and others relapsed after some traumatic event (e.g., discovering that wife was having an extramarital affair. Friedman concluded that the Brietal relaxation method was well suited for the treatment of impotence, especially erectile disorders.

Using Friedman's (1968) Brietal procedure, Kraft and Al-Issa (1968) treated two cases of impotence. A common seven-item hierarchy was used for the two men. The only additional treatment the men received was instruction to refrain from intercourse unless they felt a very strong desire to perform sexually. Both men improved and remained so in a six-month follow-up. Kraft and Al-Issa (1968) point out that it is unclear which aspects of the therapy (drugs, instructions in sexual technique or refraining from intercourse until a great need is felt) were most effective.

Contrary to Friedman's (1968) and Kraft and Al-Issa's (1968) success with the Brietal procedure, Ahmed (1968) found that continuous administration of Brietal sodium during the session caused a pain in most subjects that was intense enough to prompt anxiety and distraction. A longer-lasting drug, triopentone sodium, was used by Ahmed with no such anxiety development because one injection of the substance relaxed the patient for the entire session. Using systematic desensitization to an imagined hierarchy of stimuli, instructions in sexual technique, and encouragement to temporarily abstain from sexual intercourse, Ahmed reported improvement in all of his subjects within eight sessions. Since no subsequent literature deals with Ahmed's criticism of the Brietal method, it is difficult to evaluate his conclusions. Perhaps his procedure for the intravenous injection of Brietal sodium was different from or more painful than that of previous researchers.

In general, the Brietal method seems to have been more efficient, averaging nine 30-minute sessions, than Jacobson relaxation (Wolpe, 1958) or hypnosis (Mirowitz, 1966). Lazarus and Rachman (1957), however, report curing an impotent man in eight sessions using hypnotic relaxation. In a 17-month follow-up, the patient discussed in Lazarus and Rachman's report was experiencing no sexual difficulty. The rapid improvement by Lazarus and Rachman may have been facilitated by the short period of time, three months, the patient had been impotent before seeking treatment. In general, in other studies, the men have suffered for longer periods of time. Johnson (1965), in fact, found that recent onset of impotence aids in successful prognosis. Thus, a confident comparison between the efficiency of the Jacobson, hypnosis, and Brietal relaxation procedures cannot be made until further research is conducted which controls for the length of time during which impotence existed before therapy.

It is important to note that the use of drugs for relaxation is quite different from the use of self-induced relaxation. A first difference is that when the patient has been trained to relax by drugs he is not trained nor prepared to combat his anxiety in the real-life situation, whereas he is prepared if he has been trained to inhibit anxiety by self-produced relaxation. Since the drug studies indicate that training in self-relaxation is not crucial for success, some doubt is cast on the advocation of self-relaxation by some researchers.

Secondly, the use of drugs is interesting in regard to Davison and Valins's (1969) argument that changes in behavior are more likely to be maintained when the individual believes that he is responsible for the change. Apparently, in regard to the use of drugs with systematic desensltization treatment of impotence, changes may endure even though it is possible that the individual may attribute his ability to tolerate images of anxiety-evoking stimuli to factors outside of himself.

Group Desensitization with Relaxation

In a study investigating the relative efficacy of group systematic desensitization as compared to traditional interpretive group therapy, Lazarus (1961) concluded that systematic desensitization is better for the treatment of a variety of problems, including impotence. Matched groups of patients, each group consisting of individuals with a like phobia, participated in one of two conditions: group systematic desensitization or group interpretation. For the impotent men in the desensitization group a common hierarchy of ten items was presented consisting of "progressively intimate sexual situations requiring increasing amounts of initiative." In the first session, the group was taught muscle relaxation and told to practice relaxing at home for two 15-minute periods each day. At the second session, the therapist began presenting the hierarchy. When any patient signaled that he felt anxious, the scene was withdrawn for the entire group. After the first few disturbing scenes had been presented, each patient was asked to state the clarity of his scenes and the anxiety he felt to each. In this way, the therapist could be certain that each individual was participating fully in the procedure. New items were introduced only after all of the group members signalled no anxiety for a period of ten seconds.

The same therapist was a participant-observer in the traditional interpretation group. The interpretive procedure was based mainly on personal disclosure about feelings, memories and relationships. The group composed of impotent men was reported to have had much more empathy for one another than did the members of the other problem groups (e.g., acrophobics and claustrophobics).

Both the desensitization and the interpretive groups met three times per week and for the same number of sessions. All subjects in the desensitization group could tolerate the highest hierarchy item by the close of treatment.

For the impotent men, outcome was determined solely by the self-report of the men. All of the impotent men in the desensitization group recovered, whereas none of those in the interpretive group therapy recovered. Lazarus (1961), therefore concluded that systematic desensitization was better suited to and more efficient for the treatment of impotence than interpretive therapy.

There are a number of problems in Lazarus's study. First, he did not consider that the power of group desensitization may have been confounded by factors not present in individual desensitization. For example, it is possible that some subjects reported seeing vivid scenes or feeling no anxiety because of the social pressure to proceed through the hierarchy. The feeling of no anxiety may have been contagious in a cognitive way also, i.e., an individual sees that others with his similar fears are no longer afraid so he reasons that it is foolish for him still to be afraid. It is also possible that social reinforcement could have played a part if the others in some way indicated approval whenever an individual was able to overcome his fears. Also, since the same therapist conducted both the systematic desensitization and the interpretive group therapy, experimenter bias (Rosenthal, 1966) may have been operating.

Masters and Johnson

Masters and Johnson (1970) have developed another type of treatment for impotence. They emphasize that symptoms of impotence should not be the primary focus of treatment. Rather, they concentrate on the "marital-unit" by encouraging communication between partners during sex, and by providing an opportunity to examine "roles" assumed in sexual activity. However, many of their techniques fit well within a behavioral framework, in particular, the use of relaxation and encouragement of a gradual increase of sexual performance in an atmosphere of relaxation.

In treating erectile disorders, the main focus of Masters and Johnson's treatment is concentration on sexual arousal without pressure from the male himself or from the female partner to perform specific behaviors adequately. Such arousal, they say, must take place in a situation where both partners are relaxed. Masters and Johnson instruct the male to attend to his partner's pleasure rather than concern himself with the possibility of his own failure. When a man gives himself in such a manner to his partner, Masters and Johnson predict that an erection will be facilitated—the man is not "taught" to achieve an erection.

After the initial sessions of body stimulation aimed at giving pleasure to the other partner without demand for coitus, and the subsequent achievement of an erection, sessions follow where the partners are encouraged to show each other (nonverbally) what sexual activities each likes. After a number of erections have been obtained, the female is shown the "teasing" procedure in which she stimulates the male to erection, lets the erection subside, and then re-stimulates him to erection. Later, the female is encouraged to place herself above the male in "superior coital position" which is followed by intromission. The female is also instructed to move slowly up and down on the male's penis until the male is ready to move while the female remains quiet.

In the treatment of inability to ejaculate in heterosexual behavior, Masters and Johnson also deal with sexual behavior directly along with treatment of the "marital-unit." The therapy is based on enhancing the identification of the female as the primary pleasurable sex symbol to the male, since many of the males could masturbate to orgasm but could not perform adequate heterosexual intercourse.

The female is instructed to vigorously manually stimulate the male's penis until she produces an ejaculation. Once this is achieved, the male is told to approach his partner thinking of her pleasure and taking pleasure in her pleasure. Erection is produced and the female is told to place herself on the male as soon as he reports that ejaculation is imminent. Continued practice of such a procedure will enable the male to withhold ejaculation for longer periods of time so that his partner is also satisfied. Masters and Johnson report 14 out of 17 cures of a group of men with ejaculatory incompetence using the above method.

Masters and Johnson employ a somewhat similar technique for premature ejaculation. Briefly, the female is encouraged to stimulate the male to the plateau phase of the sexual response cycle, and then apply the "squeeze technique" which prevents actual ejaculation. The "squeeze technique" consists of the female applying pressure to various parts of the penis. The stimulation and squeeze treatments are repeated a number of times resulting in a prolonged period of time where the male is aroused but he does not ejaculate. In the second phase of the treatment, the female mounts the male for increasingly longer periods of time, removing herself only when the male indicates that he is about to ejaculate. Her removal allows him to refrain from ejaculation.

The rest of the treatment follows a similar pattern of increasing the period of sustained erection. Masters and Johnson claim only four out of 186 men with premature ejaculation failed to be cured by this method. In the treatment of premature ejaculation, as in the treatment of erectile disorders, they emphasize the role of expectancy and confidence in the treatment for success, but no systematic research has been done to evaluate the relative importance of the different factors.

Behavior Modification with Other Techniques

Mirowitz (1966) used one of four techniques to treat male impotence: 1) post-hypnotic suggestion, 2) reciprocal inhibition (he does not indicate whether he prefers self-relaxation or drug-induced relaxation), 3) re-education in sexual technique and processes, and 4) reintegrative therapy to insight. He does not discuss the relative efficacy of the four methods, but says that the techniques may be differentially effective with different patients, and that in some cases more than one technique should be used.

For a case of impotence plus fetishism, Cooper (1968) used relaxation for the treatment of the former and aversion therapy for the latter. Cooper found that even when the fetish of achieving ejaculation by rubbing a woman's silk stocking on the upper part of the thigh, had been eliminated in the patient by practicing it while under the influence of an emetic solution, the impotence was still present. Relaxation in the sexual situation restored potency.

A combination of behavioral techniques and explanatory, encouraging psychotherapy was used to treat impotence by Cooper (1969). Cooper's patients were trained to induce muscle relaxation and encouraged to relax prior to and at various stages during sexual behavior. The patients were also instructed not to have intercourse until they had held a strong erection for several minutes. Cooper also discussed with his patients their sexual anxieties as well as various aspects of sex education. In addition, he held interviews with the male's female partner to discuss with her the optimum sexual environment for the male.

Improvement was rated on the basis of self-reports by the patient and his female partner. Cooper's results showed that 7 men recovered, 12 men improved, 21 men were unchanged and 9 men were worse. He attributed the poor outcome to the long duration of impotence prior to treatment for many of the men. He also concluded that strong motivation was a major factor in the "improve" and "recover" groups. Cooper also suggested that duration time of impotence, motivation, age and premarital sexual experiences are more significant and better predictors of outcome than level of coital anxiety.

CONCLUSION

In treating impotence, it is useful to provide rewards for behaviors that are increasingly sexually adequate. Usually, the satisfaction from coition and the satisfaction of the female are rewarding for the male. Erectile problems and ejaculatory problems seem to be no great obstacle for behavior modification treatment. Systematic desensitization, relaxation in the sexual environment and assertive response training have proven highly successful. Since the therapy for impotence works best in the real life situation, and rewards are almost certain to be contingent upon performance of the desired behavior, relapse is relatively rare.

The treatment of impotence often includes techniques of re-education in sexual processes, encouragement, expectancy and insight. Most of the previous research has not yet factored out the importance of these cognitive and social aspects and how they are related to the basic behavioral methods. Further study is necessary so that the value of the many aspects of therapy can be assessed.

REFERENCES

Ahmed, S. Treatment of premature ejaculation. *Brit. J. Psychia.* 1968, **114**, 1197-1198.

Apter, I. On the psychotherapy of psychogenic impotence. In R. Winn (Ed. and transl.), *Psychotherapy in the Soviet Union.* New York: Philosophical Library, 1961.

Caprio, F. *The sexually adequate male.* New York: The Citadel Press, 1952.

Cooper, A. A case of fetishism and impotence treated by behavior therapy. *Brit. J. Psychia.* 1968, **114**, 719-731.

Cooper, A. Disorders of sexual potency in the male: A clinical and statistical study of some factors related to short-term prognosis. *Brit. J. Psychia.* 1969, **115**, 709-719.

Davison, G. & Valins, S. Maintenance of self-attributed and drug-attributed behavior change. *J. Pers. & Soc. Psych.* 1969, **11**, 25-33.

Friedman, D. A new technique for the systematic desensitization of phobic symptoms. *Beh. Res. & Ther.* 1966, **4**, 130-140.

Friedman, D. The treatment of impotence by Brietal relaxation therapy. *Beh. Res. & Ther.* 1968, **6**, 257-261.

Johnson, J. Prognosis of disorders of sexual potency in the male. *J. Psychosom. Res.* 1965, **19**, 195-200.

Kraft, T. & Al-Issa, I. The use of methohexitone sodium in the systematic desensitization of premature ejaculation. *Brit. J. Psychia.* 1968, **114**, 351-352.

Kinsey, A., Pomeroy, W. & Martin, C. *Sexual behavior in the human male.* Philadelphia: W.B. Saunders Co., 1948.

Lazarus, A. & Rachman, S. The use of systematic desensitization in psychotherapy. *South African Med. J.* 1957, **31**, 934-937.

Lazarus, A. Group therapy of phobic disorders by systematic desensitization. *J. Abn. & Soc. Psycho.* 1961, **63**, 504-510.

Lazarus, A. The treatment of a sexually inadequate man. In L. Ullmann and L. Krasner (Eds.), *Case Studies in Behavior Modification.* New York: Holt, Rinehart and Winston, Inc., 1965.

Leitenberg, A., Agras, W., Barlow, D. & Oliveau, D. Contribution of selective positive reinforcement and therapeutic instructions to systematic desensitization therapy. *J. Abn. Psych.* 1969, **74**, 113-118.

Masters, W. & Johnson, V. *Human sexual inadequacy.* Boston: Little, Brown and Co., 1970.

Mirowitz, J. The utilisation of hypnosis in psychic impotence. *Brit. J. Med. Hypotism.* 1966, **17**, 25-32.

Murray, E. & Jacobson, L. The nature of learning in traditional and behavioral psychotherapy. In A. Bergin and S. Garfield (Eds.) *Handbook of psychotherapy and behavior change.* New York: John Wiley & Sons, 1971, 709-717.

Oliveau, D.; Agras, W.; Leitenberg, H.; Moore, R. & Wright, D. Systematic desensitization, therapeutically oriented instructions and selective positive reinforcement. *Beh. Res. and Ther.* 1969, **7**, 27-33.

Rachman, S. Sexual disorders and behavior therapy. *Am. J. Psychia.* 1961, **118**, 235-240.

Roen, R. Impotence: A concise review. *N.Y. State J. Med.* 1965, **65**, 2476-2482.

Rosenthal, R. *Experimenter effects in behavioral research.* New York: Appleton-Century-Crofts, 1966.

Wilkins, W. Densensitization: Social and cognitive factors underlying the effectiveness of Wolpe's procedure. *Psych. Bull.* 1971, **76**, 311-318.

Wolpe, J. *Psychotherapy by reciprocal inhibition.* California: Stanford University Press, 1958.

26
A Case of Impotence Successfully Treated With Desensitization Combined with *In Vivo* Operant Training and Thought Substitution

ZALMON H. GARFIELD, JOHN F. McBREARTY and MARVIN DICHTER

The case reported is one of impotence treated essentially with a broad spectrum approach. An aspect of the therapeutic program previously unreported to the authors' knowledge, is the use of desensitization as a means of monitoring and controlling overly rapid and premature efforts to complete the sexual act. Control of this rapid series of behavioral components has been a repetitive problem in treating this particular behavioral deficit. The combination of thought-stopping and thought substitution in the sexual situation represents another treatment innovation.

The subject was originally referred to the senior author because alternative efforts to assist with the problem were ineffective. The patient's impotence was so anxiety-producing as to have substantially reduced his ability to benefit (or participate) from other therapy offered in the hospital for alcoholics where he was a resident.

CASE HISTORY

Mr. C., a 45-year-old robust patient, suffered with total sexual impotence for a period of one year prior to seeking help. He described its gradual onset for a period of six months to a year prior to that time. This consisted of increasing inability to maintain an erection after it was achieved. The loss sometimes occurred after intromission. Occasionally no erection at all occurred. Finally he was unable to achieve an erection at any time.

Mr. C. was a rather handsome, gray-haired man of slightly more than average height. He was trim and well built. In manner he was pleasant, soft-spoken, and tended to be both passive and submissive. He agreed with the therapist, even when within ten minutes the therapist's statements were self-contradicting, and only rarely disagreed. When he did, however, he became doggedly, almost desperately stubborn in maintaining his position. He was respectful of authority.

Patient was a resident in a center for the treatment of alcoholism at the time the problem of his impotence was approached for the first time. There was no obvious connection between his impotence and his alcoholism in that he never attempted intercourse while drunk or drinking, nor had this ever been a pattern with him. He was sober for long periods (up to six months) between drinking binges. He had been sober for five months at the time treatment for impotence took place. The therapist who treated the impotence had nothing to do with the group therapy in which Mr. C. participated, nor with any other aspect of his therapy related to drinking or other maladaptive behaviors.

History

Patient was one of four children, all siblings being female and older. He described a somewhat seductive relationship with his mother as a boy ("she would lie down with me, sometimes cuddle me or play with my ear") and a fearful, submissive relationship with his father, whom he disliked because "he was mean to my mother." His father apparently returned his distaste and singled him out for frequent beatings with a frayed hose.

The parents' relationship to each other was described as tense and angry. The mother and children conspired to deceive the father to avoid his anger. Father was Catholic, mother Lutheran. The children pretended to go to the Catholic church at the father's insistence, but they avoided actually attending whenever possible, with approval from the mother.

The father was a powerful man, dark, stern, with virtually no interest outside the home other than his work as a plasterer. He was rigid and strict in all matters, especially sexual, refusing to allow any of the children, including Mr. C., to attend dances or have a friend of the opposite sex in the home at any time. The second sister was his father's favorite. He nicknamed her "Billy," and would tease the patient about his inadequacy compared to her. As a boy, Mr. C. heavily emphasized his participation in sports and he joined the paratroopers during World War II.

Patient's sexual history showed rather sparse activity and even more sparse information. He was seduced by a somewhat older neighborhood girl when he was in high school. This relationship continued on a furtive, occasional basis in her house for about a year. In his senior year in high school, he began to date his future wife. They had intercourse a few times, but with minimal response from her.

Mr. C.'s notion about orgasm in women ranged from an early concept that few women had orgasm and then rarely, to one in which he felt it was a man's duty to produce orgasm and that he failed as a man if it did not occur. The latter was his opinion when therapy began. His notions about sexual matters were consistently a product of impression rather than education; his sexual education in both home and school was negligible. He described his ideas in this area as largely acquired from peers, including an adolescent notion that masturbation and sexual intercourse were weakening.

Somewhere in his adolescence, or perhaps his early adult years, Mr. C. became emotionally attached to the Catholic church.

After separating from his wife, following 14 years of marriage, he took up a relationship with Miss M., a woman whom he had met earlier, and with whom he had had relations, but had left. Miss M. was the third and only other sexual partner of his lifetime and with her he achieved his first satisfactory sexual adjustment. They practiced contraception by coitus interruptus. He described condoms and diaphragms as "messy."

(This conformed with an impression of overmeticulousness and overorderliness in his behavior, dress and attitudes.)

Miss M. refused to marry him until he had been sober for a year. (He was drinking heavily by this time.) She was a registered nurse, supported her mother, maintained her own home and, in general, according to Mr. C. was a "superior" person to him. She also was a woman who dominated her environment. Mr. C said he always resented Miss M.'s condition for their marriage although he "understood" it. His religious scruples apparently added to this discomfort. She was, in person, short, round, good humored, and spoke with great assurance on all matters until confronted by a vigorous counter-assertiveness. She appeared readily capable of asserting control over Mr. C.

Mr. C. reported that until his impotence became a problem, he was able to bring her to orgasm readily. He regarded this as a matter of great importance, it having never characterized his sexual relationship with his wife. This achievement became for him a "proof" of virility.

Miss M. persuaded Mr. C. to go to her church, a Protestant denomination. He felt guilty about going, however, because he felt his life made him unworthy of being in church.

Treatment

While history-taking was being completed, relaxation instruction was begun. At the same time, Mr. C. was advised to engage in no sexual activity that had not been specifically approved in discussion with his therapist. He was told to think of himself and the therapist as an engineering or coaching team; no strategy was to be executed without full approval of the coaching team.

An analysis of Mr. C.'s behavior suggested that anxiety with reference to sexual behavior began with the most remote point in time and space at which he initiated approach behavior in the direction of Miss M. Just prior to experiencing his first signs of impotence, he reported a general feeling of unworthiness, including as a part of this his relationship with Miss M. He also reported having had achievement of orgasm by Miss M. on his mind at all times when they were engaged in intercourse. This was of primary importance. As anxiety about ability to perform increased, this factor became a major preoccupation and increased his anxiety.

It was determined that based on the behavioral analysis summarized above, treatment should include:

1. Desensitization to the temporal and spatial stimuli producing anxiety while approaching a time and place suitable for sexual relations to occur.
2. Thought-stopping and thought substitution with reference to preoccupation with his partner's orgasm (Wolpe & Lazarus, 1966).
3. Practice in sexual assertiveness lagging a step or two behind desensitization and otherwise following the model described by Wolpe (1958).

In addition to the above, brief discussion took place with reference to Mr. C.'s worthiness as a human being and forgiveness as part of the Christian ethic. Mr. C. was encouraged to speak with a priest about his church association and negative feelings with reference to church attendance which appeared to be a response to his drinking behavior, as well as to the fact that he and Miss M. were not married. At the termination of the therapeutic relationship six weeks later, these discussions had had the initial effect of at least one church attendance and talk of visiting a priest.

Utilization of sexual assertiveness alone in an effort to attain the level of intercourse was attempted in this case independently by the patient early in the treatment program. It resulted in failure. It is, of course, unknown if it might have been successful if pursued more slowly in accordance with the Wolpe (1958) paradigm. It was felt at this stage, however, that the desensitization hierarchy would act as a supportive element in maintaining successful sexual approach behavior. It was also felt that it would act to inhibit responses which Mr. C.'s anxiety then would be likely to render unsuccessful. The procedure was successful in both respects.

The hierarchy constructed with Mr. C. was essentially one of temporal and spatial approach to the anxiety-producing situation, sexual behavior. Fortunately for this purpose Mr. C.'s habits and behavior tended to be quite regular. Thus, items in the hierarchy suggest the apparent remoteness of stimuli which can be anxiety-producing. They involved such items as:

1. Closing the gas station where Mr. C. was working and delivering the cash to his employer's home.
2. Driving home and rounding the corner onto the street where he lived with Miss M.

On both these items, Mr. C. had initial anxiety reactions, but they occurred only one time. As he approached more closely the sexual situation anxiety became more acute. Such items as taking a bath before going to bed and kissing Miss M. good night required several repetitions, relaxation scenes, fractionation, etc.

As the hierarchy proceeded into sexual behavior and contacts (hugging, kissing, feeling, etc.), Mr. C. was strictly enjoined, under no circumstances, to proceed beyond the hierarchy level and advised to actually lag a step behind.

This injunction and advice relieved Mr. C.'s anxiety as to maintenance of an erection at crucial moments. The results of this was that very early in the sexual situation paralleling the hierarchy, Mr. C. developed and maintained an erection. By the time he arrived at stages just prior to intromission, he was sexually extremely excited and desirous to proceed to completion.

In fact, as stated above, one time quite early in the desensitization procedure paralleled by in vivo training, Mr. C. attempted to proceed at his own discretion to complete intercourse. He failed. This experience led to close adherence thereafter to procedures agreed upon with the therapist.

The interaction of the relief of anxiety by reason of limitations placed on his actual behavior, plus relief generated by the desensitization procedure, led to steadily maintained relaxation in the situation as Mr. C. proceeded closer and closer to intercourse. His verbally expressed confidence in the therapy situation of his ability to carry the act to completion preceded by at least two weeks the actual accomplishment of the act.

It should perhaps be noted here that another method utilized by the therapist to relieve anxiety in the therapy situation as well as with reference to the sexual situation and discussion related to language. The therapist utilized common slang with reference to genitals and intercourse generally, picking up and continuing to use those expressions by Mr. C.

At the stage where Mr. C.'s confidence in ability to function sexually was quite high, such items were introduced into the hierarchy as:

1. "Miss M. plays with your prick for several minutes while you play with or suck her tits.
2. "You press against her pussy with your hard on."
3. "(Crucial item) You feel "I could put it in if I wanted to.""
4. "You decide to put it in and do so for a very little while and take it out."

At the stage of item 3 above, the subject of Mr. C.'s preoccupation with Miss M.'s orgasm was reraised.

At this time, Mr. C. was instructed in thought-stopping and thought substitution. He was told whenever during sex play he had any concern about his partner's orgasm he should instantly say to himself: "No, I will not think of that. I will think of enjoying myself." He was then instructed to think of the most pleasurably erotic situation he could while continuing sex play. Several such scenes were constructed involving situations particularly exciting to Mr. C. He was to continue these thoughts until the actual circumstances and activity became completely absorbing.

With this procedure and behavior added to his repertoire, the length of intromission was extended until it involved ejaculation. In these circumstances, as they recurred, Miss M. sometimes did not experience orgasm. The first experience of Mr. C. experiencing ejaculation took place a little more than four weeks after the first therapy session and three weeks after beginning desensitization procedures.

Mr. C. continued in therapy for several weeks beyond this point. Operant theory was utilized in designing behaviors to practice in developing further assertiveness in other areas with Miss M., her mother, in job situations, etc. These procedures were interrupted by Mr. C.'s departure from the hospital.

A footnote to this case is that Mr. C. returned to the hospital for a party. He reported at this time that he had experienced drinking "slips" sufficient to cause job loss, but that his sexual functioning had continued to remain intact up to that time.

SUGGESTIVE CONCLUSIONS

The case suggests once again the stability of responses developed by behavior-modification methods. The possible value is suggested of reinforcement and anxiety relief proceeding from feelings of strong potency in the sexual situation while being protected for a time from a test situation in a structured, authoritarian relationship. The combination of desensitization procedure with *in vivo* training appeared to accomplish this purpose, combining classical and operant conditioning methodology.

Finally the thought-stopping followed by appropriate preplanned thought substitution appeared effective in this case in eliminating a sexually inhibiting stimulus from occurring.

REFERENCES

Wolpe, J. *Psychotherapy by reciprocal inhibition.* Stanford: Stanford University Press, 1958.

Wolpe, J. & Lazarus, A.A. *Behavior therapy techniques.* New York: Pergamon Press, 1966.

27
Treatment of Erectile Failure and Ejaculatory Incompetence of Homosexual Etiology

JOSEPH LoPICCOLO, RITA STEWART and BRUCE WATKINS

In contrast to their generally high rates of success in treating problems of sexual inadequacy, Masters and Johnson (1970) report considerable difficulty in treating impotence (erectile failure) in cases where religious orthodoxy or homosexual influence are etiological factors. They state (p. 273): "It is in these two areas that so much more work needs to be done. Currently there is an inexcusably high level of failure rate in therapeutic return for patients handicapped by either of these two specific etiological influences."

This paper reports on a learning theory based treatment program developed for cases of impotence where homosexuality is involved, and illustrates the use of this program in one case.

Masters and Johnson consider erectile failure to be a fear reaction. "Fear can prevent erections just as fear can increase the respiratory rate or lead to diarrhea or vomiting" (Masters & Johnson, 1970, p. 196). They consider this fear to be a fear of failure, or "performance anxiety," which leads the male to assume a nonparticipant, "spectator" role in sexual relations. Their program aims to reduce this fear through what is basically an *in vivo* desensitization procedure, similar to that described by Wolpe (1969).

In cases of erectile failure where the male has a homosexual orientation, it seems logical to assume that lack of heterosexual arousal in addition to performance anxiety is a factor in the inability to attain and maintain an erection. A treatment which focuses only on reducing performance anxiety, and not on increasing heterosexual arousal, would seem likely to be unsuccessful in such cases.

In the case reported here, an *in vivo* desensitization program to reduce performance anxiety was used contiguously with a program designed to recondition sexual arousal to heterosexual stimuli through the directed use of fantasy and masturbation.

CASE A

The clients were two unmarried graduate students living together in a stable and permanent love relationship. Their presenting problems were the male's lack of sexual arousal to his mate, his inability to attain or maintain an erection in sexual relations with her, and his frequent inability to become aroused enough to ejaculate (ejaculatory incompetence) on those occasions when he did achieve an erection. In support of the notion that arousal reconditioning is necessary in such cases, it might be noted that the client felt genuine revulsion and disgust at the sight or touch of the female's genitals.

The male had been an overt homosexual since early adolescence, and was engaging in overt homosexual activities (mutual masturbation, fellatio, and intercourse) at the time the couple entered treatment. He had had intercourse with six or seven other women besides his mate, but each relationship terminated because of his inability to achieve erections.

The female was sexually liberal and quite experienced (more than 40 previous sexual partners). She was aware of her partner's homosexuality and did not object to it per se, but only to his inability to perform sexually with her.

What they wanted of treatment was to increase his heterosexual arousal and functioning. They both stated that they did *not* want the therapists to attempt to eliminate the male's homosexuality, which they viewed as nonpathological, but merely to enhance his heterosexuality. This was agreed to with the exception that the male was to refrain from overt homosexual activities for the duration of treatment.

TREATMENT

Both the male and the female were seen for 15 weekly sessions by a male and a female therapist (R.S. and B.W.).

One aspect of treatment involved the reduction of the male's performance anxiety through an *in vivo* desensitization approach. As this approach has been well described elsewhere (Wolpe, 1958, 1969; Masters & Johnson, 1970) it will not be detailed here. Briefly, the clients were initially forbidden to engage in any sexual activity. They were then given, each week, a "homework" assignment to increase their repertoire of sexual behaviors. In the first week only hugging, kissing and body massage were allowed. This assignment permits the male to relearn enjoyment of sensual pleasures, without any worry about whether or not he will be able to achieve an erection. In following weeks, the behaviors successively added were breast and genital touching, stimulation of the penis in a "teasing" manner (Masters & Johnson, 1970, p. 206), simultaneous masturbation and genital manipulation by each other, penile insertion with no movement, penile insertion with male pelvic thrusting, mutual genital manipulation and masturbation to orgasm, and finally, allowing mutual pelvic thrusting with ejaculation during intercourse. To eliminate performance anxiety, the timing of introduction of these behaviors was such that they were allowed only after the male client had become confident that he could accomplish them. For example, intravaginal ejaculation was not "allowed" until after the client had been unable to restrain himself from ejaculating intravaginally.

The major innovation in the treatment of this case was the arousal reconditioning procedure. A program of directed masturbation was initially used to raise the client's heterosexual arousal. At intake, the male client was masturbating several times weekly to exclusively homosexual fantasies. McGuire, Carlisle and Young (1965) have suggested that the orgasm experienced during masturbation is the reinforcer which conditions arousal to the fantasy or other stimuli accompanying masturbation. Davison (1968) and Marquis (1970) have made use of this principle in "orgasmic reconditioning" procedures designed to eliminate sexual perversions. In a manner similar to the procedures developed by Davison and Marquis, the male client was instructed to use homosexual fantasies to attain erection and approach orgasm in masturbation. At the instant of orgasm, however, he was to switch to fantasies of sexual relations with his mate. If arousal was lost, he was briefly to switch back to homosexual fantasies and then return again to fantasies of his partner. Over successive occasions of masturbation, the time of the switch from homosexual to heterosexual fantasies was gradually moved backward from the point of orgasm, until the client was finally using exclusively heterosexual fantasies during the entire masturbatory session.

One modification of Marquis's procedure was made. As is typical of male homosexuals (Annon, 1971), the client had difficulty in visualizing or fantasizing heterosexual stimuli during masturbation. To deal with this problem, the therapists provided the couple with a Polaroid camera and had them take pictures of the female for the male to use as heterosexual masturbation stimuli. This procedure worked quite well; and in the latter stages of therapy the male did acquire the ability to fantasize effectively without the aid of the pictures.

Because this fantasy-switching program worked well in masturbation, it was also used to facilitate arousal in the *in vivo* desensitization sessions with the female. The male was instructed to use homosexual fantasies as necessary to facilitate arousal in these sessions but to switch back frequently to focusing on the reality of what he and his partner were doing, and in any case always to switch back to heterosexual reality just before orgasm. This program was also successful. While initially the male was fantasizing homosexual activities during much of the time he was engaging in sexual activity with his mate, he eventually came to be highly aroused while focusing *exclusively* on the heterosexual reality.

In any type of behavioral treatment where the major therapeutic procedures are to be carried out by the client at home, there is the problem of knowing whether or not the client is following them. In the present case, both clients were required to fill out daily activity record forms at home specifying in detail their sexual activities and emotional reactions to them. These records, as well as the clients' verbal reports in therapy sessions, indicated that the clients did follow the program procedures quite faithfully.

OUTCOME

At the close of the treatment, the male was able to obtain and maintain erections solely through the use of heterosexual fantasies and activities. In addition, he was able to ejaculate intravaginally on virtually every occasion. These changes were found to have been maintained at a follow-up 6 months after termination.

Assessing outcome on the basis of global reports is, of course, unsatisfactory in a scientific sense. An attempt to deal with this problem in cases of sexual dysfunction is being made by the senior author and his students by the use of two sexual behavior inventories. As reliability and validity research on these inventories is still in progress, however, only a few scores of high "face validity" from these inventories will be reported here. These scores are shown in Table 1.

Table 1 Outcome Statistics

Variable	Time of Assessment		
	Pre-Treatment	Termination	Six-month Follow-up
1. Intercourse frequency	once/2 weeks	3 times weekly	twice weekly
2. Intercourse duration	1-5 min	11-15 min	11-15 min
3. Achieves erection—			
% of coital opportunities	25%	100%	100%
4. Achieves orgasm in intercourse, if erection achieved			
male	50%	100%	100%
female	50%	75%	75%
8. Self-rating—satisfaction with sexual relationship (scale of 1-6)			
male	2	5	5
female	2	5	5

As Table 1 indicates, treatment was quite successful in dealing with this couple's presenting complaints. One additional set of scores from our assessment inventory is also interesting, as it documents the effectiveness of the reconditioning procedure in making heterosexuality more arousing and pleasurable to the male. This inventory lists 17 different heterosexual activities, ranging from kissing to intercourse, and asks the client to rate, on a scale from 1 to 6, how pleasant he finds each activity. The mean pleasure scores in a normative sample of 63 couples with a satisfactory sexual relationship are 5·3 (standard deviation = 0·54) for males and 5·1 (standard deviation = 0·54) for females. Before treatment, the male client's score was 3·8, the female's 4·9. After treatment these scores had increased to 5·0 and 5·1 respectively, and were 5·0 and 5·3 at follow-up. Clearly, heterosexual behavior had become much more pleasurable and arousing for both clients.

DISCUSSION

The results in this case are encouraging, and suggest that the addition of an arousal reconditioning procedure to the basic Masters and Johnson (1970) program for impotence may be necessary to obtain better results in cases of impotence related to a homosexual orientation. This case is also instructive in illustrating two modifications of the arousal reconditioning procedures developed by Davison (1968) and Marquis (1970).

Usually, in this procedure the client's fantasies or *Playboy* pictures (e.g., Davison, 1968; Jackson, 1969) are used as heterosexual stimulus materials during masturbation. In this case, Polaroid pictures of the client's actual sexual partner were used. This seems to offer the advantages of providing clear and explicit stimulus materials (unlike fantasy images), and of conditioning the client's arousal *directly* to his actual sexual partner, rather than to a magazine. It seems improbable that arousal conditioned to *Playboy* models will generalize completely to the client's actual sexual partner. The Polaroid camera may therefore be a useful tool in the behavior therapist's armamentarium.

The second innovation was to have the client use his homosexual fantasies to reinforce sexual arousal in actual heterosexual behavior with his mate as well as with masturbation.

Again, it should be noted that the goal of treatment was to improve the quality of the male client's sexual relationship with his partner, and not to change his homosexual orientation. The client did report a decrease in homosexual behavior at termination, but at the time of follow-up indicated a return to its pre-treatment level. The client wanted treatment to make him heterosexually aroused and competent; and it was not necessary to decrease homosexual functioning in order to achieve this aim. He is now capable of adequate sexual functioning with both sexes. We consider that the use he makes of this capacity is a matter of his personal morality which should not be intruded upon by the therapist.

REFERENCES

Annon, J.S. *The therapeutic use of masturbation in the treatment of sexual disorders,* Paper presented at Fifth annual meeting of the Association for the Advancement of Behavior Therapy, Washington, D.C., 1971.

Davison, G.S. Elimination of a sadistic fantasy by a client controlled counter-conditioning technique. *J. abnorm. psychol.* 1968, **77**, 84-90.

Jackson, B.T. A case of voyeurism treated by counterconditioning. *Behav. res. & therapy.* 1969, **7**, 133-134.

Marquis, J.N. Orgasmic reconditioning: Changing sexual object choice through controlling masturbation fantasies. *J. behav. ther. & exp. psychiat.* 1970, **1**, 263-271.

Masters, W.H. & Johnson V.E. *Human sexual inadequacy.* Boston: Little-Brown, 1970.

McQuire, R.T., Carlisle, J.M. & Young, B.G. Sexual deviation as conditioned behavior: A hypothesis. *Behav. res. & therapy.* 1965, **2**, 185-190.

Wolpe, J. *Psychotherapy by reciprocal inhibition.* Stanford: Stanford University Press, 1958.

Wolpe, J. *The practice of behavior therapy.* New York: Pergamon Press, 1969.

Additional Selected Readings

Cooper, A.J. A case of fetishism and impotence treated by behavior therapy, *British Journal of Psychiatry*, 1963, 109, 649-652.

Cooper A.J. A blind evaluation of a penile ring-a sex aid for impotent males, *British Journal of Psychiatry*, 1974, 124, 402-406.

Dengrove, E. Behavior therapy of impotence, *The Journal of Sex Research*, 1971, 7, 177-183.

Friedman, D.E. & Lipsedge, M.S. Treatment of phobic anxiety and psychogenic impotence by systematic desensitization employing methohexitone-induced relaxation, *British Journal of Psychiatry*, 1971, 118, 87-90.

Kockott, G., Ditmar, F. & Nusselt, L., Systematic desensitization of erectile impotence: A controlled study, *Archives of Sexual Behavior*, 1975, 4, 493-500.

Lazarus, A.A. Group Treatment for impotence, *Sexology*, Dec., 1969, 22-25.

Salzman, L.F. Systematic desensitization of a patient with chronic total impotence. In Rubin, R.R. and Franks, C.M. (eds.). *Advances in behavior therapy*, 1968. New York: Academic Press, 1969, 97-104.

Ejaculatory Problems

Problems associated with ejaculation (often labeled "premature" or "delayed" ejaculation) usually occur when a man and/or his sexual partner feel that ejaculation occurs either considerably sooner, or later, than they would prefer and that enjoyment of sexual intercourse is therefore dampened by the timing of the ejaculation. The range of these problems is from men who ejaculate well before intromission (some, even before they are undressed) where the problem involves lack of voluntary control over the ejaculatory reflex, to men who engage in vigorous intercourse indefinitely without being able to ejaculate at all ("retarded ejaculation" or "ejaculatory incompetence"). This latter problem is one that appears to be relatively uncommon in comparison to the number of complaints regarding ejaculation that occurs too early. Since it is absurd—and probably dysfunctional—for any "expert" to suggest the ideal length of time between intromission and ejaculation (or even the "right" number of requisite in-and-out thrusts before ejaculation), the decision as to what is the desirable time before ejaculation remains a very personal one, which varies not only among couples, but also from time to time for each couple.

The first article consists of "Two Case Reports on the Modification of the Ejaculatory Response with the Squeeze Technique" by Tanner. The author first reviews the basic procedures for dealing with ejaculatory problems. For all of these procedures, there have been implicit or explicit cautions that they may not be effective with "psychotic" clients. Tanner's article presents two detailed case reports each of which involved one partner with a diagnosis of "psychosis." The focus in each case was on the dysfunctional sexual behaviors, problems which often are ignored by clinicians confronted with vast areas of dysfunctionality in their clients. Given the apparent success of his efforts to improve sexual behavior in these two cases, Tanner argues that methods such as those described in his article probably can be used with anyone regardless of the psychiatric labels involved.

Further, the successful focus on specific behaviors also suggests the possibility that in cases such as these, such partialization may be the treatment of choice, with the therapist dealing with specific behaviors, moving on to new problems as earlier ones come under control.

The second article, by Razani, describes a case of "Ejaculatory Incompetence Treated by Reconditioning Anxiety." This case involved a man who complained of an inability to ejaculate intravaginally associated with coital anxiety. The problem was viewed as being mediated by anxiety and was therefore treated by systematic desensitization and *in vivo* techniques (manual penile stimulation). The problem—which had persisted to that point for six years— was eliminated in five sessions.

The final article in this section is "Group Treatment of Premature Ejaculation" by Kaplan *et al.* This article describes the group treatment of four heterosexual couples in which the chief complaint for each was the male's ejaculation coming too early. The article describes the basic principles of treatment for this problem as well as its application in a group context. After a relatively brief period of treatment, at a four month follow-up, all four couples reported continued and improved sexual functioning. The average amount of therapist time spent in this efficient treatment program was only 1.5 hours per couple, thereby suggesting its appropriateness for use in the typical clinic with waiting lists or other problems in obtaining immediate treatment.

28
Two Case Reports on the Modification of the Ejaculatory Response with the Squeeze Technique

BARRY A. TANNER

Semans (1956) was the first to describe a direct, behavioral treatment for premature ejaculation. The present author views Semans' procedure as akin to operant shaping and time out from reinforcement, since the penis is manually stimulated until just prior to ejaculation, at which point the man removes his partner's hand. In effect, a reinforcer (stimulation of the penis) is withdrawn contingent upon an undesirable response (physical sensations premonitory to ejaculation). When the prejaculatory response ceases, the manual stimulation begins again, gradually increasing the duration of the erection. Clients are then instructed to lubricate the penis during stimulation, since ejaculation occurs more rapidly when the penis is wet. Semans (1956, p. 353) cautioned against using this procedure when there were psychiatric symptoms related to sexual activity.

Wolpe and Lazarus (1966) further extended this shaping procedure by adding the steps of manual stimulation with the male astride the female, insertion of the glans into the vagina without pelvic thrusting, insertion of the glans with the female alone engaged in pelvic thrusting, and then progressively deeper insertion and greater amounts of thrusting. In all of these steps the client withdrew from his wife's vagina prior to ejaculation, thereby withdrawing reinforcement. The final step involved full insertion of the penis, with ejaculation allowed only after several minutes of controlled thrusting. Other cases involved the use of relaxation to inhibit anxiety. The authors make it clear through the subtitle of their book, and with several references, that the procedures described are intended for neurotic patients only.

Masters and Johnson (1970) developed still another variant of Semans' procedure. Contained within their general treatment regime are specific steps for premature ejaculation. The male assumes a nondemand position which is intended to serve a similar anxiety reducing function as Wolpe and Lazarus' relaxation instructions, and is manually stimulated by his wife until he experiences the prejaculatory sensations. At that point, he informs her and she squeezes the coronal ridge of his penis between her thumb and first two fingers for about four seconds. This results in a loss of the premonitory sensations and a partial loss of erection. After waiting another 30 seconds or so, manual stimulation begins again. The couple is told not to have intercourse during this period, thereby

288

increasing the reinforcing value of intercourse through deprivation. Following this phase of treatment, vaginal containment of the penis with the female astride but without pelvic thrusting is attempted. Gradually, thrusting is introduced, with the female rising off the penis and squeezing when the premonitory sensations are reported. Other coital positions are used, with the male-astride position attempted last, since this is reported to be the position in which ejaculatory control is most difficult to achieve. As with Wolpe and Lazarus (1966), Masters and Johnson (1970, p. 21) state that their procedure is not intended for psychotic clients.

The two case reports which follow each involved one partner with a psychotic diagnosis, and a history as an inpatient at a state hospital. They are intended to demonstrate how methods similar to those described above can be used regardless of the psychiatric labels applied to a client.

Case Report One: The husband of the first couple was a judically committed 40-year-old, diagnosed upon admission as paranoid schizophrenic, and transferred to our hospital following two months at another state hospital. Five years before hospitalization, after 16 years of marriage, he became extremely jealous and abusive of his wife who was 10 years younger than he. He was reported to have destroyed parts of his car and his house when angry at his wife's suspected infidelity. Several years before commitment he had shot himself in the stomach when he believed her to be with another man. Prior to commitment, he had become enraged at his inability to sexually satisfy his wife, had forced her to have intercourse daily, to use a dildoe, and to look at pornographic literature before intercourse. He was finally committed following a series of homicidal and suicidal threats. At this time, he reported frequent thoughts about his wife's suspected infidelity. He also believed his penis to be undersized, and requested medication to make it longer.

Procedure: The first two sessions were spent in convincing the man that he could benefit from counseling, while at the third session he was given a stopwatch and instructed to record his time to ejaculation. He was told to begin timing when he inserted his penis in his wife's vagina, and to stop timing when he ejaculated. Directions were given over the phone to his wife who was ill and did not attend that meeting. She was asked to rate her pleasure or displeasure during intercourse on a scale which ran from "-10" through "0" to "+10." The negative numbers indicated displeasure, zero indicated an absence of emotion, and the positive numbers indicated pleasure. They had intercourse four times before the next session, thereby obtaining the baseline data.

At the fourth session, the couple was instructed in Masters and Johnson's (1970) non-demand position and squeeze technique for premature ejaculation. We also discussed the need to communicate with each other about sex. They were to practice the squeeze technique twice a week, going through the masturbation/squeeze sequence four times during each session. They were told they could engage in intercourse following each squeeze session if they wished, but should not record that data since it would be contaminated by the training session.

At the fifth session both partners reported satisfaction with the husband's sexual performance, and indicated a desire to work toward the wife achieving orgasm. They were instructed in Masters and Johnson's (1970) nonsexual stroking at this session, and in the nondemand sexual stroking for the wife at the sixth session. The man was discharged at this point and the couple failed to respond to attempts to contact them, until six months later when the husband informed us that his wife had left him to marry another man one week after his discharge.

Results: Figure 1 is a record of the wife's subjective rating of pleasure during intercourse and of the husband's time until ejaculation during the 45 days of treatment. The wife's rating of pleasure increased from zero (absence of all emotion) during baseline, to a mean of +4.8 (mild to moderate pleasure) during treatment. The ratings were lowest following the fifth session, when her adolescent son was arrested on a serious charge. No data was collected between the 16th and 40th days of treatment because of this crisis. The husband's time to ejaculation increased from a mean of 119 seconds at baseline, to a

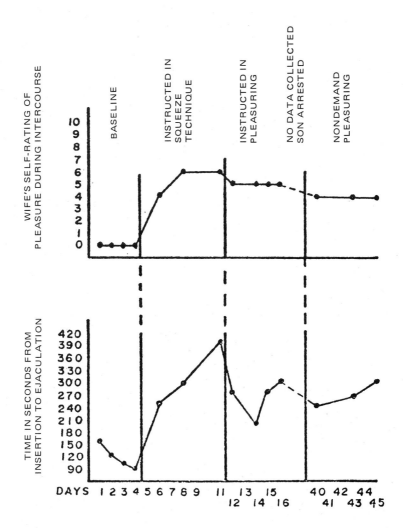

Fig. 1 A Record of the Wife's Self-rating of Pleasure during Intercourse, and of Time in Seconds from Penile Insertion to Ejaculation for Couple One.

mean of 228.1 seconds during treatment. While no quantitative data was collected at the six-month follow-up, the man stated that he continued to be satisfied with his sexual performance. However, he now complained of severe head and stomach pains which he said did not respond to medication. He said that he was under considerable pressure from holding down a job while maintaining a home for his children.

DISCUSSION

The treatment appeared to result in a considerable improvement in both the sexual and over-all relationship of the couple since the husband reported no longer feeling sexually inadequate, and his wife described him at the last interview as "a source of real strength," as opposed to the time of admission when she stated that she felt he was like one of the children. Unfortunately, the wife failed to reveal other apparent areas of dissatisfaction or of her involvement with another man. As a result, no attempt was made to work on other problem areas and the marriage was dissolved. Nonetheless, the treatment was successful in modifying the specific behavior for which it was intended.

Case Report Two: The 36-year-old wife of the second couple was admitted with a diagnosis of chronic undifferentiated schizophrenia following private psychotherapy and one previous hospitalization. At this time she was described as depressed, and was reported to have earlier said that she was talking with the Holy Ghost, and erroneously believed that she was suffering a heart attack. The couple reported premature ejaculation and infrequent intercourse for about five years prior to this.

Procedure: After two months of hospitalization the wife was instructed in the construction of a desensitization hierarchy on sex with her husband. Following group self-desensitization, she reported a slight improvement in that she could now comfortably hold hands with her husband, although she continued to view intercourse as "dirty." Two months later when she became an outpatient, sexual counseling was initiated with an understanding that it was to be brief, and that it would deal only with the couple's sexual behaviors, after which the couple would apply to a community facility.

The initial session was used to pinpoint target behaviors and begin environmental manipulation. The use of condoms was suggested at this time, since the wife objected to her husband ejaculating directly into the vaginal canal because she believed his semen was dirty. Similarly, we recommended using a radio to mask the creaking of their bed, as the wife feared that her sons would overhear the bed noise. The husband was referred to his family physician for complaints of painful ejaculation, which turned out to be a quickly treated prostate infection. Because the wife was self-conscious about her obesity and also found intercourse difficult for the same reason, she too was referred to the family physician who placed her on an unsuccessful diet and hormone shots. Finally, the couple was instructed to practice deep muscle relaxation (Wolpe & Lazarus, 1966) together in bed, and to rate their pleasure-displeasure during biweekly intercourse.

At the second session the couple reported having followed only the advice of seeing their physician, and having had intercourse one time. The need to follow instructions was emphasized, and in addition they were told to use K-Y sterile lubricant to make vaginal penetration and pelvic thrusting more comfortable for the wife. They were also asked to engage in nonsexual stroking or pleasuring with verbal feedback before intercourse, since they reported no foreplay. Instructions at the third session emphasized mutual backrubs because both partners reported enjoying this contact the most. Sessions were cancelled several times because of painful boils on the wife's thighs which interfered with intercourse. The fourth session centered around instructions to arouse the wife through sexual foreplay, and implementing a contingency contract in a nonsexual problem area.

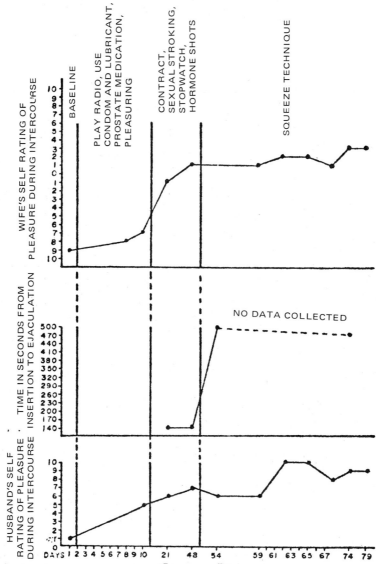

Fig. 2 A Record of Both Partners' Self-ratings of Pleasure during Intercourse, and of Time in Seconds from Penile Insertion to Ejaculation for Couple Two.

At this session the husband was given a stopwatch and asked to record his time to ejaculation. The squeeze technique was explained at the fifth session, while a contingency . contract trading meals out for intercourse was formalized at the final two sessions.

Results: Figure 2 indicates that both spouse's rating of pleasure during intercourse rose when a condom and lubricant were used, when the radio was played, when nonsexual stroking was initiated, and when the husband was treated for his prostate infection. The wife's ratings rose from -9 (extreme displeasure) to a mean of -7.5 (moderately unpleasant), while the husband's ratings rose from +1 (mild pleasure) to a mean of +4.5 (mild to moderate pleasure). An even more dramatic rise occurred for the wife when sexual stroking and hormone treatment began, moving from a mean of -7.6 (moderately unpleasant) to a mean of "0" (neutral). At this point she reported a decrease in her dread of intercourse, though no real interest in it. The husband's ratings also rose from a mean of +4.5 to a mean of +6.5 (moderate pleasure) during these 38 days. When the squeeze technique was used, the husband's time to ejaculation increased from a mean of 140 seconds to a mean of 488 seconds, while his rating of pleasure went from a mean of +6.5 to a mean of +8.3 (very pleasant). He also reported that his wife now assumed a more active role during intercourse and that she had stopped making comments such as "Hurry up and get it over with." During these same 31 days the wife's rating of pleasure increased from a mean of "0" to a mean of +1.9 (mild pleasure). The frequency of intercourse increased from zero during several months before counseling to about once a week during counseling. At the nine-month follow-up, the couple reported that the husband's ejaculatory control was the same as at termination (wife) or somewhat better that at termination (husband), that their sex in general was about the same as at termination (wife) or somewhat better (husband) and that they had sex once (wife) or twice (husband) a week despite the boils on the wife's thighs. The husband rated sex during the previous nine months at an average of +7 (moderate pleasure), while the wife rated sex during the same period at an average of +5 (moderate pleasure).

DISCUSSION

The counseling effectively increased both partners' ratings of pleasure during intercourse, the husband's time to ejaculation, and the frequency of intercourse. These improvements were reported, at the nine-month follow-up, to have been maintained, although no actual timing of ejaculatory control was provided. While it is impossible to assess the contribution of the hormone treatment, at no time did the wife report being sexually aroused or anticipating intercourse with pleasure, as would be expected if the hormones had affected her behavior.

CONCLUSIONS

The results with both couples suggest that the cautionary advice of Semans (1956), Wolpe and Lazarus (1968) and Masters and Johnson (1970) needs to be re-examined. In both couples the behaviors which were dealt with responded favorably, while other problem areas remained unchanged. It may be that couples such as these with many severe problems of long duration simply require additional behavior modification, instead of a different form of treatment. Rather than dismissing such couples as untreatable, the counselor might better continue dealing with specific behaviors, moving on to new problems as earlier ones come under control, until the couple is satisfied, or the counselor believes he can do no more.

REFERENCES

Semans, J.H. Premature ejaculation, a new approach. *Southern medical journal,* 1956, **49,** 353-358.

Masters, W.H. & Johnson, V. *Human sexual inadequacy.* Boston: Little, Brown & Co., 1970.

Wolpe, J. & Lazarus, A.A. *Behavior therapy techniques: A guide to the treatment of neuroses.* New York: Pergamon, 1966.

29
Ejaculatory Incompetence Treated by Reconditioning Anxiety

JAVAD RAZANI

An association between sexual dysfunctions and coital anxiety has frequently been noted (Allen, 1962; Stekel, 1927; Wolpe, 1958). Cooper (1969) reported a 94 percent correlation between coital anxiety and male potency disorders in a study of 49 patients. Ejaculatory incompetence (inability to ejaculate intravaginally) is an infrequent form of male sexual dysfunction. Masters and Johnson (1970) found only 17 cases in an 11-year period.

The case described below is that of a 24-year-old male with ejaculatory incompetence associated with coital anxiety. It had persisted for 6 years. It resolved rapidly with systematic desensitization in the office and *in vivo* techniques at home.

CASE HISTORY

B.M., a 24-year-old, engaged, postgraduate student, referred himself to the Behavior Therapy Unit with the complaint of never having been able to ejaculate intravaginally satisfactorily since his first attempt at coitus 6 years previously. Although able to achieve and maintain erection sufficient for intercourse, both before and during intercourse he would have doubts about his ability to perform, and at the same time become anxious about the possibility that he might impregnate his partner. As a result, even though he was able to maintain his erection intravaginally for several minutes, he would gradually lose his erection, eventually withdrawing without ejaculation. This, understandably, left him and his partner disappointed and frustrated.

Since the age of 14 he had masturbated regularly an average of three times a week with no premature emissions. He dated infrequently during his high-school years, the extent of his sexual activity being kissing and light petting. Since the onset of his sexual difficulty, he had retained a normal desire for intercourse as evidenced by his use of fantasies of women during masturbation.

Six years before his coming to the clinic, while a freshman in college, he had taken a girl friend to a motel after a dance with the intention of having intercourse (his first-ever

295

attempt). The girl expressed fear of becoming pregnant even though she had had a hysterectomy, and he became apprehensive about this possibility. He attained a firm erection, but in attempting penetration, aimed inaccurately; which resulted in an increase in his anxiety and premature ejaculation. Thereafter, he became reluctant to have intercourse; and, even though he dated off and on, did not try again until 4 years later when he became engaged for the first time.

He attempted intercourse with his first fiancee a total of seven times, but each experience ended with partial loss of erection and withdrawal without ejaculation. His first engagement lasted 13 months and ended because of the sexual dysfunction. After a 3-month period, he became engaged a second time. Four months later he came for treatment. With his second fiancee he had attempted intercourse a total of 13 times. On three occasions he was able to ejaculate intravaginally, but with much apprehension and anxiety. On eight occasions he had suffered partial loss of erection and on two occasions lost his erection before penetration. He was clearly on a path toward secondary impotence (Masters & Johnson, 1970), when he came to us. His fiancee was understanding and eager to cooperate, and he was highly motivated for treatment.

His initial clinical evaluation and psychological testings (Fear Survey Schedule, Eysenck Personality Inventory, EPAT Self Analysis Form and MMPI) revealed a somewhat shy, passive, and introspective young man who suffered from a lack of confidence in his sexual performance. He was well adjusted in his occupational and social environment, and there was no evidence of any overt interpersonal anxiety or of phobic or obsessional symptoms. His acquaintances perceived him as a warm and sensitive person and he had been able to establish several close interpersonal contacts.

He was born in a middle-class Jewish family, who were not religiously devout. His past history did not reveal any significant neurotic symptoms and he described his childhood as a happy one. There had been no discussions dealing with sexual matters at home. His one brother, 29 years old, is apparently functioning well sexually and otherwise.

TREATMENT

He was seen for five sessions each lasting 50 minutes. His first session was directed to clinical evaluation. A urological examination after this session showed no genito-urinary pathology. During his second session, he was seen with his fiancee, and a discussion about normal human sexual response ensued. He was then instructed in deep muscle relaxation. In order to decondition his fear of sexual contact, he and his fiancee were taught Semans' (1956) technique, according to which she was manually to stimulate his erect penis to the point premonitory of ejaculation and then to desist so as to allow the sensations to dissipate. The sexual arousal was expected to inhibit the fear. She was to repeat this two or three times before allowing him to go on to ejaculation. In the second and third sessions they carried out this technique several times, with the result that he no longer felt threatened by sexual contact with his fiancee. At the third session systematic desensitization was applied to the image of intravaginal ejaculation. He was able to practice coitus successfully at home with his fiancee in the female superior position described by Masters and Johnson (1970). At the fifth session he reported many successful intravaginal ejaculations after an average of 2-3 minutes of containment. At this time a switch was made to the male superior position without any difficulty. Thereafter, he was able successfully to ejaculate intravaginally with no recurrences of erective inadequacy and with mutual satisfaction. He married his fiancee shortly afterward.

Monthly follow-up (6 months until now) show continuation of satisfactory sexual performance. He has reported an increase in confidence in thinking about his performance and is able to regard sex as natural and physiological. As before, he continues to do well in other spheres of life.

DISCUSSION

Masters and Johnson state that a man with ejaculatory incompetence rarely has difficulty in achieving or maintaining the erection necessary for successful coitus. The problem usually arises during the first coital experience and continues unresolved by subsequent attempts. Pressure to succeed can become so acute that secondary impotence may develop. Masters and Johnson had a cure rate of 83.4 percent in their seventeen treated cases. Seven of the cases described by Cooper (1969) would appear to fit Masters and Johnson's description of ejaculatory incompetence. Six of these responded rapidly to treatment which consisted of deep muscle relaxation, Semans' technique, sexual education and "psychotherapy." It may be presumed that anxiety reduction was central to Cooper's successes. In the case described here, recovery followed specific deconditioning of the anxiety evoked by the coital situation.

Acknowledgment: I wish to thank Dr. Neil B. Edwards for his critical evaluation of this paper and Dr. Alan Goldstein for his advice in the treatment of the case.

REFERENCES

Allen, C. *Textbook of psychosexual disorders.* London: Oxford University Press, 1962.

Cooper, A.J. A clinical study of "coital anxiety" in male potency disorders. *J. psychosom. res.* 1969, **3**, 143-147.

Cooper, A.J. Clinical and therapeutic studies in premature ejaculation. *Compreh. psychiat.* 1969, **10**, 4.

Masters, W.H. & Johnson, V.E. *Human sexual inadequacy.* Boston: Little, Brown & Co., 1970.

Semans, J.H. Premature ejaculation: A new approach. *J. Urol.* 1956, **49**, 353-357.

Stekel, W. *Impotence in the male.* New York: Liveright, 1927.

Wolpe, J. *Psychotherapy by reciprocal inhibition.* Stanford: Stanford University Press, 1958.

Wolpe, J. *The practice of behavior therapy.* New York: Pergamon Press, 1969.

30
Group Treatment of Premature Ejaculation

HELEN S. KAPLAN, RICHARD N. KOHL,
WARDELL B. POMEROY, AVODAH K. OFFIT and BARBARA HOGAN

INTRODUCTION

A pilot study of the group treatment of premature ejaculation is being undertaken as part of the Sex Therapy and Education Program of the Payne Whitney Psychiatric Clinic of the New York Hospital–Cornell Medical Center. The following is a report of the first group, which consisted of four couples. Premature ejaculation of the male was the chief complaint of each couple. The goal of the treatment was limited to the attainment of ejaculatory control.

DEFINITION OF PREMATURE EJACULATION

Premature ejaculation is probably the most common sexual dysfunction of American males, occurring in the psychiatrically healthy as well as in patients exhibiting various forms of psychopathology. It is a condition wherein a man reaches orgasm very quickly. Definitions of premature ejaculation have varied. They have been given in terms of length of coital time prior to ejaculation, number of strokes prior to ejaculation, and, by Masters and Johnson (1970), percentage of times in which the man reaches orgasm before the woman (more than 50% equals premature ejaculation). In contrast, at the Cornell Medical Center, we believe that the essential parameter of premature ejaculation consists of the failure of the man to attain control over the ejaculatory reflex once an intense level of sexual arousal has been attained, with the result that once excited he reaches orgasm rapidly. Hence, we define prematurity as the inability of a man to tolerate high (plateau) levels of sexual excitement without ejaculating reflexly.

TYPES OF TREATMENT

Various forms of therapy have been tried to cure prematurity with varying degrees of success. These have included psychoanalytic methods, "common sense" and behavioral approaches, and, more recently, a highly effective "sensory training" technique.

Psychoanalytic treatment is based on the premise that premature ejaculation is an expression of the unconscious conflicts regarding women which derive from developmental problems in the patient's childhood. The analytic methods have been employed to uncover and resolve the patient's postulated unconscious conflicts and hostilities toward females, with the expectation that such a resolution would be accompanied by an automatic improvement in sexual functioning. Although no systematic study has been performed, the general impression is that results of insight therapy alone, at least for the relief of premature ejaculation, have been disappointing.

The "common sense" approach, which is widely espoused by the medical profession and laity alike, is based on the supposition that premature ejaculation is caused by excessive erotic sensation and that the remedy lies in diminishing this sensations. Specific techniques prescribed by physicians include the use of condoms, anesthetic ointments applied to the penis, distraction from the sexual experience in progress by nonerotic imagery, and the use of alcohol, sedatives, and tranquilizers. All of these have been unsuccessful.

Behavioral approaches have also been applied to the therapy of prematurity. These have mainly employed desensitization, on the theory that anxiety is a cause of premature ejaculation. Behavioral treatment has not been very effective.

Various pharmacological treatments have also been tried. The use of tricyclic and hydrazine antidepressants has some success while the patient uses those drugs. However, when medication is discontinued, the man again is unable to exert voluntary control over ejaculation and reaches climax quickly.

Marital therapy treats prematurity by attempting to resolve the alleged transactional roots of the symptom. Again, to date there are no reports of success of this approach.

The most successful, however, and the foundation of the Masters and Johnson approach, was reported in 1956 by the urologist James Semans, who based his treatment on "prolonging the localized neuromuscular reflex mechanism of ejaculation," which he felt was "extremely rapid" in premature ejaculation. His technique was exceedingly simple. It consisted of extravaginal stimulation of the man by his wife, until the sensation premonitory to ejaculation was attained, then interruption of the stimulation until the man could tolerate this stimulation indefinitely without ejaculating. At this point, in the eight patients who made up his study population prematurity was permanently relieved.

The Masters-Johnson approach is essentially the same. It differs primarily in substituting a "squeeze" of the penis (just below the rim of the glans) at the time of ejaculatory premonition, rather than a simple cessation of stimulation. The Masters-Johnson treatment also involves a complex, intensive format wherein the couple under treatment is seen every day for 2 weeks by a mixed-gender cotherapy team. In addition to the squeeze technique, various other exercises, including sensate focus, are included in the treatment regimen. A 98% success rate is reported by Masters and Johnson with this approach.

A WORKING CONCEPT OF PREMATURE EJACULATION

One implication of the success of the Semans type of approach is that an understanding of the original motivation roots of premature ejaculation is irrelevant for the purpose of treatment: the underlying dynamics do not have to be resolved in order for the patient to achieve ejaculatory control. Perhaps there are many remote factors which play a role in the etiology of prematurity. However, the multiple remote causes of the condition may be bypassed. It is only the immediate antecedents of the man's failure to acquire ejaculatory continence which have to be modified to cure the patient. What are these immediate antecedents? The final answer to this question is not clear. However, we postulate that for some reason, because of unconscious conflict or perhaps some other cause, the premature ejaculator has not focued his attention on the sensation of sexual arousal. He virtually does not perceive the sensations premonitory to orgasm and has therefore failed to learn control of his ejaculatory reflex. This is analogous to a child's failure to learn urinary continence because he has not perceived the sensations of a full bladder. The essential aim of treatment then becomes the clear-cut one of supplying previously deficient perceptual links to encourage the patient to be aware of and experience his sexual sensations.

APPROACH OF THE CORNELL PROGRAM

The approach to the therapy of prematurity in our program is based on these principles. As is true of the treatment of all sexual dysfunctions, the format employs exercises to be carried out by the patient and his wife in the privacy of their home which are integrated with conjoint psychotherapeutic sessions in the clinic. The primary aim of the exercises used in the therapy of prematurity is to help the man focus his attention and concentrate on, and fully experience, the sensations premonitory to orgasm. This experience must occur together with his partner because it is anxiety engendered by the sexual and marital transactions which often seems to distract the husband from abandoning himself to his sexual sensations.

Treatment begins with an evaluation session, attended by the couple, during which a detailed history is obtained of the sexual functioning of both partners. All motivated couples are accepted for treatment except those in which *either* partner exhibits active, severe psychopathology or in which the sexual symptom appears to be employed as a major defense against pathology.

The couple is given an explanation of the rationale behind the treatment, and it is made clear to the wife that, initially at least, there may be little reward for her. If she can defer her immediate gratification, a therapeutic "contract" is entered into with the couple, whereby they agree to cooperate in the recommended treatment. They are also made aware that they themselves are responsible for the success of the treatment. Finally, they are told that the prognosis for rapid relief is excellent, provided that they adhere to the treatment.

Couples are seen conjointly, usually once a week for 3-6 weeks, for a total of six to 12 times, and are encouraged to telephone their therapist should questions arise. The exercises themselves, carried out in the home, follow a two-part sequence: extravaginal stimulation, and stimulation during coitus. The exercises are based on the Semans approach. Initially, the man is stimulated manually by his wife, with four premonitory "ceases" prescribed before ejaculation is to be allowed. When improvement in control is seen, the exercises are repeated, with the penis first lubricated by vaseline, as this more closely simulates the vaginal environment. After three to six extravaginal sessions, sufficient improvement is usually attained to permit the beginning of intercourse. Intercourse is first attempted in the female-superior position, as being less stimulating to the man; with success, the lateral and then the male-superior position is attempted. The stop-short technique is used during the early intercourse sessions and is suggested for occasional use after treatment is terminated. As stated, the prognosis is excellent in that, if the couple follows the instructions and performs the exercises, the man will reach his goal of being able to choose when to ejaculate. In fact, we have treated 32 premature ejaculation couples with this approach, and of the couples who have completed therapy none has failed to attain ejaculatory continence. However, since these trials were not done under controlled conditions these promising results must be regarded with caution. Nonetheless, we were encouraged by this apparent success to hypothesize that the essential ingredients in the therapy of prematurity have been identified. Moreover, the therapy was exceedingly simple and might be more economically applied in a group setting in which several couples could be treated simultaneously.

GROUP TREATMENT

Our first group treatment for prematurely ejaculating men was undertaken with four couples, all having stable marriages, all without severe psychopathology in either partner, all previously screened and evaluated. Group sessions were 45 min long, and the group was seen once a week for 6 weeks. The group was directed by Drs. Kaplan, Pomeroy, Offit, and Mrs. Hogan*, as a task-oriented, theme-centered group, with the group process used to enhance the sex treatment. Specifically it was the objective of the group sessions to convey instructions for the exercises which the couples were to carry out at home and also deal with obstacles to sexual functioning and resistances to treatment which almost invariably emerge during the course of therapy. The group met once a week and the session began with the review of each couple's experiences during the previous week. The therapists worked with intrapsychic and transactional resistance to treatment as they emerged. As is usual in group therapy, the group dynamics were employed in the service of revealing and resolving conflicts. However, in this setting our objective was limited to the treatment of prematurity. Therefore, in contrast to the usual group therapy, where transactions between the members are employed to reveal and resolve all manner of problems, here interpretations were made only to implement sex therapy. For this reason, competiton among couples was bypasssed; emphasis was on mutual support and encouragement. Perhaps the group process can best be understood by describing the results obtained by each couple individually.

First Couple
In couple 1, the man, a 25-year-old carpenter, was married to a woman of the same age. They had been married to each other for 1½ years, and it was the second marriage for each. The wife had two children from her former marriage and was 4 months pregnant when the treatment began. She was attractive, intelligent, and easily multiorgastic. Her husband, whose early sexual experience had been with prostitutes, had been a premature ejaculator since he commenced sexual activity. On his first manual stop/start session, the

*The use of four therapists was motivated primarily by staff interest in the project. Subsequently we have been using single therapists, which is of course far more economical and seems to be equally effective.

husband twice successfully controlled his ejaculatory reflex. However, resistances emerged during the next session. He had had too much to drink, and when they began to exercise again he was unable to concentrate on his sensations and thus failed to stop in time, and ejaculated. The wife also presented obstacles. For the third exercise session, the couple did not practice the extravaginal sequence as recommended, but, with the wife's urging, the man proceeded directly to intercourse, in the female-superior position. Not surprisingly, he was unable to concentrate on the penile sensations and ejaculated immediately on insertion.

During a group discussion of these events, the wife of another couple pointed out that this man seemed to have a fear of failure that was distracting him from focusing on his sensations and that his wife also seemed fearful and was pressuring her husband. Clarification of the resistances of this couple helped the rest in getting in touch with their own previously unconscious fears of sexuality. The mutual discussion of this material was extremely helpful to all. However, the couple did not attend the third group session. They came to the fourth. A new resistance was revealed. Describing the exercises they had performed in the meantime, they reported waiting for the man's sexual sensation to cease completely before resuming manual stimulation, instead of resuming stimulation after a few seconds, per instructions. Again, resistances and anxieties were dealt with in the group. The man's sense of inadequacy and some of its roots were discussed during the session. In addition to psychodynamically oriented interpretations, it was pointed out that they were waiting too long and losing the benefit of experience with high plateau levels of excitement. It was suggested by the therapists that they have some additional extravaginal experience and then move to intravaginal stop/start. This was the couple's last session in the group. They cancelled the final meeting and were rescheduled 4 months later for followup. Surprisingly, this resistant couple had a successful outcome. At the followup meeting, they reported having followed the recommended exercise sequence, after they left the group, with the husband moving to the lateral and then the male-superior position with increasing success. The husband described a sense of control and awareness of his penile sensations. They declared that intercourse now lasted as long as they liked. She was multiorgastic on coitus, which was now a positive experience for both of them.

Second Couple

In couple 2, the man, a 44-year-old writer, had been married for 8 years to a 37-year-old woman, the second marriage for both. They were a very sensitive, intelligent couple. The woman had been in analysis a number of years previously; she had great insight and freely communicated her knowledge and impressions to other group members in a helpful way. She was sexually responsive but coitally inorgastic. The man seemed to have an essentially normal history of sexual and psychological development. His prematurity had its onset with sexual activity. The couple had read Masters and Johnson and had tried, without success, to deal with the prematurity problem by themselves. Although the marriage was basically a healthy one, the man was obsessive and constantly worried about his inability to control his ejaculation and his wife's inability to have orgasm during coitus. For this couple, treatment proceeded without the dramatic resistances demonstrated by couple 1.

The husband learned to concentrate on his sensations, which he had previously failed to do. He was very impressed with the sexual abandonment which was described by the multiorgastic wife of the first couple. He compared this with his own constricted attitudes. He was delighted with the improvement of his sexual enjoyment and ejaculatory control, when he too was able to abandon himself "selfishly" to the sexual experience. The other women in the group vociferously confronted the husband with the pressure he was placing on his wife for coital orgasm. The couple discussed this openly between themselves in the group. Two sessions later, she reported that, free from having to worry about her husband's concern for her, she was able to concentrate on her own sexual feelings and was able to experience coital orgasm. He gained satisfactory ejaculatory continence by the fifth group session. The couple could not be reached for followup.

Third Couple

Couple 3 had been married for 7 years and had one child. The man was a stockbroker, 35 years old; the woman was a teacher and social worker, 32 years old. This also appeared to be a good marriage. The man suffered from premature ejaculation. The wife, who had been in therapy for a short time, had been orgastic in the past, but not within a year of treatment. The man was suffering from a mild depression.

The treatment for this couple also progressed easily to a successful conclusion. The husband was able to participate in the exercises and concentrate on his sensation without resistance as soon as it became clear that his wife had no objections to such "selfishness." On the contrary, she was too eager to be generous. It was pointed out in group sessions that she was neglecting her own pleasures and that she too permitted overconcern for her partner to impair her sexual abandonment. During the sessions, it became clear that both partners were governed by unconscious fears that the other would abandon them. The remoter causes of this dynamic were not dealt with in the group sessions because it did not present direct obstacles to improved sexual functioning. This couple was seen 4 months later. At that time, they reported that success had continued; in addition, the wife had become orgastic again and was no longer worried about sex. The husband reported that his mild depression had lifted.

Fourth Couple

Couple 4 were two college-educated people, married to each other for 20 years. The man was 47 years old, the woman 2 years his junior and easily orgastic. To find a cure for his premature ejaculation, the man had previously spent 10 years in therapy, going two or three times a week. Although he felt that he had benefited in general from the experience, his ejaculatory control had not improved. The goal that brought this couple to the clinic was not only increased ejaculatory control for the man but also an increase in the frequency of intercourse; at the time of treatment, they had intercourse about once every 3-4 weeks.

This couple began the Semans exercises along with the others. At first there was no difficulty. The man was easily aroused in his erotic feelings, approached the exercises eagerly, and experienced a number of initial successes. Then, quite suddenly, he began to have trouble achieving and maintaining an erection.

He revealed to the group that he had encountered this problem previously and that it had been related to a feeling of pressure to perform and consequent anxiety that he might fail. The treatment regimen was modified for this couple to accommodate for his erectile difficulty. They were advised that, if necessary, additional sessions could be scheduled with them in the fall but that in the meantime they should resume the exercises in a nondemand context, that is, at the husband's discretion, with no demand for coital stimulation.

During the group sessions, it became apparent that the wife was placing obstacles in the way of her husband's progress. As his functioning began to improve, her anxiety about losing control over him seemed to motivate her to place on him excessive demands for sexual performance. Not surprisingly, this vulnerable man began to experience erectile difficulties. His wife's demands, their destructive effects, and some of their underlying sources were discussed during group sessions. Consequently, she was able to control her behavior. Relieved of the demands for performance, the man was able to respond, to obtain an erection and carry through the start/stop sequences. Soon his ability to control ejaculations extravaginally improved, and a little later, when he proceeded to insertion, he also quickly attained intravaginal control. He discovered that he was capable of having intercourse two or three times a week, and even claimed that he had had more sexual experiences in the 6 weeks of group treatment than in the past 10 years.

The alleviation of this man's symptoms required more than the modification of the immediate obstacles to sexual functioning which sufficed to help the other couples. It was necessary to deal with some of the remote roots of the problem. Both transactional and intrapsychic determinants were dealt with in the group. It emerged that he was unconsciously continuing his struggle against a controlling "mother" (i.e., his wife) via the use of sex. He had already dealt with his relationship with his mother in his previous psychotherapy; however, he had heretofore failed to make the necessary connection between this genetic material and his current sexual functioning. This was done in group. This couple was later rescheduled and seen in 4 months, by which time the man had achieved complete ejaculatory control. There were no further erectile problems, and frequency of sexual contact was once per week.

DISCUSSION

Our pilot experiment with the group treatment of premature ejaculation is gratifying on many levels. First, experience has supported our hypothesis that we have developed a useful working concept of the pathogenesis and essential treatment parameters of this condition. The hypothesis that the immediate obstacle to ejaculatory control lies in the man's failure, for multiple reasons, to perceive sensations premonitory to ejaculation requires experimental validation before it can be regarded as established. However, on an empirical level, the concept is useful. Similarly, it appears that the active ingredient of the successful therapy methods consists of overcoming the immediate obstacle to ejaculatory continence by inducing the man to experience the previously avoided perception of high levels of erotic arousal while he is with his sexual partner. This procedure may be thought of as supplying the perception necessary for learning ejaculatory continence.

From a technical standpoint, it seems that the group process can be employed to implement this treatment goal. Specifically, in the group sessions we gave directions for the stop/start exercises which are designed to overcome the alleged immediate cause of prematurity. In addition, the group process was employed to deal with obstacles and resistances which were motivated by deeper causes. How far we had to go to resolve these varied with each couple. Thus, in one instance, couple 2, very little deeper transactional and intrapsychic material was interpreted. In contrast, the problems presented by couple

4 necessitated explicit work with more complex marital interactions as well as with interpretation of the husband's unconscious conflicts and exploration of some of their genetic roots.

This treatment of premature ejaculation was based on a theme-centered, target-symptom-removal group. Success was defined as the husband's attainment of voluntary ejaculatory control with consequently prolonged coitus. The attainment of such control was indicated only if both spouses agreed that this had happened. According to this criterion, of the four couples in the pilot study, two were treated with success in the six group sessions, and the other two had gained ejaculatory continence successfully 2 months later. All four couples reported continued and improved sexual functioning at 4 months followup.

Results obtained in only one program involving only four couples cannot of course be definitive, but they are consonant with the results obtained with the single-couple treatment provided in the program, which is based on the same concept of pathogenesis and treatment. The group format seems well suited to implement the treatment procedure.

At the present time, we are seeing additional groups of premature ejaculators and their wives, using only single therapists, and the results continue to be excellent. It may be inferred that other types of sexual dysfunction may be similarly amenable to such treatment provided that the essential principles of treatment for these syndromes are also clearly delineated.

It is worth noting also that the actual amount of therapist time spent in helping four couples achieve success amounted to about 7 hours, or about 1½ hours per couple. This represents a significant reduction in therapist time from the already rapid treatment format for individual couples which is used at the Payne Whitney Clinic, where a couple is seen for an average of 7 hours. Four couples would thus have required 28 hours of therapist time.

REFERENCES

Kaplan, H. *The New Sex Therapy.* New York, Brunner/Mazel, 1973.
Masters, W., and Johnson, V. *Human Sexual Inadequacy,* Boston: Little Brown, 1970.
Semans, J. Premature ejaculation: A new approach. *South. Med. J..* 1956, 49: 353-358.

Additional Selected Readings

Kraft, T. & Al-issa, I. The use of methohexitone sodium in the systematic desensitization of premature ejaculation. *Brit. J. Psychiat.,* 1968, **114,** 351-352.

Semans, J.H. Premature ejaculation: A new approach. *Southern Medical Journal,* 1956, **49,** 353-358.

Orgasmic Dysfunction

Until fairly recently women have neither expected nor felt as much pressure to achieve orgasms through intercourse as men. Part of this difference was a result of sexism, and part was related to the physiological fact that a woman can participate in sexual intercourse when not aroused, while a man cannot.

Along with the changing status of women has come increased attention to the problems experienced by many women in not achieving orgasm through intercourse. Indeed, scientific knowledge of the female orgasm, which was quite limited only a few years ago, is rapidly expanding.

The range of women's orgasmic responses to intercourse is quite wide, with some women experiencing numerous intense orgasms at each intercourse and some experiencing very subtle, gentle orgasms or none at all. The probability of a woman experiencing orgasms in marital sexual relations seems correlated with premarital masturbation, petting, or intercourse leading to orgasm (Katchadourian & Lunde, 1975, p. 373). There are some women who do not experience orgasms—or experience them rarely—who enjoy their sexual relations and do not consider their lack of orgasms a problem. There are also others, of course, who experience frequent and satisfying orgasms but find other aspects of their sexual activities unsatisfactory. Nevertheless, there remain large numbers of women for whom the lack of satisfactory orgasms is a major concern, and orgasmic problems in women are the most frequent ones reported to sex therapists.

The problems associated with orgasm discussed in this section typically are referred to as "frigidity." However, as with the term "impotence" for men, the term "frigidity" is far from behaviorally specific, is vague, has come to acquire a pejorative connotation and often leaves women who have acquired the label of "frigid" feeling increasingly anxious, helpless, and hopeless. Despite the fact that most of the authors whose work is presented in this section use the term "frigid," it would be far more useful and less

307

harmful to clients to eschew such global labeling and to attempt to define in specific behavioral terms whatever problem the client describes. Hence, the term "orgasmic dysfunction" is used in this book. Commonly, primary orgasmic dysfunction, in which a woman has never experienced orgasm, is distinguished from secondary orgasmic dysfunction wherein the problem developed after a period of time during which the woman was able to reach orgasm. A subsidiary classification distinguishes between absolute or situational orgasmic dysfunction; in the former, the woman cannot reach orgasm under any circumstances, while in the latter, orgasm can be reached only under certain circumstances.

It should be noted that some authors (e.g., Kaplan, 1974), distinguish between frigidity (a generally sexually dysfunctional woman who derives little if any erotic pleasure from sexual stimulation) and orgasmic (or "orgastic") dysfunction, which specifically involves lack of orgasm. However, since intervention tends to proceed in similar ways in both cases, there appears little necessity to exaggerate the importance of this distinction.

The first article, by Wolpe, presents an actual case transcript involving "Correcting Misconceptions in a Case of Frigidity." In this case, Wolpe demonstrates the use of a procedure to which, generally, only passing references are made in the literature—the correcting of misconceptions. The detailed transcript shows how Wolpe initiated efforts to remove the client's mistaken idea that she somehow was sexually biologically incapable. The transcript also illustrates how Wolpe moved, in a joint interview with the client's husband, to re-communicate the existence of basic mutual affection.

The next article, Goldstein's "Conflict in a Case of Frigidity," traces from the beginning to end of treatment the case of a 24-year-old woman who initially presented "frigidity" as her only problem. Apparent factors contributing to the problem were fears of expression of her own anger and the anger of others, plus misconceptions concerning her roles of wife and mother. Goldstein illustrates the interconnections between these various areas of disturbance and the resulting therapeutic measures, including desensitization for what was seen as conditioned inhibition to sex, and a behavior therapy group with particular emphasis on her lack of assertiveness. The article concludes with an interesting discussion among several therapists who analyze with Goldstein many of the finer points of this case.

The article by Lazarus illustrates "The Treatment of Chronic Frigidity by Systematic Densitization." This is one of the early descriptions of desensitization applied to sexual problems, and clearly illustrates the process, including a detailed statement of the hierarchy used for one of the cases treated by Lazarus. Since this is an early article, it is interesting to speculate on other, additional courses of action that would be used in the seven cases considered as "failures." Although several of the clients apparently terminated before adequate treatment could be instituted, there apparently also were some who could not produce sufficiently vivid images for desensitization. Since, in most situations involving behavior therapy, more than one technique is used, it is likely that, were these cases to be encountered today, the use of the other techniques described in this book to complement or even replace desensitization would have raised the success rate substantially.

The next brief article, by Madsen and Ullmann, describes "Innovations in the Desensitization of Frigidity." The basic innovations involve having the husband present in the room during construction of the hierarchy and the development of the desensitization procedures, as well as having him actually present some of the hierarchy items. The advantages of these modifications are discussed and a case history illustrating their use is presented.

The following article, "Directed Masturbation and the Treatment of Primary Orgasmic Dysfunction," by Kohlenberg, evaluates the efficacy of directed masturbation as an adjunct to the treatment of primary orgasmic dysfunction. The directed masturbation procedure consisted of a gradual series of assignments that were to be practiced by the client, and was used with three couples who had not benefitted from a sexual treatment program modeled after that of Masters and Johnson. The results suggest that directed masturbation holds promise as an important adjunct to sexual counseling.

The final article in this section is "Secondary Orgasmic Dysfunction: A Case Study," by Snyder *et al.* In this case, a direct behavioral retraining program was employed to increase the couple's repertoire of effective sexual behaviors. An extinction and successive approximation procedure was used to transfer orgasmic responsiveness from solitary masturbation to heterosexual coitus. Concurrent with this, a direct intervention into the marital relationship was made on the grounds that nonsexual marital problems may have been contributing to the orgasmic dysfunction. The article concludes with the presentation of some interesting outcome data on the effectiveness of treatment.

REFERENCES

Katchadourian, H. & Lunde, D. *Fundamentals of human sexuality* (2nd ed.). New York: Holt, Rinehart, and Winston, 1975.

Kaplan, H.S. *The New Sex Therapy*. New York: Bruner/Mazel, 1974.

31
Correcting Misconceptions in a Case of Frigidity: A Transcript

JOSEPH WOLPE

An operation that is common and often important in the practice of behavior therapy, but to which as a rule only passing reference is made in published accounts, is the correcting of misconceptions. In the case whose first interview is reported below, a marked diminution of general anxiety followed the correction of her erroneous notions about the nature of her inability to have coital orgasms. Her intellectual acceptance of the proposition that her unadaptive responses were learned also directly facilitated her collaboration in the conditioning procedures subsequently applied.

The patient had learned from her first husband that her sexual inadequacy was due to "emotional sickness"—a view endorsed by her psychoanalyst and reinforced by her present husband and her father. When, year after year, for 10 years, the psychoanalysis produced no sign of changed sexual responsiveness, she became increasingly despondent.

A week before the transcribed interview, the husband had consulted me about her. Despite strong mutual attraction, the marriage, entered into 11 years previously, had never been satisfactory, for reasons related to the absence of his wife's coital orgasms. From an early stage in the marriage the husband had noticed that his wife was markedly irritable for days after each sexual act. She had become more and more unhappy as the years went on, going into increasingly prolonged and profound spells of depression, and frequently giving vent to tantrums and other minor acts of violence. Her psychoanalyst had diagnosed her condition as a character neurosis. At the end of 1970, she had briefly run away with a university student, a fact that had become embarrassingly widely known. Since then, she had been something of a recluse.

In the first half of the transcribed interview the patient was seen alone. The main therapeutic task at that juncture was to undermine the view that her disability was a "sickness." In the second half, the husband was included to facilitate the objective of correcting her impression that he did not really care for her. A climactic reorientation evidently occurred at the *next* interview, at which she was persuaded that there was nothing inherently wrong with her—that her sexual inhibitions were purely a matter of conditioning and, as such, capable of being removed by conditioning procedures. At the commencement of the third interview she stated: "I feel like I'm halfway home." She now had a feeling of optimism and confidence that enabled her to cooperate splendidly in the emotional reconditioning procedures that were later applied. There was never again the slightest hint of depression in the months that followed. In the course of a total of 10 interviews her basic fear of trusting people (mentioned in the transcript) was overcome, and by maneuvers based on her masturbatory orgasms, regular coital orgasms were achieved. Her widespread jealousy reactions toward other women faded away when she became aware of her own normality.

Dr.: I gather from Ed, your husband, that there is a lack of harmony in certain ways between you.[1] The question is whether there is any practical possibility of straightening out your relationship and making it mutually desirable.

Lisa: I think we're very different people. Of course most people are different; but I think that I married my husband for very neurotic reasons, and I'm sure there had to be something like that on his side, too. I've spent 10 years in therapy. You're the third doctor my husband has made me come to—not *made* me come to. I shouldn't phrase it that way.

Dr.: Well sometimes it's not a matter of therapy.[2] Anyway, before we make any decisions, let's get some facts. When did you first meet him?

Lisa: I guess I knew him casually when we were in our teenage years. I was a freshman at college when he was a senior. I didn't start dating him until after my first marriage dissolved.

Dr.: What did you like about Ed?

Lisa: He was entirely opposite from my father.

Dr.: How old were you when your first marriage dissolved?

Lisa: 20.

Dr.: You liked the fact that Ed was different from your father. Well, what was the difference?

Lisa: He was quiet and more stable; certainly emotionally more balanced. He was the type of man that I've always been attracted to—protective, I guess.

Dr.: Well, he was stable and elicited a feeling of protectiveness. Is that the essence of it?

Lisa: I don't know. I never thought about it that way.

Dr.: Did you feel very strongly attracted to Ed at that time?

Lisa: Yeah.

Dr.: How long after this did you get married?

Lisa: Six months.

Dr.: And how did you get along with him during those six months?

Lisa: Ah—it was sort of a topsy-turvy relationship.

Dr.: What do you mean?

Lisa: Well, there were certain periods of stress and strain. It was never what I would call a quiet courtship period.

---

[1] The statement was deliberately phrased in these extremely general terms so that the patient could state without constraint the issues as she saw them.

[2] Some marital incompatibilities are not resoluble by psychotherapy. This is true, for example, of intellectual differences and wide divergencies of interest. This idea was now introduced in order to suggest to the patient that she might, after all, not be "sick" as had always been assumed. As it turned out, this was the key move in the treatment of the case.

Dr.: What were the causes of the stresses and strains?

Lisa: Me, I guess. I was a very emotionally sick person at the time and I——

Dr.: Something must have upset you.[3]

Lisa: I don't know. I guess his background.

Dr.: I'm not asking you in that sense. I'm not asking you what caused the upset. I'm just asking what upset you.[4]

Lisa: Oh I don't know. I guess I was demanding and insecure and jealous of the amount of time he spent with me. I never go along on an even keel; I'm always up or down or——

Dr.: Still, what are the kinds of things that upset you?

Lisa: When he gives attention to another woman, that upsets me.

Dr.: Well, that's clear enough. Was that the sort of thing that used to happen?

Lisa: It's so long ago, I can't remember. I was in such a state of complete unreality when Ed and I were dating, I don't even remember what my behavior was like.

Dr.: But you liked to be with him and you were happy with the relationship.

Lisa: Yeah.

Dr.: But there were just some things that upset you.

Lisa: Yeah. Well, I was living at home with a small baby[5] —not exactly an ideal set-up.

Dr.: What was the sexual relationship[6] at that period?

Lisa: I don't know. For me, there never has been any sexual satisfaction, but I guess I have tried very hard because I want to hold on to him.

Dr.: So there wasn't any real sexual enjoyment for you?

Lisa: There never has been with anyone.

Dr.: You know some women will say they don't reach a climax, but they enjoy sex. You don't even enjoy it.

Lisa: Oh, I guess I enjoy it. Yeah, to a point.

Dr.: Yes?

Lisa: Yes, I guess I never really tore it apart like that.

Dr.: Well, do you get stimulated up to a point and then feel left high and dry? Do you feel frustrated?

Lisa: No, the anger has completely faded out of it for me. I'm no longer angry about it or demanding of it. I become very irritable and hostile toward Ed.

Dr.: Well, that's what I mean.

Lisa: But I don't feel that this is my fault because——

Dr.: It's not important whose fault it is.[7]

Lisa: No, but I mean, there isn't any sexual relationship—unless it comes from me, there isn't any.

Dr.: I see. Anyway, going back to that time. At that time, you were having some sex with him?

---

[3] Further deflecting from the idea of "sickness," and suggesting accountable reactivity.

[4] Patients who have had psychoanalytically-informed therapy are characteristically more ready to provide causal hypotheses than facts.

[5] The offspring of her first marriage.

[6] It should be noted how noncommittally this crucial topic was introduced.

[7] The therapist seizes every opportunity to assuage guilt and diminish self-blame. It does not matter that in this instance the patient's next remark showed him to be off-target.

Lisa: Yeah.

Dr.: And, you were enjoying it up to a point——

Lisa: Oh yeah.

Dr.: And then you were left irritated afterward?

Lisa: Yeah.

Dr.: So that tended to make you keep away from him because it was sort of punishing.

Lisa: Well, I think eventually, yes. Especially after you're married and you're legally bound to one another, you're safer and you can turn it off, so to speak, emotionally. When I went to the first psychiatrist, and Ed found out there was a problem, he completely dropped sexual approaches. In the last 10 years—if I didn't initiate it, there was nothing. Last year, we went the entire year without any sex at all. But I do feel that my therapy has been—it's been long, but it has served the purpose.

Dr.: What purpose has it served?

Lisa: Well, I have found out, I think, the reasons for my problems. I consider myself a controlled neurotic[8] now. I'm afraid to do anything.

Dr.: You're afraid to do anything?

Lisa: Right. I don't do anything at all. If I know it's dangerous to my . . .

Dr.: This is very important. Take this sexual situation. If you find that sex leaves you very upset and irritated, then it's reasonable to avoid it. It doesn't necessarily mean that your failure to respond sexually is itself neurotic. It may be, I don't know. But it may not be.[9]

Lisa: Well, it's a different feeling now. But since I returned to Ed—as I'm sure he explained to you—following the circumstances of last Fall,[10] he made an effort and I made an effort. But again he has backed off and this makes me more irritable——

Dr.: He has backed off in what way?

Lisa: He doesn't make advances toward me anymore. He tried for a while. I never rejected him in this entire period; and I was cooperative and enjoyed it and——

Dr.: So today you would like him to make advances?

Lisa: But he doesn't. And this is when I started questioning him. I said: "Ed, I am not going to any more psychiatrists because it's a two-way street." And I said: "I am tired of always being the aggressive one in our relationship." I can never be subordinate in my mind if I'm the only one who's aggressive.

Dr.: In the beginning you were the one to avoid intercourse and now he avoids it.

Lisa: Well, he avoided it during the entire 8-year period. The doctors questioned about it.[11] They felt that Ed had dropped it much too quickly when he found out that I had a mental block concerning—well, they called it an Oedipus complex, a father complex, you don't have the ability to have an orgasm.[12] It's so beyond me. A lot of girls adore their fathers—so what? After 10 years of therapy there certainly should have been some change.

---

[8] By whatever route her therapy led to this conception, it boils down to an acceptance of permanent inferiority.

[9] Like the referent of Footnote 2, a thrust in the direction of throwing doubt on the assumption of the patient's "sickness."

[10] The reference is to the affair with the student that Ed had described and that she later details.

[11] Without, however, leaving any doubt that the primary "blame" was Lisa's.

[12] This dogmatic equation would inevitably preclude any exploration of the evolution of Lisa's sexual behavior.

Dr.: I agree with you.[13]

Lisa: Here we are in the same situation, and for some reason these women are still very upsetting to me—his mother, his sister, it doesn't make any difference; it's just women in general. My mother was my competitor, so any woman is my competitor.[14]

Dr.: Well, do you think you would feel this as much if Ed were making advances to you?

Lisa: No, I wouldn't. I would feel more secure.

Dr.: That makes sense.

Lisa: As it is now, I feel very insecure. I feel any woman is a threat to me. There are certain kinds of women that are very feminine women, who seem secure enough in their own life. They don't pose a threat. But then there are those that all of a sudden bleach their hair and are dissatisfied with their home situations. To me they are threatening.

Dr.: But there's a basis for this. You realize that Ed is a person and has needs. If he doesn't come to you, maybe he feels these dissatisfied people are more accessible.

Lisa: Well, if it's that, I've disguised it to myself. Perhaps that would be too horrible for me to face.

Dr.: But you are acting as if you were feeling that way, aren't you?

Lisa: I guess.

Dr.: Apart from this sexual business, how do you get along?

Lisa: Terribly. I'm constantly irritable—we're just like two people grating against each other.[15] I do love Ed and we have three of the loveliest children. They're very stable, healthy in body and spirit. It's amazing to me. I look at them and think: "With my mental condition, how could these children possibly be the way they are?" Ed has never been around for 12 years. I guess to escape me he throws himself into work. I don't know. I guess a lot of men do. Maybe it's just a pattern of behavior. It runs in his family. His own sister never stays home and she has four children; and she is constantly going. And his brother has been through three divorces at 38. I look at all these things and I think: "Is it all me?" I've said to Ed: "I'm through with the therapy. I feel like I've been placed under doctor's care so I couldn't make waves[16] so you could go on your merry way and enjoy life while I was trying to keep the lid on, plus raise the children." I guess you get to a certain point where you just don't care.

Dr.: Have your thoughts ever turned to other men?

Lisa: Last year I went away with a college student for a few days. He was unhappy with his personal life. His family are our neighbors. He came to speak to me and I got involved. Reality just seemed to leave me. I look at it now and I think it couldn't possibly have happened. But it did.

Dr.: Was it an emotionally satisfying situation?

Lisa: Emotionally satisfying, yes. It fulfilled a need. I guess I've been looking and looking for years, but I just didn't think it would be a boy of 20.

Dr.: Well, that doesn't matter.[17] Did you have orgasms?

---

[13] Reinforcing her questioning of the analytic theory; and augmenting the statements referred to in Footnotes 2 and 9.

[14] The reason being, as it emerged, that no other woman suffered from her "abnormality."

[15] In the light of what has been said it could scarcely be otherwise.

[16] While this was not the purpose of "doctor's care," it was certainly a consequence of it.

[17] A few words to dispel any thought of censure.

Lisa: No.

Dr.: Well did you get close to it?

Lisa: No.

Dr.: What do you think is lacking—preventing you from having an orgasm?

Lisa: Well, I've been told it's an Oedipus complex.

Dr.: Never mind that.[18] What do you think?

Lisa: I just don't think that I feel adequate. I don't know.

Dr.: Can you picture any circumstances that might enter into a relationship that would let you——

Lisa: Oh—I feel that I have a fear of losing touch with reality.

Dr.: Sort of a fear of letting go, is it?

Lisa: This is what it is. I don't trust anyone enough.[19]

Dr.: Of course, really, if you have an orgasm, you're not losing touch with reality. You are engrossing yourself very very much in reality.[20] I can see that you might feel the other way, though. We find people who are afraid even to relax.

Lisa: Well, I never relax either. I don't mean just in sex, I mean in anything. And they tell me: "Don't be nervous." It's very fine to tell somebody, you know, don't be nervous, but——

Dr.: Well, I would like to ask Ed to come in and see if we can get some further orientation.

(Ed is summoned and enters.)

Ed: Good morning, sir.

Dr.: Do sit down. We've had a brief conspectus of the marital problem from Lisa's point of view, and it seems to me that there are both general and situational factors. One situational factor that seems very important to me is that, according to her account, you don't make any sexual approaches to her. Can you comment on that?

Ed: I'd say that generally it's true.

Dr.: Uh-hum. Well, there must be a reason for it. What prevents you?[21]

Ed: There's been a particularly bad spectacle, so to speak, between us over this thing. I was just turned off somewhere along the line.

Dr.: Perhaps there has been some bad communication between you. Long ago,[22] Lisa became negative toward sex because she was irritable after not having orgasms. But her feeling is different now. She now looks for signs of affection from you and would respond to them. I guess that you're not aware of that.

Ed: Well, she's told me that. Perhaps I have a block now, because of past bad experiences with her.

Dr.: Well, do you like her?

Ed: I love her.

---

[18] A further undermining of the "sickness" diagnosis and a cueing of self-exploration.

[19] This remark opens a new direction of investigation. What does she mean by "trust"? How did fear of it begin? What factors are involved?

[20] I reverted to this topic because before anything else, I wanted the basic facts about sexual responding in general to be clear in her mind.

[21] This is a characteristically behavioristic question, seeking the antecedents of the behavior. It is to be contrasted with other kinds of therapist responses at a juncture like this ... moralizing, directing, interpreting, "reflecting," etc.

[22] A thumbnail resume of the history as background to discussing the present situation.

Dr.: Do you like to be close to her?

Ed: Very much so.

Dr.: Well, how do you get there without approaching her?

Ed: I'm not following your question.

Lisa: He means how to get to first base, honey, if you don't try.

Ed: Oh, I see. Well, it's a good question but I don't have an answer.

Dr.: It's very understandable that you've become scared, like a child who has had his knuckles rapped quite a number of times. To be perfectly frank with you, a situation, can become so powerfully aversive that the approach movement cannot be made.[23] There will then be a therapeutic problem. But before trying therapeutic solutions I want to see if I can persuade you to make approaches. The fact that the three of us have been discussing the matter openly may already have facilitated action because you now know in advance, Ed, that you are going to be accepted. Would you welcome it, Lisa?

Lisa: I think it would take some effort. I've become angry to the point that I just can't predict an answer. I mean, you can become so completely turned off that it would take a longer period of time to be aroused. But I'd welcome it, sure.

Dr.: I think, Lisa, a lot depends on what we mean by an approach. An approach can take many forms. It can be just holding your hand. It can be walking into the kitchen and giving you a hug. At this stage Ed is sort of hesitant and you are sort of resentful. But since affection is mutual, action should start.

Lisa: I think that I would be very suspicious. I would feel that he was initiating it because you told him to.

Dr.: Well, that's true, but he also wants it.

Lisa: I'm not convinced of that.

Dr.: Well, how can we find that out?

Lisa: I don't know. I've spent 10 years in therapy and I haven't found out.

Dr.: I really don't see how that therapy could have helped you find this out. You said that you would be pleased if he were to approach you. If he didn't want you, he could just leave you, couldn't he?

Lisa: Yeah. Sure.

Dr.: What would be the point in his lying? Why should he pretend he wants you? Why should he endure the dissatisfaction unless he really hopes that something will work out?

Lisa: Well, I think this is true.[24]

Dr.: Therefore, I think there's a primary reason for accepting him. There is what we might call ground for an experiment. I would like to see him making approaches, small approaches, many approaches. He would be uncertain at first, but you would reinforce him. Then it would become easier for him to do it.

Lisa: I have been forthcoming since Christmas time, since I went back to Ed.

Dr.: Yes, but I mean when he makes an approach.

Lisa: I have.

Dr.: But you said he never makes an approach.

---

[23] By raising the possibility that emotional factors might render action impossible, I freed Ed from the burden of a moral imperative and thus probably made voluntary efforts easier.

[24] The purpose (and evident result) of the foregoing argument was to break down Lisa's firmly held conception of Ed's attitude toward her.

Lisa: He tried. He read this book by Masters and Johnson and then he dropped it again.

Dr.: Why did you drop it again Ed? Did you feel unwelcome or what?

Ed: Yes, to a great extent, I did. I felt that it was a failure, although at first we did have a good relationship on occasion. But then after that, if I did reach an orgasm—it was premature and Lisa said: "Why are you so fast?" Sometimes the act was just a failure.

Dr.: What is foremost here is not sex, but love, of which the sexual act is an outward expression, but not the only one.[25] There are also many small things that happen between people—small approaches where sex needn't happen, and perhaps couldn't happen. If Ed will do these things and Lisa respond positively, a strong feeling of mutual assurance will build up, from which sex is a natural offshoot, though it will not necessarily be an enormous success from the beginning. Lisa's fear of letting go may make it for the moment impossible for her to have coital orgasms. But I'm pretty sure she will eventually have orgasms with you.

Lisa: I don't think we accept each other as individuals.[26] Therefore I don't see how we can possibly have a satisfactory sexual relationship.

Dr.: Let's consider that. Sometimes people don't accept each other because they really are terribly different and incompatible. Sometimes they don't accept each other because of a succession of wrong messages. I don't really know what the situation between you is. Let's explore these things, I'll ask each of you some questions. Do you, Ed, feel attracted to Lisa physically?

Ed: Yes.

Dr.: Do you feel attracted to Ed physically?

Lisa: Yes, definitely.

Dr.: Do you have a substantial number of common interests?

Ed: We have a number of them; we have golf, we have our children.

Lisa: I took up golf to be with you.

Dr.: But it's there now.

Ed: It's there, yes.

Lisa: We enjoy it.

Dr.: What else are you interested in?

Lisa: Not very much any more.

Dr.: What could you be interested in?

Lisa: Creative things. Anything creative: I sew a lot. Things that Ed isn't interested in.

Dr.: Well, you don't have to share everything.

Lisa: Don't you have to share some things?

Dr.: Some things.[27] You have golf and you have the children.

Lisa: But golf only came about in the last 4 years.

Dr.: That doesn't matter. It's here now. What about movies and books and so on?

Lisa: We don't like the same movies at all.

---

[25] The expression of affection solely in the context of sexual intercourse is amazingly common, and a major source of marital disaster.

[26] Now, though granting mutual good-will, she expresses the idea that a fundamental incompatibility comes between them.

[27] There is quite enough mutual interest to build on.

Dr.: I think the most important thing is a feeling of mutual participation in living itself. That is more important than movies and books, to the extent that you can feel yourselves capable of building a life together, in which your house and children are an important part. Do you have any such general feeling?

Ed: Of being able to build a life together?

Dr.: Yes.

Ed: Oh, certainly I have.

Lisa: I thought you said "participation."

Dr.: Yes. I mean emotional participation in building a life together.

Ed: Well, I think that—I think we both really want that. I think this is——

Dr.: All right, Lisa, what are the things that you would like that Ed doesn't provide?

Lisa: Well, I think the most important thing is to be able to see somebody's needs.[28] And when they need you, you've got to be there.

Dr.: I'll tell you what I'd like you to do. Would you each make a list of the things that you feel come between you? As many as you can. Then I would like you to give each other these lists and indicate whether you think that anything can be done to reconcile each particular objection.

---

[28] She regards Ed as lacking in this respect.

32
Case Conference: Conflict in a Case of Frigidity

ALAN GOLDSTEIN

The case I am presenting is primarily interesting because the inceptive complaint, while important, proved not to be the central problem. The way the case unfolded is particularly worthy of note.

A 24-year-old married woman was, at the time she came for treatment, pregnant with her second child. Her presenting complaint was frigidity. She came at her husband's insistence. She described her marriage as a good one so far as she was concerned. She had been developing more and more inhibitions in the area of sexual activity, and was now anxious at the thought of it. Related to this, her own nudity had become disturbing to her, for example in the shower. She was unable to look at herself in the mirror while nude. She slept in underwear and pajamas, and felt uncomfortable if she had anything less on when she went to bed.

There were events in her childhood that could reasonably have led to her being inhibited about sex. However, the history of the frigidity had a kind of up-and-down path. She and her husband-to-be had started to have intercourse a year before they married, although she did have some ambivalence about it. Their best sexual adjustment was attained just before their marriage. For 3 months after marriage she was reaching climax about 50 percent of the time, and enjoying sex on every occasion. In the fourth month they moved in with her parents for the summer and it was at this time that the sexual inhibition began. The proximity of her parents seemed to engender a lot of guilt about sexual activity.

When they went back to school, August through December, 1966, she was able to have orgasms only every third or fourth time. She began to worry whether she would have orgasms. In December there was an occasion when she approached her husband for sex when she was feeling very aroused, and he rejected her. She said, regarding this: "I turned off and I haven't been interested since." She had a baby in July of 1967, and through September of that year they had very irregular intercourse, none of which she

*This case was presented at a seminar in the Behavior Therapy Unit of the Temple University Department of Psychiatry. Participants in the discussion were: Dennis Munjack, Robert Rugel, Gert Speierer, Joseph Wolpe and William Yoell.

particularly enjoyed. She was using a diaphragm at that time, and inserting it was beginning to make her anxious. There was a period from October to January when things seemed to be getting better, but she was afraid that it would not last. When her husband then showed some reluctance about variations in the sexual act which she wanted him to do, she was again not being able to respond sexually, feeling a rejection of her sexuality. From then on each time they attempted intercourse she found that she was not at all lubricated. It was not physically painful, but she described it as mental agony, as if she were being attacked. She continued to be compliant out of a sense of duty.

A few things in the early history seemed at the time to be important. When she was a child, up to thirteen, she had to be nude or partially so when being punished by her father. If he spanked her it would be on her bare bottom or with her underpants on only. She had a particularly vivid and disturbing memory of her sister walking nude down the hall to be punished by her father. Her parents told her about sex when she was eleven, in the presence of her brother. The visual image she got of intercourse was that her father inserted his penis and urinated into her mother—and this she found quite disgusting. Her parents were quite watchful over her contacts with young boys, and her mother would constantly warn her against sexual involvement. She remembered that the first time she was nude with her husband-to-be, her feeling was of helplessness and defenselessness, and altogether very unpleasant.

Her history in other areas was not remarkable except that she viewed her father as a person toward whom she could never express any emotion. He was a physiology professor, and this seemed to her to determine his orientation to life. His attitude on the surface was that everything was physiological and open, but he was very inhibited about any expression of feelings. She had the impression that it was up to her, her sister, her brother and her mother, all to be supportive of him and not disturb him in any way.

After two or three sessions I had become reasonably convinced that this was a case of straightforward conditioned inhibition to sex and embarked on desensitization treatment. I taught her relaxation. We set up a hierarchy involving nudity, and another relating to more and more intimate sexual contact, starting with being touched on the shoulder with clothes on, going on to kissing, and so on. The patient was asked to follow each completed item up by action at home. To facilitate this, I spoke to the husband. I described to him the plan of action. They were never to go past the point which she had reached in desensitization in the office. The patient was instructed to be particularly attentive to relationships between what was happening and how she was feeling, so that we could establish stimulus-response connections. Many things came up as we went along. For instance, at one time she observed that the touch of his toes was a stimulus to anxiety. We incorporated this into the hierarchy. We did the same with other stimuli to which she found herself responding with anxiety.

She was also instructed to follow up the desensitization to nudity by doing at home whatever she had been desensitized to in the previous session. She would stand before the mirror in less and less clothing, corresponding to her progress in desensitization. At one point, she expressed discomfort about the therapy because she felt that her husband was left out too much. We arranged for him to come into each session with her for about 20 minutes of the hour. He was in the room only while we were setting up the home assignment. I asked her if she would like him to present the scenes to her; I could make up the scenes and he would present them, but she did not want that.

She progressed steadily through the hierarchy and was able to follow up the desensitization at home right up to the point of intercourse. At that juncture she reported that she was having a tremendous amount of sexual feeling toward other men and even a girl friend, but not her husband. This led to a discussion about her feelings to her husband as a person. What now became apparent was that she felt she was continually having to hold her husband up—having to interact with him much as she had done with her father. She was never able to express anger or other negative feelings. A revealing incident took place one day when the two of them were leaving the office after a session. He had suggested an experiment that would be interesting, and as they were walking away I heard her say: "Gee, that was a great thing you thought of." The feeling I got as they went down the hall was that she was talking as a mother would to a 7-year-old.

Now, after the fifteenth session, our discussions turned away from sexual topics. She was feeling that she could respond normally sexually. She was able to tolerate her own nudity very well. She was becoming aware that she resented the responses to her husband that she had in the past considered appropriate—her protective, supportive behavior. When we talked about this she felt anger. She could see that when they married this behavior had met both her needs and his; but as time had passed resentment had built up. She had lost respect for him for not being a "man."

Several months after this shift in focus of therapy, the patient separated from her husband. At this point we talked about the necessity of her not making the same mistake again. Her attraction toward men had been determined by her past, and it was not unlikely that she would again pick the same kind of man. So we spent a good deal of time talking about her responses to different men.

A few months later she formed a relationship with someone who was quite different from her father or her husband. He was notably independent and quite different from them in appearance. She established a sexual relationship with this man with little difficulty. At times she would wonder if this association would last, fearing a repetition of the events with her husband. This was no empty fear, for it soon became apparent that her inability to express any kind of strong negative feeling was interfering with her new relationship. She would do things she did not want to do because of a feeling that she *should* do them for the sake of the relationship, and would then become resentful about it and angry at him. I persuaded her to join a behavior therapy group to learn to express appropriate negative affect and to receive feedback about how she enacted the "taking care of" role with others. A most important event occurred in the group when it was concentrated on someone else. We had formed a circle and were having a man break into this circle for purposes relative to his therapy. He tried to break in right where she was. She started, very tentatively at first, and then with more and more enthusiasm, she expressed anger directly at him. However, she kept interpolating: "You are going to hit me, I shouldn't be talking like this. Gee, I never talked to anybody like this before." But she received support from the other members for expressing herself, and the more she did it the more comfortable she became. Finally, she got into a rage. We now talked about the significance of what she had done in terms of her expectations of what would happen to her when she expressed anger. He wasn't destroyed and she wasn't either. She was directed to apply her training to her relationships outside—and she did. Her boy friend was able to take her anger without difficulty, and it seemed always to result in bringing them closer together. The issue of her assertiveness came up repeatedly in the group, of course, since such inhibitions are not dissolved with one experience. This became the most important part of therapy in terms of her avoiding a repetition of the situation she had been in with her husband. The total time in therapy was a year and a half. She is now planning marriage and has no difficulty in being expressive and has had no further inhibitions in the area of sex.

Yoell: Before she was separated did she indicate whether she wanted to save that marriage at all?

Goldstein: This was a matter of some concern to her. At first she decided that although she did not love her husband she should, as a wife, maintain a marriage—the most important thing in the world. She should do it for the children as well. These obligations were part of her upbringing. She saw her mother as really never happily married but doing the "right thing" all the time. A large part of her hesitation about separation was concern about how her mother and father would respond to it. Would she, in fact, be a bad person for not maintaining these responsibilities? She worked that out with her parents. They actually became very supportive as she was able to become more assertive. I haven't mentioned that we did assertive training quite broadly, but particularly in respect of authority figures, including the mother and father. She had had particular difficulty with self-assertion with such people.

Wolpe: What did she like about her husband in the first place?

Goldstein: Well, in the beginning she needed somebody to cling to, and he was very receptive to that. There was a feeling that he would not ever leave her. She had, just before meeting him, had a bad experience with another fellow who had broken off the relationship because he felt she was too clinging and demanded too much of him. This experience had made her more fearful of relating to another in case she would be rejected.

Wolpe: Would you say that as her marriage continued her self-sufficiency increased—in other words, there was a stage where she no longer leaned, and felt herself rather leaned on?

Goldstein: Yes.

Wolpe: Do you think that sexual rejection by her husband could have caused a feeling of abandonment? Did you have any indication of this?

Goldstein: No.

Wolpe: It is possible that she reacted negatively to his rejecting her.

Munjack: I wonder what her feelings are about success of treatment—how she views her problems now relative to how she felt when she came in.

Goldstein: She attributes her change to treatment. There is a great deal of change, without question, in terms both of her general anxiety and her inhibitions with people. She views the important thing as having learned to assert herself, particularly in the areas of negative feelings and sexuality, without feeling guilty.

Rugel: Would you say that she was aware of this interpersonal anxiety when she came to you, or did it unfold in the course of treatment?

Goldstein: It unfolded. Her first statement to me was that she was quite happy with the marriage. The picture was that she was not responsive sexually—therefore the difficulties in the marriage. If she could just get the sexual problem worked out everything could be fine.

Munjack: You mentioned that her mother and father had a similar problem between them?

Goldstein: She felt that her mother never enjoyed sex but did her duty as a wife, staying with her husband, raising the children, keeping the family together, while suffering deprivation in terms of her own satisfactions in life. This was the responsible thing to do; this was what one ought to do. This is the way she saw her parents' relationship.

Yoell: How much time was spent in assertive training in the twenty-odd sessions? I think you said there were twenty all together.

Goldstein: We had a lot more than twenty sessions. That was how long we were in formal desensitization. Assertive training started at the second or third session, at first in the context of small things in relation to her husband. One of the instances was: "When he makes a sexual approach to you, you must tell him your feelings instead of feeling that you are being assaulted while physically complying. You must let him know."

Yoell: You rehearsed how she could do this?

Goldstein: Yes. We also did assertive training in relation to the people that lived upstairs. After about the fifteenth session we extended it to her parents, dealing with small issues first and working up to the important issue of separation from her husband by about the twenty-fifth session.

Wolpe: This case is interesting in relation to our classification of frigidity. We divide cases into situational frigidity which is in response to a particular relationship, and essential or general frigidity which would be manifest in any relationship the woman might have. Here we have an example of a woman who started out not being frigid, then developed a situational frigidity which generalized, so that when you saw her she had general frigidity. There was a spread of inhibition to all sexual stimuli. Sometimes you get the opposite development. With the turning off of positive feelings to one person there may be a switching of interest to alternative sexual stimuli—though this may not go beyond fantasies of relationships with other men.

Goldstein: I think the reason she didn't have recourse to that is that fantasies and feelings in relation to other men were threatening because of her strong role orientation—her fear of being a bad wife. This seems to have accounted in large part for the spread of anxiety to nudity. It became obvious, eventually, that she was a woman with a very strong sex drive whom almost anything turned on. But at that time these extramarital thoughts were anxiety sources.

Speierer: Surely there must be some kind of insight formation during the course of therapy. The patient comes to you with a symptom, and you get her desensitized and do assertive training. And now there comes a point where there has to be a decision—and she makes it. How do you explain this kind of insight formation during behavior therapy? Is it due to the desensitization procedure or is it due to some other things you are doing and not stating so clearly?

Goldstein: From the outset, the thought of divorce, of leaving her husband or of having affairs was extremely anxiety-provoking because of the training she had had at home. Consequently, her only sexual feelings were within the relationship with her husband. When things were not going right with her husband she did not have the thought: "Oh, perhaps I don't love him" or "There is something wrong with our relationship." Intolerable anxiety would have been triggered by such thoughts. These were blocked, and she became more and more inhibited sexually. When we began to desensitize and clear the marital area of sexual anxiety, we were also lowering the anxiety related to sex in general. During the desensitization, when I would have her imagine herself doing things with her husband—kissing, lying nude in bed, she would occasionally find the thought of another man coming in; and this was extremely anxiety-provoking. At the same time she was being told that she had every right to be true to herself—that it was in no way unusual or bad that she felt sexual attraction to others or that she experienced negative feelings to her husband—or others. She was being convinced that whatever she feels is OK and that she is accountable to others only in terms of what she does overtly. Images, feelings and thoughts which were anxiety-laden before became less and less anxiety provoking. She was able to think about things that had been too loaded before. It is possible to have avoidance behavior in terms of thoughts as well as external events. So, more than insight, the anxiety attached to these thoughts became less and less until she was able to think about them freely.

Speierer: You must have some theory about how these things happen. There must be a kind of internal conversation.

Goldstein: The therapy reduced anxiety attached to these specific thoughts to a degree to which she could think about them and not have to avoid them—still anxiety-laden but not so much that she had to avoid them completely. I see the whole thing as a progression of fear reduction—fear of any kind of sexual activity—of her own nudity all the way down to overt sex with anyone she chooses; conmitantly, reduction of fear to decision-making counter to the diligent mother-and-wife role.

Wolpe: Continuing what you are saying—in a sense, the insight involved is secondary. A change has occurred, and then the subject verbalizes the change. She is not in a steel cylinder. She is living in the world, and there are sexual stimuli around every day. A year ago, if she saw a good-looking man there may have been a kind of incipient approach, but it was inhibited by anxiety. A few months later, after desensitization, if she saw that same man again she would have had an approach feeling and, in addition, an excited response. Now, perhaps, she says to herself: "God, I could have relations with that man." That is insight into what has happened to her. The insight doesn't change her. She has insight into the fact that she has changed.

Rugel: One of her insights was that she was very unhappy because of her lack of assertiveness.

Goldstein: That was the result of my propagandizing, pointing out the connection between her anxious state and her non-assertiveness. Of course, it is insight in the sense that she can say: "Oh, that applies to me."

Yoell: I wonder if it is insight—maybe I am semanticizing—rather than awareness. She now realizes this no longer bugs her. I know this, because I now can have a thought, a feeling, a reaction and I don't feel anxious. More than insight she has knowledge, she has a cognition. I behave, I feel, I think differently. This isn't an insight, it is an accomplished fact. Before when Dr. Goldstein gave me the scene it was fearful. Now he gives it to me and I sit there and say "OK Doc give me the rest." Now this is knowledge, isn't it?

Wolpe: You can use the word insight in that way, to mean an awareness, a cognition of how she responds.

Yoell: I was thinking of insight in terms of "Suddenly I have seen the picture."

Goldstein: I think the question you are raising is a different one. That is, without any change in her assertiveness, she became aware of the fact that not being assertive was destructive to her. That is insight too: recognizing a stimulus-response relationship between what happens out there and what happens inside her, or what happens between thoughts and the response at the emotional level. Of course, people who ordinarily talk about insight have a "dynamic" orientation, and for them it refers to coming to know the unconscious—

Munjack: The historical root, kind of thing. There is a paper on insight by John Paul Brady of the University of Pennsylvania that outlines different kinds of insight. Insight that something is wrong with me is one kind of insight. Then there is the insight—"It happened to me because I want to have sex with my mother"—a different kind of insight. I was particularly interested that you used the word "propagandizing," suggesting the other things that go on in psychotherapy that might be therapeutic other than behavior rehearsal, desensitization, direct correcting of inaccurate kinds of notions about the world. What did you do in the realm of propagandizing? Is that important at all?

Goldstein: I think it is important. When I said "propagandizing," what I was talking about is making order out of chaos. I described events as occurring logically in a certain S-R way. I think that just describing the logical structure of behavior is important. Now, I could have done it another way if I had been otherwise oriented. And so in this sense I am propagandizing.

Munjack: She came from a house where Mama said: "You must endure and suffer when you are married to a guy you don't dig, because of the kids," and the rest of it. I have the feeling that somewhere you sent the message to her: "The hell with that!" I have the feeling that you came out, in a sense, for a position opposed to Mother. That is what I meant by propagandizing.

Goldstein: Your point is well taken.

Munjack: How much of what you do in behavioral therapy is of this kind?

Goldstein: There are times when I take a very strong line of that sort. In this particular case it was not necessary because she brought up all these "nasty" thoughts. I said that it was natural that she would want to live a good life. I would say things like: "Not to be married is better for the children than a very bad marriage."

Munjack: Yes, I think that sneaks into a lot of therapy we do.

Wolpe: Why do you say it sneaks in? It doesn't sneak in. It is very explicit. You very frequently find a patient with an unadaptive orientation whose verbal expression is: "I must do good for my fellow men. I must think only of them. I must never be selfish"—things like that. Now, if you are going to try to overcome this patient's unassertive habits, it is very important to change his orientation so that he realizes that this is unadaptive, that it is a false set of beliefs. Then the patient is ready for the assertive training you are going to do.

Munjack: Perhaps, the word "sneak in" was inappropriate. I used it because it is not usually talked about much.

Wolpe: It is, quite often.

Munjack: Well, then I haven't heard about it much.

How about leaving? Actually, she was hung up because she was taught that somehow you should endure a bit for the kids. I guess if it becomes intolerable it is no longer an issue. She would just leave, kids or no. But in her case she was just caught in that middle ground between the guilt of leaving and the pain of staying and you kind of came out to push her, in a sense, up the grade in one direction.

Goldstein: Actually, it was my feeling at the time that it would be easier for all concerned if the marital problems could be resolved. It was her decision in the end that too many bad feelings had piled up to allow for a readjustment. Maybe just by my supporting her thoughts in this direction I opened the possibility of separation. She never asked me: "Should I separate or not?" She decided quite on her own. But I always said that it is right that you think those things. I never agreed with her mother's position that she ought to sacrifice her life.

Munjack: Still, you were exercising a value judgment.

Wolpe: Does calling it a value judgment really make a difference?

Munjack: Actually, what I am approaching is the question of attitude and the role of that in what we call behavior therapy.

Yoell: This is in line with the case where an individual is separated and tells the therapist that she has had relations with another man. Would it be a value judgment to say: "Really you are not married, are you? You are not living as man and wife. You have a contract, but you do not have any of the overt signs of being married."

Goldstein: How does one form attitudes or values to begin with? Certain attitudes that are expressed are punished, others reinforced. Parents model for children, mother models for daughter, and attitudes are built up through varied kinds of learning. A therapist as a person meaningful in the person's life may reinforce different statements. He changes an attitude, through furnishing an opportunity for new learning.

Munjack: I think that is an important aspect of what we do. Recently it has been talked about, but up to two years ago I rarely saw anything like that in behavioral literature.

Wolpe: You say it is only in the past two years. I have this kind of statement in my 1958 book.

Rugel: The power of this should not be overstated. It wasn't until she came to voice displeasure at the guy who broke into the circle that she began emotionally to change her attitude toward being assertive.

Goldstein: I think there are two ways of changing attitudes. One is, once the behavior occurs, by reinforcing it, as you are suggesting, but I think you can put on enough pressure and raise motivation sufficiently to make a change so that attitudes begin to change even in the absence of any overt behavior. By convincing the person that this is an adaptive thing to do and a healthy thing to do, even if he has not done it yet, his attitude begins to change.

Wolpe: I would say, that when you change an attitude you are changing something which is more than verbal; you are changing an emotional response. For example, a person may believe that spinach is an undesirable food. And then someone in authority says: "Spinach is an excellent food, full of iron and vitamins." Now he is positive toward spinach. Why is he positive? It seems quite clearly because the expert's statement that it is full of iron and vitamins changes the response. Spinach has become valuable, which is an emotional thing. The sentence from the authority has attached to it attributes that evoke "positive" feelings. The emotional change has come from changing the perception of the vegetable, not from changing the emotional reaction to the original perception—as happens in desensitization.

Speierer: In some recent studies on attitude change it is very much stressed that first, there is behavior change and then the cognitive change which comes automatically. In our discussion we have agreed that this is not true in all cases.

Wolpe: It must be said that in many contexts before you start conditioning, before you start any specific procedure, you do things to prepare the patient. One is to give a general orientation, "reconceptionalizing" the problem; another, in the assertive situation is to state how despicable it is to behave in an underdog fashion. A very good word for this kind of thing is "dressage"—unveiling unseen angles and aspects of things to help move the patient toward cooperating with the therapist.

33
The Treatment of Chronic Frigidity by Systematic Desensitization

ARNOLD A. LAZARUS

The term "frigidity" is associated with a wide range of conditions, most of which refer to female hyposexuality. Frigidity need not necessarily imply deficient sexual feeling or desire per se, since some women who are completely frigid in all heterosexual situations are capable of orgastic experience during masturbation. Apart from organic factors (which are responsible for a minority of symptoms in young women) frigidity may generally be regarded as a learned pattern of behavior, although some females are probably genetically unequipped to respond erotically. Frigid women may be placed on a continuum extending from those who basically enjoy coitus but fail to reach orgasm, to those for whom all sexual activities are anathema.

Acute but shortlived episodes of frigidity are not uncommon during or after pregnancy and lactation, defloration, physical illness and during periods of psychological stress. Mild or temporary frigidity may also be due to faulty sex technique and a variety of misconceptions which may usually be corrected by appropriate instruction and information. The present paper deals with the treatment of recalcitrant and persistent cases of frigidity, many of which had failed to respond to the usual run of psychiatric techniques.

While the present discussion deals with frigidity as a specific psychosexual aberration, it must be understood that several psychopathological conditions are often heralded by or result in impaired sexual functioning (e.g., endogenous depression, schizophrenia).

The patients discussed in this paper were selected from numerous cases of frigidity in our records. Excluded from the present survey are all cases in whom varying degrees of frigidity were present as a minor part of a much broader neurotic or psychotic spectrum. The 16 patients who comprise the present sample all complained of frigidity as a monosymptomatic or primary disturbance. Of the present series, five patients had been referred by general practitioners, three were referred by gynecologists, one was referred by a psychiatrist and seven had been recommended by previous patients. Cases were only accepted for therapy when medical reports excluded organic pathology. All were married. Their mean age was 24.6 years with a standard deviation of 3.8. Of the 16 women, nine had been married for two years or less, five had been married for approximately four years and two were married for more than ten years. The majority had always found coitus to be meaningless, somewhat unpleasant or utterly repugnant.

The educational level of these patients varied considerably and ranged from three professional women (a doctor, a lawyer and a grades teacher) to several housewives with only two or three years of secondary schooling. The patients were reasonably homogeneous with regard to socio-economic status and may be described as fairly typical of middle class, urban, white South African women.

Two of the women stated that they had been highly promiscuous premaritally. They both claimed, however, that they had never derived any sexual satisfaction whatsoever. One of these patients had also been fairly active extramaritally. A previous therapist had convinced her that these sexual exploits were a search for erotic sensations which had always eluded her. This knowledge made no appreciable difference to her condition. The remaining patients maintained that their sexual activities had been confined to their marriage partners.

In attempting to delineate reasonably clear-cut areas of causation, it was found that the basic etiological factors were very diverse. In some cases, the problem seemed to emanate from faulty attitudes and misplaced sexual emphasis in childhood, which resulted in conditioned avoidance responses to sexual activities. Many patients showed evidence of early or recently acquired feelings of hostility and resentment toward men in general and/or their husbands in particular. Only in one case was there evidence of a traumatic etiology. A few patients were completely unable to offer any explanation for their symptoms. In some, the basic reasons were apparently uncovered during therapy (these insights, although comforting, appeared to bear little relationship to therapeutic outcome), whereas in others, the pattern of causality remained speculative or enigmatic. In one case, the entire problem amounted to a hypersensitivity to extraneous auditory stimuli and a high degree of distractibility. During sexual intercourse this patient would be excessively upset by the sound of a distant motor car, an imagined footstep, a leaking tap, or the like, whereupon she would experience violent dyspareunia.

A direct fear of pregnancy appeared to be the underlying cause of chronic frigidity in yet another case. "The so-called safe period is a myth . . . no contraceptive is infallible and I refuse to play around with hormones . . . I have a rheumatic heart and doctors have warned me not to have any children, so I regard sex as a pretty risky business." When the therapist suggested that the impasse might be remedied by means of surgery, the patient revealed a basic phobia of doctors, hospitals and anesthetics, and required desensitization* along the latter dimension. She was consequently enabled to have a salpingectomy and subsequently experienced sexual satisfaction for the first time in her life.

The sexual reluctance of one patient followed a severe monilia infection which flared up during her honeymoon. She had irrationally attributed her illness to sexual participation and was disinclined to expose herself to the risk of further infection. It is worth noting that she had other mild obvious hypochondrical tendencies, which were treated concurrently with her sexual problems.

The following excerpt, taken from a frigid patient's notes, provides a graphic

---

*Systematic desensitization is a technique which was developed by Dr. Joseph Wolpe (1958, 1961). It consists of presenting carefully graded situations, which are subjectively noxious, to the imagination of a deeply relaxed patient until the most personally distressing events no longer evoke any anxiety.

description of the attitudes of one of the most severe cases:

"I hate every single man on this earth, bitterly. I think they are all pigs—some smaller, some bigger. When one looks at me in the street I could shoot him with a water pistol full of vitriol. I hate women who enjoy sex. I think they are just animals. I hate sexy books; they are filthy. I hate to see people kissing; it makes me feel sick. I don't want to become one of them.

"I hurt my husband's feelings whenever I can. I think he is a pig too. I don't want to have children. I would feel too much like an animal. I have nightmares about men—in my dreams they are just pigs and animals. I hate sex and everything that goes with it.

"When I have intercourse I feel like spitting. I can't stand my husband's hands on me. When I have to go to bed with him and there is no way out I feel trapped like an animal about to be slit open with a knife. I could strangle him and kick him. I hate to see him look at other women. I want to shout at him 'Animal, animal.' Men are all pigs; my father, my brothers, the whole lot!"

On studying the life histories, psychodiagnostic test profiles and similar detailed information which was routinely obtained in each case, it became obvious that the patients were not a homogeneous group with regard to temperament or personality makeup. Marked individual differences and variations in background, training and temperament were clearly noted. There was suggestive evidence, however, that the introverted patients (i.e., persons with an E score of less than 15 on the Maudsley Personality Inventory [Eysenck, 1959]) generally displayed straightforward *anxiety* reactions to sexual situations—"as soon as my husband approaches me in that way I literally feel tense if not terrified"—whereas the highly extroverted patients (i.e., those with and E score of 35 or more) tended to complain of vaginismus and similar reactions of a probable *hysterical* variety.

All the patients had received some form of treatment for their condition before consulting the writer. Five had received detailed instruction from their family doctors concerning sex technique. Three were treated by means of hormonal injections and topical ointments. Three other patients had consulted marriage guidance counselors who had embarked on a course of reassuring discussions with both husband and wife, supplemented by a recommended list of books on sex hygiene. One of the patients had undergone four years of psychoanalysis. Two had visited psychiatrists at weekly intervals for approximately six months, and the remaining two patients had been treated by clinical psychologists for one year, and five months respectively.

THERAPY

The present therapeutic program was based on the assumption that frigidity is usually the result of learned habits of anxiety relating to sexual participation. As in every effective system of therapy, the basic curative mechanism would then depend on unlearning the primary neurotic stimulus configuration.

The desensitization procedure (Wolpe, 1958, 1961) has proved highly effective in treating diverse neurotic reactions where specific rather than "free-floating" anxiety is present (Lazarus & Rachman, 1957). This technique has also been used in groups (Lazarus, 1961) and adapted for child therapy programs (Lazarus, 1960; Lazarus & Abramovitz, 1962). Bond and Hutchinson (1960) have successfully employed systematic desensitization in the treatment of exhibitionism, and Lazovik and Lang (1960) have scrutinized the value of desensitization therapy under controlled laboratory conditions. Rachman (1959) has provided an account of a 24-year-old female who had a phobia for injections, a fear of using internal sanitary pads and who experienced pain and anxiety in sexual situations. The elimination, by desensitization, of her sanitary-pad anxiety and the injection phobia effected an improvement in her sexual adjustment.

Briefly, the desensitization method involves the following three separate sets of operations:

1. The patient is taught the essentials of Jacobson's (1938) progressive relaxation. This relaxation-training program seldom extends over more than six interviews. (During the past year, however, the writer has relied extensively on a long-playing phonograph record of which he is the co-author [1962]).

2. Graded lists are drawn up of all the definable themes into which the patient's anxieties may be grouped. This construction of anxiety hierarchies implies that all important thematic elements which engender neurotic anxiety in the patient will be identified and properly ranked according to the degree of subjective disturbance aroused.

3. The anxiety-evoking items from the hierarchy are presented verbally to the imagination of the deeply relaxed patient, commencing with the "weakest" stimuli and gradually proceeding up the hierarchy to progressively "stronger" anxiety-arousing situations. New items are introduced only when patients are able to picture their preceding scenes without experiencing anxiety. It is impressed upon patients that if any item proves upsetting or disturbing they must raise their left forefinger.

The easiest cases to handle were those in which the normal erotic interchange between male and female constituted the essential anxiety component. "My mother warned me to keep away from boys so often that I even feel guilty when my husband kisses me." A patient who depicted less generalization along this theme said: "I actually quite enjoy kissing and necking, but when it gets more serious than that I just feel myself freezing up." Desensitization in these cases proceeded along a hierarchy of more and more intimate physical and sexual interchanges. In the most severe cases, the graded repertoire of noxious situations had to commence with the most casual and innocent contacts between the sexes. The thought of a flirtatious glance or an ephemeral embrace initially produced observable anxiety reactions in two of the patients. The "mildest" case along this dimension was a patient who could accept coitus in the "normal" position, but whose husband's erotic gratification depended on varying the sexual positions. "Frankly, I think that my husband needs treatment. He behaves just like an animal."

This patient's aversion to postural variations during coitus apparently emanated from feelings of fear and disgust when, as a young girl on the farm, she had on occasion been forced to witness animals copulating. She reported that ever since then, the sight of "animals doing it in the street" upset her unduly. Systematic desensitization was accordingly administered along dimensions of distance and size—the nearer the animals the worse; the larger the animals the worse. As soon as she became impervious to sexual activities in animals, her own behavior underwent a change. She became free from unnecessary inhibitions which had upset her sexual relationships. Significantly, this appeared to have consolidated her marriage and according to her husband, "saved a worthwhile marriage in the nick of time."

The patient whose sex life was undermined by real or imagined extraneous sounds responded well to desensitization methods. While hypnotically relaxed, she was asked to imagine increasingly disturbing sounds while conditions for sexual relations became less and less ideal. (As an example: "I want you to imagine that you and your husband are in Cape Town on holiday. While having intercourse you can clearly hear people walking and talking in the hotel corridor.") After 14 desensitization sessions she reported that she was able to "get lost in sex." At the time of writing, she has not experienced dyspareunia for over fifteen months.

A more detailed case presentation should lend greater clarity to some of the points outlined above.

Mrs. A, aged 24 years, had been married for two-and-one-half years, during which time she claimed to have had coitus on less than two dozen occasions. She always experienced violent dyspareunia during intercourse as well as "disgust and anxiety at the whole messy business." She could tolerate casual kissing and caressing without anxiety and at times found these experiences "mildly pleasant." The background to her problem was clearly one of puritanical upbringing, in which much emphasis was placed on the sinful qualities of carnal desire. Mrs. A's husband had endeavored to solve their difficulties by providing his wife with books on sex techniques and practices. Mrs. A had obligingly read these works, but her emotional reactions remained unchanged. She sought treatment of her own accord when she suspected that her husband had developed an extramarital attachment.

After diagnostic interviews and psychometric tests, systematic desensitization was administered according to the following hierarchy (the most disturbing items being at the head of the list):

1. Having intercourse in the nude while sitting on husband's lap.
2. Changing positions during intercourse.
3. Having coitus in the nude in a dining-room or living-room.
4. Having intercourse in the nude on top of a bed.
5. Having intercourse in the nude under the bed covers.
6. Manual stimulation of the clitoris.
7. Husband's fingers being inserted into the vagina during precoital love play.
8. Caressing husband's genitals.
9. Oral stimulation of the breasts.
10. Naked breasts being caressed.
11. Breasts being caressed while fully clothed.
12. Embracing while semi-clothed, being aware of husband's erection and his desire for sex.
13. Contact of tongues while kissing.
14. Having buttocks and thighs caressed.
15. Shoulders and back being caressed.
16. Husband caresses hair and face.
17. Husband kisses neck and ears.
18. Sitting on husband's lap, both fully dressed.
19. Being kissed on lips.
20. Being kissed on cheeks and forehead.
21. Dancing with and embracing husband while both fully clothed.

Variations in the brightness of lighting played a prominent part in determining the patient's reactions. After four desensitization sessions for instance, she was without anxiety able to visualize item 14 (having her buttocks and thighs caressed) if this was occurring *in the dark*. It required several additional treatments before she was able to tolerate this imagined intimacy under conditions of ordinary lighting.

The therapist asked Mrs. A's husband to make no sexual overtures to his wife during the period of treatment (to avoid *resensitization*). Mrs. A was desensitized three times a week over a period of less than three months.

When item 7, on the hierarchy had been successfully visualized without anxiety, Mrs. A "seduced" her husband one evening and found the entire episode "disgustingly pleasant." Thereafter, progress was extremely rapid, although the first two items were slightly troublesome and each required over 20 presentations before the criterion (a 30-second exposure without signaling) was reached. A year later Mr. and Mrs. A both said that the results of therapy had remained "spectacularly effective."

RESULTS

Of the 16 patients, nine were discharged as "sexually adjusted" after a mean of 28.7 sessions. (The mean time was somewhat inflated by one patient, who required more than 40 sessions.)

The remaining cases were regarded as failures. Patients were usually seen once a week, so that the average time period for successful therapy was just over six months. The majority of patients listed as failures usually terminated therapy on their own initiative after less than six sessions. It can safely be said that treatment was successful for every patient who underwent more than 15 sessions.

The nine recoveries were all cases in whom reasonably clear-cut areas of inhibition could be discerned, while the seven patients who reported no improvement were nearly all individuals in whom abstruse, pervasive or extreme attitudes prevailed. Some of them were inadequately motivated for therapy. Others, although evidently eager to overcome their sexual difficulties, were unable to produce sufficiently vivid images—an essential prerequisite for effective desensitization. It is worth noting that all the successful cases were undoubtedly dysthymic in character (i.e., having high scores on neuroticism and low scores on extraversion [Eysenck, 1947]).

The criterion for "cure" was an affirmative reply to each of the following three questions:

Do you look forward to sexual intercourse?

Do you nearly always reach an orgasm?

Do you ever initiate sexual activity?

Whenever possible, patients' husbands were interviewed separately and encouraged to express their opinions concerning the outcome and effects of our therapy. (In one case, statements of a patient who claimed to be cured after eight sessions were disputed by her husband: "She still treats me like a nasty dose of castor oil." The patient in question subsequently informed the therapist that her "cure" was confined to her participation in an extramarital relationship, but as her lover could not be interviewed—and as she was a most unreliable witness—the patient was technically regarded as a therapeutic failure.)

Follow-up inquiries were conducted in four cases after 15 months. Two reported additional post-therapeutic improvements in sexual pleasure and adjustment. One patient stated that she still had occasional phases of sexual indifference which seldom lasted for more than a fortnight. The fourth patient stated that she had remained sexually well-adjusted for approximately four months after therapy, until she became pregnant, at which stage she again found sexual intercourse "repugnant." A few months after the birth of her baby, four additional desensitization sessions were required to regain her previously acquired level of sexual participation and enjoyment.

DISCUSSION

From a quantitative point of view, 9 recoveries of 16 cases treated is anything but spectacular, but the writer knows of no other therapeutic approach which can achieve comparable results in the treatment of chronic frigidity.

Many frigid women condescend to have treatment in order to "please" their husbands. After their own subjective assessment of "a reasonable exposure to treatment," they terminate therapy and often utilize their own sexual disinclinations as a weapon to which they add reinforced post-therapeutic hostility. Similarly, in the masochistic female, displeasure and pain during sexual intercourse may in itself afford a certain measure of anxiety relief.

The ever-present possibility of homosexuality among frigid women should not be overlooked. One of the seven therapeutic failures spoke of "revolting but exciting adolescent interludes" with members of her own sex. Whereas she regularly achieved clitoral orgasms during masturbation, she described all heterosexual activities as "locally anesthetising." It is possible that undetected homosexual proclivities were present in some of the other therapeutic failures.

In evaluating the effectiveness of systematic desensitization in the present context, the coincidence of "manipulation" and effect was observed in the fact that in nine of 16 cases, clinical improvement occurred contemporaneously with the application of the method. It seems justifiable to conclude therefore, that in the treatment of frigidity, where specific or reasonably clear-cut fears inhibit sexual pleasure, systematic desensitization is the method of choice.

SUMMARY

An account of various cases suffering from persistent frigidity precedes a discussion of the application of Wolpe's (1958, 1961) technique of systematic desensitization therapy. By employing this psychotherapeutic procedure, nine of 16 recalcitrant cases of frigidity were discharged as "sexually adjusted" after a mean of 28.7 sessions. Follow-up inquiries strongly suggested the durability of this method and supported the conclusion that desensitization is the method of choice in those instances where specific anxieties underlie patient's frigid responses.

REFERENCES

Bond, I.K. & Hutchinson, H.C. Application of reciprocal inhibition therapy to exhibitionism. *Canad. Med. Ass. J.* 1960, **83**, 23-25.

Eysenck, H.J. *Dimensions of personality.* London: Kegan Paul, 1947.

Eysenck, H.J. *Manual of the Maudsley personality inventory.* London: University of London Press, 1959.

Jacobson, E. *Progressive relaxation.* Chicago: University of Chicago Press, 1938.

Lazarus, A.A. & Rachman, S. The use of systematic desensitization in psychotherapy. *S. Afr. Med. J.* 1957, **31**, 934-937.

Lazarus, A.A. The elimination of children's phobias by deconditioning. In Eysenck, H.J. ed. *Behaviour therapy and the neuroses.* New York: Pergamon, 1960, 114-122.

Lazarus, A.A. Group therapy of phobic disorders by systematic desensitization. *J. Abnorm. Soc. Psychol.* 1961, **63**, 504-510.

Lazarus, A.A. & Abramovitz, A. The use of "emotive imagery" in the treatment of children's phobias. *J. Ment. Sci.* 1962, **108**, 191-195.

Lazarus, A.A. & Abramovitz, A. *Learn to relax* – a recorded course in muscular relaxation. Wolhuter, Johannesburg: Troubadour Records, 1962.

Lazovik, A.D. & Lang, P.J. A laboratory demonstration of systematic desensitization psychotherapy. *J. Psychol. Stud.* 1960, **11**, 238.

Rachman, S. The treatment of anxiety and phobic reactions by systematic desensitization psychotherapy. *J. Abnorm. Soc. Psychol.* 1959, **58**, 259-263.

Wolpe, J. *Psychotherapy by reciprocal inhibition.* Stanford: Stanford University Press, 1958.

Wolpe, J. The systematic desensitization treatment of neuroses. *J. Nerv. Ment. Dis.* 1961, **132**, 189-203.

34
Innovations in the Desensitization of Frigidity

CHARLES H. MADSEN, JR. and LEONARD P. ULLMANN

The authors have treated a number of frigidity cases by systematic desensitization. The starting point was the excellent article by Arnold Lazarus (1963). Our generally favorable results confirm his approach and formulations, in contrast to those of Freudians such as Fenichel (1945). We have, however, noted some problems, and in reacting to them have deviated somewhat from Lazarus' procedure. The purpose of this communication is to describe these innovations to our colleagues for possible adoption of what may be of value and criticism of what is not.

The basic innovation comprises the presence of the husband in the therapy room during construction of the hierarchy and the desensitization procedures. The husband also performs some tasks usually assigned to the therapist, such as presentation of hierarchy items. Wolpe's (1962) report of a medical student sharing therapeutic work is the forerunner for such a procedure. A second innovation deals with the question of intercourse (resensitization) during the period of desensitization.

The advantages of having the husband participate in the treatment sessions are 1) The husband's active investment in the therapy; 2) The reduction of unwanted worries by the husband (what is happening) and by the therapist (ethical problems of interfering with the private life of the husband without his understanding and concurrence); 3) The object of therapy is generalization to an extra-therapy environment in which the husband is central; the presence and active participation of the husband should facilitate such generalization; 4) Therapy marks a new period in a relationship which, in many cases, has been characterized by discouragement that may have led the husband to make minimal responses. The husband may come to view his wife's tension responses in the extra-therapy situation with some of the objectivity with which he responds to tension during the presentation of a hierarchy item. The husband may learn concepts of gradual progress along a hierarchy such as dropping back a step when necessary and proceeding forward only when the wife is prepared to do so. In later interviews the therapist may well make explicit that the husband is the crucial person and not the therapist; desensitization may be structured to the husband as a "priming" device for his *in vivo* presentation of appropriate stimuli. Ideally, the husband would come to this insight himself, and if he does, the therapist's admiration for his perspicacity should be unstinted. 5) The presence of both partners permits conversation of ongoing events. All too often the open discussion of likes and dislikes has been extinguished and one or both partners have become so sensitive to failure that the spouse's behavior is incorrectly labeled as rejection, dislike or disinterest. In early therapeutic sessions marital partners frequently note the other's progress and provide reinforcement which they hesitate to express in "real-life" situations.

A matter which is related to the last three points raised is that of sexual relations between husband and wife during the process of desensitization. In his detailed case presentation, Lazarus (1963) counseled abstinence as a method of avoiding resensitization. Where there is vaginismus or dyspareunia (pain) this procedure should be given careful consideration. We think, however, the treatment of frigidity might optimally parallel the treatment of impotence: the partners cooperate so that behavior which the patient avidly desires is performed, but behavior for which the patient is not prepared is avoided. This is an ideal situation, and while the husband may agree to the wisdom of making a short-term investment for the sake of benefits accruing over decades, it is difficult to obtain in reality. The wife may also play a role similar to the male being treated for impotence: the pressures in our society to assume sexual maturity, as defined by intercourse and the desire to satisfy the partner, are of greater strength than the wisdom of the therapist or promises made to him in his office. Finally, we have found indifference rather than pain to be typical of the cases we have dealt with. While discouraged and less than perfectly happy, the husband's sexual reactions were generally not completely extinguished, especially since the folkways peculiar to midwestern United States are such that there are few acceptable alternatives to intercourse with an unresponsive wife.

There are more positive reasons for permitting intercourse during desensitization of frigidity. Progress may be noted and provide the strongest and most direct reinforcement for undergoing treatment procedures. While clinical in nature, we have observed that both husband and wife report that progress outside therapy frequently parallels progress on the hierarchy. We have not noted resensitization as such, but there has been valuable discussion of the behavior which led to an ending of approach responses. This may be turned to additional therapeutic advantage by adding or highlighting particular hierarchy items. The possibility of resensitization must be weighed against the potential benefits of observed change and facilitation of generalization.

A type of compromise can be achieved by the introduction of a discriminative stimulus: the hierarchy is constructed and put into actual practice under one set of temporal and geographical circumstances, while a noticeably different set of times and places is reserved for the satisfaction of the husband's sexual needs. There may well be generalization from both situations to each other, and occurrences in both are suitable for discussion during the therapy hour.

While details vary with different therapists and clients, the following case history, the most different from Lazarus' procedures, will illustrate the considerations presented above.

A young married couple, both with college degrees, were seen when the wife was three-months pregnant. The husband was enrolled in graduate school. Despite marital counseling extending over a four-month period (one year earlier), as well as appointments with physicians in unsuccessful attempts to alleviate the fear and anxiety connected with sexual contacts, no mutually satisfying sexual intercourse had occurred during two years of marriage. Intercourse was infrequent (1-3 times per month) and "usually ended in frustration for both partners." The couple reported "all arguments came about because of the sex problem." There was a history of complete sexual abstinence prior to marriage for both partners in accord with their religious and family backgrounds. (It is interesting that only one of the seven women the present authors have dealt with had ever experienced an orgasm by any technique.)

The rationale and procedures were explained and relaxation was taught during the first session. The husband was instructed to approach and continue toward intercourse only as long as the wife did not experience anxiety. When anxiety was signalled, the husband would leave her presence immediately regardless of the extent of psychological or physical involvement. The couple was seen for a total of twelve sessions. The desensitization hierarchy leading toward sexual intercourse consisted of twelve items. There was, however, a great deal of deviation from this original hierarchy through interpolation such that the final hierarchy included fifty items. The situations were expanded as to length of presentation and variety of content.

Because the husband was anxious and thus frequently avoided intercourse when he desired it, and also to help him understand the process of desensitization, during the first three desensitization sessions the husband, as well as the wife, was relaxed and asked to visualize images. Thereafter the husband presented hierarchy items to his wife. After completing five desensitization sessions, the wife experienced the first two orgasms of her marriage. Precise instructions were given to the wife as to ways to become more active during sexual stimulation. Tension reactions were still associated with oral-breast and oral-genital contacts which were included from the sixth to twelfth sessions. Time intervals between sessions were lengthened. In the six-week period between the tenth and twelfth session the wife achieved orgasm at least twelve times.

The husband reported a decrease in frequency and intensity of family arguments as well as enjoyment during sexual contacts of a nature which he had thought to be "virtually impossible." A nine-month follow-up indicated the baby was born normally and frequency and enjoyment of sexual contacts continued at the same level.

REFERENCES

Fenichel, O. *The psychoanalytic theory of neurosis.* New York: Norton, 1945.

Lazarus, A.A. The treatment of chronic frigidity by systematic desensitization. *J. nerv. ment. dis.* 1963, **136**, 272-278.

Wolpe, J. Isolation of a conditioning procedure as the crucial psychotherapeutic factor: A case study. *J. nerv. ment. Dis.* 1962, **134**, 316-329.

35
Directed Masturbation and the Treatment of Orgasmic Dysfunction

ROBERT J. KOHLENBERG

INTRODUCTION

Directed masturbation as an adjunctive procedure in sexual counseling has been suggested by Lo Piccolo and Lobitz (1971). To use this technique for the treatment of primary orgasmic dysfunction in women, a sequence of specific masturbation-related activities is assigned to the patient, who then practices the activities at home. These assignments range from a brief visual exploration of her nude body to daily 45-min sessions of manual stimulation of the genital area. Lo Piccolo and Lobitz describe the use of directed masturbation in conjunction with a treatment program involving the husband and wife modeled after the procedures of Masters and Johnson (1970).

Masturbation appears to have good potential as a treatment procedure. First, since a primary inorgasmic woman is one who has never experienced an orgasm from any source of physical stimulation, the production of an orgasm through masturbation is directly related to and is, in part, a resolution of the presenting problem. Second, Kinsey *et al.* (1953) reported that masturbatory attempts to reach orgasm in women are more success-ful than coitus. Directed masturbation would thus constitute an easier first step in acquir-ing the sexual response. Third, the orgasmic experience in masturbation permits the patient to become aware of the feelings that lead to orgasm, an awareness which can be used as a basis for communication with her mate during a conjoint sexual encounter. Four, since the patient controls the sexual stimulation during masturbation, fears related to loss of control or fears of a too-intense experience are alleviated. It should also be added that masturbation is a source of pleasure enjoyed by many people and has such value independent of therapeutic effects.

An opportunity to assess the effects of masturbation on the treatment of primary inorgasmic women occurred at the University of Washington's Center for Psychological Services and Research. The Center had been involved in the treatment of sexual problems for 2 years prior to the time of this study. During the 2 years prior to this study, the author had been involved as a supervisor or therapist with the treatment of 15 couples in which the female had been identified as a primary inorgasmic, who had completed at least

13 sessions of treatment. The basic treatment procedure was modeled after that of Masters and Johnson (1970) with the following exceptions: (1) couples were seen on a once a week basis instead of a daily schedule; (2) although the patients were told that the program would last approximately 13 weeks, the possibility of additional appointments was suggested; (3) eleven of the 15 couples were seen by a single therapist and four by a male-female cotherapist team. Masturbation was not part of the treatment program.

The success of the above type of treatment program (without directed masturbation) was as follows: Seven of the 15 couples were successfully treated in that the female reported several encounters to be highly arousing with orgasm occurring during intromission before treatment was terminated. Eight couples, however, had made minimal progress. The females reported that the sexual encounters were not arousing and that they had not experienced orgasm. Three of the latter couples were the subjects in this study.

METHOD

The couples were seen primarily on a weekly basis with an occasional 2-week period between appointments. The basic treatment plan was modeled after that of Masters and Johnson (1970). Couple 1 was seen by both a male and a female cotherapist, whereas couples 2 and 3 were seen by a male therapist alone. Masturbation as a therapeutic procedure was introduced into the treatment program after several months of the basic Masters and Johnson treatment program. Masturbation was introduced after the eighth week of treatment for couple 1, the twelfth week for couple 2, and the twenty-fourth week for couple 3.

During the therapy session in which the couple was introduced to the topic masturbation, data pertaining to prevalence and sociological aspects were presented. This session then centered around the couple's personal feelings about masturbation and the origins of these feelings. In each case, the patient (both male and female) was instructed to first look at her/himself in the mirror for 5 minutes each day and to identify the various points of anatomy of the genital area. The male was included in these assignments so that the weekly discussions of the previous week's assignment would be based on both of their experiences. The second week of masturbation instructions included touching each of the previously identified areas to find out which was most pleasant and to continue touching for a minimum of 5 minutes. The third week consisted of instructions to obtain the maximum amount of pleasure by trying various methods of stroking and pressure. As in the previous week, they were instructed to continue this procedure for a minimum of 5 minutes; however, it was permissible to continue for longer periods of time if they so desired. The fourth week included the same instructions as the third week with a 20-minute minimum duration. In all cases, the patients were instructed to use a sterile lubricating jelly to avoid tissue irritation. Both male and female were to engage in these activities but were to do so privately. The fifth week involved the introduction, if it had not spontaneously occurred, of the self-stimulating activities into the exercises that involved an interaction between the couple. Basically, the male was to show the female how he obtained maximum pleasure from masturbating and the female was to do the same. It was suggested that each individual engage in the masturbatory activity during conjoint sexual encounters, with self-stimulation gradually fading into stimulation by the mate.

At the same time that the directed masturbation was taking place, the couple was instructed to engage in at least three conjoint sexual encounters per week. These sessions involved touching for sensate pleasure and could include genital involvement if both male and female consented. The conjoint sexual encounters were to end after a 5-minute minimum duration if it was not enjoyable and pleasurable for both. Similarly, intromission was only to occur if it did not interfere with ongoing pleasurable feelings. Rear entry and lateral positions were suggested as a means of permitting concurrent genital caressing and intromission.

Subjects

The three couples described below applied for the treatment of a sexual problem at the University of Washington's Center for Psychological Services and Research. In two cases, the female reported that she had never experienced orgasm through any means. The remaining female reported that she may have experienced an orgasm about 10 years ago and was classified as primary inorgasmic due to the vagueness of her recollection. In all three cases, the women had received recent gynecological examinations which indicated no organic basis for sexual dysfunction.

Couple 1

Mrs. G., 28, had a childhood that was saturated with sexual trauma. Never having met her natural father, she lived with her mother and a sequence of temporary fathers until the age of 8. She reported that often during these early years she witnessed her mother engaging in intercourse which at times included intoxication, fighting, and injury to her mother. She had vague recollections of being sexually approached by a man her mother brought home but is uncertain about the details. The remainder of her childhood was spent with an uncle and aunt whose stringent morality was opposite to that of Mrs. G.'s natural mother. Mrs. G. expressed feelings of gratitude toward her foster parents, who provided food, shelter, respectability, and reportedly undemonstrated love. Physical contact was nonexistent and a rigid view of sex as a necessary evil was presented. She reported that she had never attempted to stimulate herself in any way. At the time of treatment, she had been married for 8 years and except for her sexual problem reported that her marriage was good. Mr. G., 30, was reared in a middle-class environment. He felt that his parents had a good marriage. He learned about sex from his two older brothers and had several coital experiences with different women before he met his wife. He reported that these experiences were good for him and also presumed they were good for his partners, although he did not know if the women reached climax. He masturbated regularly until he was married and then quit because "there was no purpose in it." Mrs. G. stated that the reason for seeking treatment at this time was that sex was an unpleasant experience and was becoming increasingly difficult to endure and was a major source of disagreement and friction in her marriage. The frequency of intercourse was approximately once per week in the early years of the marriage and currently occurred less than twice a month immediately before beginning treatment.

Couple 2

Mr. and Mrs. P. sought treatment for their sexual problem because she could "take it or leave it" and he felt she was unresponsive and only participated in intercourse out of a sense of duty. Mrs. P., 33, had read several recent articles in books about sex which suggested to her that she could be receiving a great deal more out of her sexual relationship. They had been married 11 years, and described their marriage as generally satisfactory. Mrs. P. thought she had experienced one or two orgasms elicited by her husband digitally stimulating the genital area in the early years of their marriage. At the time of the beginning of treatment, she did not like her husband to touch her "there." She could not recall masturbating. She could recall no sexually traumatic events in her childhood or ever hearing anything negative about sex or masturbation from her family. Mr. and Mrs. P. had intercourse several times with each other before they were married, which resulted in strong feelings of guilt. Neither had had intercourse with any other person. At the time treatment began, intercourse occurred two or three times a month and was rated as a neutral experience by Mrs. P. and a moderately satisfactory experience by Mr. P.

Couple 3

Mrs. F., 32, and Mr. F., 32, had been married 6 years. Intercourse was a decidedly unpleasant experience for Mrs. F., and occurred less than once a month. Mr. F. said he received some pleasure and relief from sex but it was not frequent enough. Also, he was disturbed by the fact that on those infrequent occasions Mrs. F. wanted it to be over as soon as possible. Mrs. F.'s parents had been divorced shortly after she was born. Her stepfather often accused her of being promiscuous, which Mrs. F. said was responsible for her eventual premarital behavior that involved over 30 men but seldom the same man more than twice. Mr. F. had masturbated frequently since high school and said it was necessary at the present time only because he was not getting enough sexual outlet with his wife. Mrs. F. did not recall masturbating or ever having reached orgasm through any means.

Data Collection

Four types of data were collected after treatment began: (1) the occurrence of orgasmic experiences during masturbation, (2) the occurrence of orgasmic experiences during coitus, (3) self-ratings of sexual arousal experienced during the husband-wife sexual encounter, and (4) self-ratings during the self-stimulation sessions.

The arousal ratings consisted of a 0-10 point scale (0 = not arousing, 10 = extremely arousing) that was rated by the patient after each sexual experience and was turned in at the weekly therapy session. The self-ratings of arousal were added as a part of treatment routine sometime after the initial treatment session; arousal ratings are, therefore, not available for some early treatment sessions. The couples were asked to continue the self-ratings after the termination of treatment, these post-therapy reports being used for follow-up data.

RESULTS

The highest self-rated session for each week is given in Fig. 1. The poor progress of these couples in the treatment program is shown by low ratings of the conjoint sexual encounters before directed masturbation was instituted. Although ratings were not

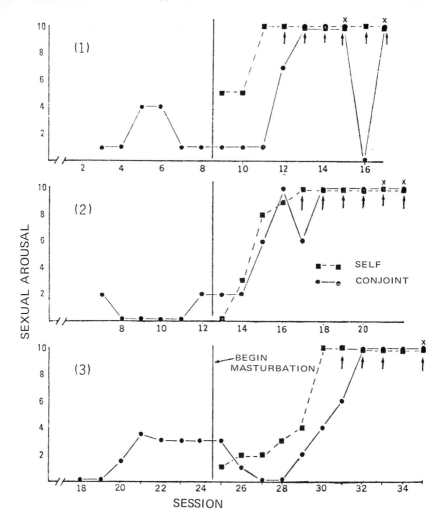

Fig. 1 Sexual arousal self-ratings and orgasms for female member of each couple. Orgasms elicited during masturbation are indicated by an arrow, orgasms occuring during intromission by an X.

obtained during the earlier sessions, all three women stated that the ratings of earlier sessions would have been similar to those shown in Fig. 1 before directed masturbation. All three females reported no orgasms, either self-induced or during coitus, before the introduction of directed masturbation.

Orgasms through masturbation were reported after 3 weeks of directed masturbation by Mrs. G., after 4 weeks by Mrs. P., and after 6 weeks by Mrs. F. The ratings of the sexual encounter involving the husband and wife also increased after directed masturbation started. It is interesting to note that increased arousal ratings of the self-stimulating experience appear to anticipate the increases in husband-wife interactions. The occurrence of orgasm during masturbation also anticipated orgasm during intromission. Female orgasmic experience during intromission occurred for all three couples several weeks after the first self-induced orgasmic experience.

Follow-up data were obtained monthly for at least 6 months following the termination of treatment. All three females reported that they were orgasmic on at least 50% of those occasions during which intromissions occurred. The average monthly frequency of sexual contacts during which intromission occurred were as follows: couple 1, 13.3; couple 2, 6.0; and couple 3, 14.0.

DISCUSSION

It would appear from the results of this study that directed masturbation can be an effective therapeutic technique. The three couples treated were shown to be difficult cases in that they did not progress under a treatment regimen that was effective with other couples. Directed masturbation resulted in successful outcomes for each couple.

The data also indicate that there is a positive relationship between the amount of sexual arousal experienced during masturbation and husband-wife sexual interactions. It appears that as directed masturbation becomes an arousing experience, so does sexual interaction. Such a relationship would be expected since the woman directly communicates the results of the masturbation experience to her mate. That is, the specific sexually arousing techniques and locations that are discovered through masturbation are integrated into the conjoint interaction. Further, the woman is able to discriminate sexual feelings from other types of feelings and can use her sexual responsiveness as a basis for providing feedback to her mate.

It perhaps can be argued that the pre-directed masturbation treatment program was not effective as it could have been particularly since the success rate and single-therapist technique (used with 11 couples) differ markedly from those of Masters and Johnson.

Although the sample involved here is small, the single therapist vs. cotherapists variable does not appear to be significant in this clinic. Two out of the four cotherapist-treated couples were failures as compared to six out of 11 single-therapist-treated couples.

Subsequent to this study, directed masturbation has been routinely introduced at the beginning of the treatment program for primary orgasmic dysfunction. An additional four couples have been treated in the manner, and all four females have experienced orgasm during coitus after 11 or fewer treatment sessions.

It should be emphasized that the directed masturbation is an adjunctive procedure and the data do not warrant the use of this technique without an adequate counseling program. One example of the necessity of a comprehensive program is the value of increased awareness and discriminability of sexual feelings obtained through directed masturbation. Unless the wife and husband can communicate during the sexual encounter, increased awareness is of no value.

REFERENCES

Kinsey, A., Pomeroy, W., Martin, C., & Bebhard, P. *Sexual Behavior in the Human Female,* Philadelphia: Saunders, 1953.

LoPiccolo, J., & Lobitz, C. The role of masturbation in the treatment of orgasmic dysfunction. Presented at meeting of Western Psychological Association, Portland, Ore., 1971.

Masters, W.H., & Johnson, V. *Human Sexual Inadequacy.* Boston: Little, Brown, 1970.

36
Secondary Orgasmic Dysfunction: A Case Study

ARDEN SNYDER, LESLIE LoPICCOLO, and JOSEPH LoPICCOLO

INTRODUCTION

McGovern *et al.* (1975) indicate that cases of secondary orgasmic dysfunction tend to be associated with a disturbed marital relationship and narrow stimulus control over the occurrence of orgasm. These data also indicate that the usual sexual retraining program leads to marked increases in self-report measures of sexual satisfaction, compatibility, and happiness, but not to increases in the rate of orgasm in intercourse. Because of this failure to accomplish the most direct goal of therapy, and following their data analysis, McGovern, Stewart, and LoPiccolo recommended two changes in the training program. In the past, the sexual therapy program involved focusing exclusively on sexual problems and avoiding intervention into nonsexual marital problems as much as possible. Thus the therapists would notice but not respond to nonsexual marital pathology except as was absolutely necessary to keep the clients following the sexual training program. Since it now appears that this procedure does not work with cases of secondary orgasmic dysfunction, a directive approach to marriage counseling was employed. The second focus of therapy in this case was an attempt to break the rigid and narrow stimulus control of orgasm which characterized the female client, as is typical in cases of secondary orgasmic dysfunction.

CASE HISTORY

The clients were a young couple in their early 20s, married for 6 months when first seen by the therapists. At intake, Mrs. A. was able to reach orgasm while masturbating, but not during genital manipulation by her husband or in coitus. She masturbated digitally, in a rigidly constrained manner. Orgasm could be attained only during masturbation while standing, and the client had masturbated in this manner since early adolescence.

Mrs. A. had initially enjoyed intercourse with her husband, which they began 6 months prior to marriage. However, due to her subsequent inability to reach coital orgasm she gradually came to find all sexual activity aversive. The frequency of intercourse had dropped from three or four times a week prior to marriage to approximately two times a month on entering treatment.

Mrs. A.'s sexual history indicated no unusual or traumatic experiences in childhood. Her parents did make it clear they were against premarital intercourse, and Mrs. A. did not engage in intercourse until she was in college and met Mr. A.

Mr. A.'s sexual history was relatively unremarkable. His previous sexual experiences included masturbation and petting; however, he did not engage in intercourse until meeting Mrs. A.

The couple began engaging in intercourse a few months after they met. Their first attempts were unpleasant experiences, due to the fear of parental discovery and pregnancy.

After several months of intercourse and concurrent with beginning oral contraceptives, Mrs. A. experienced a lessening in sexual responsiveness and mild depression. On advice of her gynecologist, the oral contraceptives were discontinued but her previous sexual responsiveness did not return.

At intake Mrs. A. reported that she thought she had been orgasmic on 40-50% of coital occasions prior to marriage, but had not experienced coital orgasm during the last several months. As treatment progressed, however, it became clear to the therapists that while Mrs. A. had been highly aroused, it was unlikely that she had ever experienced coital orgasm. She was unable to describe any of the physiological correlates of orgasm during coitus, although she was able to clearly describe these phenomena as occurring when she masturbated. As previously reported, this tendency to misperceive the orgasmic response is common in women with orgasmic difficulties (McGovern et al., 1975).

COURSE OF TREATMENT

The clients were seen together for 17 sessions over a 15-week period by a male-female cotherapy team (A.S. and L.L.). During history taking, it became clear to the therapists that, in addition to the couple's sexual dysfunction, there was also a good deal of marital disharmony. While this is consistent with the findings of McGovern et al. (1975), it was quite surprising in this case as both Mr. and Mrs. A.'s pretreatment scores on the Locke-Wallace Marital Adjustment Test (1959) were well into the range considered to indicate satisfactory marital adjustment. On the basis of the clinical material, however, the therapists decided to focus treatment on three issues: (1) training in sexual technique, (2) breaking the narrow stimulus control of orgasm, and (3) dealing with the marital problems. Despite the fact that these were carried out more or less concurrently, they will be presented separately in the interest of clarity.

Sexual Technique Training

Treatment emphasized reduction of performance anxiety, increase in verbal feedback, and acquisition of more effective sexual techniques. Since the approach is well described elsewhere (Masters and Johnson, 1970; LoPiccolo and Lobitz, 1974), it will not be elaborated on here. Briefly, the clients were initially forbidden to engage in sexual intercourse. They were then given "homework" assignments each week. During the first week, only hugging, kissing, and body massage were permitted. This assignment allowed the couple to focus on sensual pleasuring without anticipating, with anxiety, sexual intercourse. In subsequent weeks, the couple gradually moved toward intercourse by successively adding behaviors such as breast touching and genital stimulation by manual, oral, and electric vibrator means. Intercourse was introduced in a series of successive approximations starting with partial penile insertion with no movement, penile insertion with female movement, and finally full insertion with mutual pelvic thrusting and ejaculation. To eliminate performance anxiety, these behaviors were introduced only when both partners felt comfortable with the next step.

Breaking Stimulus Control of Orgasm

Annon (1971) has suggested that women who have narrow stimulus control over orgasm in their masturbation can learn new means of reaching orgasm by gradually switching from their restricted method to positions and techniques of masturbation which approximate coitus. Rather than follow this gradual stimulus generalization procedure in this case, the therapists decided to simply extinguish the stimulus response link between standing masturbation and orgasm. Mrs. A. was forbidden to continue in her pattern of standing while masturbating. The therapists explained that discontinuing her current practice was necessary in order for her to learn to respond to a wider variety of sexual stimulation. She was therefore started on a 9-step program of masturbation designed to result in coital orgasm (LoPiccolo and Lobitz, 1972). This program begins with visual and tactile exploration of the pelvic region, to locate sensitive areas, progresses to manipulation to these areas, and eventually (step 6) involves stimulation of the clitoral region with an electric vibrator. To break the previously established pattern of orgasm only while standing, the client was instructed to engage in each step of this program while lying down. Initially while learning to masturbate in this new way, the client was not aroused, but she did eventually become orgasmic. Once orgasm in masturbation while lying down was well established, the final three steps of the masturbation program were used to transfer orgasmic response to coitus (LoPiccolo and Lobitz, 1972). In subsequent weeks, Mrs. A. masturbated with her husband watching her, masturbated with her husband kissing, caressing, and embracing her, and then guided her husband's manipulation of her genitals. At this point, she began to experience orgasm during her husband's manipulation of her genitals with the vibrator. All that remained at this point was to instruct the clients to continue clitoral stimulation *during* coitus, and shortly Mrs. A. became orgasmic in intercourse.

Teaching a woman to switch, via successive approximation, her masturbation from the clitoris to the vaginal opening as Annon (1971) advocates may be inefficient, given the Kinsey *et al.* (1953) and the Masters and Johnson (1966) data that clitoral stimulation is the focus for female orgasm. Annon's procedure, involving successive changes in masturbatory focus from the clitoral shaft to the mons area, to the vulva area, and to vaginal stimulation when orgasm is imminent may, furthermore, reinforce a client's erroneous belief in the now generally discredited concept of vaginal orgasm. It may be more effective to simply teach clients to have coital orgasms through maintaining active manual stimulation of the clitoris during intercourse, as was done in this case. Annon's procedure is, however, well thought out and is reported to have produced results with one client (Annon, 1971).

Marital Problems

After emphasizing to the couple the positive aspects of their relationship, the therapists pointed out that Mrs. A.'s dissatisfaction with her career prospects was having a negative influence on their sexual adjustment. The therapists shared their impression that Mrs. A. wanted either to attend graduate school or to secure employment in some field related to her art major, rather than take a menial job to support her husband and remain professionally stagnant for 4 years while he pursued his graduate career. The legitimacy of Mrs. A.'s discouragement over what she felt was expected of her was supported by the therapists openly indicating their belief that women should be permitted the same opportunity to develop their potential as men. Meanwhile, Mr. A.'s attentive listening and expressions of concern for his wife's feelings were mentioned and reinforced with praise. This strategy was aimed at minimizing his defensiveness and maintaining her esteem for him.

The therapists informed Mr. and Mrs. A. that they were convinced that until this issue was resolved the sexual problem would probably not be alleviated. It was suggested that they thoroughly talk out their thoughts and feelings about the issue and rate their conversations on a 1 to 10 scale along a "constructive-destructive" continuum. Mrs. A. was also encouraged to write out what she felt she "should do" and what she "wanted to do" in order to insure that her value conflict would be clearly expressed in their discussions.

Several other marital problems emerged at this point: Mrs. A. felt negative about their spending too much time with their parents. She also resented the subtle pressure from Mr. A.'s mother to take a menial job to support Mr. A. She also expressed dissatisfaction with Mr. A.'s constant compliance with his parents' wishes. In response to these issues, the therapists were directive and confrontive and informed the clients that satisfying sexual relations were dependent on redefining their family as the two of them. They were encouraged to ask "What is best for *us*?"

As the couple became more aware of the interrelatedness of their difficulties, it was recommended that they begin to identify the possible courses of action for their future and start constructing a branching tentative plan (Tyler, 1969). In subsequent interviews, the clients were assisted in exploring possibilities, constructing a plan, identifying choice points, and dealing with parental attitudes. As a result of this plan construction, they were able to disengage from their parents, and agree that Mrs. A. would pursue a graduate career in art.

OUTCOME DATA

Assessment data were collected from the couple before and after treatment and at 3 months following termination of therapy. A number of scores from this assessment battery are presented in Table I. These data indicate that gains were made in all aspects of the sexual relationship. Additionally, at termination Mr. and Mrs. A. reported they were

Table 1 Outcome Data

	Pretreatment	Posttreatment	Followup
Frequency of intercourse	1 or 2 times a month	twice a week	twice a week
Duration of foreplay	15-30 min.	30-60 min.	16-30 min.
Duration of intercourse (from entry of penis until male reaches ejaculation)	4-7 min.	7-10 min.	7-10 min.
Percentage of female orgasm through genital stimulation by male	0	100	100
Percentage of female orgasm in coitus with concurrent clitoral stimulation	0	50	100

each initiating sexual intercourse about equally often, in marked contrast to their pre-therapy pattern of Mr. A.'s usually initiating. In response to the questionnaire item "Overall, how satisfactory to you is your sexual relationship?" both Mr. and Mrs. A. responded "extremely satisfactory" at the close of treatment in comparison to their responses of "slightly unsatisfactory" (Mr. A.) and "moderately unsatisfactory" (Mrs. A.) prior to treatment.

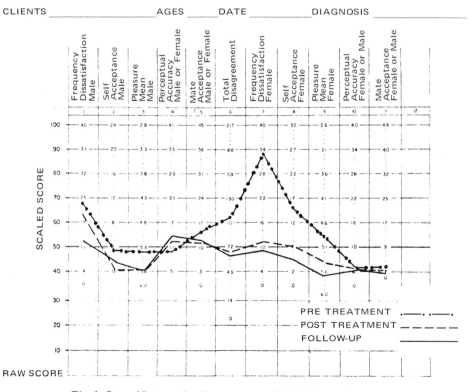

Fig. 1 Sexual Interaction Inventory profile for Mr. and Mrs. A.

As Fig. 1 indicates, Mr. and Mrs. A. made significant gains in their sexual relationship as measured by scores on the Sexual Interaction Inventory (LoPiccolo and Steger, 1974). For those scales that indicated the most pathology at intake (scales 6, 7, 8), post-treatment scores changed in the desired direction and improved by more than 1 SD.

Scores on the Locke-Wallace Marital Adjustment Test (1959) showed that the overall marital relationship improved following treatment. Mr. A.'s score increased from 132 to 146 and at followup was 142. Mrs. A.'s score increased from 120 to 134 and at followup was 128.

DISCUSSION

In this case, a directive and confrontive marital therapy plus a direct, simplistic approach to breaking stimulus control of orgasm led to a successful treatment outcome. As reported by McGovern *et al.* (1975), the usual sex therapy program had previously failed to increase the orgasmic response in coitus of six successive secondary inorgasmic women. Two other couples with secondary orgasmic dysfunction have since been seen by other therapy teams, and in both cases following the procedures outlined in this article has led to regular coital orgasm. While treatment of only three cases clearly does not "prove" the effectiveness of a set of procedures, it is hoped that this report will lead other therapists to experiment with this therapeutic strategy.

REFERENCES

Annon, J.S. The therapeutic use of masturbation in the treatment of sexual disorders. Paper presented at the Fifth Annual Meeting of the Association for the Advancement of Behavior Therapy, Washington, D.C., September, 1971.

Kinsey, A.C., Pomeroy, W.B., Martin, C.E., & Gebhard, P.H. *Sexual Behavior in the Human Female,* Philadelphia: W.B. Saunders, 1953.

Locke, H.J., & Wallace, K.M. Short marital adjustment and prediction tests: Their reliability and validity. *Marriage Family Living,* 1959, 12:251-255.

LoPiccolo, J., & Lobitz, W.C. The role of masturbation in the treatment of primary orgasmic dysfunction. *Arch. Sex. Behav.* 1972, 2: 163-171.

LoPiccolo, J., & Lobitz, W.C. Behavior therapy of sexual dysfunction. In Hammerlynck, L.A., Handy, L.C., & Mash, E.J. (eds.), *Behavior Change: Methodology, Concepts, and Practice,* Champaign, Ill.: Research Press, 1974.

LoPiccolo, J., & Steger, J.C. The Sexual Interaction Inventory: A new instrument for assessment of sexual dysfunction. *Arch. Sex. Behav.* 1974, 3: 585-595.

Masters, W.H., & Johnson, V.E. *Human Sexual Response,* Boston: Little, Brown, 1966.

Masters, W.H., & Johnson, V.E. *Human Sexual Inadequacy.* Boston: Little, Brown, 1970.

McGovern, K.B., Stewart, R., & LoPiccolo, J. Secondary orgasmic dysfunction. I. Analysis and strategies for treatment. *Arch. Sex. Behav.* 1975, 4: 265-275.

Tyler, L. *The Work of the Counselor.* New York: Appleton-Century-Crofts, 1969.

Additional Selected Readings

Brady. J.P. Brevital-relaxation treatment of frigidity. *Behaviour Research and Therapy,* 1966, **4**, 71-77.

Brady, J.P. Psychotherapy by a combined behavioral and dynamic approach. *Comprehensive Psychiatry,* 1968, **9**, 536-543.

Caird, W.K., & Wincze, J.P. Videotaped desensitization of frigidity. *Journal of Behavior Therapy and Experimental Psychiatry,* 1974, **5**, 175-178.

Chernenkoff, W., M.D. A case of frigidity. *The American Journal of Clinical Hypnosis,* 1969, **11**, 3, 195-198.

Cooper, A.J. Frigidity, treatment and short-term prognosis. *Journal of Psychosomatic Research,* 1970, **14**, 2, 133-147.

Faulk, M. Factors in the treatment of frigidity. *British Journal of Psychiatry,* 1971, **119**, 53-56.

Faulk, M. Frigidity: A critical review, *Archives of Sexual Behavior,* 1971, **2**, 257-265.

Hustead, J.R. Desensitization procedures in dealing with female sexual dysfunction. *Counseling Psychologist,* 1975, **5**, 30-38.

Kraft, T., & Al-Issa, I. Behavior therapy and the treatment of frigidity. *American Journal of Psychotherapy,* 1967, **21**, 116-120.

McGovern, K.B., Stewart, R.C., & LoPiccolo, J. Secondary orgasmic dysfunction. I. Analysis and strategies for treatment, 1975, **4**, 265-275.

Segraves, R.T. Primary orgasmic dysfunction: Essential treatment components. *Journal of Sex and Marital Therapy,* 1976, **2**, 115-123.

Wincze, J.P. & Caird, W.K. The effects of systematic desensitization and video desensitization in the treatment of essential sexual dysfunction in women. *Behavior Therapy* (in press), 1976.

Wincze, J.P. A comparison of systematic desensitization and "vicarious extinction" in a case of frigidity. *Journal of Behavior Therapy and Experimental Psychiatry,* 1971, **2**, 285-289.

Painful or Difficult Intercourse

Pain in the pelvis at the point of intromission, during intercourse or, more rarely, following intercourse are problems reported by many women. Such pain, and often the fear of such pain, can create severe problems for a woman as well as her concerned sexual partner.

The anticipation of painful intercourse will likely impair muscle relaxation and vaginal lubrication and thus set up conditions which increase the likelihood of pain occurring. Further, as the pelvic muscles tighten around the vagina as a result of anticipated pain or other factors, it may become difficult or impossible for the man to insert his penis. Painful intercourse, in general, is often referred to as "dyspareunia," while the term "vaginismus" refers specifically to the involuntary tightening of the vaginal introitus (front muscles) which makes intercourse virtually impossible.

The first article by Haslam focuses on "The Treatment of Psychogenic Dyspareunia by Reciprocal Inhibition." In this relatively early (1965) article, Haslam first describes the rationale for using deconditioning procedures to treat dyspareunia. He then presents two case histories where a simple procedure of insertion of glass dilators ("bougies")—graduated from small to large—into the vagina produced rapid and very positive changes in the problem.

In the next article, Cooper introduces "An Innovation in the 'Behavioral' Treatment of A Case of Non-Consummation Due to Vaginismus." Cooper first describes the "typical" behavioral approach (as presented in the previous article) involving training in relaxation and the use of lubricated glass dilators. He then presents a case study illustrating his modification, which essentially involves actively incorporating the husband in therapy in the clinic. While, in this case, the presenting complaint of vaginismus was apparently successfully handled, the client complained of subsequent orgasmic dysfunction.

This case does raise some issues. Although the vaginismus was eliminated,

351

some of the therapist's advice to the husband with regard to ignoring his wife's complaints of pain and suggesting that he be more aggressive, although effective and possibly necessary in this situation, may seem, especially to some women, unwarranted if not "insensitive." Indeed, although this is pure speculation, intensified training in relaxation and use of the dilators might have precluded the need for such advice. Similarly, the emphasis on "collusive psychopathology," while well taken in terms of the reciprocal reinforcement patterns between the client and her husband that might have been preventing successful outcome, adds a bit of mysterious and perhaps unnecessary level of inferential thinking to the process. Finally, although the author did express the hope that the client's lack of full orgasmic responding would disappear with time, it is unclear as to why this did not become a target for treatment using such methods as described previously in this book. Indeed, the discussion toward the end of the article regarding "frigidity"— particularly the alleged distinction between clitoral and vaginal orgasm and the possibility of some women being biologically unable to respond with vaginal orgasms—contradicts some recent research on this topic and may simply be a *post hoc* rationalization for the lack of complete success in this case (*see* Masters & Johnson, 1966, 1970). However, the controversy over the nature of female orgasmic behavior does continue (*see* Katchadourian & Lunde, 1975, for a summary of this issue), so no definitive conclusions on this can be offered. Nevertheless, this article does show how even successful treatment may raise important issues about which clinicians must be aware.

REFERENCES

Masters, W.H. & Johnson, V.E. *Human sexual response.* Boston: Little, Brown, 1966.
Masters, W.H. & Johnson, V.E. *Human sexual inadequacy.* Boston: Little, Brown, 1970.
Katchadourian, H.A. & Lunde, D.T. *Fundamentals of human sexuality* (2nd ed.). New York: Holt, Rinehart and Winston, 1975.

37
The Treatment of Psychogenic Dyspareunia by Reciprocal Inhibition

M. T. HASLAM

The inability in a woman to tolerate intercourse is a factor which causes tremendous strain in marriage and leads rapidly to dissension between husband and wife and often the eventual break-up of the union. It is therefore a condition which it is vital to treat quickly and successfully if the partnership is to be saved.

A history which commonly emerges is as follows: for some time neither partner has been prepared to seek help, through embarrassment or possibly a sense of inferiority. It is often only when matters have come to an extreme state that help is sought, the husband by this time already threatening to leave. The patient visits her G.P., or the marriage guidance center, where advice is given about the possible simple measures that may be taken to improve things. The couple are given a book to read on the art of married love, and sent away to try again. A physicial examination is then arranged, possibly by a gynecologist. The patient is examined and no physical abnormality is found; she is reassured and returns home. She is still unable to tolerate intercourse. After this, dilatation is arranged; the patient is admitted to hospital and under a general anesthetic, bougies are passed with ease. She returns home. Intercourse remains impossible, and either the marriage breaks up or the couple, discouraged, settle down to an unsatisfactory half-marriage which is punctuated by rows. Sex ceases to be mentioned. Even if at this stage the patient is referred to a psychiatrist, treatment may be lengthy or ineffective.

An explanation of psychogenic dyspareunia is offered below in learning theory terms, and two case examples are given where deconditioning has been used in treatment, with a rapid and entirely successful result.

The history given by patients presenting with the picture sketched above shows that the problem is not one of physical defect but rather one of emotional tension. Thus, one would not really expect any procedure adopted under general anesthesia to be effective in relieving the condition.

In fact the disability appears to be a spasm of the perineal muscles and contraction of the adductors of the thighs. This makes attempted intercourse painful or impossible. It is suggested that the cause of this spasm is a conditioned anxiety response which occurs as a result of the first attempted introduction of something into the vagina during conditions of stress or tension, producing pain and fear. The spasm in turn results in further attempted intercourse continuing to be painful, thus confirming the patient's fear and strengthening the conditioned response.

It was postulated therefore that methods of deconditioning should be devisable to remove the maladaptive conditioned response, and that since the act itself should normally be a pleasurable one, once intercourse had been satisfactorily achieved there should be no fear of relapse; for if a response antagonistic to anxiety can be made to occur in the presence of anxiety-evoking stimuli, in suppressing the anxiety responses the bond between the stimuli and the anxiety response will be weakened (Wolpe, 1958).

If the spasm of the muscles could therefore be relieved by some anxiety-reducing procedure, the maladaptive response would be removed. To this end deconditioning with relaxation responses and/or sexual responses (which are anxiety reducing) (Wolpe, 1958, p. 113) seemed to be appropriate.

In the two cases to be described, this type of procedure was carried out.

Mrs. T., was a married woman of twenty-two. Her previous personality showed a number of neurotic traits. She first met her husband at seventeen, and enjoyed sexual play with him but did not allow full intercourse. She did, however, as a result of close contact become pregnant and had to get married. She had this first baby at the age of nineteen. In spite of this she remained very afraid that intercourse would prove painful, and in fact at the critical moment always became so tense that she was unable to allow penetration. Satisfactory penetration had never occurred at any time, in spite of the fact that she had one further pregnancy before presenting at the clinic.

At twenty-two, after three-and-a-half years of marriage, her husband had become exasperated at her apparent inability properly to consummate the marriage, which was indeed on the verge of breaking up. The patient was very distressed about this. She obtained normal sexual excitement in every way apart from the act of penetration itself. She had been seen by her G.P. who had examined her and reassured her, but this had been of no avail.

At the first interview, a history was taken, and the patient had her disability explained to her on the above lines. The Willoughby personality schedule was administered and scored 58. She was an anxious introverted person who might be predicted, therefore, to condition readily to anxiety and generate reactive inhibition poorly. (Reactive inhibition is the weakening that occurs in a conditioned response when the stimulus is not reinforced by drive reduction. Anxiety-responses are said to generate little reactive inhibition.) It was postulated therefore that the patient might be expected to learn quickly and decondition readily, and that treatment by reciprocal inhibition methods might be fairly rapidly effective.

A physical examination was performed. This showed a normal perineum and vagina, but the patient was extremely nervous and the perineal muscles and thigh adductors were tightly contracted automatically even in the left lateral position. She complained of severe pain on the insertion of a finger.

A number four glass bougie was then passed, well lubricated, and this was maintained in position while the patient was reassured and given time to become more relaxed. The same was then done in the dorsal position, the whole procedure taking about ten minutes. Nothing more was done at this session. No drugs were given. She was advised not to attempt intercourse yet at home.

At the next session graded bougies from size four to eight were passed in the dorsal position, taking sufficient time with each one to allow her to become accustomed to them. She was shown the number eight bougie (about the size of a normal erect penis) and this fact was pointed out to her. She was then encouraged to retain the bougie herself with her fingers, and to take it out herself when she felt confident to do so. This she managed after a short time.

At the next session the patient herself passed the bougies at her own request. She was now much more confident, and was able to contract and relax her perineal muscles at will, appreciating that the reason why insertion had been, in the past, painful had been because these muscles had acted as a barrier. She was encouraged to take an active part in attempting intercourse with her husband by assisting him in his insertion, using plenty of lubricating jelly, in the belief that this activity would assist in anxiety reduction.

She returned for the fourth session with the news that for the first time in her life they had had satisfactory and normal intercourse. Both were pleased and confident. No further treatment was considered necessary, and at follow-up one month later intercourse was continuing regularly, pleasurably and satisfactorily.

The personality of the second patient to be described contrasts with the above.

Mrs. Th. was twenty-three, and had been married for two years. The marriage had never been consummated. She gave a history of having been examined *P.V.* by a general practitioner when young, and having been very scared by this. She was afraid to touch or insert anything into the vagina (e.g., a tampon). The marriage was continuing on the basis of mutual masturbation, which both parties enjoyed. The husband had had previous sexual intercourse with another girl, but was reluctant to attempt to force his wife in any way. If intercourse was attempted she became very tense and pushed him away. She had been seen by a gynecologist who had performed a P.V., which had again been painful, though no physical abnormality had been found. She had seen a marriage guidance counselor without benefit. There was a history of congenital dislocation of the hips which might have accounted for some of her fear of abducting the thighs. She had been in plaster for a long time as a child and could remember this, but the hips were now quite normal.

Their trouble had started on the honeymoon, when the husband had failed to penetrate, due to his inability to maintain an erection following a surfeit of champagne. After this, neither party had been confident and intercourse had never taken place.

The first two treatment sessions were spent as with the first patient. A Willoughby score of twenty-one was found. This confirmed the clinical impression that this girl was an extrovert, not prone to generalized anxiety, and one could predict that she would generate reactive inhibition readily, would be less self-controlled and decondition less well. A successful outcome might thus take longer to achieve.

At the third session, deconditioning was commenced. The patient was rather uncooperative and one had to proceed very slowly. Gradually her confidence increased. She tolerated the number four bougie for a short period, but was tense, arched her back and complained histrionically of pain when it was introduced. However, when the bougie had been introduced and left for a few minutes she was gradually able to relax, and in this way confidence was increased. Progress was slow, however, and it was not until the tenth session that she was able to tolerate the passage of a number eight bougie and retain it in place herself. Up till this time she had refused to contemplate passing the bougie herself at all, and had had two (unadvised) traumatic failed attempts at intercourse at home which had shaken her confidence and delayed improvement. It was decided therefore to resort to the number four bougie for the purpose of getting the patient to pass it herself, and two sessions were spent in encouraging this procedure. At the fourteenth session she succeeded in passing the number six bougie herself and departed very pleased with her accomplishment. She returned for the next session saying that intercourse had been partially successful and that her husband was at last beginning to believe in the possibility of some improvement. One more session of deconditioning was held, and following this intercourse was successful and enjoyable. Follow-up revealed there to be no further problem. The patient observed that intercourse was much easier than the passing of a rather unpliable bougie had been. Significantly no other symptoms developed to replace those removed in any of the patients seen.

DISCUSSION

The use of learning theory in the treatment of what might be considered hysterical symptoms did not result in the development of any other symptoms to replace those lost. In fact, once the problem of the dyspareunia had been overcome, these patients settled down to normal happy married lives. No attempt was made to analyze even superficially any possible hidden motives for their symptoms (if indeed any existed). The time taken to treat the patients (a total of 2-1/2 hours in the first, and 8 hours of deconditioning in the second), compares very favorably with any other psychiatric approach that might have been attempted. The value to the patients of having this situation put right so simply after two or three years of unhappiness made the time spent well worth while. Relapse can be predicted as most improbable. The technique employed involved relaxation and reassurance from the therapist in establishing a strong and confident relationship with the patient, and the anxiety-relieving properties of sexual responses could be predicted to support and continue to prevent any recurrence once intercourse was being enjoyed.

SUMMARY

A method of treating psychogenic dyspareunia by reciprocal inhibition is described. Two examples of cases where this method was successfully used, in contrasting personalities, are given.

Acknowledgments: I should like to thank Dr. W.A.L. Bowen for his assistance in providing the facilities and case material for this study.

REFERENCES

Wolpe, J. *Psychotherapy by reciprocal inhibition.* Stanford University Press, 1958.

38
An Innovation in the "Behavioral" Treatment of a Case of Nonconsummation Due to Vaginismus

ALAN J. COOPER

The majority of "behaviorally oriented" treatments for nonconsummation due to vaginismus combine a) teaching the patient how to relax the perineal muscles, b) simultaneous vaginal exploration and dilatation, preferably performed by the patient herself, and c) some form of psychotherapy (Lazarus, 1963; Malleson, 1942; Friedman, 1962; Brady, 1966). Surprisingly perhaps, active participation by the male spouse is considered unnecessary by some experts (Malleson, 1942; Friedman, 1962). Friedman has shown there was no statistical relationship between actively involving the male in therapy and the outcome of treatment.

This paper describes an innovation in treatment which consists in actively incorporating the husband in therapy, in the clinic, and in the case reported transformed a therapeutic failure into a success. This case also demonstrates the ("subconscious") collusion which may exist between such couples; this can be antitherapeutic, tending to maintain the sexual *status quo* (nonconsummation).

CASE HISTORY

The patient, aged 21, presented with nonconsummation since her marriage 1-1/2 years previously.

Before marriage she had engaged in and enjoyed petting with her fiance, but had been unable to tolerate even minimal digital penetration of her vagina, because of severe pain. Following marriage, despite numerous attempts, coitus had not been possible; mutual masturbation (clitoral stimulation in her case) to orgasm usually followed these abortive coital attempts. The patient always apologized tearfully to her husband and expressed distress at her inability to allow penile penetration. He in turn, had been sympathetic about her "dreadful pain" and reassured her that he would never purposefully do anything to hurt her.

Clinically the patient appeared to be a pleasant, cooperative woman with a hysterical type of personality. On the MPI, she scored as extroverted and nonneurotic (E-I = 34,

357

N = 10). She had positive attitudes about sex generally: thus she described herself as uninhibited; she enjoyed being kissed and cuddled and was able to reach orgasm through clitoral stimulation. She described her husband as "sympathetic and gentle . . . incapable of losing his temper or hurting anyone."

The diagnosis was that nonconsummation was due to severe vaginismus which had probably been maintained and consolidated by the submissive and sexually compliant attitudes of the patient's spouse; the symptom (vaginismus), present even before marriage seemed to be due to a marked fear of, and a desire to avoid the pain of coitus. Thus the mechanism seemed to be solely self-protective; there was no evidence that it was symptomatic of marital conflict, or was part of a personality disorder, or was otherwise subserving subconscious motives.

TREATMENT

Treatment consisted of a) teaching the patient deep muscular relaxation (Cooper, 1964) together with b) gradual vaginal dilation using glass dilators of progressively increasing size (while fully relaxed). At the end of each session, the patient was encouraged to examine and then to pass the dilators herself and thereby to gain confidence about the obvious adequacy (for coitus) of her vagina and dispel any fears that she might be "torn inside" by the male organ.

After six sessions she was able to tolerate the largest dilator in comparative comfort, and said she felt sufficiently confident to attempt coitus. She was advised to tell her husband that he should be prepared to rouse her fully, with prolonged love play; also that he was to ignore any protests of discomfort from her, since as he continued to stimulate her and to proceed with coitus she would become fully roused and relatively insensitive to pain, which would dissolve into pleasure culminating in orgasm.

After four weeks she reported that despite much effort and the cooperation of her husband penetration had not been achieved. On each occasion they had tried, she had developed muscular contractions and pain; her husband had found it impossible to proceed further, since he could not bring himself to hurt her.

The patient and her husband then were invited to attend the clinic together. The husband was told that he was oversensitive to his wife's discomfiture and, by "colluding" with her not to proceed with coitus when she gave minimal cues of pain, was partly responsible for the failure of therapy; that full sexual arousal and orgasm was incompatible with pain, which would diminish reciprocally as his wife became more excited; that he should ignore any complaints of pain either overt or implied, since it would be necessary for him by persistent and skillfully aggressive techniques to overcome his wife's resistance to full penetration; that repeated clitoral stimulation to the exclusion of coitus, with the obvious reinforcement for its repetition which orgasm must bring, was likely to diminish in her any desire for change; that his wife's vagina was more than able to accommodate his penis and that it was not possible to cause any physical damage through coitus; that his wife's spasms were protective in function and serving to prevent a situation (penetration) which she felt would be intolerably painful. He was then shown the dilators which had been previously used, and was persuaded to pass them as instructed into his (relaxed) wife's vagina; he was surprised to find that she was able to accommodate the largest without pain. Finally, he was advised that if a spasm should develop during penile penetration he should not withdraw, but should remain where he was until the spasm and associated pain disappeared, when he was to continue penetration in a leisurely and unhurried manner.

OUTCOME AND FOLLOW-UP

Although consummation (full penetration) and coitus was accomplished immediately following the joint interview, the patient failed to reach orgasm. After ten months, despite fairly frequent and sustained (technically adequate) coitus (up to seven minutes) from which she derived pleasure, she has still not experienced a sensation comparable to the climaxes she had enjoyed through clitoral stimulation. She is pleased with her new-found ability to engage in full coitus, but is disappointed about her failure to achieve orgasm. She feels, however, that with continuing experience this will become possible.

COMMENT

The present case may be considered a therapeutic success, since the limited goal of treatment—namely, relief of vaginismus and subsequent consummation—has been achieved. However, treatment by its very "success" has revealed a co-existent degree of "frigidity" (lack of coital orgasmic capacity), which persists despite regular and sustained coitus. Friedman (1962) has suggested that in some cases the symptom of vaginismus not only protects the patient from the pain associated with the "feared object" (penis), but also protects her from "finding out" about her "sexual inadequacy"—her inability to achieve coital orgasm. However, Malleson (1942) says that some women are probably biologically unequipped to respond with vaginal (coital) orgasm, however adequate the male, while being perfectly capable of immediate orgasmic response from even minimal clitoral stimulation; Malleson warns: to imply frigidity in these cases or to suggest personality immaturity is to do a grave disservice to the patient. She adds that some of these women, with increasing coital experience, may eventually become capable of responding with coital orgasm. Malleson and Friedman agree, however, that noncon-summation and frigidity, although often co-existing, are different disorders, both etiologically and prognostically, and require different therapies.

The case exemplifies the "submissive" sympathetic and gentle personality of the male partner which so often figures in the literature, and the collusive psychopathology that may exist between such couples. The treatment described here shows how it might be possible to break through this antitherapeutic collusion and transform an unsuccessful outcome into a successful one (*viz.* in terms of alleviating the presenting complaint). It is not suggested that such measures are either necessary or justified in every case, but in well-chosen cases they may be worthy of trial.

REFERENCES

Brady, J.P. "Brevital relaxation treatment of frigidity." *J. behav. res. and ther.* 1966, **4**, 71.

Cooper, A.J. "Behaviour therapy in the treatment of bronchial asthma." *Ibid.* 1964, **1**, 351.

Friedman, L.J. *Virgin wives.* London: Tavistock. 1962.

Lazarus, A.A. The treatment of chronic frigidity by systematic desensitization therapy. *J. nerv. ment. dis.* 1963, **136**, 272.

Malleson, J. Vaginismus: Its management and psychogenesis. *Brit. med. J.* 1942, **ii**, 213.

Additional Selected Readings

Clark, D.F. The treatment of hysterical spasm and agoraphobia by behavior therapy. *Behaviour Research and Therapy,* 1963, **1**, 245-250.

DeMoor, W. Vaginismus: Etiology and treatment. *American Journal of Psychotherapy,* 1972, **26**, 207-215.

Fuchs, K., Abramovici, H., Hoch, Z., Timor-Tritsch, I., & Kleinhaus, M. Vaginismus—The hypno-therapeutic approach, *The Journal of Sex Research,* 1975, **11**, 39-45.

Wilson, G.T. Innovations in the modification of phobic behaviors in two clinical cases. *Behavior Therapy,* May, 1973, **4**, 3, 426-430.

Part 2
Problems Involving Undesired
Sexual Object Choices

Homosexual Behavior

Of all the "problems" associated with human sexuality, none is as controversial as homosexual behavior, that is, sexual interest or activities between individuals of the same sex. Sexual attraction and activities between individuals of the same sex are variously viewed as a sin, an abnormality, a disease, an impairment of normal sexual development or just an alternative way of life and a variation in sexual-object choice. Only recently, the American Psychiatric Association went through a painful debate culminating in a vote on whether homosexuality was "still" a disease or just a condition. The "condition" won. This change parallels a growing openness and awareness about homosexual behavior, resulting, in part, from the gay liberation movement's efforts to educate the public.

It is difficult to determine the number of individuals experiencing problems with their homosexual behavior. For one thing, as reported by Kinsey et al. (1948, p. 639), a very large number of individuals (from 11 to 20 percent of women, and 18 to 42 percent of men) have to some extent engaged in homosexual behaviors; this is not to mention those having occasional or frequent homosexual fantasies or wishes without engaging in homosexual behaviors per se. The great majority of these people, of course, either experience no problems as a result of these activities or, if they do, seek no professional help.

Even those who engage exclusively in homosexual relationships do not necessarily perceive these behaviors as problematic. Many who have identified with the gay subculture feel their orientation is no more inherently problematic than a heterosexual orientation. Indeed, their major problems associated with their sexual orientation may be the negative attitudes of the great majority of heterosexually oriented individuals (Weinberg & Williams, 1974, pp. 93-96 and 147), and the legal prohibitions against homosexual activities in the majority of states.

Nevertheless, there are sizable numbers of individuals who reject their homosexual desires or behaviors and wish to eliminate these responses and increase their heterosexual responses, and it is to these individuals that most behavior therapy programs dealing with homosexual behavior are addressed.

Of all the areas of behavior therapy with sexual problems, homosexual behavior has received the most attention in the literature with over 80 articles available from which to choose for this book. The goal in this section, then, was to select examples of the variety of techniques and behavioral programs that have been used successfully to modify homosexual behavior and illustrate their application. This is not intended to imply that each of the techniques has been used to the same extent. In fact, perhaps the most extensive use in changing undesired homosexual behavior has been made of electric shock—aversive conditioning—and, as several articles in this book and in the Additional Selected Readings indicate, there has been considerable success with aversive measures (even though the exact mechanism of aversive therapy, i.e., that which produces the success, is, as yet, unclear; see McConaghy and Barr, 1973). However, recent years have seen some degree of de-emphasis on physically aversive methods and a corresponding increase in a wide variety of nonaversive procedures—including procedures to decrease homosexual arousal (e.g., covert sensitization), procedures used to increase heterosexual arousal (e.g., fading, classical conditioning), and procedures to decrease heterosexual anxiety (e.g., systematic desensitization).

Of note in examining success rates in altering undesired homosexual behavior is, when outcome is vigorously examined, there appears to be far greater potential for success with those individuals who have had prior heterosexual experience and fantasies than for those who have not. In the latter case, particularly, it would seem to be the clinician's job to be aware of such outcome information, to make use of it in his assessment and then to strongly consider the possibility that a more effective form of intervention than helping the homosexually-oriented client to change his sexual orientation would be to help him accept or adjust to the homosexual orientation.

The first article dealing with modification of unwanted homosexual behavior is Wilson and Davison's important review "Behavior Therapy and Homosexuality: A Critical Perspective." The authors argue that inadequate behavioral assessment in formulating appropriate therapeutic strategies characterize a good deal of the behavior therapy literature on treatment of homosexual behavior. They suggest that "homosexuality" has been too narrowly conceptualized, and that improved treatment approaches should more adequately reflect its complexity and diversity. Wilson and Davison critically examine the rationale for the predominant use of aversive procedures in behavioral treatment of homosexual behavior, and suggest a more expanded therapeutic program derived from social learning theory. Finally, they discuss the ethics and choice of therapeutic goals in behavior change programs dealing with homosexual behavior, concluding that behavior therapy might be successfully used to either eliminate homosexual behavior in cases where the individual so desires, or to help individuals with a homosexual orientation to participate meaningfully in everyday life *as homosexuals.*

The other articles in this section illustrate the various ways behaviorists have attempted to deal with homosexual behavior that the client desires to change (which, to date, has been the predominant orientation of the behavioral interventive programs involving homosexual behavior). The next article is by MacCulloch and Feldman, "Aversion Therapy in Management of 43 Homosexuals," MacCulloch and Feldman, pioneered the use of aversive procedures in attempting to change male homosexual behavior, and this article briefly describes the techniques they use, and also presents outcome data. Their technique, called "anticipatory avoidance aversion therapy" involves a mild electric shock administered when clients find pictures of men attractive; the shock and its resultant anxiety can be avoided if the client signals the picture is not attractive. This is coupled with pictures of attractive females at offset of the shock thereby pairing it with anxiety relief. (This procedure is described in detail in Chapter 48.) The authors present extensive and impressive outcome data, drawing the important conclusion that one of the major variables that may be prognostic of success is a history of heterosexual interest and practice at some time in the client's life. There are numerous issues involved in the MacCulloch-Feldman strategy (*see* Additional Selected Readings) as suggested in the previous article by Wilson and Davison. These issues involve empirical, ethical and theoretical questions about their work. To date, many of these questions remain unsolved, often subject to the ideological position of the debaters, although many of them are subject to empirical testing. But there is little question that work such as described here has been pioneering in the treatment of sexual disorders, and that MacCulloch and Feldman's research remains one of the most extensive and important attempts to apply learning principles to the treatment of undesired sexual behavior.

The brief article by Meyer and Freeman describes the "Alteration of Sexual Preferences via Conditioning Therapies." Their procedure involves a combination of conditioning clients to heterosexual stimuli while deconditioning them through aversive procedures to homosexual stimuli. Outcome data also are presented indicating a significant change in the direction of increased heterosexuality. Among the contributions of this study are a greater specification of conditioning procedures than in most other studies; emphasis on a combinations of techniques in a controlled outcome study; and an emphasis on client self-control.

The article by Huff describes an entirely different approach, "The Desensitization of a Homosexual." Huff operates on the basis that homosexual behavior may be, at least in part, a sexual adjustment necessitated by an irrational fear of the opposite sex. In this case study, Huff shows that the undesired homosexual behavior did indeed appear to be related to fear of the opposite sex for this client, and that when desensitization was used to lessen this fear, heterosexual approaches were begun.

The article by Herman, Barlow and Agras, "Exposure to Heterosexual Stimuli: An Effective Variable in Treating Homosexuality?" is an abbreviated version of a more extended description of this procedure in Volume I. In essence, the rather simple procedure consists of exposing the client to movies of a young, nude, seductive female with instructions to imagine engaging in sexual behavior with her. A second phase of the treatment involved exposure to a film depicting homosexual activities, and the third phase was re-exposure to the female film. As can be seen from the data, exposure to high intensity sexual stimuli (perhaps somewhat confounded with positive therapeutic instructions) was successful in modifying this client's sexual arousal.

The article by Curtis and Presly presents a case study of "The Extinction of Homosexual Behavior by Covert Sensitization." In this study, a client's homosexual interest was nearly eradicated using covert sensitization. As the authors point out, covert sensitization, at least in this instance, appeared to be an improvement over physically aversive treatment since no special equipment was necessary and the procedure is easily self-administered.

The next article, by Maletzky and George, "The Treatment of Homosexuality by 'Assisted' Covert Sensitization," demonstrates an interesting modification in the covert sensitization procedure (see also Volume I). Based on the authors' experience that "traditional" covert sensitization appeared somewhat impotent in changing homosexual behavior, Maletzky and George bolstered the procedure by adding an odiferous substance, valeric acid, at appropriate intervals during the application of the procedure. The authors report impressive results, maintained at follow-up, in decreasing homosexual behaviors and increasing heterosexual behaviors. This suggests the possiblity of using this procedure as a potential substitute for aversive methods, although the authors properly caution that proof of the actual effectiveness of "assisted" covert sensitization in changing undesired homosexual behavior must await more rigorous, controlled outcome research.

The brief report by Bellack describes "Covert Aversion Relief and the Treatment of Homosexuality." This is another modification of covert sensitization. In this instance, a process of "aversion relief" was added in which, after the aversive image was terminated a relief image of an attractive young woman with whom the client interacted was used. This was an apparently successful, and logically or theoretically appropriate, extension of the covert sensitization procedure.

The next article, by Rehm and Rozensky, describes the use of "Multiple Behavior Therapy Techniques with a Homosexual Client." In this case, various aspects of a client's homosexual behavior and heterosexual avoidance were modified by the use of education, self-managment, desensitization, covert sensitization, aversive conditioning, aversion relief, orgasmic reconditioning and assertive training. The authors argue, probably quite properly, that careful analysis of an individual's homosexual behavior may lead to the application of multiple techniques. Of course, in this case, it is difficult to tell which, if any, of the techniques was most significantly related to outcome. But it is, indeed, likely that the program of choice for changing undesired homosexual behavior, or for that matter, any undesired sexual behavior, would involve multiple techniques, including procedures for decreasing the undesired behavior, say, beginning with traditional or "assisted" covert sensitization (because it is quite practical to apply), use of desensitization to decrease fear of the desired sexual object choice and possibly behavior rehearsal and modeling to build social skills and approach behaviors.

The article by Blitch and Haynes presents one of the few published attempts by behavior therapists to deal with female homosexual behavior. In "Multiple Behavioral Techniques in a Case of Female Homosexuality," Blitch and Haynes use systematic desensitization, relaxation, behavior rehearsal, role-playing and manipulation of masturbation fantasies. Special features of this treatment were the use of self-report procedures, and a focus upon developing heterosexual behavior.

As mentioned previously in this volume and in Volume I, and as indicated by a recent survey of behavior therapists (Davison and Wilson, 1973), most behaviorists seem, if not preoccupied with the idea, occupied in attempts to change or convert their homosexually-oriented clients to a heterosexual orientation. Of course, most therapists encounter clients whose requests are to change from a homosexual to a heterosexual orientation; however, it is far from clear what effect intensive exploration by a therapist open to the idea of helping the client accept or adjust to a homosexual orientation would have on the direction ultimately selected by the client. Certainly, it would be unreasonable to expect most clients to consult therapists whose reputation is for converting people from their homosexual orientation, about helping clients simply adapt to their preferred homosexual orientation.

Indeed, there have been some calls for complete abolition of the "conversion" perspective from the behavioral armamentarium. A recent article (McCrea, 1976)* reviews Gerald Davison's presidential address to the 1976 meeting of the Association for the Advancement of Behavior Therapy in which Davison declared that "behavior therapists should refuse to help homosexual clients change their orientation even when they request it" (McCrea, 1976, p. 8). Davison pointed out that if, according to the behavioral perspective, sexual preference, *per se*, is not supposed to be proof of a problem, why is it that all the research and work in sexual adjustment goes in only one way—from homosexually-oriented to heterosexually-oriented? This very fact of a continuing focus on conversion " 'tends to validate the prejudice, tends to impede change, and tends to limit the options available to homosexuals' " (McCrea, 1976, p. 8).

Davison, in his speech, acknowledges how difficult it is to say "no" when somebody asks for help, but claims to be increasingly skeptical of what people really want when they ask to be changed. Part of this is related to the fact that people in American society are so indoctrinated to the view that same-sex relations are "sick" and undesirable that " 'to overlook, or to downplay, or to not take very seriously the coerciveness, inherent in bearing social stigma—to talk about people 'voluntarily' asking for change — is to be terribly naive and . . . not to be good behaviorists . . . let alone good practitioners and good people' " (McCrea, 1976, p. 8).

*The authors are indebted to Sterling Jones for bringing this article to their attention.

Despite this call from Davison, and the results of a recent survey that show that many behavior therapists are willing to help their clients become more at ease with a homophile orientation (Davison and Wilson, 1973), there is little in the behavioral literature to suggest active efforts or success at doing so. The final chapter in this section is one of the few, if not the only article to appear in the literature in which specific procedures for helping individuals who wish to maintain their homosexual orientation are delineated. The article is "The Use of Stimulus/Modeling Videotapes in Assertive Training for Homosexuals," by Duehn and Mayadas. In this article, the authors present both the rationale for and procedural descriptions of the use of assertive training (using stimulus/modeling videotapes, behavioral rehearsal, and videotape feedback) to help a 26 year old male accept his homosexual orientation. In view of an apparent increasing societal willingness to tolerate divergent sexual lifestyles, and the increasing openness of sexual minorities to assert their rights (see, e.g., "Gays on the March," *Time*, September 8, 1975, pp. 32-43), the material in the Duehn and Mayadas article may be a portent of the future; at least, such interventive options should be included in the armamentarium of all clinicians working with sexual problems.

REFERENCES

Davison, G.C. & Wilson, G.T. Attitudes of behavior therapists toward homosexuality, *Behavior Therapy*, 1973, **4**, 686-696.

Kinsey, A.C., Pomeroy, W.B. & Martin, C.E. *Sexual behavior in the human Male*. Philadelphia: W.B. Saunders, 1948.

McConaghy, N. & Barr, R.F. Classical, avoidance and backward conditioning treatments of homosexuality, *British Journal of Psychiatry*, 1973, **122**, 151-162.

McCrea, R. There are no cures, *The Advocate*, 1976, June 2, 8, 9.

Weinberg, M.S. & Williams, C.J. *Male homosexuals: Their problems and adaptations*. New York: Oxford University Press, 1974.

39
Behavior Therapy and Homosexuality:
A Critical Perspective*

G. TERENCE WILSON and GERALD C. DAVISON

In recent years, homosexuals in cities and on college campuses everywhere have organized themselves into frequently militant alliances which have strongly condemned the rhetoric of sin, and more recently of psychopathology, in terms of which homosexual orientations have traditionally been viewed. Objections to prevailing psychiatric and psychological thinking have often singled out behavior therapy (inevitably identified with the use of aversive conditioning techniques) for particular criticism (Weinberg, 1972). This reaction prompted us to enter into dialogues with gay activist groups to re-examine our own practices and attitudes. The present paper represents the findings of our review of the behavior therapy literature as well as numerous discussions with many of our behaviorally oriented colleagues, and proposes an expanded conceptualization of homosexuality.

BEHAVIORAL ASSESSMENT AND BEHAVIOR THERAPY

It is now well established that the essential features of behavioral assessment involve the specific determination of target behaviors for modification, the discovery of all relevant variables currently maintaining those behaviors, the precise sequencing of therapeutic objectives, and the careful selection of the appropriate therapeutic technique(s) for modifying these behaviors. Behavioral assessment entails the implementation of therapeutic regimens which are tailored to the individual case (Bandura, 1969; Mischel, 1968). Lazarus (1971a) stresses the "personalistic" nature of therapy, while Shapiro (1961) and Yates (1970) define behavior therapy in terms of the application of the principles of experimental psychology to the individual case. Despite the refinements that have been suggested in behavioral assessment, behavior therapy approaches to homosexual clients, particularly in research settings, have rarely reflected appropriate attention to the *diversity* of the subject.

*We are grateful to Arnold Lazarus, Gert Sommer, Steven Fishman and Barry Lubetkin for their critical reading of earlier versions of this manuscript.

Well developed among behavior therapists is the treatment-oriented research strategy of assigning large numbers of patients presenting apparently the same problem to different treatment conditions so as to compare the outcome efficacy of different techniques (Paul, 1966a). In these factorial studies the explicit assumption is that the subjects constitute a relatively homogeneous population which shares a common target behavior for modification. For example, Bancroft (1966), Birk, Huddleston, Miller and Cohler (1971), Feldman and MacCulloch (1971), Freund, (1960) and McConaghy (1969, 1970) all randomly assigned homosexual patients to different treatment conditions without any attempt being made at behavioral assessment. We question, however, the assumption that an unselected group of homosexuals will necessarily present the same homogeneous, uniform target behavior. What is specifically required are comparative studies of the relative efficacies of different behavioral techniques singly and—more importantly—in combination. And, at the more general level, what is needed is a better understanding of the complex behavior patterns labeled homosexuality, so often treated in what is probably an oversimplified and stereotyped manner. Until now, the behavior therapy literature has concentrated on the technical details of aversion therapy, the customary form of treatment, while neglecting the nature of homosexuality itself.

THE RATIONALE FOR AVERSION THERAPY

The main thrust of the behavior therapy literature to date has unquestionably been in the use of aversion therapy for altering homosexual orientation (Bancroft, 1966; Birk et al., 1971; Freund, 1960, Eysenck & Rachman, 1965; Eysenck & Beech, 1971; McConaghy, 1969, 1970; Feldman & MacCulloch, 1971; Rachman & Teasdale, 1969; Maletsky, 1973). Our survey (Davison and Wilson, 1973) of the members of the Association for Advancement of Behavior Therapy (AABT) in the United States, and of an association of British behavior therapists confirms this impression: aversion therapy is the most common and preferred method of treatment of homosexual behavior, with systematic desensitization a somewhat distant second contender. The rationale behind these treatment strategies deserves scrutiny.

Feldman and MacCulloch's (1971) use of their anticipatory avoidance (AA) technique represents the most systematic application of learning principles for the treatment of homosexuality to date. Their principal technique entails the presentation of attractive male slides followed by painful electrical shock that can be avoided if the patient responds within a given period of time to remove the male slide from view and substitute a female picture. In discussing the development of their pioneering research efforts, the authors state that they chose an aversive therapy technique so as to "win a breathing space within which the patient might acquire (or re-acquire) an interest in heterosexual behavior" (1971, p. 17). Similarly, Freund (1960), Kanfer and Phillips (1970), and Marshall (1971) all insist that homosexual behavior must be directly interrupted *before* an alternative heterosexual repertoire can emerge.

However, the documented efficacy of the AA technique (Birk et al., 1971; Feldman & MacCulloch, 1971) cannot be unequivocally attributed to aversive conditioning since the avoidance learning is confounded with the "anxiety-relief" procedure (Franks & Wilson, 1973). This confound is important since Feldman and MacCulloch consider that the reduction of heterophobic feelings is a *necessary* component of successful treatment.

In essence, they are reaffirming Bieber's (1962) contention that homosexuality is largely a function of pathological fear of the opposite sex. If the heterophobic hypothesis is correct, and given the fact that aversion-relief procedures might be effective in reducing avoidance behavior (Solyom, Heseltine, McClure, Ledwidge & Kenny, 1971), then it is reasonable to suggest that aversion-relief is the critical ingredient in the Feldman and MacCulloch therapeutic package and that the presumed importance of conditioning aversion to homosexual stimuli is irrelevant. Feldman and MacCulloch themselves remark upon this possibility (1971, p. 161). It may well be that the theoretical differences between Rachman and Teasdale (1969) and Feldman and MacCulloch as to whether it is classical or instrumental conditioning which best accounts for the success obtained with the AA technique are of minimal importance since the aversion technique is confounded with aversion-relief.

It is impossible to make any definite statement on the interactive effects of attempting to devalue homosexual arousal while strengthening heterosexual responsiveness and it is premature to assert that homosexual arousal must be reduced before heterosexual interest is increased (e.g., Thorpe, Schmidt & Castell, 1963). At least in some cases it does not seem necessary (Herman, Barlow & Agras, 1971; LoPiccolo, 1971).

Bancroft (1969, 1970) found that although aversive therapy significantly decreased penile erection to homosexual stimuli, it had little effect on clinical behavior change. Yet the only completely successful clinical outcome of the ten patients treated with aversive therapy was one in which 32 sessions of aversive therapy *failed to diminish* homosexual arousal, and heterosexual arousal developed which seemingly later accounted for the patient's totally heterosexual adjustment (Bancroft, 1969). A curious result was what Bancroft (1971) has called "paradoxical facilitation," *viz*, an increase in heterosexual erections from the beginning to the end of treatment as a function of punishment of erection to homosexual stimuli. This increase in heterosexual arousal which did not follow treatment with desensitization was significantly correlated with successful behavioral change. This result is difficult to understand at present, but it raises the possibility that aversive therapy, where effective, might be working for reasons other than those originally envisaged. On the basis of Bancroft's data it appears that aversive therapy is successful in modifying homosexual behavior to the extent that it *directly* affects heterosexual arousal rather than *indirectly* paving the way for subsequent heterosexual behavior by eliminating homosexual responses first.

Why then has behavior therapy been so wedded to the use of aversion therapy in the treatment of homosexuals? We believe that homosexual behavior has been viewed by client, therapist and society alike as undesirable at best, and pathological at worst, something which should be eliminated irrespective of heterosexual development. Rachlin (1970) points out that the most effective means of eliminating a response is to punish it directly rather than rewarding its absence. However, if the goal of therapy is to develop heterosexual arousal, then the therapeutic strategies might be different, since the best way of strengthening a response is to reinforce its occurrence rather than to punish its absence. Furthermore, we suspect that the traditional viewpoint about sexual development being the successive manifestations of a largely fixed biological drive (libido!) influences therapeutic decisions. If the sex drive is biologically determined and relatively fixed in amount, then it follows logically that the prevailing expression (e.g., homosexuality) has to be blocked so that it can be channeled elsewhere (e.g., heterosexuality).

We echo Rachman and Teasdale's (1969) surprise at the considerable success

Feldman and MacCulloch have achieved with the use of their AA technique (the efficacy of which is further substantiated by Birk et al. 1971 study), not because of theoretical reasons relating to the specifics of the conditioning paradigm involved, but because the logic of their research paradigm precluded a behavioral analysis of the presenting problem. A more complete assessment together with the use of another technique(s) might have resulted in even greater outcome efficacy. Bancroft (1970), for example, found that desensitization led to successful clinical outcome in those patients who showed heterosexual anxiety whereas aversive therapy tended to be more effective with other patients.

Another consequence of the omission of a full behavioral anlaysis relates to the Feldman and MacCulloch theory of the etiology of homosexuality. They have distinguished between "primary homosexuals" (those without prior heterosexual experience) and "secondary homosexuals" (those who have experienced pleasurable heterosexual behavior), and have hypothesized that the homosexual behavior of the former is attributable to prenatal hormonal effects whereas the latter's behavior is largely a function of social learning. Drawing a fundamental and potentially far-reaching etiological distinction like this on the basis of outcome response to a fixed therapeutic regime is extremely hazardous given the logical alternative explanation that the "primary homosexuals" were the ones to whom the AA technique was inappropriately applied and who therefore, not surprisingly, showed little evidence of change (Barlow, 1972). The plausibility of this alternative explanation is enhanced by the argument that the AA technique is effective with "secondary homosexuals" by virtue of the reduction of avoidance behavior toward members of the opposite sex, thereby allowing a preexisting heterosexual response repertoire to function. With "primary homosexuals," however, little would be accomplished by the reduction of heterophobic reactions without "building up a verbal and visual fantasy repertoire and the skills for interactions with socially acceptable partners" (Kanfer & Phillips, 1970, p. 119).

DEVELOPMENT AND MAINTENANCE OF HOMOSEXUAL BEHAVIOR

In contrast to the Freudian view that heterosexuality is the normal end-product of a naturally unfolding psychosexual development, and that homosexuality occurs only when pathological anxiety inhibits "normal" heterosexual development (Bieber, 1962), the social learning approach emphasizes that homosexuality is acquired and maintained in the same manner as heterosexual behavior (e.g., Bandura, 1969; Kinsey, Pomeroy & Martin, 1948; Ullmann & Krasner, 1969). There is still little compelling evidence showing that homosexuality is either genetically determined or hormonally based. Money (1970) has concluded that a biological predisposition toward homosexuality might exist, but "not in the ordained sense, only if the social conditions are right" (p. 432). Gagnon and Simon (1970) postulate that the primary controlling element in the development of sexual commitments is the acquisition of *gender identity* which determines what kinds of sexual acts are consistent with particular conceptions of "masculinity" and "femininity," and also what kinds of sex role characteristics make it possible for one person to see another as erotic. They also stress that sexual behavior might be influenced by nonsexual factors, as in the case of men who, having trouble handling authority relationships at work, show an increased incidence of homosexual dreams, while others, under heavy stress on their jobs, have been shown to have more frequent episodic homosexual experiences.

INCREASING HETEROSEXUAL AROUSAL AND BEHAVIOR DIRECTLY

There have been several programmatic attempts within the behavior therapy literature to directly train heterosexual responsiveness (Barlow, 1973). Davison (1968) has described a sexual reorientation technique in which the client learns to be aroused by a previously neutral stimulus through a carefully directed sequence of masturbation. Although there has as yet been no systematic study of this method, several clinical reports attest to its possible utility (e.g., Bancroft, 1966; Evans, 1968; LoPiccolo, Stewart, and Watkins, 1972; Marquis, 1970; McGuire, Carlisle & Young, 1965). A related approach is that of classically conditioning sexual arousal to a previously neutral stimulus by pairing it with another visual stimulus evocative of arousal (Rachman, 1966; Rachman & Hodgson, 1968). Another intriguing possibility lies in reinforcing penile erection to heterosexual stimuli (e.g., Rosen, 1972; Quinn, Harbison & McAllister, 1970). It is probable that future research along these lines will establish powerful means of developing sexual arousal to a variety of stimulus conditions. Of course, it must be reiterated that more than genital arousal is inherent in what Simon and Gagnon call the "scripting" of psychosexual identity, such that modes of dress, courtship behaviors, speech patterns and other social factors become the necessary concern of the behavior therapist. (There is more to sexuality than genital secretions.)

This analysis is conjectural at present, but some scattered research findings do provide some support Bancroft (1970) found that the reduction of homosexual behavior outside of treatment in his study was intimately associated with direct improvement on *heterosexual variables* like a more favorable heterosexual attitude, greater heterosexual arousal and decreased fear about heterosexual inadequacy.

MULTIFACETED BEHAVIORAL TREATMENT OF HOMOSEXUALITY

A behavioral approach based on a comprehensive functional analysis appears to be ideally suited for encouraging the development of new behavioral repertoires through the use of such procedures as modeling (Bandura, 1969), behavior rehearsal (Lazarus, 1971a: McFall & Marston, 1970), assertive training (Stevenson and Wolpe, 1960), and graded *in vivo* homework assignments. Any heterosexual anxiety could be treated by the above-mentioned methods or with the addition of systematic desensitization (e.g. Di Scipio, 1968; Kraft, 1969; LoPiccolo, 1971). However, it would be well to determine whether the anxiety is a cause or effect of homosexuality, since this might have important consequences for therapy. The elimination of heterosexual anxiety and behavioral deficits and the reinforcement of heterosexual arousal and social-sexual skills might best be accomplished by following the Masters and Johnson (1970) therapeutic model, in terms of which the homosexual would undergo graduated relearning experiences, with, ideally, an emotionally sensitive, psychologically sophisticated, and technically proficient partner of the opposite sex. The availability of a sympathetic female for initial heterosexual contact by the homosexual male seems especially important in view of Kinsey et al.'s (1948) observation that ostracism by a high proportion of females was a factor in forcing the male with known homosexual experience into exclusively homosexual patterns of behavior.

It should be noted that even those therapists who have used aversive therapy as their major technique for modifying homosexual behavior stress the fact that this method represents only one aspect of the behavior therapist's armamentarium of techniques, and specifically advocate the future use of a broad spectrum approach (Bancroft, 1970; Feldman & McCulloch, 1971).

Differences between Male and Female Homosexuals

An extremely important factor which is seldom taken into account in formulating treatment strategies for homosexuals is whether the clients are male or female (Davison & Wilson, 1973). Too much emphasis has been placed on "the homosexual" (almost invariably male—MacCulloch & Feldman, 1967, had only two Lesbians in their entire sample) without due regard for differential diagnostic and prognostic considerations relating to gender (Simon & Gagnon, 1970). Kinsey, Pomeroy, Martin and Gebhard (1953), Saghir, Robins and Walbran (1969), Simon and Gagnon (1967) and Martin and Lyon (1972) have suggested that *gender identity* is important for a full understanding of homosexuality. For instance, homosexual females share more in common with hetero-sexual women—"the start of genital behavior, the onset and frequency of masturbation, the time of entry in sociosexual patterns, the number of partners, and the reports of sexual deprivation"—(Simon & Gagnon, 1970, p. 29)—than they do with homosexual males; similarly, homosexual and heterosexual men seem to have more in common with each other than they do with homosexual and heterosexual women, respectively. Female homosexuals and heterosexuals tend much more to stay with a given partner for a length of time, to develop a romantic tender relationship prior to (and sometimes even in place of) an overtly genital one and to be less aroused than males by visual or fantasy materials (Gagnon & Simon, 1973; Hedblom, 1972). One obvious difference in therapeutic approach, then, would be considerable caution in embarking with a female on a regimen of "Playboy therapy" (Davison, 1968; Marquis, 1970), pairing masturbatory arousal with social-sexual visual stimuli to which client and therapist wish to increase attraction. (Indeed, with men also a determination must be made that masturbation is a legitimate, meaningful sexual activity for the client.)

Topography of Homosexual Behavior

An infrequently mentioned parameter of homosexuality is the topography of activities engaged in by the particular client. Would one's therapeutic approach differ, for example, if the client is a male who prefers the "active" role in anal intercourse as compared to a male who derives enjoyment from the "passive" role? It would seem that there is greater similarity between anal-intromission and vaginal-intromission both in terms of the bodily movements and the tactile stimulation involved. Does this suggest, therefore, that a homosexual who intromits in anal intercourse is somehow more oriented toward conventional heterosexual intercourse than a man who enjoys having a penis in his anus? Another example might be the comparison between the male who enjoys fellatio being done to him and the one who greatly prefers doing the fellatio. The tactile stimulation from fellatio being done by a man would seem to be quite similar to that derived from fellatio done by a woman. Is this man, therefore, "less homosexual" than the individual whose sexual enjoyment comes from having another man ejaculate into his mouth—an occurrence impossible for a male in heterosexual relations?

HOMOSEXUALITY VERSUS HETEROSEXUALITY AS THE FOCUS OF BEHAVIOR MODIFICATION

The selection of therapeutic goals is intimately associated with the therapist's theory of normal behavior development and with his own ethical standards of what *should* be. Unlike Freudian theory, the social learning approach we have advocated neither equates "normality" with heterosexuality nor homosexuality with "abnormality" (Bieber, 1962; Hatterer, 1970; Socarides, 1970). Instead, along with other forms of statistically less frequent sexual behavior, homosexuality is assumed to be acquired, maintained and modified in the same manner as heterosexual behavior (Simon & Gagnon, 1970). "Normal" and "abnormal" are seen as labels which reflect the prevailing social value judgments of society's labelers (Szasz, 1961), and many non-Western cultures even *expect* and *encourage* a degree of bisexuality (Churchill, 1967; West, 1967).

Based as it is upon social learning theory, "behavioral therapy is a system of principles and procedures and not a system of ethics. Its methods . . . can be employed to threaten human freedom and dignity or to enhance them" (Bandura, 1969, p. 87). In his illuminating discussion of these issues Bandura further points out that the choice of behavioral goals should be the *client's.* This fundamental tenet of behavior therapy conflicts not only with the traditional psychiatric practice of diagnosing homosexuals *ipso facto* as suffering from psychopathology which needs to be "cured" (American Psychiatric Association, 1968), but also with the opposition of members of gay liberation groups who deny the right of the individual homosexual to seek treatment aimed at heterosexual reorientation. The reservation that only those individuals who desire to change sexual orientation be treated with aversive therapy has been constantly expressed, and, with the possible exception of Freund (1960), aversive therapy programs have carefully avoided imposing society's values on the homosexual participants. Indeed, we have elsewhere raised the question as to whether *any* behavioral change can be imposed upon an unwilling client, who would seem to have at his/her disposal any number of countercontrol devices to nullify the intended effects of a technique (Davison, 1973).

Despite this very proper caveat, we are aware of few published reports describing programs directed toward helping homosexuals adjust more satisfactorily to a permanent homosexual identity. Fensterheim (1972) has described the successful desensitization treatment of impotence in six male homosexuals, and Lazarus (1971b) has advocated the same approach, but these are exceptions. The lack of similar clinical ventures is unfortunate, for it tends to perpetuate the erroneous public impression about behavior therapy being bent on eradicating homosexual behavior. Our discussions with behavioral colleagues and the results of our survey indicate quite clearly that *the majority* of behavior therapists would, and in fact do, attempt to foster homosexual adjustment where appropriate and reject treating homosexuals against their wishes.

Crowley's (1968) now classic statement in *Boys in the Band*—"show me a happy homosexual and I'll show you a gay corpse"—is misleading. Accumulating evidence strongly suggests that, contrary to widespread clinical belief, homosexuality can be a rewarding, healthy life style (e.g., Hedblom, 1972), and that homosexuals of either sex need not necessarily be more disturbed or manifest more signs of psychopathology than comparable heterosexual individuals (Evans, 1970; Hooker, 1957; Kinsey, et al., 1948; Loney, 1971; Saghir et al., 1969; Thompson, McCandless & Strickland, 1971; Westwood, 1960).

These findings are particularly important, for the possibility exists, however slight, that homosexuality is constitutionally determined. Despite the lack of strong supportive evidence, Feldman and MacCulloch's theory of "primary homosexuality" might prove to be correct, and—like transsexualism—be impervious to even the most comprehensive of behavior change programs. Therapy in such cases should then be directed toward assisting the individual in making a satisfactory homosexual adjustment rather than reversing sexual preferences.

Behavior therapy has much to contribute to helping homosexuals to participate fully and meaningfully in everyday life *as homosexuals*: modeling and behavior rehearsal of effective behaviors for dealing with both straight and gay people, group behavior therapy for developing a more rational perspective on common problems, increasing levels of self-esteem, and eliminating self-defeating, unrealistic standards of self-appraisal and self-reinforcement (Silverstein, 1972). On a more social-action level, behavior therapists might do well to enter into more dialogues with the various gay alliances and lend a hand in repealing laws which attempt to legislate against certain sexual activities among consenting adults and against the right to assemble publicly.

REFERENCES

American Psychiatric Association. *Diagnostic and statistical manual of mental disorders* (2nd ed.). Washington, D.C.: American Psychiatric Association, 1968.

Bancroft, J. Aversion therapy of homosexuality. *British Journal of Psychiatry,* 1969, **115,** 1417-1431.

Bancroft, J. A comparative study of aversion and desensitization in the treatment of homosexuality. In Burns, L.E. & Worsley, J.L. (Eds.), *Behaviour therapy in the 1970s.* Bristol: John Wright & Sons, 1970, 1-22.

Bandura, A. *Principles of behavior modification.* New York: Holt, 1969.

Barlow, D.H. Review of Feldman, M.P. & MacCulloch, M.J. Homosexual behavior: Therapy and assessment. *Behavior therapy,* 1972, **3,** 479-481.

Barlow, D.H. Increasing heterosexual responsiveness in the treatment of sexual deviation: A review of the clinical and experimental literature. *Behavior Therapy,* 1973, **4,** 655-671.

Bieber, I. *Homosexuality.* New York: Basic Books, 1962.

Birk, L., Huddleston, W., Miller, E. & Cohler, B. Avoidance conditioning for homosexuality. *Archives of General Psychiatry.* 1971, **25,** 314-323.

Churchill, W. *Homosexual behavior among males: A cross-cultural and cross-species investigation.* Englewood Cliffs, N.J.: Prentice-Hall, 1967.

Crowley, M. *Boys in the band.* New York: Farrar, Straus, & Giroux, Inc., 1968.

Davison, G.C. Elimination of a sadistic fantasy by a client-controlled counterconditioning technique. *Journal of Abnormal Psychology.* 1968, **73,** 84-90.

Davison, G.C. Counter-control in behavior modification. In L.A. Hamerlynck, L.C. Handy & E.J. Mash (Eds.), *Behavior change—Methodology concepts, and practice.* Champaign, Illinois: Research Press, 1973.

Davison, G.C. & Wilson, G.T. Attitudes of behavior therapists towards homosexuality. *Behavior Therapy.* 1973, **4**, 686-696.

Evans, D.R. Masturbatory fantasy and sexual deviation. *Behaviour Research and Therapy,* 1968, **6**, 17-19.

Evans, R.B. Sixteen personality factor questionnaire scores of homosexual men. *Journal of Consulting and Clinical Psychology,* 1970, **34**, 212-215.

Eysenck, H.J. *Experiments in behaviour therapy.* London: Pergamon, 1964.

Eysenck, H.J. & Rachman, S. *Causes and cures of neurosis.* London: Routledge and Kegan Paul, 1965.

Feldman, M.P. & MacCulloch, M.J. *Homosexual behavior: Therapy and assessment.* Oxford: Pergamon, 1971.

Fensterheim, H. The initial interview. In A.A. Lazarus (Ed.), *Clinical behavior therapy.* New York: Brunner/Mazel, 1972, 22-40.

Franks, C.M. & Wilson, G.T. *Annual review of behavior therapy: Theory and practice.* New York: Brunner/Mazel, 1973.

Freund, K. Some problems in the treatment of homosexuality. In H.J. Eysenck (Ed.), *Behavior therapy and the neuroses.* Oxford: Pergamon, 1960, 312-326.

Gagnon, J.H. & Simon, W. (Eds.), *Sexual deviance.* New York: Harper & Row, 1967.

Gagnon, J.H. & Simon, W. (Eds.), *The sexual scene.* New York: Transaction, Inc. 1970.

Gagnon, J.H. & Simon, W. *The social sources of sexual conduct.* Chicago: Aldine, 1973.

Hatterer, L.J. *Changing homosexuality in the male: Treatment for men troubled by homosexuality.* New York: McGraw-Hill, 1970.

Hedblom, J.H. The female homosexual: Social and attitudinal dimensions. In J.A. McCaffrey (Ed.), *The homosexual dialectic.* Englewood Cliffs, N.J.: Prentice-Hall, 1972, 31-64.

Herman, S.H., Barlow, D.H. & Agras, W.S. Exposure to heterosexual stimuli: An effective variable in treating homosexuality. Paper read at *American Psychological Association Meeting,* Washington, D.C., September, 1971.

Hooker, E. The adjustment of the overt male homosexual. *Journal of Projective Techniques.* 1957, **21**, 18-31.

Kamen, F.E. Gay liberation and psychiatry. *Psychiatric Opinion.* 1971, **8**, 18-27.

Kanfer, F. & Phillips, J. *The learning foundations of behavior therapy.* New York: Wiley, 1970.

Kanfer, F. & Saslow, G. Behavioral diagnosis. In C.M. Franks (Ed.). *Behavior therapy: Appraisal and status.* New York: McGraw-Hill, 1969, 417-444.

Kinsey, A.C., Pomeroy, W.B. & Martin, C.E. *Sexual behavior in the human male.* Philadelphia: Saunders, 1948.

Kinsey, A.C., Pomeroy, W.B., Martin, C.E. & Gebhard, P. *Sexual behavior in the human female.* Philadelphia: Saunders, 1953.

Lazarus, A.A. *Behavior therapy and beyond.* New York: McGraw-Hill, 1971a.

Lazarus, A.A. Behavioral therapy for sexual problems. *Professional Psychology,* Fall, 1971b, 349-353.

Loney, J. Background factors, sexual experiences, and attitudes toward treatment in two "normal" homosexual samples. *Journal of Consulting & Clinical Psychology,* 1972, **38**, 57-65.

LoPiccolo, J. Case study: Systematic desensitization of homosexuality. *Behavior therapy,* 1971, **2**, 394-399.

LoPiccolo, J., Stewart, R. & Watkins, B. Treatment of erectile failure and ejaculatory incompetence of homosexual etiology. *Journal of Behavior Therapy and Experimental Psychiatry,* 1972, **3**, 233-236.

McConaghy, N. Subjective and penile plethysmograph responses following aversion-relief and apomorphine aversion therapy for homosexual impulses. *British Journal of Psychiatry,* 1969, **115**, 723-730.

McConaghy, N. Subjective and penile plethysmographic responses to aversion therapy for homosexuality: A follow-up study. *British Journal of Psychiatry,* 1970, **117**, 555-560.

McGuire, R.J., Carlisle, J.M. & Young, B.G. Sexual deviations as conditioned behavior: A hypothesis. *Behaviour Research and Therapy*, 1965, 2, 185-190.

MacCulloch, M.J., & Feldman, M.P. Aversion therapy in the management of 43 homosexuals. *British Medical Journal*, 1967, 2, 549-597.

Maletzky, B.M. "Assisted" covert sensitization: A preliminary report. *Behavior Therapy*, 1973, 6, 117-119.

Martin, D. & Lyon, P. *Lesbian/woman*. New York: Bantam Books, 1972.

Marshall, W.L. A combined treatment method for certain sexual deviations. *Behaviour Research and Therapy*, 1971, 9, 293-294.

Marquis, J.N. Orgasmic reconditioning: Changing sexual object choices through controlling masturbation fantasies. *Journal of Behavior Therapy and Experimental Psychiatry*, 1970, 1, 263-271.

Masters, W. & Johnson, V. *Human sexual inadequacy*. Boston: Little, Brown, 1970.

McFall, R. & Marston, A. An experimental investigation of behavior rehearsal in assertive training. *Journal of Abnormal Psychology*, 1970, 76, 295-303.

Mischel, W. *Personality and assessment*. New York: McGraw-Hill, 1968.

Money, J. Sexual dimorphism and homosexual gender identity. *Psychological Bulletin*, 1970, 74, 425-440.

Paul, G.L. Behavior modification research: Design and tactics. In C.M. Franks (Ed.) *Behavior therapy: Appraisal and status*. New York: McGraw-Hill, 1969a, 29-62.

Paul, G.L. Outcome of systematic desensitization II. Controlled investigations of individual treatment, technique variations, and current status. In C.M. Franks (Ed.), *Behavior Therapy: Appraisal and status*. New York: McGraw-Hill, 1969b, 105-159.

Quinn, J.T., Harbison, J. & McAllister, H. An attempt to shape human penile responses. *Behaviour Research and Therapy*, 1970, 8, 213-216.

Rachlin, H. *Introduction to modern behaviorism*. San Francisco: Freeman, 1970.

Rachman, S. Sexual fetishism: An experimental analogue. *Psychological Record*, 1966, 16, 293-296.

Rachman, S. & Teasdale, J. *Aversion therapy and behaviour disorders*. London: Routledge and Kegan Paul, 1969.

Rachman, S. & Hodgson, R.J. Experimentally induced "sexual fetishism": Replication and development. *Psychological Record*, 1968, 18, 25-27.

Rosen, R.C. Effects of contingent feedback on suppression of a human elicited autonomic responses: Penile tumescence. Unpublished doctoral dissertation, State University of New York at Stony Brook, 1972.

Sagher, M.T. Robins, E. & Walbran, B. Homosexuality II. Sexual behavior of the male homosexual. *Archives of General Psychiatry*, 1969, 21, 219-229.

Shapiro, M.B. The single case in fundamental clinical psychological research. *British Journal of Medical Psychology*, 1961, 34, 255-262.

Silverstein, C. Behavior modification and the gay community. Paper presented at the Annual Convention of the Association for Advancement of Behavior Therapy, New York City, October, 1972.

Simon, W. & Gagnon, J.H. The lesbians: A preliminary overview. In J.H. Gagnon & W. Simon (Eds.), *Sexual deviance*. New York: Harper & Row, 1967. 247-282.

Simon, W. & Gagnon, J. Psychosexual development. In J.H. Gagnon and W. Simon (Eds.), *The sexual scene*. New York: Transaction, Inc., 1970, 3-27.

Socarides, C.W. Homosexuality and medicine. *Journal of the American Medical Association*, 1970, 212, 1199-1202.

Solyom, L., Heseltine, G., McClure, D., Ledwidge, B. & Kenny, F. A comparative study of aversive relief and systematic desensitization in the treatment of phobias. *British Journal of Psychiatry*, 1971, 119, 299-303.

Stevenson, I. & Wolpe, J. Recovery from sexual deviations through overcoming of non-sexual neurotic responses. *American Journal of Psychiatry*, 1960, 116, 737-742.

Szasz, T.S. *The myth of mental illness: Foundation of a theory of personal conduct*. New York: Hoeber-Harper, 1961.

Thompson, N.L., McCandless, B.R. & Strickland, B.R. Personal adjustment of male and female homosexuals and heterosexuals. *Journal of Abnormal Psychology*, 1971, **78**, 237-240.

Thorpe, J., Schmidt, E. & Castell, D. A comparison of positive and negative (aversive) conditioning in the treatment of homosexuality. *Behaviour Research and Therapy*, 1963, **1**, 357-362.

Ullmann, L.P. & Krasner, L. *A psychological approach to abnormal behavior.* Englewood Cliffs: Prentice-Hall, 1969.

Weinberg, G. *Society and the healthy homosexual.* New York: St. Martin's Press, 1972.

West, D.J. Homosexuality. Chicago: Aldine, 1967.

Westwood, G. *A minority: Homosexuality in Great Britain.* London: Longmans, 1960.

Wittman, C. Refugees from Amerika: A gay manifesto. *San Francisco Free Press*, December 22-January 7, 1970.

Yates, A. *Behavior therapy.* New York: Wiley, 1970.

40
Aversion Therapy in Management of 43 Homosexuals

M.J. MacCULLOCH and M.P. FELDMAN

A wide variety of techniques have been used in the treatment of homosexuality. They include psychotherapy, psychoanalysis, hormones and several types of aversion therapy. There are relatively few published reports involving more than a small number of patients. To date, only one series of patients treated by aversion therapy has appeared (Freund, 1960). This involved the use of apomorphine as the aversive stimulus. A satisfactory response to treatment was obtained in 25 percent of all cases, but this was only after patients referred by the courts had been excluded. The same percentage of success was obtained in a series of 100 patients treated by psychoanalytic techniques (Bieber et al., 1962). Follow-up data for this series have not been reported. The two British series which have been published obtained treatment results which were even less satisfactory than those of Freund and of Bieber et al.

Curran and Parr (1957) were able to follow up 52 out of their original 100 patients, most of whom received psychotherapy, and in only 9 was there a change of preference toward heterosexuality. Woodward (1958), reporting a series of patients treated at the Portman Clinic and referred by the courts, found that out of the 48 who completed treatment without interruption only seven had no homosexual impulse and an increased heterosexual interest and activity. Very little follow-up data are available for Woodward's series. It seems, therefore, that in the published series approximately one-quarter at best of treated homosexual patients make a satisfactory response to treatment in that they display a noticeable change in the direction of their sexual preference and practice toward heterosexuality. Such follow-up data as are available suggest prevention of relapse to be one of the major problems in the treatment of homosexuality.

METHOD OF STUDY

The present paper is a report on a series of 43 homosexual patients treated by us and our colleagues over a period of three-and-a-quarter years, by means of the technique of anticipatory avoidance learning using an electrical aversive stimulus. The minimum period of follow-up is 12 months. A preliminary report on the technique has appeared elsewhere (Feldman & MacCulloch, 1964) and a detailed description is given in an account (Feldman & MacCulloch, 1965) of the response to treatment of the first 19 patients. A survey of the results of treatment of homosexuality by aversion therapy, together with a critical account of the aversive techniques used to date, has also been presented (Feldman, 1966). A brief account of the technique used by us follows.

TREATMENT TECHNIQUE

The homosexual patient views a slide of a male which is back-projected on to a screen. He is instructed to leave this picture on for as long as he finds it attractive. After the slide has been on the screen for 8 seconds the patient receives an electric shock if he has not by then removed it by means of a hand switch (with which he is provided). If he does switch off within the 8-second period he avoids the shock. The circuit is so wired that the patient's attempts to switch off can be delayed by the therapist. A schedule of reinforcement is used so that one-third of all the patient's attempts to switch off are delayed but do eventually remove the male slide within the 8-second period; one-third are nonreinforced—that is, the patient is shocked despite his attempts to switch off—and one-third result in the picture being removed immediately. This mixture of trials has been shown to assist considerably in delaying extinction (relapse). A photograph of a female is introduced and remains on the screen for 10 seconds immediately after the male slide leaves the screen, but in order to preserve the principle of unpredictability the female slide is not introduced on every possible occasion. Finally, the patient can press his switch to request the return of the female slide should he wish to do so. Once again his request is not met on every occasion but only randomly.

The whole treatment situation and the various variables referred to above are designed to make the fullest possible use of the extensive knowledge available to us of the psychology of learning (Kimble, 1961). The slides are first set up by the patient in a hierarchy of attractiveness, and we begin with a male slide which is only mildly attractive, working up to one which is very attractive. The opposite is carried out with the female slides, beginning with one which is relatively attractive to the patient and gradually moving along the hierarchy. The aversive stimulus (unconditional stimulus) is provided by a 12-volt make/break induction coil and is controlled by a rheostat. About 24 stimulus presentations are used per session, and each session lasts for 20 to 25 minutes. On average each patient receives 18 to 20 sessions of treatment. Treatment is continued until either a change of interest occurs or it becomes clear that no change is likely. A number of patients (see below) have discontinued treatment of their own accord.

Recently we have been carrying out a controlled trial of the technique described above, in which it is compared with classical conditioning and psychotherapy. The results of this will be reported later. Both the apparatus and the treatment technique employed have been made somewhat more complicated and advanced so as to increase the degree of control over the situation exercised by the therapist.

RESULTS

Forty-three patients are reported here. We offered treatment to all those who presented; no selection criteria other than the inevitable self-selection (two potential patients declined the offer) have been used. Unless all patients are accepted for treatment no true assessment of criteria prognostic of success (*see* below) can be made. Thirty-six patients had the full course of treatment, and seven failed to complete it. Six of the seven terminated treatment after one or two sessions, and one terminated it after six sessions. The data which follow refer to the entire sample of 43, and are presented in sufficient detail to enable comparison with other published series.

Table 1   Age of 43 Patients at Referral

Age range	15-20	21-25	26-30	31-35	36-40	40 +
No.	5	8	10	8	3	9

The ages of the patients when they first presented for treatment are shown in Table 1; it will be seen that there is no great preponderance of very young patients, 9 of the sample being over the age of 40. The group who failed to complete treatment were fairly evenly distributed throughout the age ranges. Seven of the series, including one of those who failed to complete treatment, were married. Two of the series were females, and were partners in a lesbian "affair"; both were aged 18, and both completed treatment. All other patients were male homosexuals.

Table 2 presents the reason why patients appeared for treatment. Eighteen (42 percent) did so either on an order of the court, as the sequel to a court appearance, or previous to a court appearance. To some extent this is due to the fact that the Director of the Department of Psychiatry at Crumpsall is a forensic psychiatrist. Only four patients presented with symptoms other than their homosexuality, and all of them requested treatment when they learned that it was available. It is of some interest that of the seven who failed to complete treatment five presented either on an order of the court or were in some way connected with a court appearance.

Table 2   Reasons for Appearing for Treatments

On an order of the court	11
As sequel to court appearance (not on an order)	7
Pressure by wife or girl friend	2
Originally referred for psychiatric illness	4
Entirely of own accord	19
	43

We are not here presenting data on social class and other social factors, but the school performance was poor in 5, average in 13, good in 4, and 21 passed the 11+ examination equivalent; a rather higher proportion in the series had a secondary grammar school education than is probably the case in the population at large. Motivation for treatment was assessed at the first interview; this was low in 5, equivocal in 13, and strong in 25. All but one of those who failed to complete treatment were in the low or equivocal group. The age of the patient's preferred sexual partner was under 16 in only seven cases, therefore five-sixths of the sample preferred adults to young boys. There was little or no overlap here, the direction of sexual object choice being either youngsters or adults. The numbers charged and found guilty of homosexual offenses at some time previous to presentation were: one offense in 17 cases, two offenses in four cases, and three or more offenses in one case. Thus half the series had been charged and found guilty of at least one offense.

Table 3 Psychiatric Status on Presentation

Current chronic disorder	Schizophrenia defect state	1
	Personality disorder	25
	Nil	17
Acute psychogenic reaction	Yes	15
	No	28
Abnormal psychogenic development	Yes	13
	No	30

Considerable care was taken to make as full as possible an examination of the psychiatric status and personality features of the patients. The personality classification used is that of Schneider (1958). In Table 3 it can be seen that 25 of the sample had a personality disorder on presentation. In most cases this was of the kind which causes the patient to suffer rather than causing other people to suffer. One patient was displaying a post-schizophrenic defect state. Fifteen patients were displaying an acute psychogenic reaction to the circumstances, either of their homosexuality or of a court appearance associated with it, when they first presented. Thirteen displayed an abnormal psychogenic development throughout the course of their lives; that is, the development of unusual self-perceptions based either on their homosexuality or on other people's real or imagined reactions to it.

SEXUAL PRACTICES

We now present data concerning the nature and degree of our patients' sexual practices. Twenty-four of the series had been practicing homosexuality overtly for more than 10 years, and only two had never practiced but instead had exclusively utilized strong homosexual fantasy (Table 4). Several other patients were not actively practicing

Table 4 Duration of Homosexual Practice

Years of practice	0	1-2	3-4	5-6	7-8	9-10	>10
No.	2	5	1	4	1	6	24

homosexuality at the time of presentation but were using predominantly homosexual fantasy (Table 5). Twenty-five of the patients were displaying no heterosexual practice or fantasy of any kind (Table 5). Of the nine patients who did use heterosexual fantasy, only two did so to a marked degree. There were nine patients in all who were heterosexually active on presentation. Seven of these were having sexual intercourse, in

Table 5 Major Homosexual and Heterosexual Practice on Presentation

Homosexual Practice		Heterosexual Practice			
Strong fantasy only	11	Weak fantasy	7	Petting	1
Mutual masturbation	9	Strong fantasy	2	Sexual intercourse	7
Buggery	26	Dating	0	Nil	25
		Kissing	1		

five cases with their wives. All five of these patients had to utilize homosexual fantasy on at least some occasions in order to maintain an erection. In these instances, therefore, the behavior was that of masturbation per vaginam (Curran and Parr, 1957). Frequent overt homosexual behaviour was displayed by all five of these heterosexually active married patients. Both Lesbian patients were practicing heterosexual intercourse with a variety of partners. Neither patient found this pleasurable, and both felt a considerable degree of contempt for their male partners.

The data presented above on heterosexual and homosexual behavior can be combined to yield a Kinsey rating (Kinsey, Pomeroy & Martin, 1948). Nineteen of the sample had a Kinsey rating of 6 and 12 a Kinsey rating of 5, giving a total of 31 (72%) with Kinsey ratings of 5 or 6 (Table 6). One relevant comparision is with Curran and Parr's series, in which 42 percent had a Kinsey rating of 5 or 6. Only 12 of our series were rated as Kinsey 3 and 4, in whom there is a reasonably strong heterosexual component.

Table 6 Pre-treatment Kinsey Rating

Kinsey rating	0	1	2	3	4	5	6
No.	0	0	0	5	7	12	19

We next present data to demonstrate the degree to which at least some of our series had adapted to a homosexual way of life. Fifteen patients had had one homosexual "affair," seven had had two affairs, eight had had three or more affairs. An affair is the situation in which there is a sexual and emotional relationship between two males lasting several weeks or more. Only 13 of the series had never had such an affair. Finally, 21 patients frequented homosexual coteries and 22 did not.

RESULTS OF TREATMENT

It can be stated, before presenting the detailed data, that of the 36 patients who completed treatment 25 improved to a sufficient degree for their treatment to be described as successful, 11 were unimproved, and 7 failed to complete the treatment. The criteria for this are presented below. All the 25 patients who are regarded as improved have been followed up for at least one year, and many have been followed up for two years or more. Of the 11 patients who failed to improve, the majority have been followed up for at least one year. In the case of two patients who initially improved no follow-up appointments were kept. It was therefore concluded that they relapsed and they are included in the "failed to improve" group. We have lost contact with two of the other patients who failed to improve, and it is concluded that no spontaneous improvement occurred. It is assumed that the seven patients who failed to complete treatment are displaying the same sexual practices as before treatment, that is, that they have failed to improve. This should be borne in mind when comparing the data on heterosexual and homosexual practices after treatment.

Table 7 presents data on heterosexual practice at the time of the latest follow-up—that is, at least one year after completion of treatment. It can be seen that 13 patients were then having active heterosexual intercourse, and in all cases this was

Table 7 Major Heterosexual and Homosexual Practice after Treatment

Heterosexual Practice				Homosexual Practice	
Weak fantasy	2	Petting	3	Weak fantasy	5
Strong fantasy	5	Sexual intercourse	13	Strong fantasy	4
Dating	2	Nil	14	Mutual masturbation	5
Kissing	4			Buggery	9
				Nil	20

unaccompanied by homosexual fantasy or practice. Seven other patients were actively practicing heterosexually. Two were mixing socially with females and were beginning to approach active heterosexual practice. Finally, three patients out of the five shown were improved in the homosexual area and were using strong heterosexual fantasy. Two patients in the failed group continued to use strong heterosexual fantasy, as they did previous to treatment, together with overt homosexual activity. There were 14 patients as compared with 25 before treatment who had no heterosexual fantasy or practice. Table 7 also presents data on homosexual practice after treatment at the latest follow-up. It can be seen that 20 patients were neither using homosexual fantasy nor displaying overt homosexual practice. Nine patients were using homosexual fantasy; five of them, however, to only a weak degree. The remainder were still displaying overt homosexual activity.

The above data on heterosexual and homosexual behavior after treatment form the basis for Table 8, which is concerned with the Kinsey ratings of the series at the latest follow-up. It can be seen that 14 patients were Kinsey 0, nine Kinsey 1, and two Kinsey 2 (making up the 25 improved patients), the remainder all being Kinsey 3 to 6. The two patients who were rated as Kinsey 2 are included in the improved group because before

Table 8 Post-treatment Kinsey Ratings

	Improved			Unimproved and Failed to Complete			
Kinsey rating	0	1	2	3	4	5	6
No.	14	9	2	2	3	3	

treatment they were Kinsey 6, and had therefore shown a very considerable improvement. The two lesbian patients had made a very good improvement, and neither displayed any homosexual fantasy, interest or practice. One of them was still practicing heterosexual intercourse; and, compared with her practice before treatment, she did so with great pleasure and had a high regard for her partner, who was a relatively permanent one. The other lesbian patient no longer practiced heterosexual intercourse but had a good heterosexual relationship with her partner, again a fairly stable one. That 20 patients were displaying no homosexual practice or fantasy but only 14 could be rated as

Kinsey 0 is accounted for by the fact that the other 6 were still displaying an occasional and very slight degree of homosexual interest in directly observed males without, however, any subsequent fantasy. Because we are trying to make our criteria as strict as possible, it has been decided to rate these patients as Kinsey 1.

DISSCUSSION

The results of treatment of 43 patients treated by anticipatory avoidance learning are presented. We are preparing a detailed analysis of factors which are prognostic of success and failure in response to treatment with this technique, and some preliminary findings are briefly mentioned below.

DEGREE OF HOMOSEXUALITY

Table 9 compares the pre-treatment Kinsey ratings of the patients who improved with the ratings of those who failed to improve or failed to complete treatment. Two points may be made in connection with this table. Firstly, there is a tendency for ratings of Kinsey 6 to occur more often in the failed to improve and failed to complete group than in the improved group, and for ratings of Kinsey 3 and 4 to occur less frequently.

Table 9 Pre-treatment Kinsey Ratings and Response to Treatment of Improved Versus Unimproved and Failed To Complete Groups

Response	Kinsey Rating				Total
	3	4	5	6	
Improved	3	5	8	9	25
Unimproved and failed to complete	2	2	4	10	18
Total	5	7	12	19	43

Secondly, having a rating of Kinsey 6 is not necessarily a bar to a successful outcome of treatment. It can be seen that 9 of the 19 Kinsey 6 patients made a satisfactory response to treatment. However, it is of some interest to point out that a Kinsey rating is assigned on the basis of interest, practice and fantasy in the three years previous to presentation, as opposed to the entire lifetime of the individual. Of the nine Kinsey 6 patients who made a satisfactory response to treatment, six had displayed heterosexual interest and practice at some stage of their lives previous to the three years immediately before presentation, and of the other three patients none had started actively practicing heterosexually. By way of contrast, only 2 of the 10 with a rating of Kinsey 6 who either failed to improve or failed to complete treatment had had heterosexual practice or arousal in the years previous to the three years immediately before presentation. In both instances the patients were very well integrated into the homosexual world.

AGE AND SUCCESS

Table 10 shows the age range and outcome of treatment. Of the 23 patients under the age of 30, 16 made a successful response to treatment, whereas of the 20 patients over the age of 30, nine did so, indicating a tendency for the younger patients to respond better than the older ones. This was of course expected. What was not expected was that four of the nine patients who were aged over 40 made a successful response to treatment. Two of these patients were married, and therefore had an available heterosexual partner. Of the remaining two, one used strong heterosexual fantasy but had not yet progressed to social mixing. The other patient, who has been followed up for a year and a half, had reached the stage of social mixing with females and was hoping to progress to active heterosexual practice. While therefore, being over the age of 40 tends to result in a less successful outcome, there are no grounds for complete pessimism.

Table 10 Age on Presentation and Response to Treatment

Age range:	15-20	21-25	26-30	31-35	36-40	40+	Total
Improved	3	6	7	4	1	4	25
Unimproved and failed to complete	2	2	3	4	2	5	18

Personality Factors

Table 11 shows the relation between personality disorder and treatment outcome. The presence of personality disorder tends to militate against a successful outcome of treatment. However, Table 12 shows that this depends to a considerable degree on the type of personality disorder. Where there is a personality disorder of the self-insecure type, the prospects for a successful outcome are as good as in those who do not display any personality disorder. By way of contrast, where there is a disorder other than of the

Table 11 Pre-treatment Personality Disorder in Improved versus Unimproved and Failed to Complete Groups

Personality Disorder	Response		Total
	Improved	Unimproved and Failed to Complete	
Yes	12	14	26
No	13	4	17
Total	25	18	43

self-insecure type—usually of the weak-willed or attention-seeking type—then the prospects for a successful outcome are extremely poor. Three of the four patients who displayed no personality disorder and who made an unsuccessful response to treatment were very well integrated in the homosexual social world and all four were rated as

Kinsey 6. One patient who displayed a self-insecure personality disorder failed to complete treatment, having been discharged from the ward by another psychiatrist. One other patient with a self-insecure disorder made a successful response to treatment but is presumed to have relapsed because of failure to keep follow-up appointments.

Table 12 Type of Personality Disorder and Response to Treatment

Personality Disorder	Improved	Unimproved Plus Failed to Complete
Nil	13	4
Self-insecure	11	2
Other disorders	1	12
	25	18

CONCLUSIONS

The data presented above show that those patients who failed to respond to treatment tended to have a high Kinsey rating, to be over 30, and to have a personality disorder other than of the self-insecure type. There is also considerable evidence that one of the major variables prognostic of success is a history of heterosexual interest and practice at some time in the patient's life, whether or not a Kinsey rating of 6 is appropriate on presentation.

It is of interest to make a brief comparison of our patients with those of other reported series, particularly those of Woodward (1958) and Curran and Parr (1957). Of our 31 patients with an initial Kinsey rating of 5 or 6, 17 improved, whereas of Curran and Parr's 23 follow-up patients with an initial Kinsey rating of 5 or 6, only one showed a change in preference toward heterosexuality. Only seven of Woodward's sample of 48 who completed treatment showed decreased homosexuality and increased heterosexuality immediately at the end of treatment, and all of these were "bisexual" (presumably Kinsey 2, 3 or 4) before treatment. No detailed follow-up data are availabe for Woodward's series.

It is unlikely that the patient-therapist relationship, which inevitably develops even in the context of behavior therapy, can entirely account for our success rate. The rate of improvement achieved by experienced psychotherapists in comparable series of homosexual patients has in no instance exceeded 27 percent (Bieber et al., 1962). In our opinion the approximately 60 percent rate of improvement achieved in our series is mainly due to the use of an aversion therapy technique which has been carefully designed to make the most effective use of the findings of the experimental psychology of learning (Kimble, 1961). However, we are also of the opinion that verbal communication of a supportive and directive kind has been of value. Merely to treat our patients as laboratory subjects might not have been sufficient either to support them during the early period of treatment, before change becomes noticeable, or to assist them through the difficult period immediately after treatment. It is in this latter period, when the patient is learning to employ new or, at best, dormant social skills in the heterosexual area, that relapse seems particularly likely.

Recent work by Argyle and Kendon (1967) on the acquisition of social skills is of great potential value in assisting the transition from homosexual to heterosexual social adaptation. Until this more systematic approach becomes available, verbal support, even of an unsystematic nature, seems valuable. The patients in the present series were followed up at increasing intervals of time, and were on average interviewed on six to eight occasions in the year following completion of treatment.

SUMMARY

An anticipatory avoidance aversion therapy is described in the treatment of 43 homosexuals. Thirty-six patients completed treatment and 25 of them were significantly improved (14 Kinsey 0, 9 Kinsey 1, and 2 Kinsey 2). This figure (58%) is unusually high, and it is believed that the appropriateness of the learning technique is mainly responsible for the results, which have remained valid over a one-year follow-up. Some prognostic features are discussed.

Acknowledgment: We wish to thank the director of the Department of Psychiatry at Crumpsall Hospital, Manchester, Dr. N.J. De V. Mather, for his constant interest and encouragment.

REFERENCES

Argyle, M. & Kendon, A. In *Advances in experimental social psychology*. Vol 3. Ed. by L. Berkovitz. London. In press, 1967.
Bieber, I. et al. *Homosexuality*. New York, 1962.
Curran, D. & Parr, D. *Brit. med. J.*, 1957, 1, 797.
Feldman, M.P. *Psychol. Bull.*, 1966, 65, 65.
Feldman, M.P. & MacCulloch, M.J. *Amer. J. Psychiat.*, 1964, 121, 167.
Feldman, M.P. & MacCulloch, M.J. *Behav. Res. Ther.*, 1965, 2, 165.
Freund, K. In *Behaviour Therapy and the Neuroses*, ed. by H.J. Eysenck. Oxford, 1960.
Kimble, G. In E.R. Hilgard & D.G. Marquis' *Conditioning and learning*, (2nd ed.). London, 1961.
Kinsey, A.C., Pomeroy, W.B. & Martin, C.E. *Sexual Behaviour in the Human Male*. Philadelphia, 1948.
Schneider, K. *Psychopathic personalities*. London, 1958.
Woodward, M. *Brit. J. Delinq.*, 1958, 9, 44.

41
Alteration of Sexual Preferences via Conditioning Therapies

ROBERT G. MEYER and WILLIAM FREEMAN

Previous attempts to alter homosexual behavior have often been handicapped by theories of sexual behavior that focused on object choice rather than the development of general sexual behaviors (Rachman & Teasdale, 1969). The present study discusses a theory of sexuality that is essentially independent of object choice. Sexual behavior is identified as a social behavior acquired under the influence of the same family of variables as any other social behavior (Bandura, 1969). The emphasis is placed on the probability function between the eliciting stimulus situation and the consummatory situation.

An effective treatment for altering the preferred consummatory behavior from homosexual to heterosexual involves accomplishing a switch in the effective stimuli eliciting sexual arousal and penile erection; a reversal in this discriminative respondent arousal must be effected. Further, since the S indirectly controls penile erection by the stimuli he presents himself or allows to be presented to him, full responsible utilization of this indirect control in the direction of heterosexual behavior must be instructed, elicited, supported and reinforced by differential social feedback from the therapist. The present study differs substantially from previously reported conditioning studies, in taking full account of the S's indirect control capabilities and incorporating these as a specific treatment variable.

METHOD

Nine male homosexuals, 4 exclusive homosexuals and 5 with varying amounts of heterosexual experience, received 20 treatments in a clinical setting. They were instructed to abstain from homosexual activity and from masturbation while thinking of males or of homosexual activities for the period of treatment. They were instructed further to masturbate to pictures of nude females and fantasies of themselves engaging in heterosexual activities between treatments. They even were instructed to stop looking for sexually exciting characteristics in males while in public and to begin occupying themselves on such occasions by looking at the females present.

392

The actual conditioning during treatment sessions was as follows. First, heterosexual stimulus slides and homosexual stimulus slides were mixed at a ratio of 3:1 and presented to the S continuously for about 20 minutes, during which time the S administered tacto-motor stimulation to his genitals and ejaculated toward the end of the conditioning period if possible. The heterosexual stimulus slides were identified as the CS, and the homosexual slides together with the penile manipulation were viewed as the US for sexual arousal. The slide US was faded by replacement with heterosexual slides until only heterosexual stimulus slides were being presented by the tenth treatment.

The above was followed, after a brief time, by the homosexual deconditioning. Twelve sets of homosexual slides, 15 slides per set, with the sets loosely ordered on a scale of increasing homosexual attractiveness, were presented one set at a time until that set was no longer an effective elicitor of incipient sexual arousal for the S. The next more attractive set then was presented for deconditioning. A set of 15 slides was presented and the S was instructed to press a button signaling incipient sexual arousal as soon as a slide appeared sexually attractive to him. The latency of the incipient arousal response was measured and the interstimulus interval between slide presentation and the presentation of a 1-second faradic stimulation was set so that the occurrence of the incipient sexual arousal and the shock would coincide. The stimulus slide and the shock were terminated together.

Ss continued to signal during treatment whenever incipient homosexual arousal occurred, and as the response latency increased, the interstimulus interval likewise was increased. Every slide was paired with shock until the response latency approached 9-10 seconds, the frequency dropped to no more than 1 response in 15 trials, and the S reported that the picture was no longer attractive to him, but was neutral or beginning to appear repulsive.

The shock was adjusted by the S to just above pain threshold. This level was found to be an effective external inhibitor of the incipient sexual arousal response and yet not sufficiently intense to establish maladaptive conditioned anxiety responses in the Ss.

Consequently, the pairing of the previously conditioned homosexual stimulus with an external shock inhibitor that repeatedly blocked the occurrence of the conditioned sexual arousal response was viewed as having an extinction effect on the homosexual CS. Repeated occurrence of the effective CS without eliciting the CR reduced the CS to a neutral, ineffective, deconditioned state.

This can be viewed as classical conditioning in which the slide is the CS and the shock the US, if one is willing to accept nonresponding as the new CR established. The mediating conditioned anxiety construct is rejected as the CR, since the data do not support such a hypothesis, which is awkward to begin with, and seems to force the model.

Rather it is viewed here as a symmetrical reversal of what happens in establishing a CS-CR bond. Establishment calls for pairing a neutral stimulus CS with a response UR-CR which is elicited by a stimulus becoming an effective CS elicitor of the response or without the discarded US. Here we begin with a stimulus CS which is already an effective elicitor of a response CR, apply an external stimulus, which in this case repeatedly blocks the occurrence of the CR, the effect of which is to reduce the CR once again to the neutral state.

The treatment effect was evaluated throughout a 6-week baseline waiting period, through the treatment period during which Ss received 20 treatments, 2 per week, and also during the follow-up, which presently is continuing.

In addition to narrative autobiographical data, 20 different repeated measures were taken throughout the experiment. Attitude change toward 7 key concepts was measured by a semantic differential technique. The concepts were: Actual Self, Female, Heterosexual, Marriage, Heterosexual Intercourse, Male, Homosexual Life and Fellatio.

Three self-report measures included:

1. The *S's* self-assigned Kinsey Scale rating.
2. The estimation of the percent of his sexual attraction directed toward males.
3. The frequency of heterosexual orgasm per week, intercourse and masturbatory activity combined.

The three measures of the changes in the strength of sexual stimuli were:

1. *S's* ratings of the sexual attractiveness of a set of standard heterosexual stimulus pictures.
2. Sexual attractiveness ratings of a standard set of homosexual stimulus pictures.
3. The percent of the standard homosexual stimuli the *S* rated as attractive.

Changes in the differential sexual response were evaluated by 7 measures:

1. The plethysmographic measurement of the absolute magnitude of penile erection to a standard set of heterosexual stimuli.
2. The plethysmographic measurement of the absolute penile erection to a standard set of homosexual stimuli.
3. The penile erection ratio defined as the heterosexual erectile magnitude divided by the homosexual erectile magnitude at each particular evaluation.
4. The frequency of heterosexual arousal signaled during heterosexual conditioning.
5. The average reaction time of heterosexual arousal during heterosexual conditioning.
6. The average frequency of homosexual arousal per stimulus set signaled during homosexual deconditioning.
7. The average reaction time of homosexual arousal signaled during homosexual deconditioning.

RESULTS

The Friedman two-way analysis of variance indicated an over-all change in the measures in the direction of increased heterosexuality which was associated with a probability of less that .001. Evaluation of the individual pre- and post-treatment measure differences confirmed statistically significant change at a probability of less than .05 in all measures except in attitude toward Actual Self, Female and Heterosexual Marriage. However, attitudes toward these three concepts were relatively positive in the *S* to begin with and were probably a motivating factor for initially seeking treatment.

In August 1972, 5 *Ss* (2 married and 3 single) had completed their 3-month follow-up. None reported a return of homosexual desires or behavior. The average frequency of heterosexual orgasm was 3 times per week. The orgasms for the 2 married *Ss* and 1 single *S* were via intercourse. For the other 2 single *Ss*, both of whom were dating regularly, the orgasms were via heterosexual masturbation.

The other 4 *Ss* had completed their 6-week follow-up by August 1972. No overt homosexual behavior had occurred. One *S* had had one booster treatment, became engaged and began having intercourse regularly with his fiancee. The second *S* had masturbatory homosexual orgasm alone twice and intercourse or heterosexual masturbatory orgasm 18 times. The third was having intercourse regularly with his wife with no return of homosexual desires whatsoever. The last *S* has had no homosexual behavior or desires, masturbates regularly to heterosexual fantasy, but still becomes anxious on dates.

It should be noted that 4 of the 5 single *Ss* were completely homosexual at the beginning of treatment. At the August follow-up, not one had relapsed into homosexual practices and all reported no homosexual desires. Telephone follow-up at the end of 9 months indicates essentially the same results as in August, and complete data from a 1-year follow-up is available as of June 1973.

Over and above the significant results obtained, the following points are contributed in this study and are amplified in the presentation: a) the use of the multivariate approach in this type of study; b) a greater specification of conditioning procedures than in prior studies; c) the emphasis on a combination of techniques in a controlled outcome study; d) the self-controlling aspects emphasized in the instructions that the subject incorporated; and e) the fact that patients could more reliably and validly identify incipient sexual arousal than was indicated by the physiological measures.

REFERENCES

Bandura, A. *Principles of behavior modification.* New York: Holt, Rinehart & Winston, 1969.

Rachman, S. & Teasdale, J. *Aversion therapy and behavior disorders.* Coral Gables, Fla.: University of Miami Press, 1969.

42
The Desensitization of a Homosexual

FREDERICK W. HUFF

Ramsay and Van Velzen (1968) made the point that, theoretically at least, desensitization therapy appeared to be the treatment of choice for homosexuality; yet they were unable to find a case where it had been used. They reasoned that if homosexuality was, even in part, a sexual adjustment necessitated by an irrational fear of the opposite sex, as many would claim, then desensitization of this phobia should open up the way to a more socially acceptable heterosexual adjustment.

From this same rationale, aversion therapy, which has recently proved very popular in the treatment of sexual deviations (Feldman, 1966), would appear less appropriate. In aversion therapy with homosexuals the same sex is rendered fearsome too, leaving no interpersonal avenue open for sexual expression.

The following case shows in an objective fashion that, at least in this one instance, homosexuality was in some complex way functionally related to fear of the opposite sex, and further that when this fear was lessened by desensitization, heterosexual approaches began to be made.

CASE STUDY

Mr. J was an obese 19-year-old college student who complained of stage fright and of homosexuality. He said he would like to be heterosexual, but was simply not interested in women. I was able to convincingly demonstrate to him that he was indeed afraid of women rather than disinterested in them. This was done by having him close his eyes and imagine being in bed with a nude woman. To this he became very upset (sweating, tense facial expression) opened his eyes and said that he was so uncomfortable he was afraid he would have to leave the room. His homosexual behavior involved the masturbation of other adult males and self-masturbation to the fantasy of being a woman having sexual relations with a man. He did not engage in sodomy or fellatio, although he was attracted to these activities with males.

The MMPI and the Leary Interpersonal Checklist were given both before and after desensitization. Figure 1 depicting the pre-therapy MMPI profile showed Mr. J to be very complaining and disturbed. Figure 2 provides Mr. J's placement of himself, his ideal self, his mother and father on Leary's Interpersonal Diagnostic Grid (Leary, 1958). As can be seen, prior to therapy (the circles) Mr. J thought of himself as shy, passive, weak and tended to be self-effacing. This was in marked contrast to his father. His mother (who had

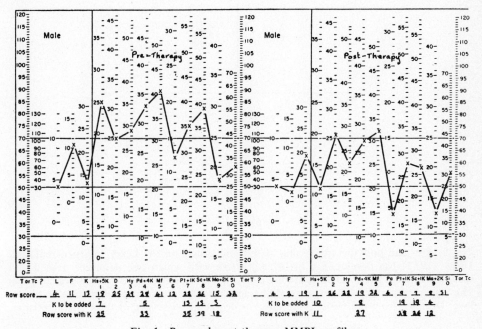

Fig. 1. Pre- and post-therapy MMPI profile.

died when he was 12 years of age) was viewed as somewhat aloof and castrating. In general, he was not identified with either his father or mother, while idealizing his father and fearing his mother.

An anxiety hierarchy to physical intimacy with women was set up and is presented in Table 1. This was accomplished in the first two therapy sessions at which time deep muscle relaxation was also taught (Wolpe & Lazarus, 1966). Desensitization, following the procedure described by Wolpe and Lazarus, was begun to the lowest anxiety-provoking situation in the hierarchy at the third session. It took 18 more sessions and a total of 170 presentations completely to desensitize Mr. J to the complete hierarchy (a session usually lasted 30 minutes). The number of presentations required for desensitization of each scene is given in Table 1. Apparently most anxiety was associated with what is usually called petting, e.g., hugging, kissing, fondling breasts, with relatively less anxiety being associated with foreplay preceding sexual intercourse and intercourse proper.

Mr. J was requested, at the beginning of therapy, to keep a day-by-day record of his sexual behavior, and preoccupations or fantasies. He was asked to keep a frequency count of 1) homosexual behavior, 2) homosexual desires and/or preoccupations, 3) heterosexual behavior and 4) heterosexual desires and/or preoccupations. No elaborate definitions of these categories was provided. At the end of therapy, three weeks after the end of therapy and for six weeks beginning five months after termination of therapy, these data were collected. To get an index of homosexuality, categories 1) and 2) were added together. The sum of 3) and 4) provided an estimate of heterosexuality. Since both homosexual and heterosexual behavior was so dependent on opportunity while fantasy

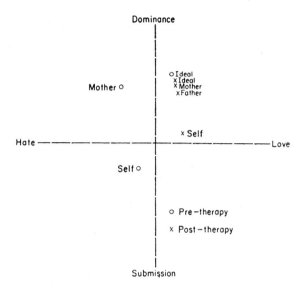

Fig. 2. Pre- and post-therapy typing of self and others on the Leary Interpersonal grid. Leary (1957) has developed a list of adjectives with which one describes oneself and specified others. The resultant data are converted into points in a two dimensional space. The dimensions are the interpersonal characteristics of dominance-submission and hate-love. Distance from the center represents the degree of possession of these characteristics.

and desire were not, this summing seemed reasonable. Figure 3 shows the frequency of homosexuality and heterosexuality from the beginning to end of therapy and for a three-week follow-up (8 on the abscissa) and a six-month follow-up (points 9 and 10 on the abscissa). Incidences occurring in therapy which were interesting are noted on the figure at the point in treatment at which they occurred. Generally, as therapy progressed homosexuality decreased while heterosexuality increased until the frequency of hetero-sexual behavior (dating females, etc.) and fantasy became greater than that for homosexual behavior. It was interesting to note that during the therapy session just following when this occurred (6 on the abscissa) Mr. J reported that he did not feel as homosexual as usual. The scene to which he was desensitized at this point was fondling the legs and thighs of a woman. Beginning with the scene of lying beside a nude girl and for each scene thereafter, Mr. J reported that as anxiety diminished he would begin to feel "sexed up." Apparently this was the first time he had such feelings to fantasies of girls.

Mr. J had never dated prior to therapy and perhaps as a "flight into health" he began to date two girls three weeks after beginning therapy. These dates were primarily asexual, involving going to concerts and crowded public events with no physical intimacy. However, by the last six weeks of therapy Mr. J found himself wanting to be alone with his dates and also felt sexually aroused by them. Six-month follow-up showed that his sexual interest in females has continued and increased (see Fig. 3, points 9 and 10 on the abscissa).

Table 1 Mr. J's Anxiety Hierarchy to Intimacy with Women (from least at bottom to most at top; No. of presentations to desensitize given in column)

Situation	No. of Presentations
16. girl moves while penis inserted	5
15. places penis in vagina	10
14. girl touches penis	6
13. nude, lying on top of girl	5
12. nude, lying beside girl	4
11. touching girl's mons, pubic hair	11
10. feeling girl's legs and thighs	5
9. fondling girl's breast	11
8. kissing girl on lips	11
7. kissing girl on forehead	22
6. looking into girl's eyes, tilting head up	21
5. hugging a girl	26
4. putting arms around girl	12
3. holding hands with girl	14
2. having a conversation with girl alone	4
1. having conversation with several girls	3
Total Number to Desensitize	170

Figure 1 shows the MMPI profile after therapy and it was obvious that Mr. J. felt less distressed. Figure 2 (the X's) shows that Mr. J's self-concept had changed considerably, coming closer to his ideal self-concept. His conceptualization of his mother had also changed from castrating, hostile to caring and instructive.

DISCUSSION

Apparently the desensitization procedure made women less aversive as sexual objects and as people from whom guidance, support and comfort might be obtained. A definite freeing of sexual interest in women was noted. The changed view of mother from hostile and punitive to supportive and loving suggests that all women were more positively valued by Mr. J. Here we have a change in attitude brought about by changing the emotional substrate of behavior. In verbal insight therapy the opposite is usually attempted, i.e., you try to change attitudes and then as a consequence emotional responding is altered. Insight which is considered the *sine qua non* of traditional psychotherapy was observed to follow desensitization or emotional change rather than precede it. Mr. J reported that he was afraid of women, an insightful statement, *after* the fear was neutralized by desensitization.

If we consider the recorded index of homosexuality (homosexual behavior plus homosexual desire) as an indication of the degree of aversiveness of women and the index of heterosexuality (heterosexual behavior plus heterosexual desire) an indication of their positive or approach value, then it will be possible to conceptualize Mr. J's therapy as the

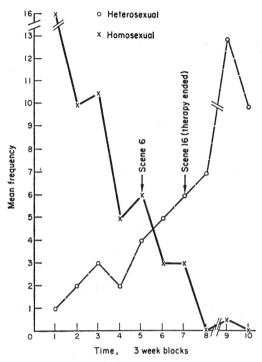

Fig. 3. Frequency of homosexual and heterosexual behavior/urges throughout therapy and for follow-up.

resolution of an approach-avoidance conflict. When the approach value of women became greater than their avoidance value, Mr. J reported he felt less homosexual and began to be sexually aroused to scenes presented in the desensitization session. It was as if homosexuality represented a compromise sexual adjustment rather than a free choice of equally available sexual objects. When the approach gradient was raised above the avoidance gradient then this compromise was no longer necessary and the selection of women as sexual objects was made. It is not known for sure why this selection was made. Desensitization just neutralized his reaction to women; there was no attempt to give them positive value. Did innate or social variables determine Mr. J's turning to women as sexual partners?

Rogers and Dymond (1954) maintained that in successful therapy the patient's self-concept and ideal self-concept become more alike. They attribute this to insight gained in a supportive, accepting interpersonal relationship. At the beginning of therapy Mr. J's self- and ideal self-concepts were very discrepant. When he was re-evaluated at the end of therapy, this large discrepency no longer existed. In other words, successful therapy, as Rogers would define it, was carried out but without the conditions he deems necessary, being met.

REFERENCES

Feldman, M.P. Aversion therapy for sexual deviation: A critical review. *Psychol. Bull.* 1966, **65**, 65-79.

Leary, T. *Interpersonal diagnosis of personality.* New York: Ronald Press, 1957.

Ramsay, R.W. & Van Velzen, V. Behavior therapy for sexual perversions. *Behav. Res. & Therapy.* 1968, **6**, 233.

Rogers, C.R. & Dymond, R.F. *Psychotherapy and personality change.* Chicago: University of Chicago Press.

Wolpe, J. & Lazarus, A.A. *Behavior therapy techniques.* New York: Pergamon Press, 1966.

43

Exposure to Heterosexual Stimuli: An Effective Variable in Treating Homosexualty?*

STEVEN H. HERMAN, DAVID H. BARLOW, and W. STEWART AGRAS

Homosexuals with little heterosexual interest prior to treatment show a poor response to aversive techniques (Feldman & MacCulloch, 1971). Anecdotal case reports (e.g., Huff, 1970) suggest that by increasing heterosexual arousal, a decrease in homosexual responding occurs. Strengthening heterosexual responsiveness is at least necessary for the treatment of homosexuality and may be sufficient, thereby avoiding the unpleasant side effects of aversion (Azrin & Holz, 1966).

Attempts to increase heterosexual behavior have been reported in uncontrolled case studies. These include systematic desensitization to heterosexual themes (e.g., Huff, 1970), shaping progressive increases in penile circumference in the presence of heterosexual stimuli with contingent administration of lime juice to fluid-deprived homosexual patients (Harbison, Quinn, & McAllister, 1970), and associating strong sexual arousal with heterosexual stimuli; e.g., Davison (1968) who paired masturbatory arousal with heterosexual stimuli.

Common to these procedures is exposure to heterosexual stimuli, often avoided by homosexual patients. This exposure alone may be responsible for the clinical effectiveness of these case studies. This notion was tested in the present study in a case of homosexuality by first exposing S to movies of a young nude seductive female, then to films of homosexual content and finally, once again, female films, while maintaining positive therapeutic instructions over all phases. If exposure is critical to therapeutic success, then increased responsiveness to females should occur during the female exposure phase, as measured in a separate test session, and should reverse or stop during the male exposure phase.

METHOD

Subject

The S was a 24-yr.-old male who had recently attempted suicide. Homosexuality began at age 13. For the last year the frequency of homosexual encounters was one to

*This paper is based on a portion of a dissertation submitted to the Department of Psychology, University of Mississippi, in partial fulfillment of the requirements for the PhD degree. Supported in part by Clinical Research Center, Grant PHS FR-91, and the Avery Fund for research in the behavioral sciences.

three per day. During this period he was arrested twice and mugged once. He had two heterosexual contacts in college, but these were initiated by the females and he was not able to ejaculate or maintain an erection.

Measures

Two measures of sexual interest were taken:

1. Penile circumference changes in response to viewing slides of nude females were recorded by a mechanical strain gauge (Barlow, Becker, Leitenberg, & Agras, 1970), using a Grass polygraph, Model 7. From a pool of 19 slides initially selected by the patient, 3 slides were shown at a daily measurement session. A fourth slide (of the female in the movie used in treatment) was also shown. Each slide was presented for a 2-min. period, during which he was instructed to "imagine yourself in a sexually arousing situation with the person in the slide." The interval between slides was 30 sec. of base-line recording or a return to base line, whichever was longer.

2. A subjective report of female arousal was obtained from a daily card sort (Barlow, Leitenberg, & Agras, 1969). Descriptions of females ("a 17-yr.-old, tall, fleshy, attractive, large-breasted female who has blond hair and an understanding personality") were constructed to form a hierarchy. Each statement was typed on a card, and the patient was instructed to read the description and put each card into one of five envelopes marked 0-4 on the basis of how sexually arousing the description was at the moment (0 = no arousal; 1, a little arousal; 2, a fair amount; 3, much; and 4, very much arousal). The number of cards placed in each envelope was multiplied by the number of the envelope. The sum across envelopes was S's heterosexual arousal score for the day. Both measures were administered in the morning.

Procedure

Base line. Nine sessions of the base-line phase were held, during which penile and card-sort measures were conducted.

Phase 1: Exposure to female. The patient was seated in a comfortable chair and instructed to imagine engaging in heterosexual behavior with the female in the film. He was cautioned against any manipulation of his penis during the session. An 8-mm. film of a nude seductive female was shown for 10 min. Film sessions were held in the evening. This phase lasted for 21 sessions.

Phase 2: Exposure to males. The S was given instructions designed to maintain a positive expectancy of continued improvement. The patient was seated in a chair and a 10-min. film depicting homosexual activities was shown. This phase lasted for nine sessions.

Phase 3: Female exposure. The female film was reintroduced as previously described and continued for 12 sessions.

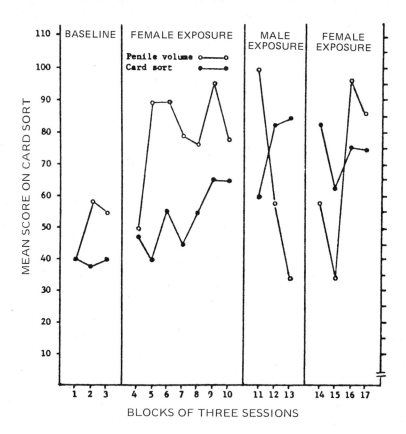

Fig. 1. Mean penile circumference change expressed as a percentage of full erection and mean female card sort averaged over 3 experimental days. (Lower score indicates less sexual arousal.)

RESULTS

Fig. 1 represents penile circumference changes expressed as a percentage of full erection and card-sort scores averaged over 3 experimental days. During base line, the patient's penile response to females stabilized between 27% and 35% of full erection. Card sort was between 38% and 40% of a score representing "much arousal" to all the hierarchy items. Behaviorally, the patient had at least four homosexual encounters, but he reported that he cruised almost continuously. All masturbatory fantasy was reported as homosexual.

During the first female exposure phase, penile responses to females increased and remained at approximately 55% of full erection. There was a concomitant increase in female card sort to 65% of a maximum score. The reported frequency of the patient's homosexual behavior declined during this period. Masturbatory fantasies became increasingly heterosexual. The patient began to date women and reported being sexually aroused by females in the environment.

In the male exposure phase, penile responses to females dropped from 57% to 25% of full erection. Card sort, however, continued to increase and reached 85% of a maximum score. Heterosexual behavior such as dating continued in the early part of this phase;

however, male responding began to increase and he stopped dating in the latter part of the phase. He began to cruise more actively and had two homosexual encounters. Masturbatory fantasies became exclusively homosexual once more.

In the final phase, the female film was reinstated. Penile responses to females increased toward the end of the phase to 55% of full erection. Card sort, after an initial decrease, continued to remain high and leveled off at approximately 75% of a maximal score. The patient soon began dating again and engaged in more heterosexual behaviors.

DISCUSSION

These findings suggest that exposure to high intensity sexual stimuli is a crucial procedure in the modification of sexual arousal in homosexuals. The effect of exposure was separated from the usual psychotherapeutic variables such as therapist attention, rapport, and expectancy of improvement, since these variables were still present during the male exposure phase and yet heterosexual arousal decreased.

The pattern of responsiveness during the testing sessions was not specific to the female pictured in the film. During exposure to this film, responsiveness increased to a slide of the female pictured in the film and also to slides of other females. The increased responsiveness also generalized to the subjective card-sort measure of arousal and to reports of behavior outside the laboratory. It should be noted that during the reversal the subjective measure followed the expectancies created by instructions and split from the objective measure. This latter finding replicates similar splits between objective and subjective measures noted in earlier experiments on homosexuality (Barlow, Agras, & Leitenberg, 1970) and other behavior disorders such as phobias (Leitenberg, Agras, Butz, & Wincze, 1971). This underscores the need for sophisticated objective measurement as well as further research on the interaction of subjective and objective measures.

It is possible that this experiment demonstrates extinction of avoidance behavior. Ramsay and Van Velzen (1968) indicated that homosexuals demonstrate strong avoidance of females. In the present study, the patient was confronted with representations of heterosexual stimuli in such a way that neither the avoidance response nor the aversive consequences could occur. Interestingly, toward the end of the experiment the patient remarked that seeing the girl in the film was like being with an old friend, in front of whom he could not be embarrassed. The present study is now being replicated on additional Ss.

REFERENCES

Azrin, N.H., & Holz, W.C. Punishment. In W.K. Honig (Ed.), *Operant behavior: Areas of research and application.* New York: Appleton-Century-Crofts, 1966.

Barlow, D.H., Leitenberg, H., & Agras, W.S. The experimental control of sexual deviation through manipulation of the noxious scene in covert sensitization. *Journal of Abnormal Psychology,* 1969, **74**, 596-601.

Barlow, D.H., Agras, W.S., & Leitenberg, H. Experimental investigations in the use of covert sensitization in the modification of sexual behavior. Paper presented at the meeting of the American Psychological Association, Miami Beach, September 1970.

Barlow, D.H., Becker, R., Leitenberg, H., & Agras, W.S. A mechanical strain gauge for recording penile circumference change. *Journal of Applied Behavior Analysis,* 1970, **3**, 73-76.

Davison, G.C. Elimination of a sadistic fantasy by a client-controlled counterconditioning technique: A case study. *Journal of Abnormal and Social Psychology,* 1968, **73**, 84-90.

Feldman, M.P., & MacCulloch, M.J. *Homosexual behavior: Therapy and assessment.* Oxford: Pergamon Press, 1971.

Harbison, J.J. M., Quinn, J.T., & McAllister, H. The positive conditioning of heterosexual behavior. Paper presented at the Second Behavioral Modification Conference, Kilkenny, England, September 1970.

Huff, F.W. The desensitization of a homosexual. *Behaviour Research and Therapy,* 1970, **8**, 99-102.

Leitenberg, H., Agras, S., Butz, R., & Wincze, J. Heart rate and behavioral change during treatment of phobia. *Journal of Abnormal Psychology,* 1971, in press.

Ramsay, R.W., & VanVelzen, V. Behavior therapy for sexual perversions. *Behaviour Research and Therapy,* 1968, **6**, 233.

44
The Extinction of Homosexual Behavior by Covert Sensitization: A Case Study

R.H. CURTIS and A.S. PRESLY

The modification of homosexual behaviour has been achieved predominantly by the techniques of aversion therapy: emetic drugs or faradic stimulation (Feldman, 1966). Rachman (1965) has enumerated the advantages of the latter, e.g. more precise control over the timing, intensity and duration of the noxious stimulus. Recent developments and variations of these paradigmatic methods have been prolific. One factor partly responsible for this increase in new techniques is that aversion therapy, although effective, is for the most part unpleasant for both the patient and the therapist, and there is an increasing reluctance to use its methods if equally efficacious and less unpleasant forms of treatment are available.

Such a technique is covert sensitization (Cautela 1966, 1967) which uses an internally produced noxious stimulus rather than an external one. A similar rationale has been employed by other workers in attempts to eliminate maladaptive behaviour without the use of chemical or electrical aversion: Lazarus (1958) required a patient to imagine being anxious when performing a compulsive ritual, and calm when resisting the temptation. Gold and Neufeld (1965) used imagined aversive stimuli in the treatment of homosexuality; Homme (1965) described a "control of coverants" technique and Kolvin (1967) used a method which he called "aversive imagery therapy." Cautela (1967) includes the following as examples of maladaptive approach behaviour which have been successfully treated by covert sensitization: alcoholic problems, obesity, homosexuality and juvenile offences. Davison (1968) used covert sensitization (he used the term "imaginal aversive counterconditioning") as a means of eliminating a sadistic fantasy in a 21-year-old student. Barlow et al. (1969) described the successful use of covert sensitization in two cases, one of pedophilic behaviour, the other, homosexual behaviour. These authors demonstrate experimentally that the crucial procedure in covert sensitization is the pairing of verbal descriptions of a noxious scene with descriptions of scenes involving the undesirable behaviour.

CASE STUDY

The patient was a 31-year-old, intelligent, self-employed male with a history of homosexual behaviour extending over seven years. He had been happily married for six years, with two children. Two factors prompted his self-referral for treatment; firstly, the frequency of his homosexual contacts had increased to at least one per week; secondly, his wife did not know of his homosexuality and he felt guilty about deceiving her. Contacts were furtive and transient; he did not seek to establish any relationship with the men involved and avoided more than one contact with the same person. Homosexual behaviour invariably took the same form, mutual manual masturbation, and the patient reported that he often felt "physically sick" after such encounters. Because of these factors, and the high motivation of the patient, a good outcome for treatment was anticipated.

At the first interview the patient completed the Sexual Orientation Method Questionnaire (Feldman *et al.*, 1966). This assesses the relative intensity of heterosexuality and homosexuality in the individual case. He has to choose between 120 pairs of adjectives; 60 relate to his sexual interest in men; 60 to his sexual interest in women. A score of 48 is the maximum in both instances. The patient on this occasion scored 48 for heterosexual interest, and 33½ for homosexual interest.

The treatment method, covert sensitization, followed that described by Cautela (1967) with one variation. Since the patient experienced difficulty in imagining himself nauseated in a homosexual situation, it was decided instead to employ an anxiety-provoking scene and to incorporate this into the imagined homosexual situation. Two "stories" were used during therapy sessions, each was presented a total of four times.

The first story was as follows:—

"S approaches lavatory in car park . . . enters and sees an elderly unattractive man . . . man approaches . . . S declines . . . man holds a knife and blocks exit . . . he threatens to injure S sexually if he does not comply with his homosexual demands . . . S manages to escape from the lavatory . . . he runs to his car, drives home and enjoys an immense sense of relief on being home and greeted by his wife. . . ."

This story was expanded in detail and lasted for approximately four or five minutes. The patient was encouraged during the recounting of the story to relax, and to visualise the scenes as vividly as possible. He reported that the story was successful in producing a high level of anxiety, and then relief at the outcome. This was confirmed by observation of overt behaviour. No psychophysiological recordings were taken.

The second story was as follows:—

"S has successfully made contact with an attractive partner . . . they are in his car . . . they are about to touch each other when S sees his wife's face at the car window . . . she is very distraught . . . he is panic-stricken . . . he pushes the man out of the car, drives home as quickly as possible . . . on reaching home he finds his wife in the house . . . it was not she whom he had seen . . . immense relief."

The great reduction of anxiety, and the sense of relief consequent to leaving the homosexual situation were emphasised strongly in both stories.

After a few presentations of this kind, the patient was encouraged to employ the procedure by himself: he later reported that he had done this successfully on several occasions, extinguishing an incipient desire to seek a contact. No homosexual contacts were made during the period of treatment, which lasted for two months, although the wish to do so arose occasionally. Follow-up in the four-month period since treatment has confirmed the patient's complete abstinence, both in fantasy and reality. Although it has not been possible to obtain confirmatory evidence from other sources, there is no reason to doubt the veracity of this patient's report.

At the end of treatment, a second Sexual Orientation Questionnaire was completed; scoring on this occasion was heterosexual interest: 46½; homosexual interest: 8.

The main consequences of the eradication of this patient's homosexual behaviour have been an improvement in his marriage through a lowering of "tension" and a feeling of "inner calm." Sexual relations with his wife have improved and there has been a general heightening of interest in the opposite sex.

DISCUSSION

This case report is intended as an addition to the scanty literature on covert sensitization. The method was chosen because it appeared to be an improvement over traditional aversion therapy in that no specialized equipment was required and the treatment can be easily self-administered. In this case no heterophobic anxiety was present (Kraft, 1969; Stevenson and Wolpe, 1960) and great benefit to the patient resulted from the elimination of homosexual behaviour without the reinforcement of heterosexual behaviour.

A common criticism of covert sensitization is that, unlike standard aversion therapy, the therapist has little control over the relevant stimuli. We do not know what the patient is thinking. This problem is shared by desensitization and is likely to be alleviated in both instances by obtaining, prior to treatment, an indication of the "goodness" of S's imagination, through the use of, for example, self-rating and picture memory (Rimm and Bottrell, 1969), together with the use of psychophysiological recordings during treatment sessions. It should be noted that although the therapist has less control over the intensity of relevant stimuli presented to the patient, he has more control over the choice of stimuli. Wilson and Davison (1969) suggest that too little attention is given, in aversion therapy, to the appropriateness of the aversive stimulus, it is usually electric shock, and consequently a good deal of reliance is placed on the process of stimulus generalisation in bringing about a change of behaviour in the real-life situation. Covert sensitization can overcome this problem by the choice of an appropriate noxious stimulus; one which is not totally unconnected with the maladaptive behaviour it is seeking to extinguish.*

REFERENCES

Barlow, D.H., Leitenberg, H., and Agras, W.S. Experimental control of sexual deviation through manipulation of the noxious scene in covert sensitization. *J. abnorm. Psychol.* 1969, **74**, 596-601.

Cautela, J.R. Treatment of compulsive behaviour by covert sensitization. *Psychol. Rec.* 1966, **16**, 33-41.

Cautela, J.R. Covert sensitization. *Psychol. Rep.* 1967, **20**, 459-468.

*The work described was carried out while both authors were at the Royal Edinburgh Hospital, Morningside Park, Edinburgh, EH10 5HF.

We wish to express our gratitude to Professor H.J. Walton for referring the patient and for his assistance throughout treatment.

Davison, G.C. Elimination of a sadistic fantasy by a client-controlled counter-conditioning technique: A case study. *J. abnorm. Psychol.* 1968, **73**, 84-90.

Feldman, M.P. Aversion therapy for sexual deviations: A critical review. *Psychol. Bull.* 1966, **65**, 65-69.

Feldman, M.P., MacCulloch, M.J., Mellor, M., and Pinschof, J.M. The application of anticipatory avoidance learning to the treatment of homosexuality—Ill. The sexual orientation method. *Behav. Res. & Therapy,* 1966, **4**, 289-299.

Gold, S. and Neufeld, I.L. A learning approach to the treatment of homosexuality. *Behav. Res. & Therapy,* 1965, **2**, 201-204.

Homme, L. Perspectives in psychology. 24. Control of coverants, the operants of the mind. *Psychol. Rec.* 1965, **15**, 501-511.

Kolvin, I. Aversion imagery treatment in adolescents. *Behav. Res. & Therapy,* 1967, **5**, 245-248.

Kraft, T. Treatment for sexual perversions. *Behav. Res. & Therapy,* 1969, **7**, 215.

Lazarus, A.A. A new method in psychotherapy: A case study. *S. Afr. Med. Jl.* 1958, **4**, 259-263.

Rachman, S. Aversion therapy: Chemical or electrical. *Behav. Res. & Therapy,* 1965, **2**, 289-299.

Rimm, D.C. and Bottrell, J. Four measures of visual imagination. *Behav. Res. & Therapy* 1969, **7**, 63-69.

Stevenson, I. and Wolpe, J. Recovery from sexual deviations through overcoming non-sexual neurotic responses. *Am. J. Psychiat.* 1960, **116**, 737-742.

Wilson, G.T. and Davison, G.C. Aversion techniques in behavior therapy: Some theoretical and meta-theoretical considerations. *J. consult. Psychol.* 1969, **33**, 237-239.

45
The Treatment of Homosexuality by "Assisted" Covert Sensitization

BARRY M. MALETZKY and FREDERICK S. GEORGE

Covert sensitization is a procedure which pairs imagined scenes of an unwanted behavior, such as homosexuality, with scenes aversive to the patient, in an effort to diminish the strength of a given response. It has been employed in the treatment of a host of maladaptive approach behavior (Cautela, 1967). However only anecdotal or single-case reports (Barlow et al., 1969; Cautela, 1966, 1967; Gold & Neufeld, 1965) have appeared regarding the treatment of homosexuality, and these have been unanimously positive. It was disappointing, therefore, in applying this technique to homosexuals, to find it ineffective. One patient complained that the stimuli "were not strong enough." Another could not adequately visualize noxious scenes. This report describes our development of a bolstered form of covert sensitization, demonstrates its application to the treatment of homosexuals and provides follow-up data to evaluate the adequacy of such treatment.

METHODS

Subjects

The 10 Ss, all referred to the authors for treatment of homosexuality, averaged 27 years of age with an average duration of homosexual activity of 14 years. All Ss but one came willingly, requesting help because of dissatisfaction with a life plagued by duplicity and the tenuousness of their homosexual relations. Subject 2, referred from court, allowed us to assess the efficacy of treatment under pressure.

Most Ss were bisexual; four of the 10 were married with children. Three others reported sexual affiliations with girl friends. Three Ss were exclusively homosexual and required desensitization to females along with assisted covert sensitization.

411

Treatment

Treatment derived from covert sensitization as described by Cautela (1966) but modified by the addition of an odiferous substance, valeric acid[1], at appropriate intervals during the procedure. All treatments were carried out by the authors.

During an initial interview, the therapist gathered historical data and emphasized that homosexuality was learned behavior which, with diligence, could be unlearned. In subsequent sessions each S was taught relaxation exercises to enhance visualization of scenes. Concurrently, he and the therapist constructed a set of scenes of past and imagined homosexual activity. At points in each scene when pleasure was escalating, noxious images, derived from each $S's$ account of what most revolted him, were introduced. These included scenes of vomiting; contact with feces, urine or insects; vile odors; and feelings of nausea. An extra scene was constructed to reward the subject for refusing the offer of homosexual activity. During subsequent sessions, scenes were presented and, at the suggestion of noxious elements, the smell of valeric acid was introduced. As the scene progressed, the Ss escaped from the homosexual situation, the odor was removed and suggestions of calm presented. An abbreviated scene is reproduced below. An asterisk notes the point of valeric acid introduction, a double asterisk its removal:

> You're at the beach with a special person, John. Imagine the ocean, the smell of salt air. You lie down behind a sand dune and start to embrace and undress each other. You can see his penis hard and stiff. He starts rubbing it back and forth. But as you get closer you notice a strange odor and you see small white worms, like lice, crawling in the hair around his penis!* You're touching them with your mouth! It's disgusting and it's making you sick. Some of them have gotten onto you. They're crawling into your mouth. Your stomach starts to churn and food particles catch in your throat. Big chunks of vomit come into your mouth. Vomit dribbles down your chin. You can see the white worms still, crawling in your puke, and you get sicker than before.** You grab your trunks, clean yourself off, and run away as quickly as you can. As you do, you feel better, your stomach begins to settle down and you can breathe deeply the fresh air of the ocean. You notice the bright blue sky, the fresh smell of the ocean and feel much calmer and relaxed.

Each scene was presented twice per session for five sessions. Three to five scenes were presented twice per session for five sessions. Three to five scenes were presented per 40-minute session and the hierarchies completed in 12-27 sessions.

Between sessions, Ss listened to recordings of scenes twice weekly, self-administering the odor of valeric acid. Subjects also sniffed the acid as they purposely sought out homosexual friends and haunts. At 3 month intervals Ss underwent "booster" sessions, similar to their last treatment sessions.[2]

[1] This substance is noncorrosive, inexpensive and readily purchased from chemical supply houses.
[2] A manual more fully explaining the treatment technique is available from the authors.

Assessment

Frequency data. Each *S* maintained records of covert homosexual and heterosexual behavior (urges, fantasies, dreams) and overt homosexual and heterosexual behavior (cruising, masturbation, petting and orgasms).

Observers' reports. An observer (wife, friend, parent) was designated for each *S* and recorded frequency of suspicions about homosexual activity.

Independent ratings. Clinical psychologists and psychiatric social workers unconnected with this study interviewed *Ss* before, just after and 12 months after treatment, and assigned Kinsey numbers (Kinsey et al., 1948) to assess progress.

The Temptation test. Each test given at the end of treatment and at 12 months consisted of a homosexual approach by a "solicitor" employed by the therapist yet unknown to the *S.* If the *S* turned down the approach, he passed; if he offered even a tentative response, the solicitor failed the *S.* Although ethical objections can be raised, objective assessment was necessary and we are unaware of any studies to indicate that widely spaced and unfulfilled "solicitations" would alter treatment or add damage to a maladaptive life-style.

RESULTS

Frequency data

Figure 1 depicts mean frequencies of homosexual and heterosexual thoughts and behavior during treatment and follow-up. These means include data from Subject 9, our only treatment failure. Mean covert homosexual activity dropped frcm 26.8 to 1.7 events per week and remained 2.1 at 12 months. Overt activity fell from 14.5 events per week

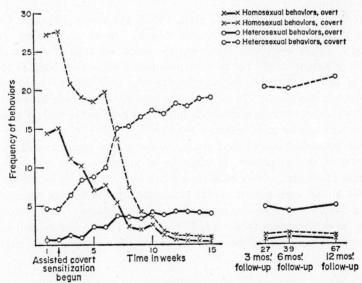

Fig. 1.

prior to treatment to 0.5 at the termination and 0.4 at twelve months. Conversely, heterosexual covert behavior increased from a mean of 4.4 to 21.8 events at 12-months' follow-up, while heterosexual overt behavior rose from 1.7 events prior to treatment to 4.6 events at follow-up. Subject 2, coerced into treatment, matched these means.

Observers' reports. Observer's suspicions averaged 15.0 per month prior to treatment, decreased to 2.6 per month at the end of treatment, and remained 1.7 per month at 12 months' follow-up.

Independent ratings. Mean ratings revealed a pre-treatment Kinsey score of 4.9 (predominately homosexual) decreasing to 1.0 (predominately heterosexual) after treatment and 0.5, (almost exclusively heterosexual) at 1 yr.

The temptation test. Subject 9 failed both tests. Subject 6 failed his 12-months' test. He was given 10 "booster" sessions, and passed two subsequent tests 14 and 20 months after beginning treatment. All other *Ss* passed all tests.

Comment

Our early efforts in treating homosexuality by covert sensitization alone did not meet with success. We persisted in developing a strengthened therapy for several reasons. Alternative methods of treating homosexuality (Madden, 1966; Marmor, 1965; McConaghy, 1971) have not yielded uniformly promising results. In addition the use of electric shock can produce resistance to treatment (Franks, 1958), aggression and anxiety (Rachman, 1969). Equipment to produce shock and present slides is expensive. The treatment described here is inexpensive, easily learned and readily applied. The success of this assisted technique may be due to the infusion of reality by smelling the odor in situations previously arousing. Valeric acid seemed appropriate as it assaults the olfactory senses with an odor benignly termed foul and adds a human decaying property especially evocative of nausea.

Unfortunately, the results of the present study are merely suggestive. Controls were absent nor were penile plethysmograph records, helpful in assessing other studies (McConaghy, 1970), employed. However, one would not suppose chance alone, or the nonspecific effects of attention, to have produced these results. Most of the data were reported by people other than the experimenter who were likely to doubt the efficacy of treatment for homosexuality. In addition, the strength of the technique was impressive. Not only was overt behavior eliminated, but covert behavior as well. A typical reaction was: "I just don't *desire* going with men anymore."

Only a controlled double-blind study, involving large number of *Ss*, can prove the effectiveness of this procedure. It might be of interest to test which of the various components of assisted covert sensitization are essential to the technique. Of clinical significance is the applicability of this procedure. The author has successfully deconditioned a spectrum of behavior using this technique, ranging from a compulsion to eat chocolate, to exhibitionism (Maletzky, 1972, 1973a, 1973b). It may well be that many forms of maladaptive approach behavior will respond favorably in future, larger trials.

REFERENCES

Barlow, D.H., Leitenberg, H. & Agras, W.S. Experimental control of sexual deviation through manipulation of the noxious scene in covert sensitization. *J. Abn. Psychol.* 1969, **74**, 596-601.

Cautela, J.R. Treatment of compulsive behavior by covert sensitization. *Psychol. Rev.* 1966, **16**, 33-41.

Cautela, J.R. Covert sensitization. *Psychol. Rep.* 1967, **20**, 459-469.

Franks, C.M. Alcohol, alcoholics and conditioning. *J. Ment. Sci.* 1958, **104**, 14-33.

Gold, S. & Neufeld, I.L. A learning theory approach to the treatment of homosexuality. *Behav. Res. and Ther.* 1965, **2**, 201-204.

Kinsey, N., Pomeroy, W.B. & Martin, C.E. *Sexual behavior in the human male.* Philadelphia: W.B. Saunders, 1948.

Madden, S.B. Treatment of male homosexuals in groups. *Int. J. Group. Psychother.* 1966, **16**, 13-22.

Maletzky, B.M. "Assisted" covert sensitization for drug abuse. *Int. J. Addict.* (in press). In *Conditioning Factors in Drug Dependence* (Ed. P.H. Blachly). Continuing Education Publications, Corvallis, Oregon. *J. Consult. Clin. Psychol.* in press, 1973a.

Maletzky, B.M. "Assisted" covert sensitization for exhibitionism. *J. Consult. Clin. Psychol.* (in press). 1973b.

Maletzky, B.M. Behavioral treatment of drug abuse, Presented to the Fifth Western Institute of Drug Problems, Portland, Oregon, 1972.

Marmor, J. *Sexual inversion.* New York: Basic Books, 1965.

McConaghy, N. Aversion therapy of homosexuality: Measures of efficacy. *Amer. J. Psychiat.* 1971, **127**, 1221-1224.

McConaghy, N. Subjective and penile plethysmograph responses to aversion therapy for homosexuality: A follow-up study. *Brit. J. Psychiat.* 1970, **117**, 555-560.

Rachman, J.J. & Teasdale, J. Aversion therapy: An appraisal. In *Behavior therapy: Appraisal and status* (Ed. C.M. Franks). New York: McGraw-Hill, 1969, 279-320.

46
Covert Aversion Relief and the Treatment of Homosexuality

ALAN S. BELLACK

Homosexuality is a behavioral complex involving sexual arousal to same sex figures and either arousal or non-arousal to opposite sex figures. When lack of heterosexual activity is a function of anxiety, systematic desensitization can be utilized as the sole method of treatment or as an independent adjunct of a technique focusing on homo-sexual arousal. This approach does not teach or increase heterosexual interest so much as removing barriers to existing interest. When no such interest exists, treatment involves the much more difficult task of making opposite sex figures sexually arousing. Feldman and MacCulloch (1971) have attempted to deal with that problem with an aversion-relief paradigm. They paired electric shock with same sex pictures and followed shock termina-tion with opposite sex pictures. The relief associated with shock termination was expected to become conditioned to opposite sex figures, thus giving them a positive valence, but heterosexual behavior was not increased. Accretion of a positive valence to a stimulus is not equivalent to sexual arousal to that stimulus, even if the stimulus is of a "sexual" nature. The physiological and cognitive responses to slides, electrodes, shock and shock termination do not appear compatible with the physiological and cognitive responses associated with sexual arousal.

An alternative to the use of faradic aversion that might avoid that difficulty is a cognitive aversion such as occurs in covert sensitization (Cautela, 1970). As suggested by Feldman and McCullough for faradic aversion relief, termination of the aversive stimulus in conjunction with presentation of a heterosexual image should result in the condi-tioning of a positive association to that image. Use of an individually designed cognitive image rather than pictures of opposite sex nudes should maximize the sexual interest. The images could also be elaborated over trials and reproduced by the patient outside of treatment, facilitating transfer. A third advantage is the physiological response of the patient. The patient in covert sensitization is trained in deep muscle relaxation and relaxed when the aversive image is terminated. Paul (1969) has reported that such relaxa-tion results in a strong parasympathetic nervous system (PNS) response. Masters and Johnson (1966) have likewise shown that sexual arousal is a PNS response. This similarity of physiological activity combined with self-produced heterosexual imagery and the positive response associated with termination of aversive imagery should facilitate the generation of sexual arousal. The following case report describes this approach.

The patient, a 22-year-old, unmarried exclusively homosexual male had had no history of satisfactory heterosexual experience and had not dated a woman in the two years prior to treatment. The first four treatment sessions were devoted to history taking and training in deep muscle relaxation; treatment proper was begun in the fourth session. The patient was first put into deep relaxation. The therapist then described a nightclub and directed the patient to form an image of an attractive male, imagine himself slowly approaching the figure, becoming increasingly dizzy and nauseous and finally vomiting on him. Each scene averaged about 5 minutes in duration, with a variable interval (3-6 minutes) between repetitions. Aversion relief was instituted in session seven. The relief image was an attractive woman with whom the patient interacted. Over repetitions, the interaction involved increasingly intense sexual activity, culminating in intercourse. The aversive image was terminated with instructions to forget the image and to relax. After an interval varying between 15-30 seconds, the relief image was presented and maintained for 3-6 minutes. The patient was then told to forget that image and to relax. The aversive sequence was represented after 90 seconds. Session nine was followed by a four-week hiatus due to term break and then five more sessions of aversion relief.

Treatment inadvertently took the form of an ABAB own-control design. The first four weeks served as a non-specific treatment period followed by five weeks of treatment, four weeks of no treatment and five more weeks of treatment. Homosexual arousal showed no diminution through the first five weeks of contact. The patient reported notable diminution after six weeks and reported experiencing no arousal after the eighth week. He also reported one satisfactory experience of masturbation to heterosexual imagery after the eighth week (ninth session). The four-week period of no-contact followed and at the tenth session, the patient reported having had an overt homosexual experience, being regularly aroused by males and unable to become aroused heterosexually. Covert sensitization-aversion relief were reinstituted in session ten. At session 11 he again reported the absence of homosexual arousal and reported heterosexual arousal and masturbation at session thirteen. Treatment was then stopped for summer vacation. When seen again two months later, the patient reported that he had not experienced homosexual arousal, had been dating regularly, and had sexual intercourse several times with considerable satisfaction. Treatment was then terminated; he was recontacted four months later and reported that he was maintaining a heterosexual adjustment and had rejected the advances of a previous homosexual partner.

Several factors suggest that the behavior change was a function of specific treatment components. One aspect of support is the reported failure of previous treatment and the direct relationship of behavior change to onset and offset of the current treatment. Within each treatment period, reports of sexual behavior change and implementation of the different treatment components occurred in the expected fashion. Homosexual arousal declined after covert sensitization; heterosexual arousal increased, followed by masturbation to heterosexual images after experience with covert aversion relief. While these results are encouraging, one must be careful in making conclusions based upon single case reports. Replication in a controlled experimental design and with other than self report as a dependent variable seems warranted. The separate components of the paradigm should also be investigated. Physiological recordings would clarify the general responsivity under each condition. The actual sexual response manifested should also be examined; both pupillography and penile plethysmography could be used for such specification.

REFERENCES

Cautela, J.R. Covert reinforcement. *Behavior Therapy*, 1970, **1**, 33-50.
Feldman, M.P., & McCulloch, J.J. *Homosexual Behavior: Therapy and Assessment.* Oxford: Pergamon Press, 1971.
Masters, W.H., & Johnson, V.K. *Human Sexual Response*, Boston: Little, Brown, 1966.
Paul, G.F. Physiological effects of relaxation training and hypnotic suggestion. *Journal of Abnormal Psychology*, 1969, **74**, 425-437.

47
Multiple Behavior Therapy Techniques with a Homosexual Client: A Case Study

LYNN P. REHM AND RONALD H. ROZENSKY

Descriptions of behavior therapy frequently report the use of multiple techniques with a single client (e.g., Mahoney, 1971). Frequently in dealing with homosexuality two broad classes of behavior, homosexual approach and heterosexual avoidance, are treated by separate techniques (Kendrick & McCullough, 1972; Feldman & MacCulloch, 1971). Still, in nearly all these studies these classes of behavior are each treated by a single method. The following case illustrates a more detailed analysis of sexual behavior, and a matching of each form of response with a treatment intervention. In contrast to the diffuseness of what Lazarus (1971) terms "broad spectrum behavior therapy," this report describes the specification of response topographies, and the resulting application of a specific therapy technique to each.

CASE HISTORY

The client, a 21-year-old male veteran, was referred for behavior therapy to the second author. Originally, he had complained of difficulty in finding a job and of fainting spells for which no organic cause could be ascertained. He had started group psycho-therapy and had only then revealed that he was very concerned about his homosexuality: thus, the referral.

His history included several homosexual experiences at age 12 which were initiated by a group of neighborhood boys. He experienced these as frightening, and their memory continued to be anxiety-provoking for some times. From 14 to 17, the client had an active heterosexual life including intercourse with several girls. From 17 to 19, in the army, his frequent sexual experiences were exclusively homosexual. He attributed his homosexual behavior to drinking and the unavailability of women. Upon discharge, he met a girl and quickly became engaged. He worried considerably about his readiness for marriage, and broke off the engagement. He concluded that he was a homosexual, and that his heterosexual orientation in high school was only an attempt to "compensate." For the next 2 years his life increasingly centered on homosexual behavior. At the time of his referral, most of his friends were homosexual. His sexual experiences were almost exclusively single occurrences resulting from being picked up while hitchhiking or meeting males in bars. He had approximately 16 such contacts per week. He reported feeling no attraction to females and considerable discomfort at any approach to them, due to a feeling that he "couldn't make it with a girl any more." He stated that he was disgusted with his homosexual life and felt pessimistic about the possibility of change since his friends had told him homosexuality was a "deep seated personality problem" which was almost impossible to "analyze out."

TREATMENT

An initial behavioral analysis revealed three target behaviors. These were 1) verbal-cognitive misconceptions about the nature of homosexuality, 2) verbal-cognitive hetero-sexual anxiety, and 3) overt-motor homosexual approach responses.

Therapy focused sequentially on these target behaviors. Each was approached with a technique deemed best able to modify its particular topography.

Changing Conceptions of Homosexuality

The client's statements about homosexuality included many misconceptions and inaccuracies. Thus, an informational-educational strategy was the focus of the second and third weekly sessions. The therapist gave the client an account of homosexuality as a learned pattern of behavior. Conceptions of homosexuality as a sickness or as a constitutional personality type were discounted. Discussion of these and related issues recurred sporadically throughout therapy. After these initial discussions, the client reiterated his strong feeling that for him homosexuality was dissatisfying in the long run and that he wanted to work toward an entirely heterosexual orientation. The therapy proceeded on this basis.

Reducing Heterosexual Anxiety

The two other potential target behaviors were the simultaneous focus on the next series of sessions. The client's heterosexual anxiety occurred in response to imagined or anticipated heterosexual situations. For this response topography, desensitization using imaginal stimuli was deemed appropriate. A 10-item hierarchy of heterosexual approach situations was constructed, and relaxation training begun. Three items were covered in the first three desensitization sessions. At the next session (Week 8) the client reported gleefully that he had struck up a lengthy conversation with a girl on a long bus ride. He reported that his confidence in his ability to approach girls had been restored and that the remaining hierarchy items no longer aroused anxiety. Desensitization was therefore discontinued.

Deconditioning Homosexual Approach

Beginning at the same time as the desensitization, a second target behavior was attacked—overt approaches to males in hitchhiking, bar and washroom situations. The initial focus was on the first response in the chain that led to the homosexual acts. Since this behavior could not be reproduced in the office, it was decided to approach it by a combination of self-management and covert sensitization.

The self-management program began at the third week by requesting the client to report weekly on the number of homosexual and heterosexual contacts (including extended conversations and dates as well as physical contacts). It was assumed that besides providing objective data, the monitoring of homosexual contacts was an aversive event that might serve to reduce the frequency of these contacts. The aversiveness of having to report the number of homosexual contacts was confirmed by the client in subsequent weeks. At Week 8, the client was given the graph of overt behavior which he

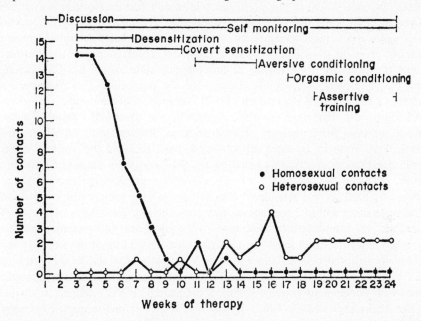

Fig. 1. Sexual behavior reported by the client and timing of various treatment techniques.

carried with him in his wallet. He reported that with each homosexual or heterosexual contact, he thought of the negative and positive aspects of entering them on the graph. This modification of the method was intended to strengthen reinforcements by making them more immediate.

Covert sensitization was also initiated at the third week. During Weeks 3-8, the client was seen in successive sessions of 45 minutes each with a break in between to separate the desensitization and covert sensitization procedures. Although the homosexual response reproducible in covert sensitization is an imaginal one, it was assumed that the overt behavior also involved imaginal stimuli, and that transfer would occur. A typical scene covered in covert sensitization involved entering a bar, noticing an attractive homosexual male, approaching him and striking up a conversation. Descriptions of increasing nausea and vomiting were introduced progressively earlier into the sequence over trials. The technique was carried out in Weeks 3-10. At that point the client reported 2 weeks without a homosexual contact and said that homosexual bars had lost their attractiveness. All subsequent contacts resulted from hitchhiking which remained the client's primary mode of transportation.

Altering Homosexual Fantasies

During these last weeks of the covert sensitization program, the client began describing a slightly different aspect of homosexual behavior which became the target for the next procedure. He reported that, although he was engaging in less overt homosexual behavior, his homosexual fantasies in other environments were increasing. Arousing fantasy images were occurring in response to attractive males noticed on the street, or elsewhere. In order to treat this particular response, a faradic aversion technique was employed in Session 7. Using a Farrell Instrument Co. AV-6 Visually Keyed Conditioner, slides of males and females were presented to the client. He could terminate a male slide and escape or avoid a randomly delayed shock by a button push. The button also advanced the projector to a female or heterosexual slide shown for 15 seconds. An interval of 15 seconds with no slide preceded the next trial. This procedure is an adaptation of Feldman and MacCulloch's (1971) aversion relief paradigm.

All slides were first rated for attractiveness by the client and a matched subset of slides was set aside for a post-test of generalization. The remaining slides were divided into sets of 10 arranged by rated attractiveness. Set 1 included the five least attractive male slides and five most attractive female slides. Set 2 contained the next 5 slides in each sequence, and so on, for a total of 5 sets. Conditioning began with the presentation of the first two sets. Each set was considered completed when the subject had avoided each of the five male slides within 2 seconds on two consecutive presentations of the set. Then the next set was introduced. In these sessions the client saw 140 presentations of male slides, received a total of 52 shocks and reached criterion on four of the five slide sets. At this point he reported that the slides were no longer attractive and he was not noticing attractive males on the street. But since he was still experiencing frequent homosexual fantasies with no apparent external stimulus, the procedure was modified to a paradigm more like Marks and Gelder's (1967). He was instructed to visualize specific fantasies and to signal when he had a clear image, whereupon the therapist administered a shock of short duration on this signal. After two sessions of this the client reported that these fantasies had essentially disappeared.

Modifying Masturbation Fantasy

Upon inquiry in Session 16, the client reported that despite the disappearance of the spontaneous fantasies he continued to find that homosexual fantasies aroused him when he wished to masturbate. He complained that heterosexual fantasies were not sufficiently arousing. At the next session he was instructed in the use of Marquis' "orgasmic reconditioning" procedure (Marquis, 1970), whereby he was progressively to switch from homosexual to heterosexual fantasies at successively earlier points in the mastubatory sequence beginning with a switch just before orgasm.

Increasing Heterosexual Approach

During these same sessions that client discussed the fact that, although he was feeling quite successful in his efforts to control his homosexuality, he nevertheless was discouraged about his heterosexual life because he was having difficulties in his relationships with females. As a consequence Sessions 19-24 were spent in assertive training with role-playing and discussion of situations involving approach to females. At this point therapy was terminated.

RESULTS AND FOLLOW-UP

Overt behavior as monitored and recorded by the client is shown in Fig. 1. Homosexual contacts were defined in terms of actual sexual behavior with a male. Heterosexual contacts were defined more broadly as any prolonged interaction with a female, whether social (e.g., a date) or sexual. The client did have intercourse with several females during the latter weeks of the program.

Table 1 Slide Ratings

	Therapy Slides		Test Slides	
	Homosexual	Heterosexual	Homosexual	Heterosexual
N	19	20	13	13
Pretest	1·00	3·45	1·38	3·62
Post-test	− 0·84	2·20	− 0·23	3·54
t	− 5·792*	− 7·812*	− 4·864*	− 0·449

*$p < 0.001$.

Subjective ratings of homosexual and heterosexual slides were made at Week 10 before beginning aversive conditioning and after the procedure was terminated at Week 14. The ratings were made on a nine-point scale from +4 as most attractive to -4 for most unattractive with zero as the neutral point. After the pre-test, the neutral and positively rated slides were divided into therapy and test sets. The test slides were seen by the client only at the time of the two ratings while the therapy slides were used in the aversive conditioning and aversion relief procedures. Table 1 illustrates the fact that the homosexual slides lost their attractiveness following the aversive conditioning procedure, and the effect seemed to generalize to the matched group of homosexual test slides as well. Contrary to expectations, the heterosexual slides used in the aversion relief paradigm also decreased significantly in attractiveness. This effect did not seem to generalize to the test slides.

At a follow-up interview 40 weeks after termination, the client reported that he had had one homosexual encounter shortly after termination of treatment. It was initiated by the driver of a car with whom the client had hitched a ride. He described the incident as unpleasant and felt that it was a test of his therapy which proved that homosexuality was no longer attractive to him. He also reported that he was dating a girl regularly and felt that this relationship was a close and satisfying one. He had completed his high-school equivalent General Education Degree, had begun courses at a local community college and was working part-time.

DISCUSSION

Although the treatment techniques are confounded in this case, and therefore do not lend themselves to specific causal interferences, the case nonetheless illustrates a general organizing principle for behavior therapy. The principle is that techniques should be chosen and applied according to the topography of the various responses to be modified. This contrasts with approaches which deal with homosexuality as a single behavior complex (e.g., Feldman & MacCulloch, 1971). It also contrasts with the use of multiple behavior therapy techniques simply to increase the power of therapy (e.g., Gershman, 1970).

This principle assumes that behind homosexuality may be various behaviors that are relatively independent of one another. These behaviors may be classified in Lang's (1968) terms as verbal-cognitive, overt-motor and physiological-autonomic. Any individual will manifest some subsets of these classes of homosexual behaviors in a unique pattern. Individuals seeking therapy for homosexuality differ in their manner of making homosexual contacts; in the form of overt homosexual behavior; in the degree of masturbation to homosexual fantasies; in the degree of subjective and physiological arousal to pictured or fantasied homosexual stimuli; in the degree of identification as "a homosexual"; in the degree of association with a homosexual community, *inter alia*. Similar distinctions could be made with regard to the same individual's heterosexual behavior.

Thus, a behavior therapy program for the modification of homosexual behavior ought to be essentially a multiple-baseline, single subject design experiment in which the various responses are sequentially modified by a series of techniques. The goal therapy is the modification of each of these responses through the application of a specific technique.

The sequencing of these applications remains a separate problem. Mahoney (1971) reported a sequence of treatments in "order of acceptability to the patient." Laboratory research on punishment (Johnson, 1972) suggests that it is more effective when an alternative response is available in the organism's repertory. It follows that in dealing with homosexuality the therapist should consider strengthening alternative sexual responses prior to, or at least concommitant with, suppressing homosexual responses. In the case described here, the attitudinal responses were approached first since some degree of acceptance or understanding of a behavioral model is probably a prerequisite for following a behavioral program. Next, overt homosexual approach responses were the focus of intervention since these behaviors resulted in powerful reinforcements which were likely to maintain a variety of correlated homosexual responses. Such sequencing may not be entirely predictable in advance. In the middle of therapy the client in the present case described the occurrence of homosexual fantasies of a type which he had not described earlier. Responses fairly low in strength became more salient once other responses had been weakened. Sequence as well as selection of techniques requires individualized application.

Acknowledgment: The authors would like to thank Arnold Freedman and Lynn Rickert for their consultation and facilitation with this case at the Oakland V.A. Hospital, Pittsburgh.

REFERENCES

Feldman, M.P. & MacCulloch, M.J. *Homosexual behavior: Therapy and assessment.* Oxford: Pergamon Press, 1971.

Gershman, L. Case conference: A transvestite fantasy treated by thought-stopping, covert sensitization and aversive shock. *J. Behav. Ther. & Exp. Psychiat.* 1970, 1, 153-161.

Johnson, J.M. Punishment of human behavior. *Am. Psychol.* 1972, 27, 1033-1044.

Kendrick, S.R. & McCullough, J.P. Sequential phases of covert reinforcement and covert sensitization in the treatment of homosexuality. *J. Behav. Ther. & Exp. Psychiat.* 1972, 3, 229-232.

Lang, P.J. Fear reduction and fear behavior: Problems in treating a construct. *Research in Psychotherapy.* Ed. by Shlien J.M.), Vol. 3, Washington, D.C.: American Psychological Association, 1968.

Lazarus, A.A. *Behavior therapy and beyond.* New York: McGraw-Hill, 1971.

Mahoney, M.J. Sequential treatments for severe phobia. *J. Behav. Ther. & Exp. Psychiat.* 1971, 2, 195-197.

Mahoney, M.J. Research issues in self-management. *Behav. Therapy.* 1972, 3, 45-63.

Marks, I.M. & Gelder, M.G. Transvestism and fetishism: Clinical and psychological changes during faradic aversion. *Brit. J. Psychiat.,* 1967, 113, 711-729.

Marquis, J.N. Orgasmic reconditioning: Changing sexual object choice through controlling masturbation fantasies. *J. Bahav. Ther. & Exp. Psychiat.,* 1970, 1, 263-272.

48

Multiple Behavioral Techniques in a Case of Female Homosexuality

JOSEPH W. BLITCH and STEPHEN N. HAYNES

Although there are many reports of the application of behavioral techniques to male homosexuals (Feldman, 1966), a search of the literature has revealed no cases of behavioral treatment of female homosexuality. The degree to which the theories and techniques derived from the study of male homosexuals are applicable to female homosexuality is an unanswered question.

For the most part, the behavioral treatment of homosexuality has focused on the homosexual behaviors per se, typically using aversive conditioning techniques (Feldman, 1966). However, several investigators have pointed out the deficiencies of this approach and have drawn attention to the importance of heterosexual anxiety in the etiology and maintenance of homosexual behaviors (DiScipio, 1968; Gray, 1970; Haynes, 1970; Huff, 1970; Kraft, 1969; LoPiccolo, 1971; Stevenson & Wolpe, 1960). If homosexuality is often in part a function of an irrational fear of the opposite sex, then aversion therapy with no attempt directly to reduce or eliminate the heterosexual anxiety would not be expected to yield optimum results. In fact, aversion therapy might sometimes merely add a phobic response to homosexual behavior in addition to the already present heterosexual phobic response.

Assuming that many homosexuals experience anxiety in heterosexual situations (Ramsay & Van Velsen, 1968), an anxiety-reducing technique such as systematic desensitization should serve as an integral part of the therapy program, in the expectation that the removal of the phobic anxiety will increase the probability of heterosexual behavior. Once heterosexual anxiety is decreased, there is still the necessity for building in an adequate repertoire of behaviors with the opposite sex to replace homosexual activity in the client's response hierarchy (Haynes, 1970; Marshall, 1971). Suggested methods for facilitating the acquisition of these sexual and social skills include behavior rehearsal and assertion training techniques (Levin et al., 1968; Wolpe, 1969).

Relaxation plus training in its use to decrease anxiety in extra-therapy situations has been shown to be an effective therapeutic technique (Zeisset, 1968), especially when used as an adjunct to other kinds of intervention. Once training in the relaxation component of systematic desensitization has occurred, the additional effort expended for the training in its application can be expected to yield large returns as a self-treatment procedure to be used in present or future anxiety producing situations.

McGuire, Carlisle and Young (1965) suggested that many sexual deviations occur through a gradual process of masturbating to a memory of an event which was not necessarily stimulating at the time of the initial experience. The stimulus value of the memory increases because of its occurrence during subsequent masturbation. This hypothesis offers a reasonable explanation of how the deviant behavior is maintained between overt incidents (Evans, 1968). McGuire et al.'s (1965) technique of altering fantasies occuring during masturbation has been used with such deviations as voyeurism (Jackson, 1969) and sadism (Davison, 1968) and other deviations (Marquis, 1970), but there has been very little consideration of its application to treating female homosexuals.

CASE HISTORY

Miss B. was an attractive 22-year-old college junior who was actively engaging in both homosexual and heterosexual behavior. She had experienced about eight or nine manual genital contacts with three girls over the 4 months immediately preceding therapy. She first had heterosexual intercourse about 6 months earlier to a total of about 20 coital experiences, most of them with one man. She described herself as afraid and upset during intercourse, but doing it to prove to herself and others that she was not homosexual: "If you go with a guy, people won't think you're homosexual." Although Miss B. had no apparent masculine behavior, she was usually the aggressor in homosexual behavior. Satisfying her partner was the most stimulating aspect of her homosexual behavior, although she seldom reached climax herself. The idea of homosexuality had connotations of constitutional predisposition and underlying causation that were very upsetting to her and at the same time substantially lessened the pressure for her to assume responsibility for the behavior.

PROCEDURE

Initial Stages of Intervention

Miss B. was seen for 14 50-minute sessions during a 7-week period. The early sessions consisted primarily of information-gathering and discussion of the rationale of the treatment with the client. An initial goal of therapy was for her to accept a behavioral orientation to homosexual behavior and normalcy as discussed by Ullmann and Krasner (1969). Although she had stated she wanted to lose the urge to homosexual behavior, other alternatives (such as becoming less anxious with homosexual behaviors) were discussed in order to allow the therapist more to clearly discern her goals and commitment to change. An informal contract was established that she would consistently attend the therapy sessions and perform extra-therapy assignments.

Explicit information was gathered concerning specific behavioral and environmental stimuli associated with the occurrence of both homosexual and heterosexual behaviors. (Relative emphasis on homosexuality was progressively decreased in later sessions.) The gathering of this information was initiated during the therapy session but soon became a homework assignment to be discussed at each following session. An example of the use of this information was the instruction to abstain from alcohol and marijuana for the next 2 months and to stay off the bed of her most frequent partner, thus eliminating what seemed to be important early stimuli in a chain leading to overt homosexual behavior.

Relaxation and Systematic Desensitization

Included in the relaxation training was instruction in its use to inhibit anxiety in various situations (*see* Zeisset, 1968) such as test situations and public speaking engagements.

An initial single hierarchy was divided into "being touched" and "touching" hierarchies of 14 and 10 items respectively. The items in these two hierarchies were similar to those in a hierarchy designed by Bentler (1968) which started with one minute of continuous lip kissing and ended with mutual oral manipulation of genitals to mutual orgasm.

Behavior Rehearsal and Role-playing

An attempt was made to overcome Miss B.'s social deficiencies—training her to accept compliments and to communicate more effectively with new people. In each of these and other social areas (e.g., disagreeing with friends or asserting her feelings) new behaviors were learned through behavior rehearsal and role-playing. To facilitate generalization, psychology graduate students were utilized in specific role-playing assignments with her, initially in the therapy room and subsequently in other places, such as the campus student center.

Manipulation of Masturbation Fantasies

Miss B. reported that the pre-therapy ratio of homosexual to heterosexual masturbation images was about five to one. Orgasm was reached in almost all of her 10-15 masturbations per week. As suggested by McGuire et al. (1965), Miss B. was told that the fantasy immediately preceding orgasm was very conditionable and that regardless of the stimuli associated with the early phases of masturbation she should switch to heterosexual stimuli during this period. A daily chart of masturbation images and frequency was begun. In addition, she was instructed to attempt progressively earlier image switches when the masturbation image was initially homosexual.

RESULTS

At the termination of 7 weeks of therapy Miss B. said that she had experienced no homosexual contacts for 5 weeks. She had had one near contact but had been able to walk away. Heterosexual anxiety appeared greatly decreased both in terms of the hierarchies and as reported in extra-therapy social situations. She was dating and interacting in groups more frequently and generally reported increasing self-assurance in interpersonal interactions.

Of the eight masturbations the first week of charting, four were to homosexual images, two to heterosexual images and two shifted from homosexual to heterosexual images before orgasm. The second week there were zero homosexual, three heterosexual and six shifted images; and the third week two homosexual, seven heterosexual, and three shifted. These figures show both an increase in heterosexual images and an absolute decrease in the frequency of masturbation.

Follow-up

At a 2-month follow-up Miss B. reported that she felt much happier, more at ease, and much better able to respond adaptively in social situations. There had still been no overt homosexual behavior since the second week of therapy. Masturbation had stablized at about seven or eight times per week with no homosexual images. She reported having several satisfying relationships with males. She was again assured that if any problems arose which she could not handle the therapist would be available. In light of her current social and sexual behaviors, more positive feelings toward herself, and her understanding of a self-controlled behavioral approach to personal problems, this need is not predicted.

DISCUSSION

The results of the present case study demonstrate that certain behavior therapy techniques previously used in the treatment of male homosexuality and other sexual deviations, can be useful in treating female homosexuality. In Miss B's. therapeutic success several factors may have contributed—her intelligence, her strong commitment to change, the presence of basic heterosexual social skills and sexual behavior, and the fact that the onset of homosexual behavior was recent.

The desensitization sessions demonstrated the need for the therapist to be constantly aware of the need for stimulus shifts during the desensitization procedure. One such need arose when Miss B. signaled increased anxiety when "gentleness" cues were inserted. It became apparent that Miss B. associated these cues with seduction and sexuality. Their special anxiety eliciting characteristics had to be taken into account. Another problem was evident when Miss B. signaled anxiety to items relatively low on the hierarchy. She explained that she was thinking not only about the particular items, but also of what they might lead to in a sexual chain. This problem was apparently eliminated simply by instructing her to confine her thoughts to the items presented. Therapists should always be on the lookout for the client's idiosyncratic ways of responding.

When an analysis is made of the specific environmental stimuli associated with sexually deviant behavior and behavioral techniques are applied accordingly, when alternative behavior is instituted, and when the client is given as great a share of the therapeutic responsibility as feasible, then success may be expected in a reasonably short time.

Acknowledgments: The authors would like to express their appreciation to Bill N. Kinder and William E. Gore for their assistance in role-playing and Robert E. Deysach for help in the preparation of the manuscript.

REFERENCES

Bentler, P.M. Heterosexual behavior assessment II: Females. *Behav. Res. & Therapy.* 1968, **6**, 27-28.

Davison, G.C. Elimination of a sadistic fantasy by a client-centered counter-conditioning technique. *J. Abnorm. Psychol.* 1968, **73**, 84-90.

DiScipio, W.K. Modified progressive desensitization and homosexuality. *Brit. J. Psychol.* 1968, **41**, 267-272.

Evans, D. Masturbatory fantasies and sexual deviations. *Behav. Res. & Therapy.* 1968, **6**, 17-19.

Feldman, M.P. Aversion therapy for sexual deviations: A critical revision. *Psych. Bull.* 1968, **65**, 65-79.

Gray, J.J. Case Conference: Behavior therapy in a patient with homosexual fantasies and heterosexual anxiety. *J. Behav. Ther. & Exp. Psychiat.* 1970, **1**, 225-232.

Haynes, S.N. Learning theory and the treatment of homosexuality. *Psychother: Theory, Res. & Prac.* 1970, **7**, 91-94.

Huff, F.W. The desensitization of a homosexual. *Behav. Res. & Ther.* 1970, 8, 99-102.

Jackson, B.T. A case of voyeurism treated by counterconditioning. *Behav. Res. & Therapy.* 1969, **7**, 133-134.

Kraft, T. Treatment for sexual perversions. *Behav. Res. & Therapy.* 1969, **7**, 215.

Kraft, T. Systematic desensitization in the treatment of homosexuality. *Behav. Res. & Therapy.* 1970, 8, 319.

Levin, S.M., Hirsh, I.S., Shugan G. & Kapche R. Treatment of homosexuality and heterosexual anxiety with avoidance conditioning and systematic desensitization: Data and case report. *Psychotherapy: Theory: Res. & Prac.* 1968, **5**, 160-168.

LoPiccolo, J. Case study: Systematic desensitization of homosexuality. *Behav. Therapy.* 1971, **2**, 394-399.

Marquis, J.N. Orgasmic reconditioning: Changing sexual object choice through controlling masturbation fantasies. *J. Behav. Ther. & Exp. Psychiat.* 1970, **1**, 263-271.

Marshall, W.L. A combined treatment method for certain sexual deviations. *Behav. Res. & Therapy.* 1971, **9**, 293-294.

McGuire, R.J., Carlisle, J.M. & Young, B.G. Sexual deviation as conditioned behavior: A hypothesis. *Behav. Res. & Therapy.* 1965, **2**, 185-190.

Ramsay, R.W. & Van Velzen, V. Behavior therapy for sexual perversions. *Behav. Res. & Therapy.* 1968, **6**, 233.

Stevenson, I. & Wolpe, J. Recovery from sexual deviations through overcoming non-sexual neurotic responses. *Am. J. Psychiat.* 1960, **116**, 737-742.

Wolpe, J. *The Practice of behavior therapy.* New York: Pergamon Press, 1969.

Ullmann, L.P. & Krasner, L. *A psychological approach to abnormal behavior.* Englewood Cliffs: Prentice-Hall, 1969.

Zeisset, R.M. Desensitization and relaxation in the modification of psychiatric patients interview behavior. *J. abnorm. Psychol.* 1968, **73**, 18-24.

49

The Use of Stimulus/Modeling Videotapes in Assertive Training for Homosexuals

WAYNE D. DUEHN and NAZREEN S. MAYADAS

INTRODUCTION

The past decade has witnessed a proliferation of experimentation with a variety of alternate sexual lifestyles. While these may be discounted as merely intriguing and transitory, there is increasing evidence (Cogswell & Sussman, 1972; Olsen, 1972; Otto, 1970; Sussman & Cogswell, 1972) which suggests that the socially sanctioned heterosexual relationship is no longer the only alternative available; other forms of sexual lifestyles are becoming an integral part of the social structure. Therefore, it is necessary to expand, perhaps substantially, the range of public tolerance for a variety of sexual lifestyles. While there may be considerable confusion, resistance and conflict regarding the incorporation of these emerging values into society, it would be a disservice both to the clients and community, if the helping professions were to abdicate their responsibility of providing service to those individuals who have selected alternate sexual lifestyles. In essence, sexual behavior is in a state of flux, just as on a more general level, traditional male/female roles are being redefined. The sexual mores of yesteryear are giving way to a continuum of increasingly complex interpersonal relationships (Berger et al., 1972; Margolis & Margolis, 1973; O'Neill & O'Neill, 1960; Ramey, 1972).

If current trends are preliminary indicators of the future, the clinician must re-examine not only the adequacy of his practice skills but the value premises upon which they rest. Sexual counseling is confronted with a new and exciting challenge. It cannot ignore the developing gap between a variety of sustained sexual preferences and the community's legal, economic and ethical sanctions against such practices. Specifically, the helping professions must devise new practice methodologies to serve the interest of these groups and in so doing enlist support for public tolerance of variant sexual lifestyles.

Recently clinicians have recognized the necessity of developing new interventive formats. Cogswell and Sussman (1972) state that professionals will increasingly be confronted with a variety of sexual lifestyles which will present different needs, problems to be solved and issues to be resolved. As such, professionals will need to incorporate notions of "pluralism in their diagnosis and treatment frameworks" thereby providing patients with increased outcome options. Consistent with the above thinking is Varley's (1972) suggestion that as more alternative lifestyles become available which complement individual needs and drives, professionals will be required to use new models for assessment and treatment.

Although the above concerns have been raised, little attempt has been made to identify the knowledge base and specific practice skills which may be applied to problems of variant sexual lifestyles. Constantine et al. (1972) suggest that the professional "facilitate alternative paths of communication" (p. 272). How these objectives are to be achieved through clinical practice skills are not delineated. Gochros (1972) puts forth a number of practice objectives for direct intervention, but procedures of treatment are not explicated.

ALTERNATE SEXUAL LIFESTYLES

For purposes of this paper, alternate sexual lifestyles are defined as those overtly acknowledged interpersonal sexual relationships which deviate from traditional monogamy. Examples of these are group and communal living arrangements, premarital and extra-marital sexual relationships, swinging, homosexuality, spouse swapping, bisexuality, etc. The above behaviors are generally forbidden because they violate societal expectations regarding the "who," "when," "where" and under "what" circumstances sexual behaviors can occur. Individuals who engage in alternate sexual lifestyles are often subject to social ostracism, contempt, ridicule, harassment, punishment and denial of their sexual as well as other human rights (Gochros, 1972).

Societal condemnation of sexual variants frequently permits two avenues of choice for those involved in these lifestyles: (1) to conform to standards and deny self-fulfillment, or (2) to defy societal regulations and thereby be victimized. In selecting either one of these avenues the individual may withdraw, clandestinely engaging in variant sexual behavior while superficially conforming (non-assertion), or may reactively exaggerate his variant sexual lifestyle (inappropriate assertion). Based on this rationale, assertive training was viewed as uniquely suited for treating individuals with variant sexual preferences. The clinical skills in assertive training described below are derived from a model of practice (Duehn & Mayadas, 1975; Stuart, 1974) which puts major emphasis on client determined outcomes.

ASSERTIVE TRAINING

Assertion training has recently received much attention as a therapeutic technique for directly shaping assertive behaviors (Fensterhein, 1972; Friedman, 1971; Hersen et al., 1973; McFall and Lillosand, 1971; Rose, 1975). Assertive behaviors consist of action oriented skills of social competency which enable the individual to appropriately affirm himself. More specifically, these behaviors are related to the degree of self-expression, passive/active orientational life sets, verbal and non-verbal communicational congruence and interpersonal risk taking (Alberti & Emmons, 1970; Eisler et al., 1973; Wolpe, 1969). This definition is consistent with the recent empirical research of Rathus (1973) and Hersen et al. (1973). Rathus (1973) developed a statistically validated quantitative scale for measuring general assertiveness in which four items were found to be correlates of assertiveness: boldness, outspokenness, aggressiveness and confidence. Similarly, Hersen et al. (1973) identified the following behavioral referents of assertion: duration of looking, verbal reply, affect and loudness of speech, and overall assertiveness.

When applied to practice, training in assertion utilizes a variety of techniques in combination. Its major components are modeling, behavioral rehearsal (role playing), social reinforcement, contingency contracting, home assignments and follow-up. The client is provided with numerous, detailed and vivid displays of a specific assertive interpersonal or personal skill to be learned; he is given considerable opportunity, training and encouragement to behaviorally rehearse or practice the modeled behavior; and he is provided with feedback regarding the degree to which his enactments approximate those of the goal behaviors. These components have a long and substantial history of demonstrated effectiveness as behavior change methods (Hersen et al., 1973). Their systematic use and evaluation in the treatment of variant sexual lifestyles, however, has been minimal (Fensterheim & Baer, 1975). The present paper, therefore, sought to examine their utilization in enhancing social interactional behavior of individuals selecting homosexuality as an alternate lifestyle.

Application of Assertive Training to Homosexual Lifestyle

The goals of assertion training are to make the sexual variant (1) at ease with his chosen lifestyle, (2) cognizant of other alternative, interpersonal behaviors and concommitant behavioral repertoires to enact these behaviors, and (3) familiar with ways of eliminating those problematic interpersonal behaviors contingent on client's desired outcome. The approach discussed here utilizes stimulus/modeling videotapes, behavioral rehearsals and videotape feedback. The stimulus/modeling videotapes were developed from our own clinical experience, reviews of the literature and problems presented by the specific client-in-treatment.*

Despite the evidence which points to the efficacy of utilizing stimulus/modeling (S/M) tapes in clinical settings, therapists have been reticent to develop and incorporate these technological tools and techniques into their practice (Mayadas & Duehn, 1975). In treatment, the S/M tapes are combined with behavioral rehearsals, videotape feedback, home assignments and presented to the client in the following sequential order:

1. A stimulus tape of assertive and non-assertive behaviors to stereotypic reactions toward homosexuality in a variety of specific but commonly occurring situations is presented.
2. Therapist discusses with client the latter's cognitive and affective reactions to stimulus tape.
3. Focused feedback (Stoller, 1972) of stimulus tape: (Tape is stopped at selected intervals in order to emphasize behavioral components of assertion).
4. Behavioral Rehearsal: Client and therapist role-play assertive behaviors relative

---

*The videotape "Coming Out: Assertive Training for Living," upon which this study is based, may be procured by writing to the authors. The authors especially wish to thank members of the North Texas Gay Task Force and AURA, Fort Worth, Texas for providing much of the stimulus and modeling content which was incorporated into the tape.

to client situation and goals. These behaviors are videotaped for playback and discussion.

5. Step four is repeated until behavior is performed to mutual satisfaction of client and therapist.

6. Home Assignment: Finally, specific behavioral rehearsals and assignments to be carried out through covert and actual role enactments as well as in actual situations are given. Projected reactions of self and others are discussed.

Case Illustration

A 26-year-old male accepting his homosexual orientation sought help with social and interpersonal problems incurred in his decision to "come out." During the initial assessment interviews, he identified skill deficits in the following impinging situations: (1) Informing family and friends of homosexual lifestyle; (2) Handling stereotypic reactions (ridicule, ostracism, spectator curiosity, etc.); (3) Ambiguity regarding extent of self-disclosure ("Whom to tell and how much?"): and (4) Repercussions of self-disclosure (possible job loss, severance of friendships, etc.). Baseline data relevant to specific problem situations were collected and pretest measures of assertion were taken over a period of two and a half weeks (five sessions).

Following the assessment phase, the client was seen for six one-hour weekly sessions. Assertive skills related to "coming out" were depicted in a variety of independent interpersonal situations. A further consideration in S/M tape development related to the importance of selecting a representative sample of commonly experienced social encounters, so that when combined with complementary behavioral rehearsals and relevant home assignments generalization of assertive behaviors would be enhanced (Lazarus, 1971).

The assessment phase and descriptions of those S/M vignettes selected for use in the treatment of this client are described below:

PHASE I — ASSESSMENT: PRE-TREATMENT

Sessions 1 to 5: Assessment Interviews: Content included inventory of the problem areas, problem selection, behavioral specification, contracting, commitment to cooperate, assessment of frequency, duration and controlling contingencies of behaviors (Gambrill et al., 1971).

As part of assessment procedures client's reaction to the stimulus portion of the S/M tape was videotaped (i.e., both the assertive and non-assertive responses to the stimulus segment of the taped vignettes were withheld). Ratings of this tape served as the pre-treatment baseline measures of assertiveness (Gottman et al., 1972).

PHASE II — TREATMENT

Session 6: S/M Tape: Cocktail party. Assergive and non-assertive verbal and non-verbal response to social ridicule.

Session 7: Report back, if home assignments are successfully completed, present S/M tape depicting assertive and non-assertive behaviors in disclosing gay orientation to close friend.

Session 8: Report back, if home assignments are successfully completed, present S/M tape of assertive and non-assertive models where sexual orientation is disclosed to a family member.

Session 9: Report back, if home assignments are successfully completed, proceed to next S/M tape. Assertive and non-assertive responses to turning down sexual overtures in a gay bar.

Session 10: Report back, if home assignments are successfully completed, present S/M tape in which gay friend is introduced to heterosexual acquaintance.

Session 11: Report back, review of home assignments, and final role enactment of cumulative assertive behaviors.

Home assignments (which included covert and overt behavioral rehearsals and actual behavioral performances) consistent with the treatment session focus were prescribed throughout phase II.

PHASE III – EVALUATION: POST-TREATMENT

Sessions 12-16: Post-treatment measures of responses to stimulus portion of S/M tape are recorded (same procedure as pre-test, see Sessions 1 to 5 – Phase I). Data on the six measures listed below were collected following Treatment Phase II. Specifically, post-treatment measures were taken one week, two weeks, one month, three months and six months following the last treatment session (Session 11 – Phase II).

Pre- and post-treatment responses to the stimulus tapes were rated on six behavioral components of assertiveness adapted from Hersen et al. (1973) with one modification. In keeping with Fensterheim and Baer's (1975) observations that the verbal behavior of the sexual variant is usually defensive, rather than offensive; a measure (5 point scale) of client's defensive-offensive verbal behaviors was included in the investigation.

Means were computed on all six measures from ratings of two independent judges. Using an interrupted time-series single subject design, multiple t tests were applied to determine differences between pre- and post-treatment measures (Gottman et al., 1972). Suitability of t test application for single subject interrupted time-series analysis was indicated by the stability of baseline data on all six criterion measures during the five pre-treatment sessions.

The results were as follows: Duration of looking, ($t(4) = 2.38$, $p < .05$; Duration of reply, $t(4) = .38$, p n.s.; Loudness of speech, $t(4) = 2.18$, $p < .05$; Defensive-offensive, $t(4) = 2.86$, $p < .05$; Affect, $t(4) = .65$, p n.s.; and Overall assertiveness, $t(4) = 3.42$, $p < .05$. These results indicate that client showed significant improvement on four selected assertive measures. Client's subjective assessment of therapeutic gain was consistent with the independent ratings. Content analysis of "report back" revealed that client was able to disclose his homosexual orientation to friends and family and effectively (assertively) deal with others' and his own reactions. He indicated a lessening of anxiety in selected social situations where homosexual overtures were made and when specific derogatory comments were directed towards him.

DISCUSSION

The case presented in this paper is illustrative of a client outcome oriented practice model which employs assertion training in enabling individuals to pursue alternate sexual lifestyles with a minimum of discomfort. This is in contrast to most reported (Hersen et al., 1973) implementation of assertive training where treatment is directed toward normative behaviors. Self-determination and recognition of individual worth have been time honored value concepts of clinical practice. The methodology and therapeutic procedures explicated here operationalize these values. Implicit in assertion training is the conviction that each individual has the right to live his life as he selects, as long as his chosen sexual lifestyle does not impinge on the freedom of others.

The results of the specific case discussed here suggest that observation of assertive and non-assertive models in combination with behavioral rehearsals and focused videotape feedback facilitate acquisition of assertive responses to specific problematic situations encountered by homosexuals who declare their alternate lifestyle.

The results further suggest that with contextual modification this model and its procedures can be applied to a variety of sexual behavioral patterns. Increasingly, therapists have access to videotape equipment. With little cost, stimulus/modeling tapes can be developed to meet the particular needs of their clientele. Preliminary efforts have been made by the authors in the areas of parent-child communication (Duehn & Mayadas, in press), and marital counseling (Mayadas & Duehn, 1975).

To date, most research in assertive training has been carried out primarily as analogue to treatment rather than in actual treatment itself. The practice model and treatment skills explicated in this paper are but a first step in this direction which needs further exploration. The methodology needs to be tested with larger samples and other client populations. The differential effects of modeling, behavioral rehearsal, and videotape feedback should be further examined in both single case design studies and through more controlled experimental procedures. Although assertion training has implications to be successfully applied to a wide variety of target sexual lifestyles, few practitioner-researchers have systematically examined these effects. Concommitant effects of an assertion program on other behavioral repertoires of the sexual variant warrant empirical investigations.

Finally, clinicians would do well to incorporate assertion training techniques into practice with sexual variants. The products of this treatment, interacting with the community, would have an increasing influence on the public's attitude and tolerance toward such behaviors. This action oriented practice stance would encourage the development of individual self-expression while increasing community's awareness of pluralistic behavior patterns and values.

REFERENCES

Alberti, R.E., & Emmons, M.L. *Your perfect right: A guide to assertive behavior.* San Luis Obispo, Calif.: Impact, 1970.

Berger, B., Hackett, B., & Millar, R.M. The communal family. *The Family Coordinator,* 1972, **21,** 419-427.

Cogswell, B.E., & Sussman, M.B. Changing family and marriage forms: Complications for human service systems. *The Family Coordinator,* 1972, **21,** 505-516.

Constantine, L.L., Constantine, J.M., & Edelman, S.K. Counseling implications of co-marital and multilateral relations. *The Family Coordinator,* 1972, **21,** 267-273.

Duehn, W.D., & Mayadas, N.S. Behavioral rehearsals in group counseling with parents. *Groups,* in press.

Duehn, W.D., & Mayadas, N.S. Entrance and exit requirements of professional education. Paper presented at the 21st Annual Program Meeting, Council on Social Work Education, Chicago, March, 1975.

Eisler, R.M., Miller, P.M., & Hersen, M. Components of assertive behavior. *Journal of Clinical Psychology,* 1973, **23,** 295-299.

Fensterheim, H. Behavior therapy: Assertive training in groups. In C.J. Sager & H.S. Kaplan (Eds.), *Progress in Group and Family Therapy.* New York: Brunner/Mazel, 1972.

Fensterheim, H., & Baer, J. *Don't Say Yes When You Want to Say No.* New York: D. McKay, 1975.

Friedman, P.H. The effects of modeling and role-playing on assertive behavior. In R.D. Rubin, H. Fensterheim, A.A. Lazarus, & C.M. Franks (Eds.), *Advances in Behavior Therapy.* New York: Academic Press, 1971.

Gambrill, E.D., Thomas, E.J., & Carter, R.D. Procedure for sociobehavioral practice in open settings. *Social Work,* 1971, **16,** 51-62.

Gochros, H.L. The sexually oppressed. *Social Work,* 1972, **17,** 16-23.

Gottman, J.M., McFall, R.M., & Barnett, J.T. Design and analysis of research using time series. *Journal of Clinical Psychology,* 1972, **39,** 273-281.

Hersen, M., Eisler, R.M., & Miller, P.M. Development of assertive responses: Clinical, measurement and research. *Behaviour Research and Therapy,* 1973, **11,** 505-521.

Hersen, M., Eisler, R.M., Miller, P.M., Johnson, M.B., & Pinkston, S.G. Effects of practice, instructions, and modeling on components of assertive behavior. *Behaviour Research and Therapy,* 1973, **11,** 443-451.

Lazarus, A.A. *Behavior Therapy and Beyond.* New York: McGraw-Hill, 1971.

Margolis, C., & Margolis, J. Alternate lifestyles and sexual tolerance. *The Humanist,* 1973, **33,** 19-20.

Mayadas, N.S., & Duehn, W.D. A stimulus modeling videotape for marital counseling: Method and application. Paper presented at the National Association of Social Workers' 20th Anniversary Professional Symposium, Hollywood-by-the-Sea, Florida, October, 1975.

McFall, R., & Lillosand, D. Behavioral rehearsal with modeling and coaching in assertion training. *Journal of Abnormal Psychology,* 1971, **11,** 313-323.

Olsen, D.H. Marriage of the future: Revolution or evolutionary change? *The Family Coordinator,* 1972, **21,** 383-393.

O'Neill, N., & O'Neill, G. *Open marriage: A new life style for couples.* New York: M. Evans, 1960.

Otto, H.A. *The family in search of a future.* New York: Appleton, Century and Crofts, 1970.

Ramey, J.W. Emerging patterns of innovative behavior in marriage. *The Family Coordinator,* 1972, **21,** 435-456.

Rathus, S.A. A 30 item schedule for assessing assertive behavior. *Behavior Therapy,* 1973, **4,** 398-406.

Rose, S.D. In pursuit of social competence. *Social Work,* 1975, **20,** 33-39.

Stoller, F.H. The use of videotape feedback. In L.N. Soloman & B. Berzon (Eds.), *New perspectives on encounter groups.* San Francisco: Jossey-Bass, 1972.

Stuart, R.B. Behavior modification: A technology of social change. In F.J. Turner (Ed.), *Social Work Treatment.* New York: Free Press, 1974.

Sussman, M.B., & Cogswell, B.E. The meaning of variant and experimental marriage styles and family forms in the 1970's. *The Family Coordinator,* 1972, **21**, 375-381.

Varley, B.K. Future shock and the mental health professions. Paper presented at the Southwestern Regional Meeting, American Orthopsychiatric Association, Galveston, Texas, November, 1972.

Wolpe, J. *The practice of behavior therapy.* New York: Pergamon, 1969.

Additional Selected Readings

Barlow, D.H. & Agras, W.S. Fading to increase heterosexual responsiveness in homo-sexuals, *Journal of Applied Behavior Analysis,* 1973, **6**, 355-366.

Barlow, D.H., Agras, W.S., Abel, G.G., Blanchard, E.B., and Young, L.D. Biofeedback and reinforcement to increase heterosexual arousal in homosexuals, *Behaviour Research and Therapy,* 1975, **13**, 45-50.

Canton-Dutari, A. Combined intervention for controlling unwanted homosexual behavior, *Archives of Sexual Behavior,* 1974, **3**, 367-371.

Davison, G.C. & Wilson, G.T. Attitudes of behavior therapists toward homosexuality, *Behavior Therapy,* 1973, **4**, 686-696.

Denholtz, M.S. An extension of covert procedures in the treatment of male homosexuals, *Journal of Behavior Therapy and Experimental Psychiatry,* 1973, **4**, 305.

Feldman, M.P. & MacCulloch, M.J. Avoidance conditioning for homosexuals: A reply to MacDonough's critique, *Behavior Therapy,* 1972, **3**, 430-436.

Feldman, M.P. & MacCulloch, M.J. *Homosexual behavior: Therapy and assessment.* Oxford: Pergamon, 1971.

Freeman, W. & Meyer, R.G. A behavioral alteration of a sexual preferences in the human male, *Behavior Therapy,* 1975, **6**, 206-212.

Gray, J. Case conference: Behavior therapy in a patient with homosexual anxiety, *Journal of Behavior Therapy and Experimental Psychiatry,* 1970, **1**, 225-232.

Herman, S.H., Barlow, D.H., & Agras, W.S. An experimental analysis of classical condi-tioning as a method of increasing heterosexual arousal in homosexuals, *Behavior Therapy,* 1974, **5**, 33-47.

Hinichsen, J.J. & Katahn, M. Recent trends and new developments in the treatment of homosexuality, *Psychotherapy: Theory, research and practice,* 1975, **12**, 83-92.

Kendrick, S.R. & McCulloch, J.P. Sequential phases of covert reinforcement and covert sensitization in the treatment of homosexuality, *Journal of Behavior Therapy and Experimental Psychiatry,* 1972, **3**, 229-231.

Larson, D.E. An adaptation of the Feldman and MacCulloch approach to treatment of homosexuality by the application of anticipatory avoidance learning, *Behaviour Research and Therapy,* 1970, **8**, 209-210.

MacCulloch, M.J., Birtles, C.J. & Feldman, M.P. Anticipatory avoidance learning for the treatment of homosexuality: Recent developments and an automatic aversion therapy system, *Behavior Therapy,* 1971, **2**, 151-169.

MacDonough, T.S. A critique of the first Feldman and MacCulloch avoidance conditioning treatment for homosexuals. *Behavior Therapy,* 1972, **3**, 104-111.

McConaghy, N. Aversive and positive conditioning treatments of homosexuality, *Behaviour Research and Therapy,* 1975, **13**, 309-319.

McConaghy, N. & Barr, R.F. Classical, avoidance and backward conditioning, *British Journal of Psychiatry,* 1973, **122**, 151-162.

Truner, R.K., James, S.R.N. & Orwin, A. A note on the internal consistency of the Sexual Orientation Method, *Behaviour Research and Therapy,* 1974, **12**, 273-278.

Fetishistic Behavior (Inanimate Objects)

Fetishistic behavior involves sexual attention and activity directed specifically toward an inanimate object—usually an item of clothing—or toward a particular part of the body. While most people may learn to associate a particular part of a body (such as breasts or buttocks) or clothing (such as a negligee) with sexual arousal and thus react erotically to that stimuli, fetishistic behaviors generally involves total involvement with the object to the exclusion of other sexual stimuli.

Usually the individual with a fetishistic orientation (almost always a man) involves the object in his masturbatory fantasies and/or activities, and may choose to ejaculate in or on the object.

One of the earlier articles to appear describing a behavioral approach to fetishistic behavior is Kushner's "The Reduction of a Long-Standing Fetish by Means of Aversive Conditioning." This case study demonstrates the use of aversive methods (electrical) to successfully eliminate a fetish involving women's underwear that lasted some 21 years. Once the fetishistic behavior and fantasy was eliminated, Kushner used a modification of desensitization to deal with the client's "impotence" in engaging in sexual intercourse.

The next case report by Bond and Evans describes "Avoidance Therapy: Its Use in Two Cases of Underwear Fetishism." Based on their review of the literature, the authors designed an approach-avoidance procedure utilizing faradic stimulation that produced rapid positive results in both uses. This article illustrates both the procedure, and an interesting follow-up method in which both clients were seen, after the major treatment had been completed, over progressively increasing periods of time (e.g., weekly for eight weeks, every two weeks for three sessions, and then once a month). This is probably the recommended method of termination for most programs in that the booster sessions increase resistance to extinction of desired behavior and reinforce the decrease in undesired behavior, while at the same time gradually decreasing the client's reliance on the therapist as he attempts new behaviors in the natural environment.

The final article in this section by Kolvin reports on "Aversive Imagery Treatment in Adolescents." Based on his own reluctance to use physical aversive methods, Kolvin developed the procedure of "Aversive Imagery Therapy." This consists of the evocation in imagination of the specific eroto-genic stimulus and the immediate disruption of it by the evocation of a noxious aversive stimulus (i.e., some stimulus or situation that was particu-larly aversive to the client). The article reports the use of this procedure with a fetishist (and a petrol addict), using as the aversive stimulus the fear of falling as dreamed by the client. Kolvin acknowledges that he used conven-tional supportive methods (psychotherapy) in conjunction with his behav-ioral procedure, so that the effects of both are confounded.

Of course, the similarities between this procedure and the more systematic covert sensitization (see Volume I) are probably obvious. While there were no single case reports such as Kolvin's involving the use of covert sensitization specifically with fetishistic behavior that could be located in the literature, it would seem that covert sensitization— for both theoretical and empirical reasons (such as the success of that procedure with similar problems)—to treat problems involving fetishistic behavior and other prob-lematic sexual behaviors to be described in subsequent sections would be a primary candidate for use when the situation involves the necessity for decreasing undesired sexual behaviors. This would seem especially so if the client and/or the therapist are reluctant to use actual physical stimuli such as involved in faradic stimulations, or when such equipment is not available.

50

The Reduction of a Long-Standing Fetish by Means of Aversive Conditioning

This is a case study of the successful treatment of a fetish of approximately 21-years' duration. The patient was a 33-year-old male whose alcoholic father deserted the family when he was a child and who, from the age of about four or five, experienced a series of placements in relatives' homes, foster homes, orphanages, day camps and so forth. He described his mother as probably being a schizophrenic who blamed the Communists for her difficulties and who felt everyone had a double, good and bad. He was the middle child of three boys. He places the onset of his fetishistic behavior at about 12 years of age. This consisted of his masturbating while wearing women's panties that he usually took from clothes lines. If these were not available, he masturbated when stimulated by pictures of scantily clad women or by fantasies of women wearing panties. He was a shy, retiring child and as he grew older he became more aware of the abnormal nature of his behavior, felt increasingly inadequate and unmasculine, and resorted to body-building and boxing as a means of proving his virility. After a brief period in the Marine Corps and two failures at attempted intercourse, wherein he found himself impotent, the patient consciously set forth to prove his virility by joining a tough gang, drinking, brawling, and earning the reputation of being a "cop fighter." As a result of assaulting a policeman he was sentenced to a reformatory for 26 months. A few years later, while slightly intoxicated and influenced by a friend of his from the reformatory, he broke into a hotel room, stole some luggage, was apprehended, and sentenced to six years in prison. While incarcerated he was removed from the exciting stimuli and the fetishistic attraction was considerably reduced. He rejected the overtures of the prison "wolves" but wondered why he was so often singled out as their homosexual target. Following this sentence he asked for treatment for his perversion. He recognized that while the fetishism did not directly get him involved with the law, it was nevertheless responsible for his antisocial behavior as a compensatory mechanism. When he began treatment he was tense, tormented and obsessed by the impulses, and increasingly guilt-ridden and self-depreciative following the act. He was bright and very well motivated for treatment. He had had no previous treatment.

A number of factors determined this particular choice of treatment, that is, the attempt to reduce symptoms through aversive conditioning. First, formal psycho-analytical treatment, the conventional treatment of choice for such a condition, was not available. Second, other methods appear to have been unsuccessful since there are only four cases in the entire psychiatric literature claiming a cure (Raymond, 1960) and, finally, the author had become particularly interested in the application of learning theory principles to clinical problems. The fetishistic behavior was conceptualized as being the product of maladaptive learning and it was proposed to extinguish the symptoms through aversive conditioning by means of electric shock.

It was recognized that a danger existed in possibly conditioning the patient adversively to normal sexual stimuli. As such, careful discriminations would have to be made in the procedure. It was also verbalized to the patient that masturbation per se was not being attacked, but rather the type of fantasies and the acting-out with which it was associated. The idea of "panties-woman" was also differentiated from "panties-masturbation" or "wearing panties." No efforts were made to deal with the patient's problems from the conventional "dynamic" point of view.

TREATMENT

The first two sessions were spent in obtaining a history. The patient recalled that the onset of the disturbing behavior occurred when he became curious and sexually excited watching girls sliding down a sliding-board with their panties exposed. It was at this same period in time that he was introduced to masturbation and he soon recognized experiencing similar sensations as when he watched the girls. His fantasies during masturbation quickly were centered about the girls and their panties and shortly this association was firmly made. This explanation for the development of such a fetish is certainly more parsimonious than the "dynamic" explanations involving castration threat, symbolism and so forth. The above explanation for his behavior was briefly explained to the patient as well as the general approach and rationale that were to be used. He understood the method and was strongly motivated to undertake the treatment regimen.

On the third session, the patient was connected to a Grayson-Stadler PGR apparatus by means of two fingertip electrodes. A conditioning circuit was used to establish a baseline for this shock. Adjustments in the circuit had to be made that still did not deliver as strong a shock as desired, but since it was experienced as uncomfortable it was decided to proceed. Approximately three-and-one-half melliamperes were delivered.

At each session, anywhere from four to six different stimuli were presented, immediately followed by shock. The patient was instructed to tolerate the shock until it became so uncomfortable that he wanted it stopped. He was then to signal for termination of the shock by saying "Stop." Twelve such stimuli were presented each session in random order. Approximately one minute elapsed between the sensation of the shock and the presentation of the next stimulus. The stimuli consisted of a magazine-size picture of the rear view of a woman from the middle of the back to the knees wearing panties; an actual pair of panties which was placed in his hand; and imaginal situations in which the patient was asked to imagine himself wearing panties, imagining a clothes line with panties on it, and imagining himself standing in front of a lingerie shop window. The picture and the panties were always used, with the imaginal situations varying at each session depending upon his reports of particular areas of sensitivity. Discussion was limited as much as possible to the patient's response to the shock and his reaction to the fetish between visits. Each session lasted between twenty and thirty minutes. He was seen three times a week.

After 41 shock sessions (14 weeks of treatment) conditioning was halted since the patient reported no longer being troubled by the fetish. Changes in the intensity of the fetishistic attraction and behavior were reported as early as the second shock session and progressed gradually with increases and decreases in the degree to which the patient was troubled by them. These fluctuations frequently reflected the degree of anxiety generated by extra-treatment conditions. Heightened anxiety often resulted in an increase in the fetishistic behavior that could conceivably be considered an important means by which the patient had learned to reduce the effects of tension and stress. As progress developed, the patient indicated that he had more and more difficulty in eliciting fetishistic fantasies during his masturbation. Soon, the nagging quality of the urges, the self-conflict and torment that accompanied his submission to these urges, and the self-depreciation that went along with it, were markedly reduced. Approximately one month following the termination of the shock sessions, spontaneous recovery of the fetishistic behavior occurred, but in a much milder form than the original. The patient was prepared for this in advance by the therapist and was not discouraged. It was decided to give him a reinforcement or booster session as suggested by Raymond (1960). About two days later when the patient appeared for the booster session he reported no longer being disturbed. Nevertheless, two successive reinforcement sessions were given for good measure.

By this time visits were spaced weekly and during the next phase of treatment the patient's impotence was dealt with. The desensitization approach reported by Wolpe (1958) was utilized and the impotence was relieved quickly to the extent that the patient is now leading a full and satisfactory heterosexual life. In brief, this approach considers the sexual difficulties to be related to high anxiety states that the patient associates with this activity. In order to reduce this anxiety he is instructed to engage in sex play and stimulation with his partner but is told that he is under no circumstances to attempt to engage in intercourse. This immediately results in a lessening of anxiety since it precludes failure. After a few such contacts the patient is further relaxed and as a result is more sexually responsive. He is told that only when he has both a very strong erection and an overwhelming desire to have intercourse is he to do so and then he is to enter immediately and let himself go, disregarding efforts to prolong the act or to try to please his partner. If instructions are followed expressly success is readily achieved that allows for a continued development of satisfactory coital expression. As can be recognized, this approach requires the full cooperation and understanding of the female partner.

Three months following the reinforcement sessions, the patient was to appear in court for two driving offenses, one of which could possibly result in a jail sentence. He was naturally apprehensive and tense, and indicated that he had been thinking of the fetish again although he could readily dismiss it from his mind. It is possible that, due to the stress he was under, he resorted to his long-term method of seeking gratification and stress reduction, that is, through the fetish. One more reinforcement session was therefore given. The court hearing worked out satisfactorily and, after an eighteen-month follow-up, he no longer complained about the fetish.

At last report the patient is married and has a family and reports that he is doing well. He indicates that he has occasional fleeting thoughts of the fetish or is reminded of it when exposed at times to advertisements, and so forth, but he has no difficulty in thinking of other things and does not dwell upon it as in the past. He reports that occasionally when either fatigued or sexually unexcited he resorts to the fetishistic fantasies in order to attain a climax during intercourse. These instances are not the rule, however, and nevertheless would represent a substantial improvement over his former condition.

The Minnesota Multiphasic Personality Inventory was administered three times during the course of treatment: first, at the time of admission; second, 14 weeks later at the point at which the aversive conditioning phase was terminated following the initial reduction in the fetishistic impulses; and third, as a follow-up measure six months later. The findings reflect no basic change in the personality make-up that is primarily of an obsessive, schizoid type. However, there was a notable reduction in the inner conflicts, together with a marked reduction in the aggressive acting-out components that were so evident in the first two records. Along with this, some of his suspicious and distrustful attitudes toward society were reduced. The Taylor Manifest Anxiety Scale taken from the three records also reflects a steady decrement in anxiety level. All in all, both behaviorally and psychometrically, the patient was less anxious, more relaxed, and there was considerably less conflict than when he was first seen.

This approach directly attacks the widely held and strongly entrenched position that symptoms serve a defensive purpose and/or are indicative of underlying disturbance. Such being the case they must not be removed without first substituting new defenses lest more serious decompensation occur or other disabling symptoms take their place. Prohibition against the removal of fetishistic objects has been raised by Freud (1928) and Stekel (1930) who believed that homosexuality would result. It was also felt that impotence or strong sadistic drives would result from their removal. In this particular case, homosexuality has not occurred. To the contrary, this man is no longer impotent and enjoys a very active heterosexual life and has so far no difficulty with acting-out aggressive impulses. Recent works by Raymond (1960), Eysenck (1960), Franks (1958), Sylvester and Liversedge (1960), and others strongly support the application of experimentally validated procedures based upon learning theory to clinical material and offer considerable evidence to refute objections such as those raised. Raymond (1960), in a case similar to this, successfully treated a fetishist by giving an emetic drug every two hours day and night for a week in conjunction with the fetishistic object. A nineteen-month follow-up revealed no recurrence of the perverted behavior.

In retrospect, it is felt that perhaps a stronger shock might have further reduced the time of treatment. An increase in the number of trials per session might likewise contribute to this end. Also, in the future, should the opportunity again present itself, partial reinforcement will be utilized with the expectation of greater prevention of extinction of the new response.

This case points up the efficacy of such an approach, rooted in a substantial body of experimentally validated material, on a condition heretofore highly refractory to psychotherapeutic intervention. Its promising application to disorders of a compulsive nature should be investigated further.

REFERENCES

Eysenck, H.J. (Ed.) *Behaviour therapy and the neuroses.* New York: Pergamon, 1960.
Franks, C.M. Alcohol, alcoholism and conditioning: A review of the literature and some

theoretical considerations. *J. ment. Sci.*, 1958, **104**, 14-33.

Franks, C.M. Conditioning and abnormal behavior. In H.J. Eysenck (Ed.) *Handbook of abnormal psychology*. New York: Basic Books, 1961, 457-487.

Freud, S. Fetishism. *Int. J. Psycho-anal.*, 1928, **9**, 161-166.

Raymond, M.J. A case of fetishism treated by aversion therapy. In H.J. Eysenck. (Ed.), *Behaviour therapy and the neuroses*. New York: Pergamon, 1960, 303-311.

Stekel, W. *Sexual aberrations: The phenomena of fetishism in relation to sex*. New York: Liveright, 1930 (2 vols.).

Sylvester, J.D. & Liversedge, L.A. Conditioning and occupational cramps. In Eysenck, H.J. (Ed.), *Behaviour therapy and the neuroses*. New York: Pergamon, 1960, 334-348.

Wolpe, J. *Psychotherapy by reciprocal inhibition*. Stanford, Stanford, Calif.: Stanford University Press, 1958.

51

Avoidance Therapy: Its Use in Two Cases of Underwear Fetishism

I.K. BOND and D.R. EVANS

During the past decade several attempts have been made to treat fetishism by aversion therapy (McGuire & Vallance, 1964; Rachman, 1961; Raymond & O'Keefe, 1965). Fetishism, like alcoholism (Evans & Day, 1966), may be considered as a learned response, which by the time of treatment is an habitual response. Support for this contention may be seen in the finding that conventional therapy has little effect in the treatment of this malady, while aversion therapy has proved more successful. The treatment pattern to be reported here was designed to further increase the potency of aversion therapy. The regimen is the result of a critical review of earlier methods and recent findings in learning theory.

CASE HISTORIES

Case 1

G.W., a 16-year-old Protestant, Canadian male, was first seen in February 1966. He was suffering from a fetish to female underwear, namely brassieres and panties. An only child of middle-class parents, he was adopted at the age of 21 months. Nothing is known of his genetic antecedents, but it is interesting that he was a hyperkinetic child. The boy had always been rather "cold," withdrawn and odd, but was not considered psychotic. It was though that he demonostrated a character disorder invariably found in sexual deviates. The boy was of average intelligence but his scholastic record was poor, as he was apathetic and without ambition. Physical examination was negative. His fetishistic activities began at the age of 11, and he had been "acting out" on the average of twice monthly since that time. His technique was to raid clothes lines at a distance from his home. At first he stole the articles and hid them some distance from the scene; he did not don them or masturbate with them. Of late he had taken to tearing up the objects, often on the spot, and this change in behavior seemed to be activated by aggressive sexual fantasies. He alleged that he had never masturbated, thus lacking the normal history of masturbation for a boy of his age.

His fantasies were heterosexual and fetishistic, and he showed no evidence of other deviations. His father was rather obsessive and domineering, the mother gentle and compliant; but there was no evidence that their handling of the boy had any etiological importance. As in all displacement phenomena, G.W. was more likely to "act out" when aroused or frustrated. He was finally expelled from school as a result of raiding girls' lockers and eventually was charged in the Juvenile Court. He was sent to stay with relatives in another province, but his abnormal activities continued unabated. After eight months of psychotherapy, including treatment with drugs without benefit, he was referred for behavior therapy.

Case 2.

F.B. was first seen in March 1966. He was a 19-year-old, single Canadian male, of the Roman Catholic faith. His home life was one of deprivation. He was an only child; his father deserted the household before he was born. His relationship with his mother was not good, and at 17 he moved into the home of an aunt. He was of average intelligence but at age 17 had reached only grade 10. He had been employed as a newspaper office boy, shipper and punch press operator. A serious industrial accident in September 1965 resulted in loss of most of the fingers of his left hand.

F.B. had formed a sexual liaison with a 27-year-old separated woman with five children. She gave birth to a sixth an illegitimate child fathered by the patient. This infant suffered from a cardiac abnormality. F.B. abandoned his mistress and became promiscuous; he recently had a venereal infection. He was a primitive individual, with the character disorder of inadequacy and immaturity. His fetishism had begun only two years previously at the age of 17 and consisted of raiding clothes lines for panties and slips approximately once a month, which he fondled while masturbating. These activities increased when he was frustrated in his normal sexual activities. At the age of 17 he was an exhibitionist for a brief period, but this activity was curtailed following treatment and he began his fetishistic activities. He was physically fit, and appeared to be normally heterosexual except for his deviation. He had not received any consistent psychiatric treatment for his fetishism before the treatment described in this report.

THEORETICAL CONSIDERATIONS

The majority of early attempts to treat fetishism by avoidance therapy involved the pairing of the fetishistic object with the noxious effect of apomorphine (Cooper, 1963; McGuire & Vallance, 1964; Rachman, 1961; Raymond, 1956). Recent work by Barker (1965) has shown that faradic stimulation or shock is to be preferred to apomorphine as the avoidance stimulus. His major point is that the temporal contiguity between the deviant response and the avoidance stimulus is more easily controlled when shock is employed. As a result of these opinions, more recent attempts to treat fetishism by avoidance therapy have used the pairing of the deviant response with shock (Feldman, 1966; Kushner 1965; Oswald, 1962).

All the studies reported above had been based on a classical conditioning pattern in which the deviant response was paired with a noxious stimulus. Solomon and Brush (1956) cite extensive evidence to suggest that an instrumental pattern in the form of avoidance conditioning should be preferred to classical aversive conditioning. According to his two-process avoidance theory, Solomon (1964) indicates that less extinction occurs when the avoidance response is followed by a second response.

Church (1963) showed that a two-choice situation, in which one response is punished and the other is not, leads to facilitation of response differentiation. Others, such as Kushner (1965), have indicated that booster sessions at varous intervals following aversion or avoidance therapy are required to maintain suppression of the deviant response.

In an attempt to incorporate the recent advances in aversion (avoidance) therapy and learning theory. Evans and Day (1966) designed an instrumental avoidance treatment for alcoholic drinking behavior. This present report concerns a modification of the above procedure applied to the treatment of two underwear fetishists.

In a review of avoidance conditioning, Feldman and MacCulloch (1965) concluded that anticipatory avoidance learning is to be preferred over other forms of avoidance conditioning because the technique produces good acquisition and a very high resistance to extinction. For this reason the method to be reported was designed as an approach avoidance pattern. It was also designed to incorporate those variables outlined by Feldman and MacCulloch (1965) which contribute to resistance to extinction of the avoidance response. It will be noted, for example, that partial reinforcement is employed because the method is instrumental in nature.

It was decided that the conditioned stimulus would be the handling of underwear because it is the first step in the response chain when the patient steals underwear. As reason gives way to action during such an incident (Steffy, 1965), it was thought more appropriate to develop a conditioned response of avoiding underwear rather than entreat the patient to exert cortical control as would be done in psychotherapy.

TREATMENT PROGRAM

After the history had been taken on the two patients they were given the treatment program. The apparatus consisted of a two-compartment dispenser box. Under each compartment was a light, which indicated to the subject which object was to be taken. The fetishistic objects were placed in the first compartment and the neutral objects were placed in the other compartment. The therapist was equipped with a control box with two three-position switches. The three positions of each switch were: light with shock; off; light. In the light-with-shock position an electric shock was given to the patient at a given delay after the light went on. The delay was controlled by a Hunter decade interval timer, and the shock was initiated with a Hunter shock stimulator. The shock electrodes were attached to the ring and index fingers of the subject's nonpreferred hand. The shock was set in each session at 10 volts higher than the subject's reported upper threshold.

The first compartment contained 20 fetishistic objects and the second compartment contained 20 neutral objects, such as matches, a cigarette box, a pencil, and so forth. The fetishistic objects were presented in random order, with the exception that no more than two such objects fell in succession. A neutral object was presented after each fetishistic object or objects if two fell together. The remaining places in the 40 item session were neutral objects. The neutral objects were never associated with shock, and the fetishistic objects were related with shock on a 70 percent schedule. Eight such sessions were held on a weekly basis, and each session lasted about 30 minutes. The delay for the first two sessions was 6 seconds, the next two 4.5 seconds, the next two 3.0 seconds, and the final two 1.5 seconds.

The patients were instructed to remove one object from a compartment whenever the light under a compartment went on. The object was to be placed in a box provided at the patient's preferred side. As soon as the object was placed in the box, shock was terminated.

RESULTS

Case 1.

The patient agreed to cooperate in the treatment program. He was seen on a weekly basis for eight sessions and by the third session he no longer reported any urges to steal underwear. He was then seen for three twice-weekly sessions and he is now seen on a monthly basis, after which he will be seen every three months until February 1967. It will be remembered that before treatment he raided lines twice weekly and the urge to do so was continuous. Since the initiation of treatment (six months) no further incidents have occurred and since March 1966 he has no urge to act out.

Case 2.

The patient agreed to cooperate in the treatment offered. As in the first case, he was seen on a weekly basis for eight weeks and reported no urge to act out after the fourth session. He was then seen every two weeks for three sessions, and is now seen once a month. As in the first case, no further acting out has occurred since the initiation of his treatment and he has had no urge to do so since May 1966.

DISCUSSION

While the patients are still in therapy, the major part of their treatment has been concluded. They are now going through a process of booster sessions in an effort to maintain their immunity from the deviant response. This procedure, strangely enough, is reminiscent of the treatment for allergies with allergens. In comparison to their former states, the patients have to date shown encouragingly normal behavior. It is probable that if they can abstain from their deviant behavior for a sufficient period of time, normal outlets for the control of sexual arousal will develop. It has been found that variations on this theme are most useful in the treatment of homosexuality, pedophilia, exhibitionism, voyeurism and other forms of sexual deviation.

SUMMARY

A pilot study in the use of a modified form of avoidance therapy in the treatment of fetishism is described. The theory and method are reported in conjunction with their use and result in two cases of underwear fetishism.

REFERENCES

Barker, J.C. *Brit. J. Psychiat.,* 1965, **111**, 268.

Cooper, A.J. *Brit. J. Psychiat.,* 1963, **109**, 649.

Church, R.M. *Psychol. Rev.,* 1963, **17**, 369.

Evans, D.R. & Day, H.I. A preliminary report on conditioning of an avoidance response to alcohol drinking. Paper presented at the annual meeting of the Canadian Psychological Association, Montreal, June 1-3, 1966.

Feldman, M.P. *Psychol. Bull.,* 1966, **65**, 65.

Feldman, M.P. & MacCulloch, M.J. *Behav. Res. Ther.,* 1965, **2**, 165.

Kushner, M. The reduction of a long-standing fetish by means of aversive conditioning. In: Case studies in behaviour modification edited by L.P. Ullmann and L. Krasner, 1965, Holt, Rinehart and Winston, Inc., New York: p. 239.

McGuire, R.J. & Vallance, M. *Brit. Med. J.,* 1964, **1**, 151.

Oswald, I. *J. Ment. Sci.,* 1962, **108**, 196.

Rachman, S. *Amer. J. Psychiat.,* 1961, **118**, 235.

Raymond, M.J. *Brit. Med. J.,* 1956, **2**, 854.

Raymond, M. & O'Keefe, K. *Brit. J. Psychiat.,* 1965, **111**, 579.

Solomon, R.L. *Amer. Psychol.,* 1964, **19**, 239.

Solomon, R.L. & Brush, E.S. Experimentally derived conceptions of anxiety and aversion. In: Nebraska symposium on motivation, edited by M.R. Jones, University of Nebraska Press, Lincoln, Neb., 1956, 212.

Steffy, R.A. A plan for an aversive conditioning therapy for pedophile offenders. Papers presented at the meeting of Correctional Psychologists, Montreal, August 29, 1965.

52
"Aversive Imagery" Treatment in Adolescents

ISRAEL KOLVIN

INTRODUCTION

Adolescents with persistent compulsive disorders or disorders with a compulsive component have always constituted a major psychotherapeutic problem. Generally, the response to traditional psychotherapy has not been impressive, but it is especially poor in the intellectually dull and verbally unforthcoming. The author knows of no published work which claim any measure of success with this later group.

In these circumstances he was led to an *exploration* of a variation of behavior therapy. Both chemical and electrical physical aversion techniques have now been widely used for such conditions as alcoholism and sexual perversions (Rachman, 1965). However, due to a reluctance to use physical methods with adolescents, the author considered possible ways of deconditioning the unwanted behavior by the use of noxious aversive stimuli at an imagery level.

The inspiration for the technique derives from three major sources—first, Wolpe (1958) in his description of psychotherapy by reciprocal inhibition indicated it was not necessary to present actual objects; Franks (1958) pointed out that it was not essential to use a nausea-inducing agent to produce conditioned aversion; and finally Lazarus and Abramowitz (1962) used "emotive imagery" in the treatment of children's phobias.

"Aversive Imagery Therapy" essentially consists of the evocation, in the imagination, of the specific erotogenic or compulsive stimulus and the immediate disruption of it by the evocation of a noxious aversive stimulus.

An account is given here of a fetishist and a petrol addict.

METHOD

The patient's help was enlisted in drawing up a list of "dislikes" which consisted of situations or experiences which were for him unpleasant. The only use made of this list was to ascertain for the particular patient the maximum noxious stimuli. In addition, an attempt was made to ascertain the precise fetishist situation.

Thereafter, the patient was taken into a darkened consulting room where he reclined on a couch and closed his eyes. He was encouraged to conjure up imagery according to a story related by the therapist. Empirically it was found that vivid imagery was more easily produced when the adolescent was in a relaxed state. A colorful story of the crucial event was now presented and the patient was asked to visualize accordingly. By careful observation it became apparent when the patient was just becoming affectively excited, i.e., motor tension, breathing, expression, etc. At this stage the aversive image was introduced, in a suggestive and vividly descriptive manner. The response was immediate and in the main reflected in the patient's expression of distaste. In this way the full erotically toned course of events was truncated and the sequence of events unpleasantly anticlimaxed.

With the fetishist, outpatient sessions were conducted twice weekly; this was determined by geographical considerations. With the petrol addict, the sessions were undertaken daily for 5 days a week. Each session consisted of two to four trials. In the case of the fetishist, the treatment was supplemented by an exposition of the biology and psychology of normal sexual behavior, and simple explanations and reassurance and indications of how to advance toward achieving socially acceptable heterosexual relationships.

THE PATIENTS

Case X, Fetishist Aged 14

The parents separated following an unhappy and argumentative marriage. The father is reported to be an irresponsible, unstable and inadequate psychopath. Mother is an intelligent, warm and insightful person who has managed to maintain reasonable standards in the face of considerable economic adversity.

X was the fourth child. His early development was normal. The first discordant note was the presence of severe shyness in the immediate preschool period followed by some excessive anxiety on first attending school. At school his progress was poor and he was described as academically slow. Then at the local secondary school he was considered educationally backward and found his way into the lowest stream. At this latter school he stole a sum of money from one of the teachers and was placed on probation for one year; he apparently complied satisfactorily with the terms of the probation order.

At the age of 14 he was charged with indecent assault on three women. It was suspected that he had committed a further series of similar offenses which the victims had not reported. X's description of the acts suggests that they were essentially unplanned. On certain occasions when he saw a young woman wearing a skirt, he would be overcome by a kind of trembling and other emotions which he did not have the language to describe; he would feel compelled to run after her and put his hand up under her clothes. He would then run away trembling with exhilaration, excitement and fear.

His mother described him as a quiet, shy, solitary boy who is prone to be solemn and sulky. She added that he erected barriers around himself and it was difficult to get through to him.

At the clinic he revealed himself as a serious-minded person, pleasant but shy, timid, reserved and verbally unforthcoming. He reluctantly admitted to anxiety and guilt about his frequent masturbation and also reported a number of frightening dreams. On the Mill Hill Vocabulary Scale (1948) he was rated as grade V and on the Progressive Matrices (1938) he was rated as grade IV. During the course of the early interviews the boy denied any psychosexual knowledge. His problems were explored with him during a psycho-therapeutic approach but progress was limited. This was thought to be due to the boy's dullness and inaccessibility. He remained plagued by the urge to commit the above-mentioned acts. At this stage it was decided to decondition him with an aversive technique.

His list of unpleasant experiences included some food fads and other minor dislikes, but the only major distressful situation for him was falling in his dreams and looking down from a precarious situation or from a great height. It was decided to use this unpleasant falling experience from his dreams as the noxious stimulus. Seven half-hour sessions were undertaken over a period of 3 weeks. One month later some reinforcement was administered. Toward the end of therapy the mother reported that the boy was more approachable, less difficult and less inclined to sulk. The probation officer who had known him for some time claimed that there was some evidence of "a growing maturity." The boy denied experiencing any further compulsive urges.

Case Y. Petrol Addict Aged 15

At the time of referral Y was at a residential school for the educationally subnormal. There he was described as a sensible, even-tempered youth, hardworking to the extent of being obsessional and extremely stable except in the area of his addiction. On occasions, after sniffing the petrol, he would pass out completely; and it was these attacks of unconsciousness which eventually after some 7 years, brought the addiction to light. Y had even gone to the length of breaking into a shed in order to obtain petrol.

At interview, the school's description was confirmed. He was a sturdily built youth who proved to be intense but friendly, forthcoming to a limited extent, and intellectually dull. He denied sipping the petrol though he did admit to having once tasted it. He said he enjoyed the smell of it. In addition, it both made him feel "smashing" and also resulted in what can be described as expansive visual hallucinatory experiences in the form of cowboy pictures. He preferred being on his own because this provided him with the opportunity of seeking out petrol. His main interests were television, work and snooker.

The background history is as follows—Y's milestones, except for late speech development, were apparently normally achieved. The school psychologist reported that in the early school years he was stubborn and difficult but these remitted on his admission to the residential E.S.N. school. His I.Q. (Terman-Merrill) was 63. His EEG was slightly immature.

The family is an intellectually dull one—both parents are dull, and two other siblings are educationally subnormal. The parents are described as reliable and conscientious farmworkers.

There were grave doubts about whether any form of treatment would be efficacious because of Y's intelligence and his persistence. It was eventually decided to try a form of aversion therapy. A list of unpleasant experiences was obtained, but, as in the first case, his main aversion concerned heights and falling. Again, this was used as a noxious stimulus. Twenty half-hour sessions were undertaken on consecutive days except for weekends.

Thirteen months after the completion of treatment the patient is well and has not returned to his petrol-sniffing habits. This is indeed satisfactory in view of Ackerley and Gibson's (1964) statement in their review of a dozen cases of lighter-fluid sniffing: "Up to the present time the social agencies' and Juvenile Courts' methods of controlling the long-standing 'sniffers' who can be considered addicted have not been successful."

PROGRESS

Soon after the initiation of treatment both patients became mildly distressed. They then asserted that they were no longer experiencing the unwanted urges and claimed that they would no longer act in the undesirable manner. (This closely parallels Raymond's experience with adult fetishists.) They were persuaded to remain in therapy and completed the course of treatment without any further untoward reactions.

When there was evidence that a distaste or an aversion had developed (at the imagery level) for the compulsive and sexually provocative situation, the close supervision of the boys was relaxed. Both reported that the previous urges and desires had completely disappeared.

FOLLOW-UP

The length of follow-up is indicated below:

> Petrol addict 13 months, no relapse reported.
> Fetishist 11 months quite well. 13 months after the completion of treatment he accused a neighbor's wife of an illicit affair. When confronted, he claimed that he had been misled by a friend and that he had behaved "stupidly." That this may not be the reflection of a highly moral attitude but a different expression of a sexual problem has to be borne in mind. 17 months afterwards, X working and apparently quite well.

DISCUSSION

Adolescents suffering from perversion or addictions are nearly always a major treatment problem. Though many drop this behavior once it comes to light, or alternatively, rapidly respond to probationary supervision or simple measures instituted at a psychiatric clinic, there is a small percentage who do not respond. Unfortunately, up to the present, in this latter group the repertoire of treatments available has been small and their efficacy dubious. The aversive drug and shock therapies available for older perverts and addicts are, in relation to children and adolescents, still regarded with disfavor ethically and aesthetically by psychiatrists.

However, the writer considered these disorders so gravely handicapping and of such serious consequence to the adolescent, that any method that may be beneficial could not be lightly discarded. The benefits accruing from the removal of the symptoms in certain cases would far outweigh the moral and ethical objections, especially if more acceptable aversive techniques could be evolved. The use of aversive imagery was examined from this point of view; and in the case of this particular group of boys was considered worthy of exploration.

Some major criticisms of aversion techniques with sexual perversions is that they fail to remove the underlying psychopathology and in addition, could result in the patient developing an aversion to all sexual relations—even normal ones. The writer has tried to minimize this risk by supplementary explanations and reassurances about normal heterosexual relationships. He therefore combined both "aversive therapy" and psycho-therapy in the case of the fetishist. These are unusual but not unique bedfellows as a number of behavior therapists have recently expressed the view that it is "practical to submit some cases to both" concurrently (Meyer & Crisp, 1966; Gelder, 1964).

It must be admitted that aversive images are not ideal aversive stimuli. They have the disadvantage that the timing of the noxious stimulus is difficult; in this respect they can, however, be considered to be at least more accurate than aversive drug techniques. The technique also depends on the capacity of the patient for visual imagery and for life-equivalent autonomic responses to pleasant and unpleasant imagery. Then there are the inevitable questions about the propriety of using drug and faradic shocks with adolescents. In the writer's experience most parents of adolescents and the adolescents themselves are reluctant to consider any treatment which incorporates a form of punishment; in this respect faradic shocks are viewed more antipathetically. In the few cases, completed and current, there have been no serious objections to aversive imagery therapy. More problematic is the choice of the noxious stimuli—neither of the two boys had any major dislikes and the only important noxious situation for both was falling in their sleep and looking down from great heights. So far there has been no substitution of the disorder by any other specific type of behavioral or sexual abnormality.

It must be pointed out that in both cases the home, in spite of previous unsettlement, was at the time of referral to the clinic reasonably stable and supportive. It is impossible to say what part this has played in the apparent sustained improvement.

A method bearing some resemblance to the above was previously described by Gold and Neufeld (1965). The main difference and similarities of the two methods are delineated in the following table.

Table 1

The Gold & Neufeld Technique	The Kolvin Technique
A. 4 components	A. 3 components
1. Relaxation.	1. Relaxation.
2. Desenzitization technique to over-come fears of failure.	2. Aversive imagery.
3. Imaginary aversive therapy.	3. Psychotherapy.
4. Discrimination learning technique which teaches the patient to actively reject and choose the two alternatives presented in the same session.	

Table 1 (Cont.)

The Gold & Neufeld Technique		The Kolvin Technique	
B.	Imaginary therapy consists of a gradual deconditioning process	B.	Aversive Imagery consists of the evoca- of the compulsive or erotogenic stimu- lus and the immediate disruption of it by a noxious one.
C.	More elaborate technique	C.	Less elaborate technique.

SUMMARY

A technique of "Aversive Imagery" in the treatment of intellectually dull and verbally unforthcoming adolescents is described. Two cases are discussed, namely a fetishist and a petrol addict. With the fetishist the treatment was supplemented by psychosexual instruction, education and reassurance about acceptable heterosexual relationships. The fetishist recovered in eight sessions, the petrol addict in twenty sessions. Later inquiries revealed no relapses but the fetishist merits prolonged follow-up.

Acknowledgment: I should like to thank Dr. V. Pillai for his help in one of the above cases, and Miss L.J. Wright of the Newcastle Child Psychiatry Unit for her secretarial assistance. I am also grateful to Dr. A.W. Drummond and Dr. P. Leyburn for referring the above cases. Also Mr. I. Mottahedin for advice on certain theoretical aspects.

REFERENCES

Ackerly, W.C. & Gibson, G. Lighter fluid "sniffing." *Am. J. Psychiat.,* 1964, **120,** 1056-1061.

Franks, C.M. Alcohol, alcoholics and conditioning. *J. ment. Sci.,* 1958, **104,** 14-33.

Gelder, M.G. Behaviour therapy and psychotherapy for phobic disorders. Paper read at *Sixth int. Congr. Psychother.,* London, 1964.

Gold, S. & Neufeld, I.L. A learning approach to the treatment of homosexuality. *Behav. Res. & Therapy.* 1965, 2, 201-204.

Lazarus, A. & Abramovitz, A. The use of "emotive imagery" in the treatment of children's phobias. *J. ment. Sci.,* 1962, **108,** 191-195.

Meyer, V. & Crisp, A.H. Some problems in behaviour therapy. *Br. J. Psychiat.,* 1966, **112,** 367-381.

Rachman, S. Aversion therapy: Chemical or electrical? *Behav. Res. & Therapy.* 1965, 2, 289-300.

Raymond, M.J. Case of fetishism treated by aversion therapy. *Br. med.J.* 1956, 2, 854-856.

Wolpe, J. *Psychotherapy by reciprocal inhibition.* Stanford: University Press, 1958.

Additional Selected Readings

Clark, D.F. Fetishism treated by negative conditioning, *British Journal of Psychiatry,* 1963, **109**, 404-407.

Marks, Isaac M. & Gelder, M.G. Transvestism and fetishism: Clinical and psychological changes during faradic aversion, *British Journal of Psychiatry*, 1963, **109**, 711-729.

Rachman, S. Sexual fetishism: An experimental analogue, *Psychological Record,* 1966, **16**, 293-296.

Raymond, M. & O'Keeffe, K. A case of pin-up fetishism treated by aversion conditioning, *British Journal of Psychiatry*, 1965, **111**, 579-581.

Stevenson, Ian, & Wolpe, Joseph. Recovery from sexual deviations through overcoming non-sexual neurotic responses, *American Journal of Psychiatry,* 1960, **116**, 737-742.

Strzyzewsky, J. & Zierhoffer, M. Aversion therapy in a case of fetishism with transvestistic component, *The Journal of Sex Research,* 1967, **3**, No. 2, 163-167.

Cross-Dressing Behavior

Cross-dressing behavior (usually performed only by men)—often called "transvestitism"—involves achieving sexual enjoyment from wearing the clothes characteristic of the opposite sex.* According to Kinsey's (1948) data, very few men who engage in transvestite behavior seek or desire sexual contacts with other men. Rather, they are heterosexually oriented men who get erotic satisfaction from being perceived as a woman by themselves or others.

The article by Gershman involves "A Transvestite Fantasy Treated by Thought-Stopping, Covert Sensitization and Aversive Shock." The client was a 22-year-old college student with a cross-dressing fantasy whose origin apparently dated back to preschool days. In six sessions, the fantasy was successfully eliminated by a combined use of thought-stopping, covert sensitization and aversive shock. In the conclusion of the article, a case conference discusses questions concerning goals, procedures, timing of approaches and practical issues. As with all case studies, especially those using multiple techniques, the issue of what produced the successful outcome cannot be clearly delineated. For the clinician—who can simply replicate the program modifying it when necessary—whose main concern is alleviating the client's stressful situation, this is probably less of a problem than it is for the researchers whose job it is to ferret out which of the procedures if any are most responsible for any changes produced, or whether the entire package may be necessary. Of course, the process is a highly reciprocal one as clinicians feed data into researchers' programs and researchers present their results to clinicians who then attempt to test them out in actual practice.

The second article dealing with the problem of cross-dressing behavior is

---

*In contrast, those individuals with a transsexual orientation may wear the clothes of the "opposite" sex; however, they *perceive* themselves as of that sex, and, further, usually get no particular erotic gratification from the clothes.

Lambley's "Treatment of Transvestism and Subsequent Coital Problems." In this case, successful heterosexual behavior was established in a 26-year-old man who was manifesting undesired cross-dressing behavior by means of rewards for heterosexual imagery and planned heterosexual encounters. Subsequently, erectile failure was eliminated by use of a series of *in vivo* graduated sexual experiences, and ejaculatory failure was successfully treated by orgasmic reconditioning.

REFERENCES

Kinsey, A.C., Pomeroy, W.B. and Martin, C.E. *Sexual behavior in the human male.* Philadelphia: W.B. Saunders, 1948.

53

Case Conference: A Transvestite Fantasy
Treated by Thought-Stopping, Covert Sensitization
and Aversive Shock*

LOUIS GERSHMAN

Mr. M., 22, is a college senior who complained of a transvestite fantasy that dominated his sex life. This had been treated unsuccessfully at a Psychological Services Center before he was referred to me for behavior therapy. Since the case involves only six sessions, I shall describe what took place at each of these.

FIRST SESSION

Early recollections date back to a pre-school memory of fighting with his sister, while taking a bath with her, about who should wear a plastic raincoat in the tub. In kindergarten he remembers being especially attracted to a little girl friend who wore a plastic raincoat. In elementary school he loved to wear a raincoat, especially of the plastic kind, but because he was afraid his friends might call him a sissy, he often desisted. By the time he entered junior high school, M.'s affinity for raincoats had extended to girls' boots. In the eighth grade, he bought a pair of girls' boots and walked outdoors in the deep snow, which hid the boots. To the question: "How did you feel when you put on these boots," he answered: "Nothing special, I just liked the idea of wearing the raincoat and the boots."

One day, at age 14, while rummaging in the basement, he discovered a woman's dress. He slipped it on and inspected himself in a large mirror. After disrobing, he masturbated. The sexual arousal during the early years of his problem was elicited by wearing women's garments. For example, he would put on boots or a raincoat and then proceed to masturbate. For the last 5 years, however, imagining himself in any kind of women's apparel has been a sufficiently exciting stimulus to be followed by masturbation. He enjoyed the act for itself, without associating with it any other thought, feeling, or imagery.

*This case was presented to a seminar conducted by Dr. Joseph Wolpe at the Eastern Pennsylvania Psychiatric Institute. Participants in the discussion were: Gregory Woodham, M.D., Joseph Wolpe, M.D., Alan J. Goldstein, Ph D. and Jorn Bambeck, Ph D.

M. made several trips to the basement in his early high school years for the purpose of dressing in women's clothes. One day, after draping himself in an old dress, raincoat and boots, he heard his sister's footsteps on the cellar stairs. He quickly hid, terribly frightened. After she left, he masturbated and removed the clothes. During the next year he had several experiences involving wearing a maid's uniform and his mother's underwear, boots, raincoat and scarf. He would venture outdoors only in the dark, not willing to risk recognition.

Starting with his sophomore year in high school, he dated girls from one to three times weekly. There was no petting, but after each date, he masturbated. As a junior in high school, he stopped dressing in girls' clothing. The fantasy of imagining himself in girls' attire was sufficient to elicit masturbation. A few years later in college, he participated heavily in sports, and masturbation decreased to approximately twice weekly.

The previous summer he had met a girl, Jessica, at a seashore resort whom he liked very much and with whom he had his first sexual intercourse. This had evoked in him depressed feelings about his sexual potentiality. The intercourse was disappointing: he described it as "Scary—it was just like masturbating." Before and during the sex act, he could not get rid of the image of himself in girl's clothing. "It's as if my girl isn't there. The fantasy takes over and sticks with me." This generated the thought that he was perverted. Subsequent sex experiences with Jessica always had the same sequel.

SECOND SESSION

I probed the family relationships. M.'s father was a strict military career man, who routinely punished his children for violations of protocol. M. had learned to fear him, becoming more or less alienated from him since early childhood days. These feelings had persisted until about a year earlier when he had received a warm reply to a letter he had sent his father from aboard ship while carrying out compulsory duties as part of his naval training. For the first time in his life, he sensed that his father really did care for him. Ever since, M. has been able to communicate more freely and satisfactorily with him. His mother, on the other hand, was M.'s refuge. In the early days, to escape the ire of his father, he would run to mother. This pattern of behavior continued throughout his growing-up years. As M. says: "Everything about her was golden and great." Both parents argued incessantly, often in the presence of the children. M.'s mother had confided to him about a year previously that the only reason that she hadn't left her husband was her concern for the children.

Going steady with Jessica has helped M. to gain a different perspective about his relationship with his parents. (Jessica herself is being counseled at the University Psychological Services Center.) In serious discussions about life, the future, etc., she has convinced M. that the real problem in his life is his mother. According to Jessica, M.'s dependence on his mother and his inability to relate in proper masculine manner to his father are the causes for his sexual difficulties. I should point out that M. had confided to Jessica his masturbation problems but not his transvestite proclivities. It was due to Jessica's persuasiveness that M. sought psychological treatment.

I explored more specifically the fantasy, trying to pinpoint where, when and in what circumstances it appeared. Stimuli such as the following were effective in its arousal:

seeing girls in class, at lunch, in the hallways, etc, and pictures of girls in magazines. Generalization had become so rampant that any female apparel was a sufficient stimulus to evoke the fantasy no matter where he was.

Woodham: Will you say once again what the fantasy is?

Gershman: He imagines himself clothed in women's apparel. This is tipped off by any of the above stimuli I just mentioned.

Wolpe: Does the fantasy also lead to sexual desire or not?

Gershman: Yes and no. For many years, the masturbation which followed the fantasy seemed to be sufficient in itself. At the present time, it would be difficult, especially since M. has already had heterosexual experience, to say that this is true.

Wolpe: I'm puzzled about one thing. You speak about masturbation being sufficient. Where do you make the separation between the impulse that leads to masturbation and what you call sexual desire?

Gershman: According to M., when he looks at a girl at the present time, his desire can go in two directions: to heterosexual desire or to fantasy. He seems to make this distinction in his own mind. It is not apparent what specific circumstances are necessary to swerve his response in one direction or the other.

Wolpe: Is it something like this? He looks at a woman. His impulses could branch off in either of the two directions. He is sexually aroused and will usually move toward gratification in fantasy and consequent masturbation; but may be impelled toward normal sexual relations in favorable circumstances.

Gershman: He was unable to have an erection unless he conjured up the fantasy. From the very first experience with Jessica last summer, he could not maintain an erection unless he had the fantasy. Unless he had the image, he could not even get an erection.

Goldstein: Did he say specifically why he wanted treatment? Does he want to get rid of the fantasy or does he want to enjoy sexual intercourse?

Gershman: Both. He wants to marry this girl. He realizes that he cannot have intercourse without calling forth the fantasy. With serious prospects of marriage facing him, he is very much concerned. He is bothered about this "perversion." He wants to get rid of it.

I would like to mention a few other stimuli that help to evoke the fantasy. Rain is an effective stimulus. Rain, you will remember, is associated with raincoat, a female object which was so important in his early years. Also, when he sees girls' clothing hanging, for example, in a closet, department store, etc., the image is inevitably elicited.

At this session, I initiated treatment. I started with the "stop" technique (Wolpe, 1969), using it in this manner: I asked him to evoke the fantasy, to stop it, and then to shift to something which was reinforcing. Since I had already found out that he likes to read and to tinker with mechanical things, I asked him to focus on interesting scenes of this sort after stopping the image. We practiced this sequence in the office several times. After about the fourth or fifth repetition, it was obvious that he would be able to do it on his own. As a homework assignment, he was required to carry out this sequence three times daily, approximately six times at each session, adding up to a minimum of 18 times per day.

I emphasized the deliberate evocation of the fantasy. The purpose was mainly to institute the factor of control. Naturally, he would also get this fantasy during the day without purposely arousing it. He was directed to make use of the "stop" technique on these occasions also.

At this session I also started a covert sensitization[1] scene (Cautela, 1967).

Goldstein: Excuse me. Is this because you anticipated lack of success in the "stop" technique?

Gershman: No. Not exactly for that reason . . .

Goldstein: Just an additional measure?

Gershman: Right. According to my treatment program, covert sensitization was the next step. I had no way of telling how successful the "stop" technique itself would be, but I never really expected it to be sufficient by itself. It was a necessary beginning because in addition to the positive effects which could evolve from making use of a tool that is always available, I wanted to institute greater self-control efforts in my patient.

Wolpe: Did you have any concern about doing away with sexual arousal?

Gershman: No. I realize the significance of your question. However, the kind of sexual arousal that M. wanted was disturbed by these images. For instance, in making love to his girl, the intrusion of the image impeded real sexual arousal for his girl.

Goldstein: You said before that he wasn't able to get an erection without the image?

Gershman: That is correct. If he maintained the image, then he was able to engage in sexual follow-up.

Goldstein: Pleasurably?

Gershman: Yes, but primarily in a physical sense. The knowledge that what he was doing was not right was beginning to disturb him.

Wolpe: Then was he able to sustain the erection?

Gershman: Off and on. Though he got the erection, it was not to his satisfaction. At times, he would have an orgasm and other times, none. It was an on-and-off proposition, creating anxiety. What plagued him most was the fact that he could not regard the girl as his girl because he was not responding to her as he ought. It bothered him that when he had difficulty in erecting and coming to climax, he would have to call forth the image to help.

Wolpe: Is this fantasy that he has a stereotyped fantasy?

Gershman: It varies. He's not always wearing the same undergarments, or clothes, or raincoat.

Goldstein: What is he doing in the fantasy?

Gershman: He is not doing anything. He sees himself dressed in these clothes.

Goldstein: Just standing there?

Gershman: Yes. In the past, when he put on the clothes, he would observe himself in the mirror. Sometimes this was reinforcing. Other times, however, the view was disappointing. The reinforcement, as you can see, was intermittent.

---

[1] This consists essentially of pairing the image one wishes to attack with an aversive image, that, for example, produces nausea.

THIRD SESSION

M. was very enthusiastic about his success with the "stop" technique. He was able to conjure up an image purposely and to eliminate it. This was very encouraging. With further probing, he estimated his success to be about 60 percent. The greatest difficulty in stopping the image occurred at bedtime. During the week he had made love to Jessica three times: having an erection three times, and an orgasm each time; but he had had to conjure up the fantasies on each occasion.

I discussed with him my intention of associating the fantasy with aversiveness by making use of the covert sensitization technique and perhaps other aversive methods. I explained my reasons for doing so. Because of his success with the "stop" technique, he was highly motivated to go along with my suggestions.

For homework, I gave him the following: 1) Continue with the "stop" technique, 2) repeat the covert sensitization scenes at least twice during the day, and 3) associate his feces with the image. Direction for the latter called for his deliberately placing his head close to his feces and conjuring up the image. In leaving the toilet area, he was to feel relieved, breathe fresh air—following the covert sensitization routine. M. pointed out that it was his house job to clean the cat's litter two or three times during the week. He despised doing this. I required him as the fourth item in his homework schedule to associate the fantasy with the cat's litter in the same way as with the feces.

FOURTH SESSION

It was obvious even before we started that M. was feeling very chipper. He eagerly pointed out that the only time he had had any fantasies during the past few days was when he let them appear. He could stop them any time he wanted. He was enjoying the newly found control which the "stop" technique had given to him. Also, he had had intercourse with Jessica the previous night, had an erection without a fantasy and penetrated her without a fantasy. This was the first time he had done this. "I felt like I was on Cloud 9 last night," he said. However, he was unable to have an orgasm, because Jessica was very tired and he had had to stop. He felt he could have had it without conjuring up the image if the intercourse had continued.

Several other significant things had happened this past week. As a result of stomach trouble, he had vomited five times over a period of a few days. Remembering the important association that had been stressed between the image and aversiveness, every time he vomited in the toilet bowl, he brought up the image—boots, raincoat, often the total image—in fantasy. He had also cleaned the cat's litter twice, making use of the same type of aversive association. A few days earlier Jessica had come into his apartment wearing a raincoat and he had succeeded immediately in stopping the image which was evoked. Also, whenever he had looked at nude female pictures in *Playboy* magazine which one of the boys in his house brought in, he was sexually aroused toward Jessica. There were no exceptions.

During the session I made use of several convert sensitization scenes and revived his vomiting experiences in imagery. In both instances, I followed this with the image of Jessica in the nude and M. and Jessica in sexual intercourse.

At this time I speculated whether merely to continue the ongoing procedures, or to try by other means to accelerate change. I decided to add aversive shock. My reason was that since aversiveness was working well, why not introduce another weapon to the arsenal to make it even more effective. I used shock in this manner. I had M. deliberately call forth the image, and say "Stop," upon which I shocked him and then immediately gave him the pleasurable image of himself and Jessica in sexual intercourse. I gave him a portable shocker and assigned him to use this technique the following week in addition to continuing the assignments of the week before.

Goldstein: Then the "stop" is conditioned to the shock?

Gershman: Yes.

Goldstein: The stopping is made aversive?

Wolpe: I am puzzled that you brought in this shock technique when you were doing so well without it.

Gershman: Well, I was thinking of Guthrie who points out that a learning process is improved when the desirable response is made in different situations with different stimuli present.

Wolpe: Will you spell this out?

Gershman: Guthrie contends that for successful learning of a skill that can be widely used we have to practice the behavior in different situations. He gives as an example, I believe, a person who is learning to play a piece of music on the piano, or learning a poem, etc. When he practices the piano, he is always in the same room, in the same position, in the same chair, facing in the same direction, the walls are always the same color—everything's pretty much the same. In other words, the stimuli are more or less the same. But when he plays the piano in some other room where many stimuli would naturally be different, he will tend to falter. Therefore, if we can build up a wide range of experiences, there is a greater probability of comprehensive learning taking place. In S-R learning terms, what we are doing is to connect numerous stimuli with a particular response. This strengthens the whole S-R situation.

Wolpe: I don't see the relevance here when you were trying to *eliminate* a response.

Gershman: I was trying to eliminate the fantasy response. My aim was to strengthen the elimination process. Remember, the "stop" technique is something M. will always have available. If I could strengthen it, why not?

Wolpe: Well, I think there is also another question here. What are you inhibiting? You are using the word "Stop" to inhibit a response and then you are following that with a shock. Is there not a danger of producing an inhibition of inhibition?

Gershman: I felt that the association of the stop and shock being used in a practically simultaneous manner would make out of both stimuli a simple totality.

Goldstein: Do you have any reason to think that it was more effective this way?

Gershman: It was very effective.

Wolpe: Was it neccessary?

Gershman: This is debatable. My interpretation was that it would add strength to the whole situation.

Goldstein: Does he use "Stop" while engaged in intercourse?

Gershman: Yes.

Goldstein: Wouldn't that be perhaps a contraindication to the use of shock therapy, because the shock would also evoke anxiety?

Gershman: No. Remember, I had been seeing this boy only a few times, and I felt that the success which I was having could very well wear off with time. I didn't want to chance that. I felt that shock could be used very effectively at this particular time as a strengthening process.

Wolpe: I can't argue against a measure that you say has succeeded. What I'm concerned about is the possibility of negative effects on responses to normal sexual stimuli, since these are being paired with aversive consequences.

Gershman: Remember, that following shock, I make use of the image of pleasant sexual intercourse with his girl. This was very reinforcing for him. If I had perhaps made use of some other image, a neutral image, for instance, what you are suggesting might very well occur. But I deliberately made use of sexual intercourse per se as a pleasant experience that *followed* the image-cum-shock.

Bambeck: Guthrie's postulate is really weak and not of much value, don't you think?

Gershman: My impression is that Guthrie is on firm ground with this postulate. As you know, it is difficult to test much of Guthrie's theory because of the multiple S-R movements that are involved. However, empirically Guthrie's ideas are quite practical. As a matter of fact, we can translate this particular postulate into Skinnerian or Hullian terminology without any trouble.

FIFTH SESSION

M.'s feelings about the fantasy image were undergoing radical change. It had become repugnant, sickening. This was the significant theme of the whole session. He had had two intercourse experiences with Jessica during the week. The first time he had for a quite a time maintained an erection without the fantasy. He again had to stop without reaching orgasm because Jessica was tired. Again he felt that he could have reached it if he had been able to continue. The second intercourse was retrogressive. Because he desperately wanted to have the orgasm that he had missed the last two times, after a few minutes he deliberately called forth the image which eventually led to an orgasm. I explained to him in learning terms that this sequence was to be avoided at all costs.

Goldstein: If you are going to operate from a conditioning model and you have a CS, the image, and you want him to develop orgasmic potential without the image that is attached to other stimuli, then why not make use of the CS you have at your disposal. It may be the only one you'll ever have.

Gershman: What are you referring to?

Goldstein: I'm saying that he has only had orgasms under a very specific stereotyped condition. This can be to your advantage rather than disadvantage in developing normal sexual arousal.

Gershman: No, the orgasm is unpredictable: sometimes it comes, sometimes it doesn't. According to M., he feels confident that the orgasm could come without the image. The previous night he was tight and frustrated and since he had experienced two frustrating sexual experiences, he called forth the image deliberately. The image was no longer the problem. He controlled it. Previously, the image was the problem. Now, he can stop it anytime he wants. What are you suggesting?

Goldstein: I'm suggesting that when he has intercourse, he should call up the image if that is what is required to have an orgasm. We can predict in terms of straightforward conditioning that all the other stimuli in the situation will become conditioned to the response of orgasm.

Gershman: However, this image is very repugnant to him now.

Goldstein: I understand this, but the point is you've got to have another response which is an alternative one before you knock out the one which is unadaptive.

Gershman: I agree with the logic of your statement, but my interpretation of the conditions is different. I am trying to overcome the necessity of achieving success by evoking the image, which has been the uncontrollable variable for so many years.

Goldstein: It's the same principle as treating a homosexual through aversive training without being concerned about first giving him an alternative response to females.

Gershman: What you are saying is that when he has sexual intercourse he should purposely bring up the image and then have his orgasm.

Goldstein: Yes.

Gershman: What would we be doing? Strengthening the association between the orgasm and the image which already existed before and which we are trying to get rid of.

Goldstein: It's the unconditioned stimulus in this particular situation.

Gershman: Sure, but there are other important unconditioned stimuli also present. You are really suggesting that he continue what was for him normal before the treatment, and for which he came for treatment—that in the sexual situation, he should evoke the image, get raised excitation and then have the intercourse. It seems to me quite reasonable that if we can eliminate the image, there will be some measure of direct conditioning of the erotic response plus erection to the sexual situation—bypassing the image. In this way we can hope to build up the sexual response without the image—which essentially seems to have happened here. At the present time, there's no question about the increase in sexual desire without the image. As a CS the image is quite weak, now, sickening. By merely seeing Jessica in the nude now, he is always sexually stimulated. It was different before. What you are saying makes a great deal of sense, in homosexual cases, but I would not do it in this case unless it was the only alternative left.

Wolpe: Isn't there evidence that one can get conditioning of sexual responses without orgasm?

Gershman: I believe so.

Bambeck: Before he started treatment and when he had to use the image to elicit orgasm, or even an erection, how did he feel immediately after intercourse?

Gershman: Disappointed. Because to him this intercourse was just like the masturbation process.

Bambeck: Wouldn't this make the idea invalid about trying to link the image, the fantasy, with satisfaction, since the consequence was really disappointing?

Gershman: I think so. All techniques used—stop, covert sensitization, and shock—were for the purpose of eliminating the fantasy. If we were to do what has been suggested, we might very well bring back the bogey man once again—the fantasy—and associate it with a high reinforcement. I think we would be back where we started.

Goldstein: I would suggest to you that the fantasy played a large part in conditioning him to respond sexually to Jessica. Had he not had a girl friend and you had used the same treatment approach, you would have closed off a possibility of normal sexuality. Apparently, what has happened is that enough has developed to make sexual responsiveness transferable.

Gershman: I think that makes good sense. The existence of a girl friend to whom he was highly motivated was definitely important.

Wolpe: I had a case about 3 years ago which was not dissimilar to this one. A young man of about 22 couldn't enjoy sexual intercourse unless he had an image of a large female who would be punishing him in some way. He was finally able to enjoy normal sexual intercourse after the image was eliminated by aversive conditioning.

Goldstein: May I ask you a question about a side issue. Did this person that you treated begin masturbation at a very young age—like 6? The reason I ask is because every time I've seen a case where there is a very stereotyped sexual response in terms of the stimuli that are elicited, there always has been a history of very early masturbation. Apparently, the younger one starts, the more stereotyped the response becomes. I don't know.

Gershman: M. also started masturbating at an early age.

Goldstein: There was a girl I saw who could only masturbate by crossing her legs in a particular way and imagining that she had to urinate. It started when she was very young, 6 or 7. When she was in a car, she would cross her legs and the motion of the car would masturbate her. The reason she got away with it was that she told her parents she had to go to the bathroom. So it developed into a very stereotyped kind of a response just as we have here. I wonder if the age at which one starts . . .

Wolpe: You're raising a question with wide ramifications. Very little work has been done on the specific factors that play a part in neurotic conditioning. It's about time somebody began working on the kind of questions you're raising in relation to this case, and similar questions in relation to other kinds of cases. What are the factors that determine neurotic conditioning of different kinds? What are the factors that favor homosexual conditioning? What are the factors making for a predisposition to agoraphobia?

Goldstein: I think one has to be careful about getting into the same bind that analysts do, by depending upon subjective reports of occurrences in the past, which are not terribly reliable. When delving into what happened when someone was 6 years old, one could get "information" to confirm an analytic model or "information" to confirm any other model.

Wolpe: There are obviously methodological problems, but the researcher has to insure that his information is reliable. When you are pressing for details of a past that is hazy, there is a factor at work that inclines people to give you the information that you want. But if you were to interview 100 fetishistic cases and a large percentage were spontaneously to tell you that they masturbated at the age of 6 or so, this would be, I think, impressively unusual.

SIXTH SESSION

This session took place several weeks later. It was short. M. was having no trouble with erection or orgasm. During the past 2 weeks, he had engaged in intercourse several times without difficulty. He was looking forward to his marriage with Jessica the next month. Most of the session dealt with a review of the techniques which had been used to counter-condition the fantasy-masturbation sequence. M. was most cheerful, was looking forward to the marriage and feeling extremely confident that he would be able to function normally. On leaving, he agreed that if any difficulty were to arise in the future, he would contact me immediately. Six months have passed without any telephone call.

REFERENCES

Cautela, J.R. Covert sensitization. *Psycholog. Reports.* 1967, **20**, 459-468.
Wolpe, J. *The Practice of behavior therapy,* New York: Pergamon Press, 1969.

54
Treatment of Transvestism and Subsequent Coital Problems

PETER LAMBLEY

According to Lukianowicz (1959) transvestism is the sexual deviation characterized by the desire to wear the clothes of the opposite sex, sometimes combined with the desire to be a member of that sex. Stoller (1971) has distinguished seven groups of cross-dressers of which fetishistic cross-dressers, transsexuals and homosexual cross-dressers are the most commonly found in clinical practice.

Conventional psychotherapeutic treatment of transvestic disorders has been disappointing, the literature revealing little in the way of convincing treatment programs (Feldman, 1966). Behavior therapy has, however, shown considerable success, in particular the aversive-shock treatments used by Marks and Gelder (1967) and the social learning method described by Bentler (1968). Bentler, preferring to avoid the use of noxious stimulation, employed rewards for heterosexual imagery in his transvestite adolescent patients, combined with planned heterosexual contacts. He successfully treated three fetishistic cross-dressers. The present report describes how Bentler's technique was applied to the treatment of an adult, and how a complicating factor—orgasmic failure—was dealt with by methods described by LoPiccolo et al. (1972) and Davison (1968).

CASE HISTORY

S was a 26-year-old graduate student who referred himself for treatment following an examination failure. He had been cross-dressing from the age of 10, and put his failure down to the excessive amount of time that he spent cross-dressing (4 times a week). When younger, his cross-dressing had taken the form of masturbating while wearing his mother's high-heeled shoes; but it had gradually extended to the stage that he dressed completely as a woman, masturbating in front of a mirror.

S had at no time experienced a desire to obtain a sex-change operation. He had had no homosexual experiences or homosexual fantasies. Heterosexual contact had been restricted to heavy petting with occasional girl friends, but he had never been steady with a girl for longer than a few weeks. Introduced to the idea of heterosexual assertive training, he readily undertook to cooperate in the program.

TREATMENT

Formal treatment began with twice weekly sesions of 1 hour duration devoted to studying S's patterns of sexual activity and imagery. He reported that in addition to his cross-dressing he masturbated nightly to an image of himself dressed as a female. Occasionally, however, he would masturbate to fantasies of females wearing the same type of clothing he himself wore. Infrequently he would daydream of being seduced by a woman dressed in these clothes, but he had never masturbated to this.

He was encouraged to concentrate as much as possible on the latter image and to imagine himself being so seduced while masturbating, at least once a week. At the same time heterosexual encounters were planned for S—going to parties and on dates. Behavior rehearsal and *post hoc* analysis of these encounters were used to improve his skills. Initially, he reported some difficulty in attaining masturbatory ejaculation while imagining an heterosexual situation, but made good progress in his interaction with females.

After 5 weeks, S met an old girl friend and became involved in a relationship during which he was able to achieve intravaginal ejaculation on one occasion. Encouraged by his success he was able to masturbate to the image of being seduced by this girl wearing his female clothes. Cross-dressing dropped to once a week, although he still had cross-dressing fantasies on most nights.

By the end of the seventh week S had stopped cross-dressing, preferring to spend his time with his girl friend. He was able to masturbate to heterosexual fantasies at least three nights a week and felt that a complete break with his old pattern of behavior was imminent.

Toward the end of the eighth week, however, he and his girl friend attempted intercourse again and he was unable to maintain an erection. This caused him to feel dubious of his sexual ability, and aroused feelings of rejection in his girl friend. S was reassured that this problem can arise in the early stages of heterosexual intercourse, especially in the context of his prior habits. During the following week his confidence further deteriorated, on failing to maintain erection on three out of five attempts. The interpersonal situation was also severely strained.

S and his girl friend agreed to come in together in order to tackle the problem. A technique similar to that used by LoPiccolo et al. was put before them, to be followed carefully during a 3-week period. Briefly they were not to have intercourse, but were given *in vivo* tasks at each session (twice a week) commencing with only kissing and hugging, building up to heavy petting during the second week. S was able to re-experience heterosexual feelings after the second week. The third week's target was to advance to intercourse, but S was unable to relax sufficiently to achieve intravaginal ejaculation despite a prolonged erection.

S was seen alone on the day following the orgasmic failure and instructed in orgasmic reconditioning (Davison, 1968; Marquis, 1970). He was asked to attempt intercourse that night, but instead of his usual heterosexual fantasy was to use a cross-dressing one, since this had invariably stimulated him to ejaculate adequately.

The next day S reported successful intercourse and was advised to continue with the cross-dressing fantasy for at least 1 week. Since during that week intercourse was successful on three out of four occasions, he was asked once again to attempt intercourse using the heterosexual fantasy. He performed satisfactorily at the first attempt and continued, apart from a temporary relapse into cross-dressing fantasies 3 weeks later, to achieve ejaculation with heterosexual fantasies.

Follow-up sessions were continued weekly for three months, until S felt able to cope on his own. Assessment after 6 months showed no relapse and S reported that while he still had occasional cross-dressing fantasies he regarded this as a temporary state of affairs secondary to his interest in heterosexual activities.

REFERENCES

Bentler, P.M. A note on the treatment of adolescent sex problems. *J. Child Psychol. Psychiat.,* 1968, **9**, 125-129.

Davison, G.C. Elimination of a sadistic fantasy by a client controlled technique: A case study. *J. abnorm. Psychol.* 1968, **73**, 84-90.

Feldman, M.P. Aversion therapy for sexual deviations: A critical review, *Psych. Bull.,* 1966, **65**, 65-79.

LoPiccolo, J., Stewart, R. & Watkins, B. Treatment of erectile failure and ejaculatory incompetence of homosexual etiology. *Behav. Ther. & Exp. Psychiat.,* 1972, **3**, 233-236.

Lukianowicz, N. Survey of various aspects of transvestism in the light of our present knowledge. *J. Nerv. Ment. Dis.,* 1959, **128**, 36-64.

Marks, I. and Gelder, M.G. Transvestism and fetishism: Clinical and psychological changes during faradic aversion. *Brit. J. Psychiat.,* 1967, **113**, 711-729.

Marquis, J.N. Orgasmic reconditioning; changing sexual object choice through controlling masturbation fantasies. *Behav. Ther. & Exp. Psychiat.* 1970, **1**, 263-271.

Stoller, R.J. The term transvestism. *Archs gen. Psychiat.* 1971, **24**, 230-237.

Additional Selected Readings

Barker, J.C. Behaviour therapy for transvestism, *British Journal of Psychiatry*, 1965, **111**, 268-276.

Barker, J.C., Thorpe, J.G., Blakemore, C.B., Lavin, N.I., & Conway, C.G. Behaviour therapy in a case of transvestism, *The Lancet*, March, 1961, 510.

Blakemore, C.B., Thorpe, J.G., Barker, J.C., Conway, C.G., & Lavin, N.I. The application of faradic aversion conditioning in a case of transvestism, *Behaviour Research and Therapy*, 1963, **1**, 29-34.

Dupont, Henry. Social learning theory and the treatment of transvestite behavior in an eight year old boy, *Psychotherapy: Theory, Research and Practice*, Winter, 1968, **5**, 44-45.

Lavin, N.I., Thorpe, J.G., Barker, J.C., Blakemore, C.B., & Conway, C.G. Behavior therapy in a case of transvestism. *Journal of Nervous and Mental Disease*, 1961, **133**, 346-353.

Morgenstern, F.S., Pearce, J.F. & Rees, W. Linford. Predicting the outcome of behaviour therapy by psychological tests. *Behavior Research and Therapy*, 1965, **2**, 191-200.

Exhibitionistic Behavior

"Exhibitionism" is a term used to describe a wide variety of behaviors ranging from individuals who like telling sexual stories at parties to women who like wearing exotic clothes. However, exhibitionistic behavior, here, refers to the individual deliberately uncovering his genitals in a situation which is likely to provoke shock from those involuntary observers who are chosen to witness the disclosure. Once again, the behavior is almost always performed by a man.

According to Gebhard et al. (1965, p. 394), the average age of men convicted for "exhibitionism" is 30. About 60 percent of these men were or had been married. Gebhard also found a very high recidivism rate for "exhibitionism" with over 40 percent of the men having four or more previous convictions.

The first article in this section is "The Application of Learning Theory to the Treatment of a Case of Sexual Exhibitonism" by Wickramasekera. In this case Wickramasekera applied a combination of techniques involving systematic desensitization to the aversive stimuli of adult females, and the shaping of a response (heterosexual approach response) incompatible with the anxiety evoked by the sexual stimuli of adult females. The treatment of the problem, which had been in existence for some five years, was apparently quite successful as indicated by two follow-ups with the client and his finance (who, at the ten-month follow-up, had become his wife).

The article by Reitz and Keil describes the "Behavioral Treatment of an Exhibitionist." The background for this rather unique treatment of a long-standing (25 years) case of exhibitionistic behavior is described in detail. Essentially, that treatment involved having the client exhibit himself under office conditions witnessed by nurses, a procedure similar to Serber's "shame aversion therapy" described in Volume I. The client reportedly reacted with shame, guilt and embarrassment. At a 14-month follow-up, the client reported freedom from any exhibitionistic behavior.

In the following article, MacCulloch, Williams and Birtles report on "The Successful Application of Aversion Therapy to an Adolescent Exhibitionist." In this case, a 12-year-old boy was given conventional psychotherapy upon his referral to a clinic for treatment of exhibitionistic behavior. However, impending police action following a further act of exhibiting himself called for a more rapid resolution. The method of anticipation avoidance aversion therapy which had been used successfully to change undesired homosexual behavior was modified for use in this case, and is explained in detail in the article. (Of course, although the client and his mother did agree to use of this aversive procedure, there was nevertheless an obvious element of coercion involved given the entrance of the police onto the scene.) The treatment, which consisted of 18 20-minute sessions, resulted in a successful reduction in the client's exhibitionistic behavior and in his sexual orientation toward and masturbation fantasies about older women. Follow-up at five months found recovery in all respects maintained.

The final article in this section, by Lutzker, demonstrates "Reinforcement Control of Exhibitionism in a Profoundly Retarded Adult." This brief but important case study eschews aversive techniques and illustrates how social reinforcement for behavior other than that which is exhibitionistic was used to reduce exhibitionistic behavior in a "retarded" institutionalized adult, a not uncommon problem in such settings. This is the only case that could be located in which reinforcement was used to deal with this problematic behavior, and while, as Lutzker notes, its use may be restricted to institutional settings, its possibilities as an alternative to aversive procedures should not be overlooked.

REFERENCES

Gebhard, P.H., Gagnon, J.H., Pomeroy, W.B. & Christenson, C.V. *Sex offenders.* New York: Harper and Row, 1965.

55
The Application of Learning Theory to the Treatment of a Case of Sexual Exhibitionism

IAN WICKRAMASEKERA*

This case history describes the apparently successful treatment of a patient who had been an exhibitionist for more than 5 years. The particular techniques combined desensitization and the shaping of a response incompatible with anxiety.

HISTORY

The patient, a 23-year-old, white, single man, was referred to our clinic by the dean of his university because he had been apprehended by the local police for sexual exhibitionism. The police agreed not to press charges if the student would secure treatment.

The patient's parents occupy very prominent places in the social and religious life of the community. In high school and at the time of treatment the patient was an A student, very active in athletics and prominent in the social life of the campus.

The examining psychiatrist diagnosed the patient as Sociopathic Personality Disturbance and noted in his report that the prognosis for behavior change was poor in view of the fact that the patient had a history of exhibitionism dating back to his 13th year.

The patient had shared a room with his two younger sisters during his early childhood and had a problem controlling his masturbation in adolescence. His earliest recollection of overt sexual exhibitionism was standing unzipped in the shadows of a barn whose doors overlooked a highway. In the ensuing years the patient continued to exhibit himself on the average about once a month at windows and while driving his car in strange towns. Complaints had been either "hushed up" or explained away on the basis of indiscretions. Careful questioning revealed that the preferred sexual object was a young (age 8-14 years) immature female. The patient had gone "steady" twice in his life, but

*The author would like to acknowledge his appreciation to Dr. W. Steinman and Dr. S. Bijou for critically reading the manuscript, and to the staff of a mental health clinic in Southern Illinois for their cooperation with the treatment program.

had dated many different girls briefly. At the time of the arrest, he had been engaged for two years and was shortly to be married. His financee was a senior in a different college and she was apparently quite religiously oriented.

PRE-TREATMENT STATUS OF RESPONSE

Starting about two months prior to his arrest, the patient had begun to expose himself more frequently and in many *more* locations (outside junior high schools, in public libraries, in stores, while driving his car close to the sidewalk at traffic lights and stop signs, etc.). Previously he had exposed himself only at his window and driving his car with his pants open through strange towns. Now he was exposing himself consistently in at least seven additional physical locations.

The rate of the response had also increased. Previously he had no recollection of ever exceeding one or two exposures a month, but in the two months prior to the arrest, he had at times exposed himself as many as ten times per week.

He also reported that he was restless most of the time, unable to concentrate and generally "jumpy." He noted that he was considering postponing his approaching marriage due to his "poor health."

Until the time of the arrest, the patient had been able to keep all knowledge of his exhibitionism carefully concealed from his fiancee. Physical contact between them had never gone beyond kissing and holding hands. In fact, he admitted that in all his heterosexual experience he had never touched a female's genitals, though on one occasion he had lightly fondled a girl's breasts through her blouse. The patient firmly asserted that his avoidance of all sexual contact was exclusively due to religious scruples. He denied homosexual contact of any type, either in childhood or adolescence. His masturbatory fantasies, which were exclusively heterosexual, always stopped short of actual sexual intercourse.

The patient reported that in the past when the impulse to expose himself arose but the location was "dangerous" he would seek relief in solitary masturbation. However, he added that more recently masturbation seemed less pleasant to him.

On the basis of the above information the following diagnostic hypotheses were formulated: 1) The patient was fearful of sexual contact with adult females and specifically of vaginal contact. 2) The alternative masturbatory response was becoming progressively less reinforcing. 3) The religious scruples were rationalizations.

THEORETICAL VIEWS OF THE ETIOLOGY OF EXHIBITION

Psychoanalytic theory asserts that the exhibitionistic response is a defense against castration anxiety. Castration anxiety is among other things traced to the vagina dentata hypothesis (Fenichel, 1963), which may suggest a vaginal phobia. In terms of a 2-factor learning theory, this would imply that certain stimulus configurations (young females in this case), which have been paired in early childhood with aversive stimuli, typically elicit anxiety and the performance of the exhibitionistic instrumental response in their presence is anxiety reducing. This formulation regards *young* females as having acquired on a contiguity basis anxiety-evoking properties for the exhibitionist. The act of self-exposure and the perception of his intact penis has somehow acquired the ability to reduce this drive (anxiety). But the exhibitionistic response probably persists because young females lose their aversive properties, and since the exhibitionistic response is a form of solution learning, it comes to be increasingly maintained by sexual drive reduction. Hence, a response originally acquired on the basis of anxiety reduction comes to be increasingly maintained by sexual drive reduction.

BEHAVIOR MODIFICATION PLAN

Two approaches seemed open, but the second one seemed to have more long term merits.

1. Contingencies could be manipulated to restore even temporarily the reinforcing properties of the masturbatory response. The prediction would be that as masturbation increased in frequency, the more "dangerous" exhibitionistic response would decrease in frequency.

2. An alternative approach would attempt to shift the sexual approach responses from young females to adult females and to increase the amount of associated reinforcement from mere exposure to actual physical contact and intercourse with adult females. The first step in remediation then would be to associate "relaxed" rather than "agitated" responses with the sexual stimuli of adult females. The next step would be to set up contingencies in which the patient's sexual approach responses toward adult females would have a high probability of reinforcement.

PREPARATION OF PATIENT FOR TREATMENT

After the psychological testing was completed and a comprehensive picture assembled of the patient's current life space, a meeting was scheduled to explain the treatment plan to the patient and to secure his consent to implement it. In a matter of fact manner, it was explained to the patient that had he been born in a different time or into a different sex, he could probably have continued to practice exhibitionism and live a productive and profitable life (e.g., as a burlesque artist). But that at the present time and in the present location the penalties of self-exposure were severe, as the patient had found out (he had been asked to drop out of school till "cured.") The therapist then told the patient that he believed that the patient's lack of sexual experience with adult females was due to the patient's fear of sexual contact with adult females. This fear, he pointed out, had lead to a legally prohibited means of sexual expression. The therapist also remarked that he considered the patient's talk about religious scruples rather flimsy camouflage. Initially the patient responded with anger to these observations and vigorously repeated his claim to religious scruples. The therapist then explained that the primary goals of the treatment, should he agree to accept them, would be to desensitize (principle was explained) his fear of sexual contact with adult females and to shape his sexual responses more in the direction of heterosexual intercourse. The therapist predicted that when the patient started having heterosexual intercourse, he would lose interest in his potentially dangerous exhibitionist behavior. The therapist pointed out that the active participation of the patient's fiancee would be vitally important to the treatment procedure. The therapist stressed the fact that since the patient was engaged to be married, the conventional social prohibitions against premarital intercourse were somewhat more relaxed. But he also emphasized the fact that the proposed treatment procedure was purely experimental, even though it seemed to make good sense. The patient and the therapist also discussed the fact that with the use of conventional treatment procedures the prognosis for recovery was poor and the duration of treatment was indefinite. The patient was also told that if he would prefer to undertake conventional treatment, arrangements could be made for such services either in the present clinic or with a private practitioner. He was then given the names of several private practitioners and directed to go and home and think further about this choice. The patient was strongly encouraged to discuss in confidence with his minister his present predicament and the choice he had between the lesser of two imperfect solutions. He was also requested to discuss the treatment plan with his fiancee (who for the first time had learned about his sexual deviation after his arrest.)

A few days later the patient indicated that he was willing to take the experimental treatment and an appointment was scheduled with him and his fiancee. The patient's fiancee felt that before treatment commenced she should marry the patient. This inclination was strongly discouraged by the therapist on two grounds: 1) The treatment was purely experimental and there was no guarantee that it would succeed. 2) There was a possibility that should the treatment succeed, the present basis of their mutual attraction would dissolve and that the patient would develop a wider interest in females.

Initially the patient's fiancee raised numerous objections to the second part of the treatment plan on both religious grounds and the possibility of pregnancy. The therapist admitted that there were serious moral issues involved here. He noted that the discovery of the patient's problems did not seem to have disrupted her plans to marry the patient and she apparently still loved him and was eager to assist with his social rehabilitation. At the close of the interview, both the patient and his fiancee tentatively agreed to try the experimental treatment plan.

TREATMENT TECHNIQUES

The first step in the treatment plan was to train the patient in relaxation and this was largely accomplished with the use of a tape and relaxation instructions. From here on the desensitization procedure described by Wolpe (1958) was used consistently. Instruction in the tensing and relaxing of his muscles were also recorded on a tape the patient purchased, and the tape was used as a guide to his practice of relaxation at home. The relaxation training period took approximately three one-hour sessions. But between clinic sessions, the patient engaged in distributed practice of these exercises 1 to 1½ hours daily. Even after the desensitization proper had begun, the patient continued to practice muscular relaxation at home.

The construction of the anxiety hierarchy provided additional evidence of the patient's aversion for the sexual stimuli of adult females. For example, one of his homework assignments was to construct in rough form a hierarchy starting with strictly social contact between himself and adult females and terminating in sexual contact. He was also required to contruct a similar hierarchy for young females. The scenes covering social contact with adult females were on the average 25 words long, but those covering sexual contact with adult females were on the average only 3 words long. During hierarchy refinement the patient was observed to be sweating and restless as the sexual imagery of adult females was approximated.

As the desensitization procedure approached its middle phase (in the 7th session) it was decided to start the shaping of an additional response incompatible with the anxiety evoked by the sexual stimuli of adult females. The patient was assigned selected readings with progressively more heterosexual erotic content (care was taken to avoid material containing reference to young females). This was perceived as the first step in shaping bolder heterosexual approach responses to adult females. For example, the first step was reading a lightly sexually toned passage from Steinbeck for five minutes in the sixth session. After he had completed reading it, he was reinforced with verbal approval "very good," "fine," etc., and a smile. These reading sessions were seldom in excess of ten minutes and he typically read two to three passages with continuous reinforcement ("very good," "fine," etc.). At the termination of this technique in the 12th session, he was reading passages from books like *Fanny Hill*, etc., and did not seem to need verbal reinforcement to keep up this type of reading at home. Previously he had reported being unable to read even moderately heterosexual erotic content for presumably religious reasons. The purpose of this step was to direct his mediating responses (verbal behaviors or thoughts, etc.) into the area of the sexual stimuli of adult females.

The next step was to set up a series of trips with his fiancee to both neighboring towns and to distant large towns for recreational purposes (ball games, plays, movies, zoos, etc.) and these were scheduled toward the terminal phase of the desensitization procedure. The first of these trips was scheduled in between the 12th and 13th session of treatment. Before each trip, the patient was explicitly told how far his petting behavior should go and strictly forbidden to go beyond the prescribed points. These points were fondling of breasts, stomach, legs, thighs, and finally genital areas. Before these trips were scheduled, the therapist explained to the subject's fiancee the rationale of the treatment and the importance of consistently and clearly reinforcing his limited sexual approach responses. For example, on the first trip the patient was explicitly restricted to kissing and the fondling of his fiancee's breasts. These restrictions on the extent of his sexual responses were generally reduced as he continued to report greater comfort and feelings of competency in his sexual relationship. After the initial stages of this shaping procedure, both the patient and his fiancee began to take an active interest in the treatment.

As the desensitization and shaping proceeded concurrently, the patient spontaneously reported a phasing out of his impulse to exhibit himself and his exhibitionistic ruminations. However, at least on two occasions during the initial stages of treatment (between the 2nd and 4th sessions) the patient reported that while returning home from a distant town where he had searched fruitlessly for employment, he had driven a number of blocks with his pants unzipped. On both occasions the exposures had occurred in areas where young females were at play.

During the 14th session of the treatment phase the therapist recommended that the patient move out of his parents' home and attempt to support himself independently. This recommendation was made because it was the therapist's judgment that the patient's parents and particularly his mother were reinforcing what seemed to be his dependent attitudes. When this recommendation was first made in the 2nd session of treatment it was ignored, but when it was repeated in the 14th session of treatment, it was quickly implemented.

TERMINATION

Treatment was terminated after the 18th session. At this time the patient and his fiancee reported a very satisfactory sexual relationship between them. According to the patient's report at termination, he had not exposed himself since the 4th session of treatment (a period of approximately 2½ months). The frequency of his sexual relationships with his fiancee had risen from nearly zero to a mean of two relationships (mainly petting and coitus) per week. There was no evidence of "symptom substitution," even though a deliberate effort was made to look for it in the final interview. There were no indications of homosexual preoccupations or other deviant preoccupations. The patient reported an increased ability to concentrate and freedom from the pre-treatment restlessness. Also both he and his fiancee reported their relationship was "deeper and more real" to them now. At termination the patient had secured employment and was making tentative plans to complete his education and get married.

FOLLOW-UP

In the first follow-up six months after treatment the patient and his fiancee were separately asked: 1. Has there been any recurrence at all of self-exposure? 2. (a) Have you had any new disturbing thoughts, feelings or motor responses? (b) Have you re-experienced any old disturbing behaviors of the above type? 3. How frequent and satisfying is your present sexual relationship? 4. How often do you have thoughts and feelings about self exposure? The patient responded to the first and second questions in the negative. He reported that his sexual relationships with his fiancee have increased to a mean of about three intimacies a week since the termination of treatment (this was confirmed independently by his fiancee), and he described their relationship as "extremely" satisfying. In response to the 4th question, he stated that just after the termination of treatment he had sporadically had thoughts and feelings about self-exposure and particularly at times when he felt "low." But recently these thoughts and feelings had become "very infrequent."

The patient's fiancee, to the extent she could, confirmed his descriptions. They were to be married very shortly.

In an identical follow-up procedure ten months after termination (the patient had now married his fiancee) both persons' responses were substantially the same as four months previously. The only difference being that the patient could not recall any thoughts or impulses to self-exposure in the last four months.

CONCLUSION

The unique feature of this treatment consisted in that the extinction of the anxiety associated with the sexual stimuli of adult females was accomplished by training the patient in not merely one but two responses incompatible with anxiety. The sexual stimuli of adult females was paired with relaxation responses and sexual approach responses. The interference theory of extinction (Kimble 1961) would seem to predict more lasting extinction under such conditions. The brevity of the treatment was probably due to at least three factors. One, the treatment procedure involved the manipulation of very powerful reinforcement contingencies (sexual stimuli). Two, the desensitization procedure was run nearly *concurrently* with shaping of an incompatible response (heterosexual approach responses). Three, it is our experience (Wickramasekera, 1967) that changes in cognitive and affective responses are most effectively induced by first changing the patient's motor responses. The self-evident nature of the patient's changed motor behavior may increase his feeling of "hope" and reduce his resistance to cognitive manipulations. Hence, treatment may be accelerated by a snowballing "placebo" effect.

Nearly all published studies of the behavioral treatment of sexual deviations up to date have used one form or another of "aversion therapy" (Feldman, 1966). These have been either "punishment" (Azrin & Holz, 1966) or avoidance conditioning procedures. The present study suggests that sexual deviatons may also be treated through the shaping and positive reinforcement procedures. This study illustrates an alternative approach which may have some merit, but the lack of proper controls makes it impossible to draw any firm conclusions from the data.

It seems relatively inefficient to provide "insight" into a patient's insecurities and immaturities till we have been able to set up contingencies of reinforcement that help patients to emit more mature behavior and secure reinforcement for it. After "symptomatic recovery" has been induced, any sort of plausible rationale (Freudian, existential, Adlerian, R.T., etc.) of the etiology of the disturbance, which will hopefully function to prevent further unadaptive learning, may be explored with the patient, particularly if the therapist feels an obligation to "explain" and the patient a need to "understand how it all got started in the first place." But the matter of etiology would seem peripheral to the immediate problem of behavior modification.

REFERENCES

Azrin, N.H. & Holz, W.C. Punishment. In Honig, W.K. (Ed.), *Operant behavior, areas of research and application.* New York: Appleton-Century Crofts, 1966.

Ellis, A. *Reason and emotion in psychotherapy.* New York, Lyle Stuart, 1963.

Feldman, M.P. Aversion therapy in sexual deviations. *Psychological Bulletin,* 1966, **65,** 65-78.

Fenichel, O. *The psychoanalytic theory of neurosis.* London: Rontledge and Kegan, Paul, 1963.

Kimble, G.A. *Conditioning and learning.* New York: Appleton-Century-Crofts, 1961.

Krasner, L. & Ullmann, L.P. (Eds). *Research in behavior modification.* New York: Holt, Rinehart & Winston, 1965.

Mensh, I.N. Psychopathic conditions, addictions and sexual deviations. In Wolman (Ed.) *Handbook of clinical psychology.* New York: McGraw Hill, 1965.

Wickramasekera, I. The use of some learning theory derived techniques in the treatment of paranoid schizophrenia. *Psychotherapy, Theory, Research and Practice.* 1967, **4,** 22-26.

Wolberg, L.R. *The technique of psychotherapy.* New York: Grune and Stratton, 1957.

Wolpe, J. *Psychotherapy by reciprocal inhibition.* Stanford, Calif.: Stanford University Press, 1958.

56
Behavioral Treatment of an Exhibitionist

WILLARD E. REITZ AND WILLIAM E. KEIL

Behavioral treatment of exhibitionism has typically been directed toward desensitizing the individual to situations which had previously led to exhibiting behaviors. In addition, encouragement, direct tuition and rewarding more assertive social behaviors have been included in such treatment (Bond & Hutchinson, 1960; Dengrove, 1967). More recently, aversive treatment has been paired with taped descriptions of sexually deviant acts (Abel et al., 1969). The treatment of the case described in the present report was unusual, being similar to the "shame aversion therapy" independently reported by Serber (1970). What led to this treatment will be pointed out as the case unfolds.

CASE HISTORY

The patient had been exposing himself in the window to a neighbor lady across the street. This neighbor reported him to the police. He had previously been caught about a year before referral, but was not charged because he entered psychiatric treatment. He was told that if he exhibited again, he would be jailed, in treatment or not.

Background

When first seen, the patient was 36 years old, married, the father of six girls. He had recently been fired from his factory job because of his behavior. His exhibitionism began, as he recalled it, when he was 11 or 12 years old when he exposed himself to his teacher, a 30-year-old woman. Shortly thereafter, he had begun exposing himself quite frequently in his own home to his sister's girl friend. This pattern went on for about a year, but during this time he also began exhibiting to a 32-year-old married woman across the street through his window. He exhibited to this woman over a period of about two years.

He estimates that he subsequently exposed himself an average of 4 or 5 times a month over the next 22-23 years. The general pattern was constant. No preference was noted regarding the places he chose for exhibiting—beaches, pools, streets, trains, cars, work, home neighborhood. With regard to choice of object, he admitted a preference for "young, pretty girls." He typically exposed in an erect state until he caught the girl's attention, at which time he would fondle and manipulate himself. Never did he manipulate to the point of orgasm while being observed, and rarely, if ever, afterward. On numerous occasions there were sequential repetitive acts of exhibition to the same woman over a period of a half a day. Often he exhibited when depressed "to get me out of depression."

Despite all this activity, he was "turned in" very infrequently—only three times. Once he was detained overnight and fined. He claims that he rarely, if ever, thought about the consequences, but simply did it because "the pressure built up." Afterwards, he would "feel bad" but not before.

Personality

The patient appeared clinically to fit a standard pattern often seen in exhibitionists—a quiet, submissive, "nice guy" with well-developed feelings of inadequacy, inferiority and insecurity in interpersonal and social relations. In addition, he displayed significant elements of depression and, on occasion, spoke openly of suicide. He described himself as being very "weak willed."

Past Treatment

On three previous occasions, he had sought psychiatric treatment in which a dynamic approach had been taken. Emphasis had been placed on his feelings of inferiority and the feelings of strength and manhood likely to result from exhibiting himself in a fully erect state. He had refrained from exhibiting while being treated the first two times. During the third treatment, however, he had exhibited, and was reported and caught.

TREATMENT

The patient was referred for behavior therapy. Various alternatives were discussed with him. Originally it was intended to use a traditional Wolpean desensitization technique. This procedure was described and the patient was given an initial relaxation session. Construction work both inside and outside the hospital, however, severely reduced the potential of this technique. It was then decided to consider pairing electric shock with appropriately selected slides. But the patient had made plans to move into a new home in three weeks. He was concerned about the move since there was a pool close by and he had often exhibited in such surroundings. To obtain and arrange the slides would take too much time.

We then discussed the possibility of exhibiting to live females in the office. We noted that the patient became acutely embarrassed. He could scarcely imagine such a procedure. This led us to think that just such a procedure would best utilize the short time available before his move. After further discussion, the patient agreed that it might work and despite his embarrassment agreed to proceed.

Four volunteer psychiatric nurses were selected as stimuli. A meeting was held with the nurses and the patient to outline the procedure and rationale. The office was to be treated as a waiting room. The patient was supplied with magazines to read and the nurses were to come in singly for 15 minutes each. They were to bring "ward work" with them to complete during the session. The patient was to exhibit himself as nearly as possible as he would in real life knowing that at the end of 15 minutes the nurses would get up and leave. Conversation was to be avoided. Initially, there would be two 15-minute sessions per visit, twice a week. The nurses were instructed to react with indifference. They were told to "look at him as though he was handling a cigarette." Afterwards, the first author would talk to him to monitor and evaluate the procedure.

The patient was informed that what he had been told in past treatments was not being contradicted. The present treatment, however, took a different line. It was pointed out to him that he had very rarely been punished for exhibiting and that he found it very satisfying (reinforcing). The aim was to have him experience the act with little or no reinforcement (neutral reaction from girls) and mild to moderate punishment from himself (shame, embarrassment, guilt).

Course of Treatment

Initially, the patient reported difficulty in exhibiting. He reported being strongly embarrassed, ashamed and guilty, while doing it, but, nevertheless, continued. Ten 15-minute sessions were implemented before he moved to his new house. A similar schedule was continued for several weeks after the move; and then a tapering off began.

Several events of interest took place during treatment. For example, it was discovered that when the girls *looked* at him, he felt unable to continue fondling himself and lost his erection. It was therefore decided to increase the frequency and length of time looking at him. The effect of this was that he was often unable to obtain or maintain an erection during the session. He then requested not to be made to expose himself at all, but to talk to the girls. This request was granted. It was seen as an opportunity for him to confront those to whom he had exhibited and discuss his feelings openly.

It was also discovered in the course of the treatment that he was "afraid" to masturbate. He felt that if he got sexually aroused he would automatically exhibit. This problem was attacked by pointing out that he could initiate masturbation under conditions where it would be impossible to exhibit.

In doing so, he discovered that masturbation sharply reduced his need to exhibit, and was more pleasurable as well as less socially undesirable. At times, subsequently, when he was tempted to exhibit, he forgot about the possibility of masturbation. He was then asked to carry a small novel object on his person at all times which he would not ordinarily carry, to remind him of it. This appears to have been a useful stimulus to his memory.

Follow-up

It is now over 20 months since the initiation of treatment and 14 months since termination. In a recent follow-up interview, the patient reported continued freedom from exhibitionistic behavior and a greatly reduced impulse toward it. He has worked steadily at a position he obtained just after treatment began.

With regard to his marriage, he reported continuing to enjoy sexual relations with his wife, and increased general marital satisfaction. His social life had been broadened and he had regained the athletic skills he once possessed. There was a virtual absence of the once characteristic depression.

REFERENCES

Abel, G.G., Levis, D.J. & Clancy, J. Aversion therapy applied to taped sequences for deviant behavior in exhibitionism and other sexual deviation: A preliminary report. *J. Behav. Therapy & Exp. Psychiat.*, 1970, **1**, 59-66.

Bond, I.K. & Hutchinson, H.C. Application of reciprocal inhibition therapy to exhibitionism. *Can. med. Ass. J.*, 1960, **83**, 23-25.

Dengrove, E. Behavior therapy of the sexual disorders. *J. Sex Res.*, 1967, **3**, 49-61.

Serber, M. Shame aversion therapy. *J. Behav. Ther. & Exp. Psychiat.*, 1970, **1**, 213-215.

57

Successful Application of Aversion Therapy to An Adolescent Exhibitionist

M.J. MacCULLOCH, C. WILLIAMS AND C.J. BIRTLES

The term exhibitionist derives from an article by Lasegue (1877) and has been defined by Kraft-Ebing (1912) as ". . . men who ostentatiously expose their genitals to persons of the opposite sex, whom in some instances they even pursue, without, however, becoming aggressive." This definition is still accepted in its essentials. Kraft-Ebing described two major categories of exhibitionist: patients in whom genital exhibition may be a symptom of a mental deterioration syndrome (organic psychosyndrome) and those in whom it is the outcome of an impulsive-compulsive drive.

Reports of successfully treated cases are relatively rare. In 1947 Sperling described a single case seen on 5 days per week for 2½ years. The 600 sessions of analytically oriented psychotherapy resulted in the eventual marriage of the patient.

The use of conditioning techniques for the treatment of exhibitionism has been more recently described. Bond and Hutchinson (1960) successfully treated a single exhibitionist by reciprocal inhibition. A further single case (Kushner & Sandler, 1966) demonstrated the successful use of a partial reinforcement schedule with imaginal stimuli. Recovery was maintained at a follow-up period of 12 months. Evans (1968) treated 10 exhibitionists by a paradigm stated to be based on the anticipatory avoidance technique of Feldman and MacCulloch (1965). Their subjects were asked to fantasize aspects of their sexual deviation in response to material projected on a screen. After a random delay period of 3-6 seconds, shock was administered, and terminated by the instrumental escape response of advancing the slide projector. Five of their 10 subjects, who reported normal heterosexual masturbatory fantasy prior to treatment, reached the success criteria after a median of 4 weeks. The remaining subjects, who had exhibitionistic masturbatory fantasies prior to treatment, required a median of 24 weeks' treatment to achieve the same degree of improvement. Evans highlights the importance of masturbatory learning trials in the genesis and maintenance of sexual exhibiting behavior.

The present paper reports the application of anticipatory avoidance aversion therapy to a single adolescent who showed persistent exhibiting behavior, using apparatus which represents a technical advance over previously published techniques.

CASE SUMMARY

K was referred at 12 years of age by his family doctor because of complaints from female neighbors in February 1969. He was a reticent, neat, tidy, physically well-developed young man, who only divulged his inner thoughts as his confidence was gained over several exploratory sessions.

He was an adopted child whose developmental and emotional milestones appeared normal on retrospective questioning of the parents. He had suffered no separations, emotional or sexual traumata; neither did he have any physical illness or educational difficulties. At an interview, K said: "I love women's bodies," and that female bras, pants, suspenders, petticoats and stockings sexually excited him. It seemed that he was highly preoccupied with women's bodies and underwear.

One month before we saw him a female neighbor had complained to the patient's mother that he had entered her house and searched for her teenage daughter's underclothes. K described the incident: "I went into the house through a door I knew would be open, looked at the daughter's clothes and went to the mother's room. I took off my clothes and went to dress in them [the mother's clothes] ."

Just before we saw him, the patient had exhibited his genitals to two women of 25 years or more when he had been left alone at home for several hours. These acts had followed a characteristic sequence. When he was alone in the house, and particularly when bored, he experienced a compulsive thought to expose his erect penis to older women, i.e., women of more than 25 years, who, by preference, should have large breasts and buttocks and well-shaped legs. He experienced an inner sense of resistance to these thoughts which he regarded as "wrong." However, they were followed by a train of compulsive thoughts to undress and exhibit himself. He positioned himself naked behind the drape of the lounge curtains, and waited for a suitably attractive older female to walk past the house. As she drew level he stepped into view (at times actually out of the home front door) and achieved orgasm when the victim appeared startled. If orgasm did not occur, he masturbated to a fantasy of himself exhibiting to the female. He also masturbated twice daily to a fantasy of himself "handling" older women. His mother's underclothes were also masturbatory items.

Although he was interested in girls of his own age, he was shy and socially unskilled with them. It was decided, as a preliminary measure, to undertake psychotherapy aimed at reducing tension about approaching girls of approximately his own age in social situations. This enabled him to talk more freely about sex, but 2 months later he again exhibited himself to a woman of 25.

Five months after our first meeting he reported a 3-month absence of further exhibitionist acts and exhibitionist masturbatory fantasy, and said that female peers were coming to occupy more of his thoughts.

Two months later a letter was received from the Chief Superintendent of Police of K's home area, stating that the patient had exhibited himself to the wife of a policeman. There seemed the strong possibility that this case might be brought to the notice of the Director of Public Prosecutions. A rapid means of suppressing further socially unacceptable (maladaptive) behavior was therefore sought to ward off a court appearance.

TREATMENT

The possibility of aversion therapy was put to the mother and the patient, who agreed to it after a full explanation of the technique and its implications. First, an analysis was made of the stimulus response sequences involved in the behavior, to render them compatible with the most effective form of aversion therapy at our disposal (Feldman & MacCulloch, 1964; MacCulloch & Feldman, 1968). It seemed probable that the initial stimulus to provoke sexual arousal and its consequent chain of exhibitionistic behavior was "seeing" or fantasizing well-developed mature females. There was ample evidence that the patient masturbated to female lingerie, and to "pin-ups" of older women. There seemed to be a disproportion in his sexual interest between girls of his own age, and women over 25.

It was proposed to reduce the age of the patient's heterosexual approach objects: in short, to make women of over 25 years the CS_1 (stimulus to be associated with shock onset) and girls of his own age the CS_2 (stimulus to be associated with shock avoidance), and to apply the modified form of faradic anticipatory avoidance aversion therapy as described by Feldman et al. (1969).[1]

Measurement of sexual attitude

The Sexual Orientation Method (Feldman et al., 1966) is a technique of assessing changes in sexual orientation during aversion therapy in homosexual subjects. In the present case, the object choice of the patient was women over 25 years, and the aim of the treatment was to lower the age of preference to girls of his own age. The method was therefore modified by substituting "women of 25 years plus" for "men," and "girls of my own age" for "women." Apart from these changes the adjective pairs and the scoring remained the same as the standard form of the method.

This modified questionnaire was completed by the patient just before the first session of anticipatory avoidance aversion therapy, and repeated prior to sessions 3, 4, 5, 8 and 13; and at 6 and 14 weeks post-treatment.

Apparatus

Further refinements of the technical developments successively described in Feldman and MacCulloch (1964); Feldman and MacCulloch (1965) and Feldman et al. (1969), was as follows:

a) *Treatment.* A single Kodak Carousel 'S' projector was modified so that it could be operated by both the therapist and the patient. Three slides were used, a blank, the CS_1 and CS_2. Figure 1 shows the operating circuit.

The projector was set to display the conditional stimuli on to a white desk top; in the between-trial intervals the projector was still running but using a blank slides. Presentation of the CS_1 and CS_2 was achieved by advancing or retarding the projector magazine.

[1] The successful treatment of a similar case (of age-inappropriate heterosexual object choice) in a man in his early 20s is reported elsewhere (Feldman, MacCulloch and MacCulloch, 1968). In that case, the subject was capable of sexual arousal only by women of 35 plus years.

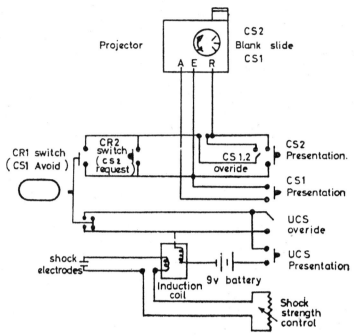

Fig. 1. Operating Circuit of Avoidance Conditioning Equipment

b) *Data Logging.* The projector operating switches were monitored by a series of switches in mechanical parallel, whose output was recorded on 8-channel punched tape. The details of the encoder are reported elsewhere (MacCulloch, Birtles & Bond, 1970; Birtles, 1970).[2]

Method

A series of slides (CS_1) of fully developed women of 20-plus year was prepared. The slides were rank-ordered by the patient using the method of paired comparisons (Woodworth and Schlosberg, 1962); and eight were used in treatment. A hierarchy of slides of a second group (CS_2) of sexually immature females of approximately the patient's age, was constructed in the same way; and six were used in treatment.

The technique is described in detail by Feldman and MacCulloch (1965) together with preliminary results on the first 19 patients. Essentially, the method relation to HS/S represents the application to the treatment situation of laboratory-derived escape-avoidance learning.

The slides of older females and young females were arranged in ascending and descending orders of attractiveness. The former signaled shock onset and hence anxiety, which was avoided if the patient removed the slide from the screen within 8 seconds; the

[2] Details of the aversion/data logger "hybrid" apparatus, together with the computer program (MACRO 9) are available from the authors.

onset of the latter was associated with shock avoidance, and consequent anxiety relief. The technique thus combined aversion to older females and desensitization to young ones within the same treatment system.

Once the patient was avoiding consistently he was placed on a treatment program comprising three types of trial: reinforced (R) in which his avoidance response succeeds immediately; delayed (D) in which, by special arrangement of the circuitry, the patient's attempts to switch off fail for a period of time within the 8-second period which elapses between the onset of the older female slide and recurrence of shock. He does eventually succeed before 8 seconds have elapsed. The length of time for which he is delayed may be either 4½, 6 or 7½ seconds, after the onset of the slide, varied randomly; (NR), the patient's attempts to switch off are not allowed to succeed and he has to sit out the 8 seconds and receive a brief shock of aversive strength. The shock and the slide terminate simultaneously. The program consists of one third of each type of trial, varied randomly.

When the patient reported that 1) his previous attraction to the current older female slide had been replaced by indifference or even actual dislike, and 2) he attempted to switch off within 1 to 2 seconds of its appearance, we proceeded to the next older female slide and repeated the process.

As mentioned above, we also attempted to associate relief from anxiety with the introduction of the young female slide. However, such a slide was not introduced at every trial, to preserve what we consider to be the important principle of reducing generalization decrement—that is, reducing the disparity between the treatment situation and the real-life situation, in which of course, attempts to approach the desired females are not always likely to meet with success. We allowed the patient to request the return of the young female slide after it had been removed. (The young female slide was always removed by the therapist and not by the patient.) The patient was provided with a switch, which he could use in order to bring the young female slide back to the screen. However, his request was met in an entirely random manner, sometimes being granted and sometimes not, so that he could not predict the consequences of his attempting to

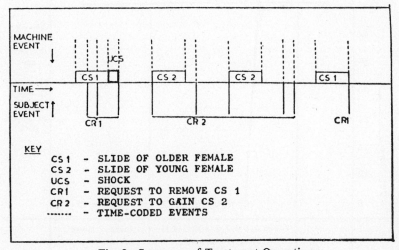

Fig. 2. Sequence of Treatment Operations

switch off the older female slide, nor of his "asking" for the return of the young slide. The whole situation was designed to lead to the acquisition of two responses: avoidance of older females and approach to young females.

Figure 2 summarizes the treatment sequence.

The patient was given 18 20-minute sessions of anticipatory avoidance aversion therapy, using eight CS_1 and six CS_2 slides.

RESULTS

Clinical. The prime aim of this therapy was to prevent *all* further exhibitory behavior in order to avoid legal proceedings against the patient; he was therefore interviewed before each aversion therapy session. After three sessions he reported a gradual increase in the ease with which he could prevent exhibitory fantasy, and the fantasy of older women during masturbation. At the completion of treatment he was able to control the start of the cognitive chain which had previously led to the exhibitory behavior, although 25 percent of his masturbatory fantasy was still concerned with older women. At six-week follow-up he reported that his masturbatory fantasy exclusively concerned girls of his own age and the compulsive ideas about exhibiting himself were absent. The situation remains unchanged at the latest follow-up at 5 months. His heterosexual skills are improved, he has a 13-year-old "girl friend" who visits his home, and he reports a lessening of anxiety in heterosexual relationships.

Psychometric: Sexual Orientation Measure. The scoring system for the Sexual Orientation Measure is so designed as to give scores between 6 and 48 on the two stimulus classes—in this case "women of 25 plus years" and "girls of my own age," where high

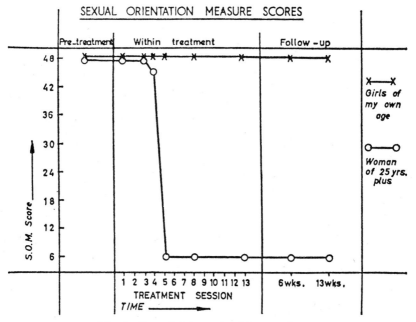

Fig. 3. Sexual Orientation Measure Scores.

scores indicate the direction of sexual orientation of the patient. From Fig. 3 it will be seen that on first presentation K attained a maximum score on both scales indicating a high positive attitude to both girls of his own age and women over 25 years.

The fall in score in relation to women of 25 plus years paralleled the increase in the patient's ability to control his compulsive thought.

We would like to suggest that aversion therapy of this type is a potent component of the behavior therapist's repertoire provided that it is judiciously used. The main usefulness of aversion therapy appears to be in situations where maladaptive approach behavior cannot be relieved.

REFERENCES

Birtles, C.J. A data logging system for behavioral studies. M.Sc. Thesis, University of Birmingham, 1970.

Bond, I.K. & Hutchinson, H.C. Application of reciprocal inhibition therapy to exhibitionism. *Can. Med. Ass. J.* 1960, **83**, 23-25.

Evans, D.R. Masturbatory fantasy and sexual deviation. *Behav. Res. & Therapy.* 1968, **6**, 17-19.

Feldman, M.P. & MacCulloch, M.J. A systematic approach to the treatment of homosexuality by conditioned aversion. Preliminary report. *Am. J. Psychiat.*, 1964, **121**, 167-172.

Feldman, M.P. & MacCulloch, M.J. The application of anticipatory avoidance learning to the treatment of homosexuality. I. Theory, technique and preliminary results. *Behav. Res. & Therapy.* 1965, **2**, 165-183.

Feldman, M.P., MacCulloch, M.J., Mellor, V. & Pinschof, J.M. The application of anticipatory avoidance learning to the treatment of homosexuality, III. The sexual orientation method. *Behav. Res. & Therapy.* 1966, **4**, 289-299.

Feldman, M.P., MacCulloch, M.J. & MacCulloch, M.L. The aversion therapy treatment of a heterogeneous group of five cases of sexual deviation. *Acta psychiat. neurol. Scand.*, 1968, **44**, 113-123.

Feldman, M.P. MacCulloch, M.J., Orford, J.F. & Mellor, V. The application of anticipatory avoidance learning to the treatment of homosexuality. Developments in treatment technique and response recording. *Acta Psychiat. Neurol. Scand.*, 1969, **45**, 109-117.

Feldman, M.P. & MacCulloch, M.J. *Homosexual Behaviour: Therapy and Assessment.* Oxford: Pergamon Press, 1970.

Kraft-Ebing, R. Von *Psychopathia sexualis*. 12th Ed. New York: Rebman, 1912.

Kushner, M. & Sandler, J. Aversion therapy and the concept of punishment. *Behav. Res. & Therapy.* 1966, **4**, 179-186.

Lasegue, E.C. *Les exhibitionistes. Troisieme series.* France: L'union medicale, 1877.

MacCulloch, M.J. & Feldman, M.P. Aversion therapy management of 43 homosexuals. *Brit. Med. J.,* 1967, **2**, 594-597.

MacCulloch, M.J. & Feldman, M.P. Personality and the treatment of homosexuality. *Acta psychiat. neurol. Scand.,* 1967, **43**, 300-317.

MacCulloch, M.J., Birtles, C.J. & Bond, S. A free space-time traversal data-logging system for two human subjects. *Med. & biol. Engng*, 1969, **7**, 593-599.

Sperling, M. The analysis of an exhibitionist. *Int. J. Psychoanal.,* 1947, **28**, 32-45.

Woodworth, R.S. & Schlosberg, H. *Experimental psychology.* New York: Holt, Rinehart and Winston, 1962.

58
Reinforcement Control of Exhibitionism in a Profoundly Retarded Adult *

JOHN R. LUTZKER

Social reinforcement in the form of praise and attention has been shown to control the behavior of normal children and institutionalized adults. Excessive crying (Hart, Allen, Buell, Harris & Wolf, 1964) and regressed crawling (Harris, Johnston, Kelley & Wolf, 1964) behaviors were changed through social reinforcement procedures. Classroom behavior also has been controlled through the use of social reinforcement (Broden, Bruce, Mitchell, Carter & Hall, Lund & Jackson, 1968). Extreme social isolation in two schizophrenic male adults was modified by contingent social reinforcement (Milby, 1970). Exhibitionism, however, has been treated previously through aversion behavior therapy techniques (Abel, Levis & Clancy, 1970). The present study used social reinforcement for behavior other than exhibitionism to reduce exhibitionism in a retarded adult male.

METHOD

Subject. Fred was a 52-year-old profoundly retarded male resident of a state school for the retarded. He frequently was seen exhibiting himself; i.e., he often had his pants fastened, but unzipped, which allowed his penis to be fully visible outside of his pants. He also frequently approached staff members and visitors to be hugged; therefore, the use of social reinforcement was the first consideration as a treatment procedure.

Setting. The entire study took place in two wards in the building in which Fred was a resident. The treatment procedures in this study were applied by the regular attendant-nursing staff of the building.

Apparatus. The attendants used a portable timer (Foxx & Martin, 1971) to time each interval. The timer was attached to a clipboard on which was placed the data-scoring sheets that were used for recording Fred's behavior during the study.

Procedure. Four training sessions of 2 hours each were scheduled for the residents of the wards in the building. That is, across the day and afternoon shifts, there were 8 hours that were to be used for training and activity periods. The present study was conducted

*Parts of this study were supported by a grant from the Maternal and Child Health Service, Project Number 906. The author expresses gratitude to the participating staff at North Building at the Fernald School and to Jerry Martin and Andrew Wheeler for their helpful advice.

during those time periods each day. During the 9 days of base line, the attendant was instructed to set the timer for 10-minutes intervals throughout each 2-hour training period. When the buzzer on the timer sounded, the attendant observed whether Fred was exhibiting himself. A response of "yes" or "no" then was written by the attendant next to the appropriate time on the data sheet. Thus, the measure indicated whether the behavior was occurring at the end of each 10-minute interval.

It had been observed that the attendants paid attention to Fred and occasionally hugged him regardless of whether or not he was exposing himself; therefore, during the baseline condition they were told to treat Fred as they always had.

The exhibition behavior was easily defined and observed. Reliability checks were made by a second observer for a 1-hour sample in each condition of the study. During the reliability checks, the second observer made an independent written response regarding the occurrence or nonoccurrence of the behavior after the buzzer sounded. When these records were compared, there was 100 percent agreement between the two observers for each reliability session.

On the tenth day, the treatment condition was begun. The attendant was told to continue to observe Fred at the end of each 10-minute interval and record the occurrence or nonoccurrence of the exhibition behavior. However, they were instructed further that if Fred was engaged in any behavior other than exhibiting himself at the end of the interval, he was to be hugged and told: "Good, Fred, your pants are on right." Thus, he received differential social reinforcement for any behavior other than exhibiting himself (DRO). If he was exposing himself at the end of the interval or during the interval, he was ignored.

The extinction condition involved the removal of the social reinforcement. The attendant continued to make a written response after every 10-minute interval, but provided no hugs or praise during that condition. The procedure, thus, differed from baseline in that some reinforcement from the attendant may have been provided during base line, but during the extinction phase there were specific instructions to provide no social reinforcement. The purpose of the extinction condition was to examine if the social reinforcement was the effective variable in producing the reduction of the exhibitionism in the DRO condition.

The procedures during the second treatment condition (DRO) were identical to the procedures during the first treatment condition.

After the forty-sixth day, a staff shortage prevented the systematic application of the program. The attendant was told to hug Fred about every other interval after which he was not exposing himself. Two days later were used as follow-up in which the data again were collected; however, the social reinforcement was provided to Fred for every other interval at the end of which he was not exhibiting himself.

RESULTS AND DISCUSSION

Figure 1 represents the percent of intervals at the end of which Fred was exhibiting himself. The percent was determined by dividing the total number of intervals ("yes" and "no" responses) into the number of "yes" (exhibition) responses.

As can be seen in Fig. 1, the percent of intervals at the end of which exhibition behavior occurred during baseline ranged from 4 to 40, with a mean of 15 percent. The

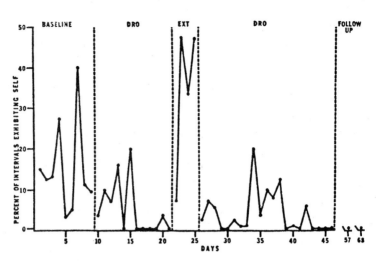

Fig. 1. Percent of Intervals the S Was Observed Exhibiting Himself.

range in the first DRO condition was from 0 to 20 percent, with a mean of 5 percent, although there were 5 days of 0 percent in the last 6 days of that condition. The range of exhibitionism in the extinction phase was from 7 to 48 percent, with a mean of 34 percent. The percent of exhibitionism during the second DRO condition ranged from 0 to 20 percent, with a mean of 4 percent. The last four consecutive days show a 0 percent rate of occurrence. Finally, the two follow-up days also show a 0 percent rate of occurrence of the exhibitionism.

The results of this study demonstrate that exhibitionism was reduced in a retarded adult by applying differential social reinforcement for other behavior. The reinforcement was in the form of a hug and praise from an attendant who supervised Fred on each shift. An attempt to look systematically at changes in the amount of reinforcement was prevented by a staff shortage in the building. However, on the 2 follow-up days, the amount of reinforcement was reduced and no occurrences of exhibitionism were observed.

While social reinforcement has been effective in controlling behavior in a variety of settings, exhibitionism previously has not been studied as a function of reinforcement control. Rather, behavior therapists most frequently have used aversion techniques for the treatment of exhibitionism in noninstitutionalized Ss. The procedures in the present study may be restricted to institutional settings; nevertheless, an alternative treatment method for exhibitionism was demonstrated. Further examination of reinforcement control of exhibitionism in other settings with Ss who are not retarded is suggested.

REFERENCES

Abel, G.A., Levis, D.J. & Clancy, J. Aversion therapy applied to taped sequences of deviant behavior in exhibitionism and other sexual deviations: A preliminary report. *Journal of Behavior Therapy and Experimental Psychiatry*. 1970, **1**, 59-66.

Broden, M., Bruce, C., Mitchell, M., Carter, V. & Hall, R.V. Effects of teacher attention on attending behavior of two boys at adjacent tasks. *Journal of Applied Behavior Analysis*. 1970, **3**, 199-204.

Foxx, R.M. & Martin, P.L. A useful portable timer. *Journal of Applied Behavior Analysis*. 1971, **4**, 60.

Hall, R.V., Lund, D. & Jackson, D. Effects of teacher attention on study behavior. *Journal of Applied Behavior Analysis*. 1968, **1**, 1-12.

Harris, F.R., Johnston, M.K., Kelley, C.S. & Wolf, M.M. Effects of positive social reinforcement on regressed crawling of a nursery school child. *Journal of Education Psychology*. 1964, **55**, 35-41.

Hart, B.M., Allen, K.E., Buell, J.S., Harris, F.R. & Wolf, M.M. Effects of social reinforcement on operant crying. *Journal of Experimental Child Psychology*. 1964, **1**, 145-153.

Milby, J.B. Modification of extreme social isolation by contingent social reinforcement. *Journal of Applied Behavior Analysis*. 1970, **3**, 149-152.

Additional Selected Readings

Bond, I.K., & Hutchinson, H.C. Application of reciprocal inhibition therapy to exhibitionism, *Canadian Medical Association Journal,* 1960, **83**, 23-25.

Evans, D.R. Masturbatory fantasy and sexual deviation, *Behaviour Research and Therapy,* 1968, **6**, 17-19.

Fookes, B.H. Some experiences in the use of aversion therapy in male homosexuality, exhibitionism and fetishism-transvestism, *British Journal of Psychiatry,* 1960, **115**, 339-341.

Lowenstein, L.F. A case of exhibitionism treated by counter-conditioning, *Adolescence,* 1973, **8**, 213-218.

Quirk, D.A. A follow-up on the Bond-Hutchinson case of systematic desensitization with an exhibitionist, *Behavior Therapy,* 1974, **5**, 428-431.

Ritchie, G.G. Jr. The use of hypnosis in a case of exhibitionism, *Psychotherapy: Theory, Research and Practice,* 1968, **5**, 40-43.

Rooth, F.G., & Mark, I.M. Persistent exhibitionism: Short-term response to self-regulation and relaxation treatment. *Archives of Sexual Behavior,* 1974, **3**, 227-248.

Wickramasekera, I. Aversive behavior rehearsal for sexual exhibitionism, *Behavior Therapy* (in press), 1975.

Wickramasekera, I. A technique for controlling a certain type of sexual exhibitionism, *Psychotherapy: Theory, Research and Practice,* 1972, **9**, 3, 207-210.

Pedophiliac Behavior

Pedophiliac behavior refers to the behavior of adults who fantasize or directly involve children in their sexual activity. Most pedophiliac behavior is exhibited by adult males with young females. Homosexual pedophilia (*see* Chapter 60) is rare. In 85 percent of reported pedophiliac attacks, the adult is either a relative, family friend, neighbor or acquaintance of the child (Katchadourian & Lunde, 1975, p. 341). Such activities may create considerable emotional problems for the child, either directly from the experience, or indirectly through the anxiety, anger and confusion of the parents. However, physical damage to the child is rare, occurring in only two percent of cases, although threats of violence occurred in about one third of the cases reported. Intercourse is rarely attempted, and the actual physical contacts between the men and the girls usually is limited to general fondling and, perhaps, stroking of the childs' external genitals.

The average age of men convicted of pedophiliac acts is 35. Only 25 percent were over 45 and only 5 percent were considered "senile." About 75 percent of the offenders had been married at some time in their lives, and they tended to be both conservative and moralistic (Gebhard et al., 1965).

The articles reported in this section comprise all of the individual case studies dealing with pedophiliac behavior that could be located in the behavioral literature.

The first article is "Classical Conditioning of a Sexual Deviation" by Beech, Watts and Poole. Based on problems which they saw as associated with the use of aversive methods to decrease undesired behavior, the authors attempted to use a classical conditioning paradigm to help a young man who had been engaging in pedophiliac behavior. The therapy employed pictures of young girls as the unconditioned stimulus and pictures of mature women as the conditioned stimulus, in which pictures of the latter were paired with pictures of the former after they had produced sexual excitation. Interestingly, this treatment led to a decrease in attraction to the young girls, and an increase in attraction to older, more "age-appropriate" females.

The article by Edwards describes an unusual but interesting use of "Assertive Training in a Case of Homosexual Pedophilia." The case of homosexual pedophiliac behavior of some 10 years' duration apparently was seen at the point when the client's family was disintegrating as a result of this sexual problem. At the first session, the client was trained in thought-stopping in an effort to diminish his preoccupation with pedophiliac fantasies and the anxiety they produced. Over a period of a month during which the client was not in treatment, the thought-stopping appeared to be notably effective. When he returned to treatment, the client was schooled in assertive training which appeared to lead to an elimination of the interpersonal anxieties that had interfered with desired heterosexual functioning and possibly led to the pedophiliac behavior. After a total of 13 interviews and at a six-month follow-up, the client reported that he had successfully attained the desired social and heterosexual functioning. The article concludes with a discussion of the intervention program by the author and several other clinicians.

The next article is Rosenthal's "Response Contingent versus Fixed Punishment in Aversion Conditioning of Pedophilia." In this case study, a long-standing situation involving pedophiliac behavior was treated by aversion conditioning therapy. Rosenthal reports that although the typical fixed punishment (pairing) aversion paradigm was largely unsuccessful, prompt and dramatic progress was obtained with a response contingent (shaping) paradigm, in which shock intensity was held constant while shock duration was made a function of response latencies (i.e., imagining the pedophiliac behavior). Follow-up data extending over 32 months from final routine booster sessions revealed maintenance of both behavioral and imaginal changes.

The final article in this section is "An Automated Fading Procedure to Alter Sexual Responsiveness in Pedophiles," by Laws and Pawlowski. In this article, an automated stimulus fading procedure was used to strengthen sexual responsiveness to adult stimuli in two individuals who previously had engaged in pedophiliac behavior (one of whom wished to retain a homosexual orientation but be more responsive to adults). Slides of children and adults were superimposed and one faded out and the other faded in when the client produced an erection above a designated criterion. If responding fell below this criterion, the fading process was reversed. The results show that when a slide of an adult was faded into a child and a covert self-instruction procedure was initiated to decrease response to the child, both clients produced high sexual responding to adult slides and decreased responding to slides of a child. Hence, this non-aversive fading method of altering sexual responsiveness to children may, with further research, prove to be extremely useful in helping individuals change their sexual responsiveness. Of course, it should be noted that both clients in this study were confined for the criminal offenses of "pedophilia," and it is difficult to determine the influence that the probability of reducing future confinement following altered sexual response had on enhancing their motivation for treatment and potential for change.

REFERENCES

Gebhard, P.H., Gagnon, J.H., Pomeroy, W.B. & Christenson, C.V. *Sex offenders,* New York: Harper and Row, 1965.

59

Classical Conditioning of a Sexual Deviation: A Preliminary Note

H.R. BEECH, FRASER WATTS AND A. DESMOND POOLE

The methods most commonly used by psychologists in the treatment of sexual deviation are designed to reduce the level of inappropriate behavior. This emphasis upon eroding the old deviant response has certain well-documented limitations, apart from the obvious point that blocking one form of sexual expression may not be expected to lead logically to the spontaneous emergence of patterns deemed by society to be "appropriate." It is not necessary to list these shortcomings here, but simply to point out that viable alternatives to such strategies as aversion therapy must be sought. It is to this problem that our report is addressed.

One might expect classical conditioning to be a method which could be used to develop responsiveness to a previously neutral sexual stimulus. The studies by Rachman (1966) and Rachman and Hodgson (1968), for example, would encourage one to believe that transfer of capacity for sexual arousal from one stimulus complex to another is technically feasible, and that such a procedure might be adapted to the special problems of sexual deviancy, in the hope of avoiding many of the complications of aversion therapy.

On the one hand, the CS or neutral stimulus in such a treatment program clearly has to be an appropriate sexual object, i.e., one which society might judge to be "normal" and "acceptable," and to which no ascertainable sexual responsiveness can be detected at the outset of training. On the other hand, the UCS would be chosen in terms of its existing capacity to produce the desired reactions (subjective feelings of sexual excitement and matching erectile responses). However, an interesting departure from a more typical classical conditioning paradigm arose from the decision to use a CS and a UCS that were as similar as possible.

At the outset, it had been our intention to consider the additional use of aversion therapy after any successful sexual transfer had been effected. The outcome of doing this could not be anticipated, but it was thought possible that the stimulus to sexual arousal at the end of training would be remote from the original UCS and that any aversive reaction to the original UCS which was created might not transfer to the new stimulus to sexual arousal. In this connection, it is of interest to note that no such further step was needed and that the development of "adaptive" sexual responses was paralleled by a reduction in "pathological" sexual interests.

CASE REPORT

Subject

A male student of 21 years who found immature girls sexually arousing and who actively sought out opportunities for voyeuristic experiences of this kind. His desire for treatment seemed to stem partly from a fear of the social and legal consequences of his impulses and partly from a desire to lead a "normal" heterosexual life.

Procedure

A series of photographs of nude females, ranging from the immature (totally without secondary sexual characteristics) to the "fully mature" (well-developed "calendar" pin-ups) were presented to the subject in random order for 10 seconds each. He was instructed to fantasize sexually to them, and the latency and amplitude of his penile plethysmographic response to each stimulus was measured. He was also asked to rate these photographs on a 5-point scale extending from "very attractive to me" to "repugnant to me." These two measures were found to be well correlated and clearly confirmed that the most immature females were the most evocative but that no sexual reactivity could be elicited to the pictures of the more mature females. Four groups of pictures were then assembled, ranging from very young and often prepubertal females (Group I) which could serve as UCS immediately, to sexually mature females photo-graphed in provocative positions (Group IV) to which no response other than repugnance was manifested.

At the beginning of treatment Group I stimuli were used as the UCS and Group II the CS. When the latter had come to elicit full responses they became the UCS and Group III the CS. In the final stage, Group III served as the UCS and Group IV the CS.

Nine CS-UCS pairs were used at each stage of the conditioning procedure. A CS was presented for 5 sec. then removed and replaced by a UCS which was presented for a maximum of 30 seconds, or until such time as a plethysmographic response was obtained (the subject being instructed to attempt to create a sexual fantasy to each stimulus). When the UCS was withdrawn, a blank card was presented and the subject was given mental arithmetic tasks to perform until any penile response which had been evoked had returned to basal level. The next pair of stimuli was then presented. The latency and amplitude of the penile response to each stimulus were recorded. After the presentations of the entire sequence of stimuli, two members of the class of photographs being used as CS were presented, unaccompanied by any UCS, in order to assess the progress achieved. The conditioning sessions extended over three months at the rate of two each week.

Results

Penile responses were successfully conditioned to all the photographs used. After three weeks of treatment the subject reported having experienced sexual arousal with mature females outside the treatment situation, and that his interest in young females was declining. He began to indulge in limited forms of adaptive sexual behavior, but claimed that he was more aroused by simply looking at females than by coming into more direct physical contact with them. However, a few months after the termination of the formal parts of the treatment program he had satisfactory intercourse. Though his sexual behavior continued to be somewhat inhibited, it undoubtedly became much more appropriate than before treatment began.

COMMENT

It appears that the classical conditioning of sexual responsiveness is a potentially viable technique and that, within limits, it can be successfully applied clinically. Furthermore, the technique has certain advantages over aversion therapy as a strategy for change.

Apart from any obvious implications this study might have for a treatment strategy, the possibility of a new theoretical orientation is suggested. In this individual patient, the emergence of a new sexual orientation was accompanied by a reduction in pathological responses, and this may indicate the existence of radically different mechanisms in sexual deviancy from those ordinarily put forward by conditioning theorists.

It is recognized that the present investigation is essentially exploratory and suffers numerous deficiencies of design and control. However, one of us (Beech) is now engaged in a larger scale and more sophisticated replication.

REFERENCES

Rachman, S. Sexual fetishism: An experimental analogue. *Psychological Record.* 1966, **16**, 293-296.

Rachman, S. & Hodgson, R.J. Experimentally induced "sexual fetishism": Replication and development. *Psychological Record.* 1968, **18**, 25-27.

60

Case Conference: Assertive Training in a Case of Homosexual Pedophilia*

NEIL B. EDWARDS

The behavior therapy literature contains few reports on the treatment of pedophilia. I have been able to find only two such reports. Stevenson and Wolpe (1960) successfully treated one pedophile by assertive training, and Barlow, Leitenberg and Agras (1969) one by covert sensitization. I chose assertive training as the primary treatment modality for the following case.

The patient, a 40-year-old physician, was referred to me by Dr. Wolpe late in June, 1971, for the treatment of three problems: sexual activity with his three sons (now aged 13, 9 and 5) for about 10 years; numerous long-standing interpersonal difficulties, mainly with his wife but also with other adults; and mild, episodic impotence with his wife for 2 years. What precipitated him into behavior therapy was his wife's discovery that he had persuaded his eldest son to take an active role in one of their sexual encounters, i.e., to penetrate the patient anally. Even though she had known for almost 2 years about the sexual activity between the patient and the boys, this new development was the last straw. The marriage had been very shaky for the past 2 years, but the wife now saw no possibility of reconciliation even if he were cured. This was the climate when the patient came to see me. He was leaving in a couple of days for a month in the Mediterranean, which was to be the beginning of a legal separation.

The patient, a slim, athletic white male, looking perhaps 10 years younger than his stated age, seemed initially somewhat anxious in telling me his story but, as the session progressed, became quite comfortable. He immediately stated two of the chief complaints already mentioned, the pedophiliac behavior and the episodic impotence. The third complaint—his difficulties in peer interpersonal relationships—unfolded as he told his story. His pedophiliac behavior with his children had started soon after he discovered that his wife had had an affair. Its frequency was variable but averaged about once every 2 weeks. It involved all three sons and consisted mainly of his rubbing his penis between the

*This case was presented at a seminar in the Behavior Therapy Unit of the Temple University Department of Psychiatry. Participants in the discussion were: Jack Almelah, Paula Bram, Edna Foa, Jay Razani, David Soskis, Joseph Wolpe and Edward Zuckerman.

boy's buttocks to the point of orgasm. Since his wife's discovery of this behavior 2 years ago, it had been a continual source of argument. Despite her pleas, however, he had been unable to stop. It was during these 2 years that he had begun to have trouble maintaining erections during their infrequent attempts at intercourse. Sex between them had been largely unsatisfactory ever since.

Regarding his background, he is the elder of two children, the younger being a married sister. He described his mother as "somewhat overbearing. She always wanted me to do more than I was doing at the time." He said that she taught him to be compulsive and was largely responsible for his becoming a doctor. His father was much more quiet than his mother but "when he did say something people listened." He was a stern disciplinarian yet tended to be "overly fair." The patient described himself as having the latter characteristic also. His father didn't show much emotion. He was very successful in business and provided a substantial income for his family. The patient got along better with his father than with his mother but said of his father: "He never really stuck up for me during my childhood." He recalls his childhood and adolescence as not very happy and during high school he pretty much "cut off relations" with his parents, i.e., he just avoided interacting with them as much as possible. He has maintained this stance to the present.

His peer heterosexual adjustment had always been, at best, tenous. Although he dated during high school he had no sexual intercourse until age seventeen when he twice had intercourse with prostitutes. On both occasions he contracted gonorrhea. This was quite frightening and succeeded in turning him off sexual intercourse for several years. About 1 year after his second gonorrheal infection he had his first pedophilic experience with the 4-year-old son of a friend.

He met his wife when he was in medical school. He did not court her very avidly at first because she wanted to go to parties a lot, which he couldn't do because of his studies. However, about 6 months after they met, they had intercourse. This enthused him so much that they were engaged 2 months later. During this 2-month period they took a 1-week vacation together in Florida. At that time "she was all for sex," but became upset when he got one room for them in Florida. However, they did have sexual intercourse frequently during their vacation. After the trip she went back to her parents' home to prepare for the wedding and he back to medical school. When he came up for the engagement party she acted somewhat coolly toward him. On the wedding night there was no sex because she was drunk on champagne. The first sexual intercourse after the wedding was on about the fifth day. She had become less keen on sex, and almost immediately began "sitting around moping." This unexpected behavior began to turn him off. Even so, he continued "trying all sorts of ways to get sex" for a few months. Gradually, however, his efforts waned, and after about a year of marriage coitus was down to once every 2 or 3 months. Two years later, she started seeing another man. Though she claimed that sex was not involved, he was very broken up by this and told her to leave. She did leave for about 3 weeks "to think things over." During her absence he changed his mind and wanted her back. However, she had consulted a lawyer and wanted a divorce. He reluctantly agreed, and after 9 months of legal separation the divorce was finalized. Two months later they remarried. Sexually, she was now the aggressor! He found this irritating; and again within a year they were back to coitus once every 2 or 3 months, a frequency which continued to be the mode. It was about a year after their remarriage that he started turning to his children for a sexual outlet.

His relationship with his wife was strained on several other scores also. Without his knowledge her parents had practically forced her to marry him, mainly because they did not approve of the friends she had been spending time with; and they saw the patient as a "good" opportunity for her. Although their constant prodding had merely augmented the good feelings she had for him, when he found out about it after they had been married several months, he was very bitter. Also, during the early years of the marriage they were prone to many arguments. She was "bored to death" but unwilling to take up sports, reading or any other activity. She was the type of person who watned to be given a good time but did not want to invest much of herself. He described her as a "nervous" person who would ride in a car practically holding on to the ceiling. He, on the other hand, had always been quite adventuresome. She was a chronic overspender. He had not been able to speak to her assertively on any of these issues. When an incident occurred, he would be sullenly angry for 2 or 3 days.

He had been in psychoanalysis for about a year 5 years earlier. He felt that it had helped him to like himself better—so that he had even decided that his pedophilia might be acceptable.

At the end of the first interview I did three things: 1) Since even when not engaging in pedophiliac behavior he was troubled by pedophiliac thoughts every day or two, I demonostrated thought-stopping, and told him to use it whenever the thoughts came to his mind. 2) I told him to avoid sex with anyone during the month he was away, and to concentrate on getting to know people instead. 3) I gave him initial instructions on assertive behavior, and told him to start practicing it. We agreed to meet three times a week on his return from the Mediterranean.

After he came back from the Mediterranean for his second session, he reported that the thought-stopping was working well; the frequency of the pedophiliac thoughts having decreased to once or twice a week. He was back with his wife and had had several good erections but, following instructions, had not attempted intercourse. I felt he was fairly well into assertive training. He had read the book *Your Perfect Right* and found very helpful its 30-odd examples distinguishing nonassertive response, assertive response and aggressive response. He told his wife that from now on he would be in control of the money; also that she could either go along with outside activities or stay at home, but was not to mope. At the third session, I congratulated him on these assertions and went on to instruct him in the expression of positive feelings. I also began to smile whenever he referred to his wife as "the wife" as was his wont. After about three sessions of this, he was routinely referring to her by her first name. However, when I started the smiling, he brought out some more feelings about her. What he disliked about her mainly was what she had been keeping him "one down." If she provoked him, he would be unable to assert himself, but stay angry for several days, feeling dissatisfied that he was not gettings things straightened out. He was not beginning to feel that he was gaining some control.

At the fourth session he reported that he had again stated clearly that he would be the decision-maker on finances, on the bringing up of the children, and "as a matter of fact, on all things." She was argumentative and angry at first, but he felt himself in control the entire time. She ultimately accepted his edict which he found a highly satisfying experience. He then told her that her sexual aggressiveness upset him because she had challenged him on the "no sex" issue and become seductive. He had, however, felt like sex with her on several occasions. Since he seemed ready to approach her, I instructed him to do so but assume at least equality in control, not to allow her to domineer.

At the fifth session he reported intercourse which he had initiated, culminating in simultaneous orgasms. He had had one disturbing experience—an erection while watching cartoons with the kids. He was worried that this would continue, but I assured him that it was merely a habit that would extinguish. There were a couple of episodes where he had missed opportunities for assertion. His eldest son, having had an accident on a motorcycle and suffered an acromioclavicular separation, needed to go to hospital to have it set. The boy was dressed in Bermuda shorts, but his mother made him get into "dress-up clothes." The patient let that one go because he did not feel that strongly; it was not important to assert himself. On another occasion, his wife had rescinded an order to the children. I instructed him to tell her that when there was an issue of discipline between him and the children upon which she differed from him, she should first discuss it with him. That was where the session ended.

By the next session he had got down to dealing with the discipline issue. Also, on one occasion he had become angry with his wife when she was upset and critical over the clothes he was wearing. He had walked out angrily, but about 15 minutes later told her not to get upset over little things. I congratulated him not only on the assertive behavior, but also on the fact that he had cut down brooding time from days to 15 minutes. Another successful assertion occurred when he overheard his wife speak about motorcycles to a doctor whom he disliked very much. The doctor started on a rampage about people who ride motorcycles and how dangerous they are. The patient did not speak directly to the doctor because he was not involved in the conversation, but became angry that his wife was saying nothing in his defense. When the doctor left he told her please to stick up for him in the future because it made him angry for her to just stand there and accept negative remarks about something he felt very positive about. When his wife's parents one day decided to invite themselves over, he told them: "No, when I'm ready, I'll invite you." Later, feeling he had made his point, he told his wife to call them up and let them come over for a drink. When they had had a drink and relaxed for an hour or so, he indicated to them that it was time to leave, which they did.

His wife was soon "falling in very nicely" with his policy toward her parents. Before the seventh session she told her parents (who had previously been quite "nosey") that the patient's problems and hers were none of their business. They had intercourse twice with mutual orgasms. Sex had been initiated either by him or mutually every time, and his wife seemed pleased with the increased sexual activity. He was quite pleased also with his ability to influence his environment. There was one difficulty that he mentioned. His wife was a bit piqued at times that he was closer to the children than she. The children had a very good general relationship with him. During his absence in the Mediterranean, she had transmitted some guilt to them about the sexual activities. Apparently she was still doing this in subtle ways. He told her at this time not to do this any more, and that the way to get close to people was to do *positive* things for them and say *positive* things to them.

At the eighth session he reported that things were going very well. Once he had awakened in the middle of the night with a very good erection, nudged his wife, and they had very good intercourse.

During the days between the eighth and ninth sessions, he spent a good deal of time explaining to his wife what assertive training was all about and why it would be good for her and the children as well as for him. He reported during his ninth session that he had misinterpreted a secret conversation between his wife and their eldest son as one of his wife's "subversive sessions." Although he was angry he let it ride to see what would happen. He found later that this had been a wise course of action—the son had been in some minor trouble with the police (breaking lumber at a construction site) while the patient was in the Mediterranean and was afraid to tell the patient about it. The wife advised the son to tell the patient about it, and the next day without prodding he did. The patient reacted positively in the sense: "I'm glad you were able to tell me about it." He told his wife of his misgivings and apologized—then congratulated her on her course of action.

His wife continued to move toward him. Before the tenth session she thought it would be great fun to get on to motorcycles and ride over to her parents' house dressed in mod clothes, since they disapproved of both motorcycles and mod clothes. He thought that this was a very nice symbolic action and told her so. He also reported that she was getting better at expressing her positive feelings toward the children. However, she had expressed a concern about "being behind" and that maybe she should come in to see me. He told her not to, that it was his treatment. I told him to modify this a little bit by telling her: "Of course you'll be behind. I'm the one that's getting therapy and I have to pass it on to you second hand—but by working together you'll catch up." He agreed that this would help her to feel less "one down."

At the eleventh session he stated that the novelty of being assertive was wearing off, that it was becoming a habit. I expressed a great deal of pleasure at this.

At the twelfth session he reported that his wife was now finally convinced that her "confidence" sessions with the eldest son were somewhat subversive in terms of family interaction and that she had agreed that they should stop. He had told her to stop reinforcing the guilt in this son and that his own now nonexistent pedophiliac behavior was not to be discussed any more. He was handling the in-laws very well except for one problem: they were already talking about coming down for Christmas "for a week." From past experience he knew that a week could easily turn into 2 months. He had already told them it was all right to come for a few days but no longer. They had agreed, with very little bad feeling. One day the eldest son had told his mother that the patient had driven recklessly on one occasion when they were riding the motorcycle together. She had said: "If you have something to complain about concerning your father, you must have it out with him." They had had very satisfactory sexual intercourse twice since the previous session. She was feeling very good about how things were coming along.

The thirteenth session was the last. He reported that he had had a minor lapse. He had allowed three issues to build up and had gotten too angry to speak out. However, he recognized it in time and was able to express to his wife that he was angry and why, and in a couple of hours it was all over. He felt at this point (and I reinforced it) that it would be a good idea for him to apologize to her for letting these things build up. He and his family were leaving for Oregon in a few days. We agreed that he call me periodically, and, if necessary, come to see me.[1]

Wolpe: What was the total time span?
Edwards: Four weeks. Thirteen sessions. We started on August 2 and the last session was August 30.
Wolpe: That's certainly quite a transformation.

---

[1] As of December, 1971, the patient reported via the telephone that he was still doing well in all areas.

Edwards: The rationale for the treatment came from a case report (Stevenson and Wolpe, 1960).

Wolpe: Actually, that paper reports two cases of homosexuality and one of pedophilia.

Edwards: It seemed that in each case the primary difficulty was in relationships with peers, and essentially these were the target of treatment here.

Wolpe: I would like it understood how much Dr. Edwards has achieved. When this man and his wife came to see me at the end of June, there was a spectacle of shipwreck. The family was disintegrating and the marriage virtually at an end. When I asked the wife whether she felt there was any chance at all of restoration of her affection for him if he were to assume normal patterns of sexual behavior, she said it was out of the question. She and the boys were antagonistic to him and yet, in a way, understanding. They regarded him as a lost soul. To have restored an apparent normality and a satisfactory set of relationships in the course of 1 month is a splendid achievement.

Bram: Would you describe the thought-stopping that you said you had instructed in the first session to use?

Edwards: I had him relax after giving him a mini-session on relaxation training. Then I got him to visualize. He couldn't very well visualize just the pedophiliac thought, but he could visualize a time when he was with his eldest son and the thought occurred to him. When he indicated that it was clear in his mind I slammed my fist on the desk and shouted, "Stop." He jumped that high and said he could probably reproduce that autonomic response with just the word.

Bram: In regard to the thought-stopping on his own, would you describe how that was done?

Edwards: Well, he was instructed not to try to visualize the thoughts, but when they did occur, to try to reproduce the session in the office at that moment. Even though there had been only one trial in the office he reported that it was working—just visualizing what I had done in the office and the word, "Stop." Every time this caused an autonomic response, and the thought went away and decreased in frequency over the month between seeing me the first time and the second time. Actually, there wasn't any time to give him any detailed instruction in thought-stopping, so I used a short-cut.

Soskis: Do you formulate the results of the assertive training on the basis that making these assertive responses brought about a conditioned inhibition of the interpersonal anxiety, which allowed his normal heterosexual tendencies to come through?

Edwards: That's the way I would formulate it, yes.

Wolpe: Fear seems to be the usual basis of homosexuality. In a lot of cases the fear is of physical contact and in these desensitization is indicated. Where there is fear of assertiveness the answer is to train in assertive behavior. What I would very much like to see—and I think that the spate of cases that we are now having makes this very possible—is a study of a systematic program of treatment of homosexuals and related sexual deviants, guiding the treatment by the analysis of the individual case. This means giving assertive training where needed, using desensitization where indicated, and only when having done both of these things to exhaustion and finding no important change—only then using aversive forms of treatment. My guess is that such a program would reveal that only a minority of cases need aversion therapy.

Bram: One case I had last year worked out in exactly the same way as today's, and I have just started treatment of two more that I think will result in similar findings. How much do you feel that your results rested on the frequency with which you saw the patient. I am interested in this 13 sessions, three times a week for 4 weeks.

Edwards: The more I see, the more convinced I am that it's much better to see a patient for a month, three times a week, than it is to see them for 13 sessions weekly—on the whole. There are certain cases where it is not appropriate. Certainly—at the June 1971 Institute,[2] a whole lot of people got significantly better after being seen about a dozen times in 3 weeks.

Bram: I raised the question because I had found a similar kind of result in a patient I had seen intensively over a short period—not because it had been planned that way, but because the patient was due to leave and go elsewhere and there was just no choice.

Edwards: Each time he came in, the episodes were fresh in his mind, and the affect was still somewhat attached to them, so that it just seemed that the whole treatment period was alive with things to do.

Zuckerman: Just one question—I thought you said there was a month during his Mediterranean trip after you first saw him. You're not including that time in your 4 weeks of treatment.

Edwards: No. I suppose I should say 2 months.

Soskis: Were there any episodes of pedophiliac behavior following his return from the Mediterranean?

Edwards: No.

Soskis: So, really, in a way—

Edwards: He was better when he came back. He had more than one complaint, though.

Wolpe: What about pedophiliac impulses? When were they last noted?

Edwards: The last time that one occurred with any affect was the time when he was watching the cartoons. That was about in the middle of treatment and he got worried because he got an erection sitting there in his robe. After that, he sometimes thought about his previous activity, but whatever was attached to it of any pleasurable quality was gone. That's a self-report, a subjective evaluation, but that's what he said. He now thought of it more in terms of the effect it might have on his children and of how he would handle it if it came up.

Razani: What about the eldest son and his relationship with his father?

Edwards: The relationships between the father and his sons are now again very close. Except for the eldest son, who has a special attachment to the mother, they look to him for advice on most matters. I felt that the wife's actions toward the end of therapy were decreasing the frequency of the eldest son's approaches.

Razani: Because of the homosexual activity with the father wasn't there a fear in too much closeness?

Edwards: On a few occasions, the son did express anxiety to the mother. The patient had instructed his wife to tell the son to come to him to discuss it which the son then did. That was about the middle of treatment. And it was worked out very nicely. The son had difficulty in expressing it, but he did get it out and it was resolved. This would not happen in the future. They were not to worry about what happened in the past, but to go on and live a good life in the future.

Almelah: How long does it usually take to develop thought-stopping or to develop

---

[2] This is an annual month-long training course in behavior therapy.

assertion in a person who may not be quite as intelligent and articulate as this patient?

Edwards: I usually find that one trial of thought-stopping is quite effective. It may need reinforcement, but the way I did it one trial can be quite effective.

Almelah: I can understand the paradigm that you created, but what happens when you and the banging of your fist aren't present?

Edwards: I defer to Dr. Wolpe to answer that one because my experience is limited.

Wolpe: You actually stop the patient's thoughts by the explosive sound that you make while he is talking. And you then say to him: "This—what I've done—you can do. You can stop your thoughts by interrupting them by a sharp switch of attention." You also tell him that there will be a tendency for the thoughts to come back, so that he has to keep on stopping them to build up a habit of stopping undesirable thoughts. Very often, people manage this very well, provided they really apply themselves to the job of stopping the thoughts. One important thing that should be noted in a case like the present one is that stopping is only an auxiliary measure—a way of removing an anxiety source that is an obstacle to the real treatment, which in this case was removing interpersonal anxiety through assertive training. There are, however, cases of obsessional thinking in which thought-stopping has succeeded as the primary method (*see*, for example, Yamagami, 1971). However, most obsessions and compulsions need more than just thought-stopping.

Foa: Is it better to displace the unwanted thought verbally or with an image?

Edwards: It varies with different patients. Some find it better to use the verbal stimulus; others find a visual stimulus quite adequate. My patient used a scene in which he was thinking of having sexual activity with his son while they were on a boat in the middle of lake. He used that scene in my office. After that, he was instructed merely to use the thought-stopping when the thoughts occurred.

Foa: How did you know when he started to see the scene?

Edwards: I had him lift his finger. And after I did my thing I said: "There, it went away, didn't it?" And he said "It sure did."

Almelah: Did he laugh?

Edwards: Yes, he did. He jumped about that far off his seat and then he laughed. He said he felt quite certain that he could reproduce the autonomic response. When he came back he reported that he had maintained that ability throughout the month. He was a very good patient. He was willing to try his utmost, and he did.

Zuckerman: The result is very impressive. But I think the explanation is open to question. There is a whole bunch of ways of interpreting it. I don't think that necessarily the idea of assertive training inhibiting anxiety is the only way of explaining it. What about the mere fact of your defining or redefining both of their roles? It seems that these people were floundering and were pretty mixed up about where to go. You provided them with specific roles and put your pressure behind them. To me, that's another way of looking at it.

Wolpe: What could you propose as a control experiment?

Zuckerman: Control for what? For my hypothesis?

Wolpe: You say perhaps it was not the assertive training.

Zuckerman: No, I don't mean that. Assertive training is part of defining his role; you're the man in the house, you're supposed to do these things; your wife is supposed to do those things. They seem to be floundering and it is just a matter of getting back on that track with these sanctions of a psychiatrist.

Edwards: I don't think the two are mutually exclusive. I was very forceful with this guy—there's no doubt about it. I put my "all" behind this particular aspect of therapy.

Zuckerman: It seems to me that if you want to do a control experiment, that's the variable that needs to be varied—the influence of the therapist through such messages as "I have a solution to this; I have treated other people like this." It seems to me that this influence—the weight of psychiatry—could be eliminated in the design simply by explaining to the subjects beforehand that this was an experimental treatment.

Wolpe: The nonspecific effects that you call "the weight of psychiatry" were to some extent shown ineffective in the history of this case. After previous psychiatrists had failed, change followed the procedures Dr. Edwards described. We believe that the main factor was the deconditioning of anxiety.

Almelah: I don't see where the anxiety necessarily fits in. I wasn't that impressed with this guy's being very anxious when in bed with his wife.

Edwards: His anxiety was not related to sexual situations, but to interpersonal situations where an assertive response would have been appropriate.

Wolpe: We develop confidence in the therapeutic relevance of a specific procedure when change repeatedly follows its use. I would like to refer to Dr. Edwards' statement that it might be better to give treatment three times a week for 4 weeks than once a week for 12. It certainly seems to be an advantage in cases like this one, in which so much is involved. But it is a question that we ought to study in general. We might also study the merits of very long sessions.

REFERENCES

Alberti, R.E. & Emmons, M.L. *Your perfect right.* St. Louis Obispo, Calif., Impact, 1970.

Barlow, D.H., Leitenberg, H. & Agras, W.S. The experimental control of sexual deviation through manipulation of the noxious scene in covert sensitization. *J. Abnorm. Psychol.*, 1969, **74**, 596-601.

Stevenson, I. & Wolpe, J. Recovery from sexual deviations through overcoming of non-sexual neurotic responses. *Am. J. Psychiat.*, 1960, **116**, 737-742.

61

Response-Contingent versus Fixed Punishment in Aversion Conditioning of Pedophilia: A Case Study

TED L. ROSENTHAL

When electrical aversion therapy is used for sexual disorders, the usual treatment paradigm involves presenting shocks of relatively constant intensity and duration to the deviant actions and stimuli (e.g., fetish objects), or their imaginal representations. The severity and duration of shock do not typically depend on the precise features (e.g., latency) of the deviant behavior, but rather on its sheer occurrence or presence. In reviewing this literature, Rachman and Teasdale (1969) pointed out the method is best described as a punishment procedure, rather than as classical (Pavlovian) conditioning as has sometimes been claimed. Nevertheless, there is involved a consistent pairing of the same basic punishment to all the deviant responses. Also, lengthy follow-ups have rarely been reported of cases so treated. The present case study describes a chronic pedophiliac who failed to benefit from the foregoing fixed punishment paradigm. When, instead, the duration of shock was made to depend on his rapidity in attaining deviant arousal images (shaping paradigm), substantial and rapid improvement was obtained. Both his behavioral gains and inability to generate pedophiliac covert fantasies persisted in follow-ups continued over 3 years from the completion of the basic aversion therapy program.

CASE STUDY

Background

The subject was a 31-year-old divorced man of mildly retarded intelligence with a history of repeated child-molesting offenses, the first having occurred when he was age 16. Although he had never inflicted penetration or violence on little girls, court authorities were considering permanent imprisonment to protect the community when he was referred after his third arrest. Several other episodes of fondling and manipulating the genitalia of female children, kin to his former wife, had gone unreported to the police but had prompted the divorce. Between arrests he spent considerable time in prisons and nearly 4 years in state mental hospitals where, although described as cooperative, he had failed to benefit from diverse inpatient treatment programs. His third arrest came soon after discharge from a hospital to a local nursing home, in order to evaluate his suitability for such a semicustodial placement. While visiting his parents, he slipped away and molested a 6-year-old girl at a near-by school playground, and was later arrested. He was then referred for aversion therapy. Its painful nature was fully explained to him, and he was made to discuss the matter with his attorney and probation officer, who both recommended attempting treatment as preferable to life imprisonment. After these consultations he determined to enter treatment, throughout the course of which he was kept in the county jail except when brought to the therapy sessions. His tenuous legal status precluded a reversal phase (undoing and then reinstating avoidance training) once progress had been made. Medical examination confirmed his physical competence to undergo faradic aversion and, because psychometric evidence revealed severe worry and neuroticism, he was first trained in deep muscle relaxation to permit his achieving calm before and between shock presentations.

Treatment

From magazines and mail-order catalogs, some 100 pictures were selected as being tempting to him; the 49 most arousing pictures were used as stimuli for actual conditioning. In common, these pictures showed pretty little girls, most often in demure frocks, undergarments or revealing sun- and bathing-costumes. He was instructed that, when given a picture, he should study it and signal by finger movement when he felt sexual arousal, or imagined himself in erotic contact with the child, or both. All shocks were administered by a Maudsley Hospital portable apparatus (powered by a 6-volt lantern battery), through electrodes on his palm or wrist. In preliminary (baseline) trials unreinforced by shock, he proved able to attain arousal and deviant images very quickly, with all latencies 1 second or less. Periodically in training, instead of the pictorial stimuli, he was told to imagine the most tempting scene he could involving sexual contact with a child, and shock was applied to that self-produced image. In an average 2-hour session, some 40 to 50 shock presentations were given. A total of 26 training sessions were conducted, typically twice per week, during a period of nearly 4 months.

The earliest sessions used fixed punishment pairings such that when a deviant image was attained, it was followed by a shock varying unpredictably between lower and maximum intensity values and with durations ranging from 1 to 6 seconds. After six such sessions, little increase was found in the latencies of imagining deviant behavior. This discouraging pattern prompted adding to the shock a simultaneous, unpleasant high-frequency sound administered through earphones. Various punishment combinations of shock intensity plus sound were explored in the next three sessions, but as shown in Figure 1, negligible progress was achieved, and the aversive sound was henceforth eliminated. Through the ninth session, there were no spontaneous reports of the taboo image ever disappearing or of any difficulty in his attaining such images.

Next, the possibility of confining intensity to the highest values and using 6- or 7-second durations was explored through session 15. Although, for the first time, he reported that the "picture" disappeared during shock, and even at its onset on some trials, his response latencies failed to increase much, as shown in Figure 1. Also, there was no evidence of decreased temptations toward children or of difficulty in attaining deviant

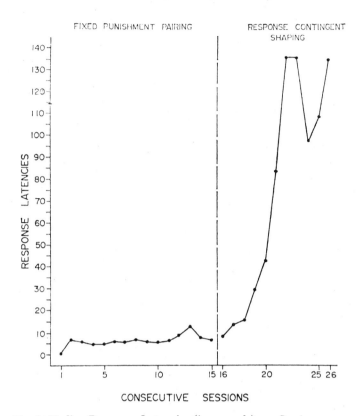

Fig. 1. Median Response Latencies (in seconds) per Session.

images. It seemed evident that progress had been insufficient and, with the man's lifelong freedom at stake, to continue with "gentle" changes seemed unwarranted. The paradigm pairing image attainment with relatively fixed shock intensity and duration had not brought him marked benefit, and a very different shaping paradigm was adopted.

In this method, shock intensity was kept constant at the highest level, and shock duration was varied as a function of his response latencies, but without his knowledge. When latency increased, shock duration was lessened but, on decreasing (or constant) latencies, duration was made moderately (or slightly) longer. Further, any large drops from prior, longer latencies were punished by lengthy shock durations. With this response contingent shaping paradigm, a duration of 5 or 6 seconds became, relatively speaking, a reward for a long latency response. In contrast, if a latency came much shorter than its immediate predecessors, such backsliding might be punished by shocks lasting up to 120 seconds. Fortunately, durations longer than 30 seconds were rarely needed.

A few sequential excerpts will illustrate the contingent but changing relationship in seconds between response latency (L) and consequent shock duration (D). In session 17, the first 12 trials proceeded as follows: L = 11, D = 6; L = 10, D = 9; L = 9, D = 15; L = 8, D = 21; L = 9, D = 15; L = 9, D = 15; L = 6, D = 36; L = 11, D = 6; L = 11, D = 6; L = 11, D = 7; L = 13, D = 5; L = 12, D = 7; rest. In session 18, trials 27 through 38 proceeded as follows: L = 17, D = 7; L = 16, D = 16; L = 16, D = 16; L = 16, D = 17; L = 15, D = 21; L = 17, D = 7; L = 17, D = 7.5; L = 17, D = 8; L = 16, D = 17; L = 20, D = 5; L = 21, D = 5;

L = 23, D = 5; rest. All 18 trials of session 21, when progress was especially rapid, proceeded as follows; L = 32, D = 15; L = 47, D = 9; L = 51, D = 6; L = 61, D = 5; L = 65, D = 5; L = 69, D = 5; L = 69, D = 7; L = 77, D = 5; L = 81, D = 5; L = 85, D = 5; L = 89, D = 5; L = 95, D = 5; rest; L = 114, D = 5; L = 110, D = 8; L = 111, D = 8; L = 124, D = 5; L = 130, D = 5; L = 134, D = 5; session ended early as reward. As can be seen, rest breaks were also made contingent on progressively longer runs of higher latency responses and, when possible, sessions were typically ended upon emission of a clearly higher latency toward the end of the allotted treatment time. The shaping paradigm thus combined punishment for attaining deviant images, with variations of shock duration intended to shape longer latencies through Skinner's (1938) method of successive approximations.

Instituted at the 16th session, and continued thereafter, this shaping paradigm produced dramatic and rapid increases in his latency of forming deviant arousal images. Figure 1 illustrates the differential pattern of latencies under the fixed punishment versus shaping paradigms. Further, the shaping procedure brought encouraging, spontaneous verbal evidence. In session 21 he stated for the first time: "It's getting to where I don't want to get the image at all. It takes a long, long time to bring that thought in." In session 24, he reported inability to produce any arousal and that, after trying but failing to attain tempting images, he was responding just "to get the shock over." Such statements continued in both final sessions, along with reports of his not having felt any child-related "urges" for a number of weeks. In light of his progress, treatment was suspended and a trial probationary period out of prison was arranged.

Booster and Follow-up Data

Five months later he was seen for 2 booster-test sessions. Prior telephone reports by the probation officer had continued to disclose no difficulties for the client with pedophiliac activities or temptations. In the booster-test phase he performed much as at the end of treatment with a median latency of 115.5 seconds and continued statements of inability to attain deviant imagery or impulses. Thus, his latencies during booster sessions averaged over 17 times greater than those obtained through use of the original, fixed punishment, paradigm, This case has since been followed periodically for more than 32 months without change in status. There have been no suggestions by deed or in fantasy that the child-molesting problem has recurred.

CONCLUSIONS

This case study may provide the first description of a promising new aversion therapy technique. When, as here, the usual fixed punishment paradigm proves insufficient, the response contingent method now presented may invite consideration. By holding shock intensity constant, and varying duration as a function of response latency, both long-standing child molesting behavior and temptations to perform it were eliminated. These changes were maintained after extensive post-treatment follow-ups. A problem with the shaping technique described is its demand for sustained, acute therapist attention to judge appropriate durations to deliver to various response latencies. This is a general issue when one response feature (occurrence) must be addressed by consequences that depend on another aspect (latency). Recent work on giving different feedback to multiple physiological measures (Schwartz, 1972) suggests that electronic programming equipment might be used to ease the burden on therapists who adopt the response-contingent aversion technique.

It is of further interest that a method aimed at slowing the latency of image production appeared to bring cessation of more overt child molesting temptations and actions. Other reports of successful behavior modification, whether by aversion therapy (Marks & Gelder, 1967) or diverse fear reduction technique (Bandura et al., 1969), have also shown parallel effects between ideation and overt symptom removal, reminiscent of the present results.

REFERENCES

Bandura, A., Blanchard, E.B. & Ritter, B. The relative efficacy of desensitization and modeling approaches for inducing behavioral, affective, and attitudinal changes. *J. Pers. Soc. Psychol.*, 1969, **13**, 173-199.

Marks, I.M. & Gelder, M.G. Transvestism and fetishism: Clinical and psychological changes during faradic aversion. *Br. J. Psychiatry.* 1967, **113**, 711-729.

Rachman, S. & Teasdale, J. *Aversion Therapy and Behavior Disorders.* Coral Gables, Florida: University of Miami Press, 1969.

Schwartz, G.E. Voluntary control of human cardiovascular integration through feedback and reward. *Science.* 1972, **175**, 90-93.

Skinner, B.F. *The Behavior of organisms: An experimental analysis.* New York: Appleton-Century-Crofts, 1938.

62

An Automated Fading Procedure to Alter Sexual Responsiveness in Pedophiles *

D.R. LAWS and A.V. PAWLOWSKI

The necessity of direct behavioral intervention for the alteration of dysfunctional and maladaptive sexual behavior, rather than more traditional psychotherapeutic approaches, has been increasingly recognized in recent years. The use of behavioral techniques to alter sexual response may be seen in clinics for the treatment of sexual dysfunction (Hartman & Fithian, 1972; Masters & Johnson, 1970), in the client's own home (LoPiccolo & Lobitz, 1972; Marquis, 1970; Serber, 1974), as well as in the laboratory (Barlow & Agras, 1973; Laws & Pawlowski, 1973; McCrady, 1973). One of the more novel approaches was that reported by Barlow and Agras (1973) where a stimulus fading technique was used to increase heterosexual responsiveness in homosexuals. Using slides of nude females superimposed on slides of nude males, the male slide was faded out and the female faded in each time the subject met a criterion of penile response. Although homosexual arousal remained high throughout, these investigators reported about a 25 percent to 30 percent increase in heterosexual arousal in postfading generalization sessions.

Aversive conditioning has long been a favored behavioral treatment used to alter sexual orientation (see, for example, Marks & Gelder, 1967). The deliberate application of painful stimulation to clients raises serious ethical problems (Rachman & Teasdale, 1969), and alternatives to aversive conditioning should be actively sought. The nonaversive stimulus fading procedure reported by Barlow and Agras (1973) represents a significant step in this direction.

This paper describes a pilot study that also used a nonaversive fading technique. Although the present technique bears some similarity to that of Barlow and Agras (1973), it differs considerably in terms of goals and procedures. First, the approach reported here attempted to alter age interest within a sexual orientation, rather than to alter sexual orientation itself. Second, in the present technique (a) a continuous session rather than a

*The opinions or conclusions stated in this paper are those of the authors and are not to be construed as official or as necessarily reflecting the policy of the Department of Health of the State of California. Portions of this paper were presented at the meeting of the American Psychological Association, New Orleans, September 1974.

discrete trial procedure was used and (b) the fading process was automatically controlled dependent upon changes in the subjects' sexual response, that is, above-criterion response produced fading in one direction and below-criterion response reversed the fading.

METHOD

Subjects

Subjects were selected for the investigation on the basis of three criteria: (a) reported sexual disinterest in adults and/or (b) reported sexual dysfunction with adults, and (c) current involvement in scheduled social interactions with adults as part of their therapeutic program at the hospital.

Subject 1 (S1) was a 44-year-old male confined for the offense of female pedophilia. He had a continuous history of this behavior for the preceding 28 years. He stated a marked preference for girls 8 to 10 years old with long blonde hair and reported that his sexual fantasies were almost exclusively devoted to these persons. His actual sexual behavior with children consisted primarily of kissing, fondling, and cunnilingus. He had been married for the past 21 years. He reported difficulty in sexual relations with his wife, to the extent that he frequently had to use sexual fantasies of children in order to accomplish coition. When he presented himself for treatment he stated that he and his wife were devoted to one another and that he wanted to save the marriage. He expressed fear that "I might be locked up for the rest of my life if I don't do something about this attraction to children"

Subject 3 (S3) was a 22-year-old male confined for the offense of male pedophilia. He had an 11-year history of homosexual behavior with boys 12 to 13 years old, usually in the form of fondling and mutual fellatio. When he presented himself for treatment, he stated that he had had limited sexual experience with adults and that it had been largely disappointing and unsuccessful. He stated that he definitely desired a homosexual orientation but wished to be more responsive to adults.

Apparatus

Apparatus for the procedure consisted of two Kodak carousel projectors, a Barlow-type penile transducer (Barlow, Becker, Leitenberg, & Agras, 1970), a specially designed criterion response sensor, a stepping motor that controlled lamp illumination in the projectors, a Beckman RM Dynograph, a counter that accumulated all time above criterion in seconds, and various electronic components that controlled the procedure.

Operation

Changes in the penile response were recorded on a polygraph and were simultaneously displayed on a relay meter in the criterion response sensor. The relay points in the meter were set at the desired criterion. When a criterion erection was emitted, the sensor operated the stepping motor controlling lamp illumination. If the subject continued to maintain an above-criterion erection, the stepper continued to operate, dimming out the lamp in Projector 1 and brightening the lamp in Projector 2. If the subject fell below criterion, the fading reversed, that is, Projector 2 dimmed out and Projector 1 brightened up again. The fading then was continuous; the direction of the fade was determined by the level of the subject's arousal.

Experimental Room

A quiet, secluded room in the hospital was divided in two; half contained the programming equipment, and half was the subject room. The projectors stood on a wall shelf in the equipment room and shone through a glass window into the darkened subject room. The subject sat in a comfortable reclining chair that faced a movie screen hung on the wall. Next to him was a small table on which a speaker produced white masking noise.

Stimuli

Subjects were asked to examine a collection of slides of nude adults and children of both sexes. They were asked to pick as many slides as possible of children whom they found sexually attractive, and as many as possible of adults who were attractive, or at least not unattractive. These slides formed the basic pool of stimuli used in the study.

Data

There were three types of data: penile circumference changes, percent of time above criterion, and subjective reports of the subjects.

Penile circumference changes.
Penile changes were recorded by Barlow-type gauge (Barlow et al., 1970) and a Beckman polygraph. Response changes were not the basic data of the investigation but were recorded in order to (a) have a permanent record of response changes with all forward and backward steps indicated and (b) have a check on the accuracy of the criterion sensor. The subject put the transducer on and reported when his penis was flaccid. A predetermined zero point was then set on the polygraph. He then stimulated himself to full erection with the gauge on. When he reported full erection, a predetermined maximum point was then set on the polygraph. The criterion response sensor was adjusted to trace with the polygraph pen; for example, 70 percent on the meter equaled 70 percent elevation on the polygraph record.

Time beyond criterion.
The basic data of the study are the percentage of the session time that the subject's response was above criterion. This was obtained by dividing the number of seconds accumulated on the counter by the total seconds of session time.

Subjective reports.

Both subjects were extensively debriefed following each day's session as to what had occurred, what fantasies were used, how they felt that day, and so forth. Subsequently each subject prepared a written account in response to two questions: (a) What did you do in each of the fading procedures, and how did you feel about it? and (b) Have you noticed any changes in your attitudes toward adults, or any changes in physical attraction?

Procedure

Before any training sessions were begun, the entire procedure was explained to the subjects. We told them, considering their extensive sexual histories, that we did not realistically expect the arousal value of children to change very much, if at all. What we hoped to do was to use that learned arousal to train a different kind of behavior, responsiveness to adults, an alternative that could be equally reinforcing not to mention legal.

When the fading procedure began, one slide was in full illumination and the other superimposed slide so dim that the image was invisible. If the subject emitted the criterion response, the stepping motor controlling the projector lamps began operating 10 seconds later. As long as the response remained above criterion, the stepping motor operated at a preset interval until 16 equal steps were completed, resulting in the initially bright slide being faded out and the initially dim slide brought to full illumination.

Baseline.

Each subject was asked to pick the most arousing slide of a child and the most attractive (or least unattractive) slide of an adult for purposes of baseline assessment. Each slide was then shown to the subject for 30-minute sessions on 2 consecutive days while penile response was monitored and time above criterion recorded. The subjects were instructed to imagine themselves in a sexual situation with the person depicted in the slide.

Fading: child to adult.

These 30-minute sessions began with the child slide fully illuminated and the adult invisible. The subjects were instructed to fantasize to the slide of the child, then, when fading reached the point where the sexual characteristics of the adult were visible, to switch the fantasy to adults. We did not expect this to be any easy task for the subjects so the reversing feature was programmed. We reasoned that, if the subject fell below criterion and the adult faded back to the child, this would enable him to recapture his erection and start the fading back to the adult. In these first fading sessions the same two slides from the baseline period were presented at a 10-second fading interval.

A second series of child to adult fading sessions was also conducted. These were identical to the first series except that each subject's preferred slides were placed in a random order of presentation so that he was unable to predict which child would be paired with which adult on any day. This method of slide presentation was maintained throughout the remainder of the study. The interval between fading steps was also changed from 10 seconds to 5 seconds.

In both child to adult fading series the criterion for fading was set at 70 percent of maximum erection.

Fading: adult to child.

These sessions began with the adult slide fully illuminated and the child slide invisible. The subjects were instructed to imagine themselves in a sexual situation with the adult and attempt to become aroused. In addition, they were given two instructions for the alteration of fantasy. First, if they became aroused to the adult and the child began to fade in they were to allow the image to become visible. When it was clearly in view, they were instructed to covertly use self-instructions such as: "Why am I attracted to this kid? Kids aren't as much fun as adults, and they always get me into trouble. I don't want to do this anymore, and I don't want to be excited by kids."

They were told that use of these covert self-instructions would interrupt any fantasies associated with children and assist them in losing their erections. Second, when the adult faded back to clear visibility, they were to again try to become sexually aroused. When they began to feel aroused they were to use self-instructions such as: "Now this is much better. She [or he] is much more attractive than that kid. This is what I ought to be doing."

The covert manipulation of these two sequences is similar to the use of thought stopping (Lazarus, 1971) followed by the introduction of competing thoughts that focus on the desired goal of the treatment. These two sequences were to be repeated as often as the subject could manage within the session.

There were three series of adult to child fading sessions. The sessions were identical except that the criterion was successively raised from 70 percent to 80 percent for S1 and from 70 percent to 80 percent to 90 percent for S3 in an effort to strengthen responsiveness to the adult. In the first series of adult to child fading the session time was 30 minutes for S1 and 15 minutes for S3; subsequently all session times were 15 minutes in duration.

Responsiveness tests (T1 through T5).

Following all fading series, tests were conducted that were identical to the baseline period. These sessions were initially 30 minutes in length and were conducted on 2 consecutive days. Beginning with the third test (T3), these test sessions were shortened to 15 minutes and were conducted consecutively on the same day. Stimuli for the responsiveness tests were whichever slides appeared in the random order for that day, with the exception of the first test (T1) where the same slides from the first child to adult fading series were used.

RESULTS

Child to Adult Fading

The data for all phases of child to adult fading are shown in Fig. 1. The data points indicate the total session time that the penile response exceeded the criterion, and the abcissas show the session days with vertical lines separating the various phases of the investigation. The first phase was a baseline period (B) followed by the first fading series where the same two slides were shown exclusively, and the first test (T1). The second phase was the second fading series where various slides were presented in random order, followed by the second test (T2). The criterion for fading was 70 percent in both series.

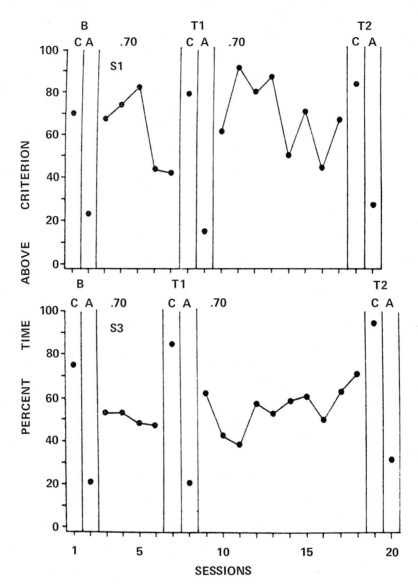

Fig. 1. Child to adult fading. Data points represent the percentage of session time that penile response was above indicated criterion. In panels designated B, T1, and T2, slides of children (C) and adults (A) were presented alone.

The fading step interval was decreased to 5 seconds on the 1st day of the second series for S1 and the 2nd day of that series for S3.

Subject 1.

Baseline assessment for S1 showed that he was highly responsive to the child slide presented alone (70%) and showed very little response to the adult (23%). In the first fading series he averaged 62 percent time above criterion. Initially he was able to stay aroused and keep the adult faded in for long periods, but this responsiveness diminished toward the end of the series. T1 showed that indpendent responsiveness to adults was even lower than in the baseline period.

S1 complained of satiating to the slides, so the randomized order was devised for the second fading series. Presentation of varied stimuli resulted in a higher average percentage of time above criterion (68%), but responsiveness was again variable toward the end of the series. T2 showed a continuing low independent responsiveness to adults.

Subject 3.

Baseline assessment for S3 also showed a high independent responsiveness to children (75%) and a low response to adults (21%). S3 averaged 50 percent time above criterion in the first fading series, indicating that the child image was present as often as the adult. T1 showed that independent response to adults was the same (20%) as that during baseline.

S3 also complained of satiation, so a randomized order of slide presentation was constructed for him as well. Presentation of varied stimuli resulted in a gradual increase in the percentage of time beyond criterion after an initial drop, averaging 55 percent for the second series. T2 showed about a 10 percent increase in response to adults.

Figure 2 shows two 12-minute samples of polygraph tracings for the two subjects that are representative of their response patterns in the second child to adult fading series. In the top two panels we see that S1 took almost 4 minutes to exceed the criterion the first time, faded the adult into clear visibility, then gradually lost the erection to about 40 percent of maximum. Between the 6th and 7th minute he recaptured the erection, completed the full 16 fading steps, and remained above criterion for the rest of the period although the small rapid traverses of the pen indicate struggling on his part. This eventual performance of a full fade and holding the response above criterion for long periods was typical of S1's behavior in this series.

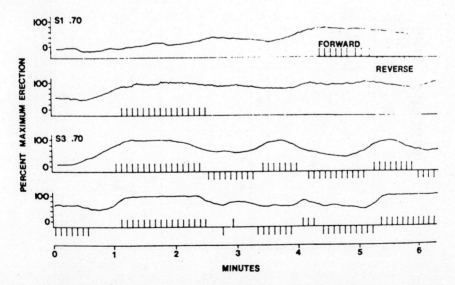

Fig. 2. Penile response record for 12 minutes of child to adult fading session for both subjects. Ordinates indicate the percentage of maximum erection. Upward pointing events indicate forward fading steps and downward points reverse fading steps.

In the lower two panels we see that S3 achieved full erection in slightly over the 1st minute, fading the adult in completely, but then immediately lost it and faded the child back in, regained it, lost and regained it again in somewhat over 5 minutes. By the 7th minute he was rapidly producing full erection and holding it at 100 percent for the full 16 steps, fading in the adult. He remained highly responsive and by the 11th minute produced another full erection and faded the adult in. This up-down pattern of response was typical of S3's behavior in this series.

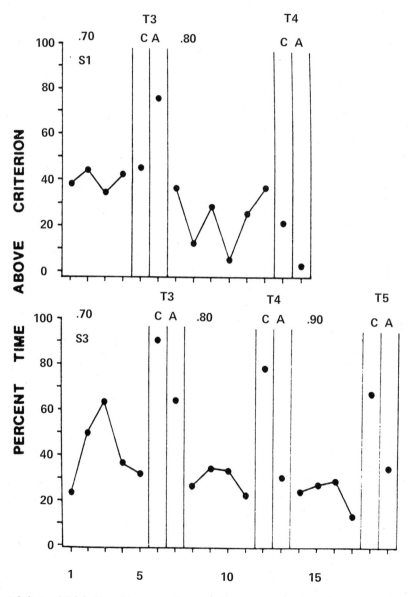

Fig. 3. Adult to child fading. Large panels are fading series with differing criteria for fading indicated. In panels designated T3, T4, and T5, slides of children (C) and adults (A) were presented alone.

Adult to Child Fading

Figure 3 shows the data for all phases of adult to child fading sessions. These fading series were the same as the preceding ones except that the criterion for fading was raised to 80 percent in the second series for S1, and to 80 percent in the second series and to 90 percent in the third for S3. The percentage of session time above criterion would be expected to fall during these sessions due to the subjects' use of the covert self-instructions; subjects were to meet the criterion, fade in the child, and lose the erection as quickly as possible using the covert procedure.

Subject 1.

The upper panel of Fig. 3 shows the data for adult to child fading for S1. In this reversed fading procedure S1 proved able to produce criterion erections to the adult stimulus and lose the erection with the child faded in, and then repeat this performance. With the fading criterion at 70 percent, he averaged 40 percent time above criterion. The test (T3) for the first adult to child fading series showed him to be highly responsive to the adult presented alone (75%) and for the first time showed diminished responsiveness to the child (45%). In the second fading series with the criterion at 80 percent, more variability developed, evidenced by his inability to repeatedly meet the criterion on the 2nd and 4th days. The average percentage of time above criterion for this series was 24 percent. The test (T4) for the second fading series showed a further diminished response to the child (21%), but also quite low response to the adult (3%) due to his inability to produce more than one criterion erection.

Subject 3.

The lower panel of Fig. 3 shows the data for S3 for adult to child fading. S3 also proved able to produce criterion erections in this reversed procedure. With the fading criterion at 70 percent, he averaged 41 percent time above criterion. However, his performance was marked by variability on the 2nd and 3rd days when he had difficulty in losing the erection once the child was faded in. He was able to master this by the 4th day, and thereafter his performance was stable. The test (T3) for this series showed continued high responsiveness to the child (91%) but also high responsiveness to the adult (65%). In the second fading series the criterion was increased to 80 percent, and the percentage time above criterion fell to an average of 31 percent. The test for the second fading series (T4) showed continued high responsiveness to the child (79%) and moderate response to the adult (32%). The final fading series resulted in an average percentage time above criterion of 25 percent. The final test (T5) showed S3 to be still highly responsive to the child (69%), and the responsiveness to adults remained stable in the moderate range (37%).

Figure 4 shows two 12-minute samples of polygraph tracings from the adult to child fading series with the criterion at 70 percent. The top two panels show the first 12 minutes of S1's behavior as he gradually produced the response to the adult, faded the child in, lost the erection, faded the adult back in, and repeated the performance. Responding characteristic of S1 may be seen at the points designated "S" (covert self-instruction). At the 10th forward step he had the child faded in, began the covert self-instruction, which produced a precipitate drop of about 20 percent in the response each time.

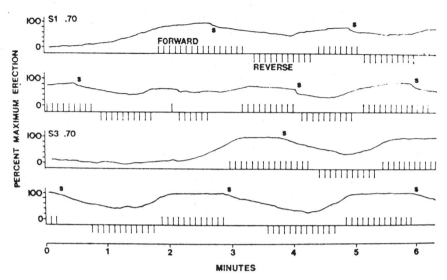

Fig. 4. Penile response records for 12 minutes of adult to child fading for both subjects. Points designated S indicate subject's use of covert self-instruction.

S3's performance was quite dissimilar. He was also slow to produce an erection to the adult, but as in the child to adult fading series, he was also slower in losing it once the child was faded in (note response at "S" points). His performance in adult to child fading was characterized by much slower overall response than he had shown previously (see Fig. 2).

DISCUSSION

This pilot investigation failed to demonstrate the effectiveness of an automated stimulus fading technique when a slide of a child was faded into a slide of an adult. Following child to adult fading, we were unable to show an independent response to adults. After two series of child to adult fading, response to adults presented alone was either lower or insubstantially higher than that shown in the baseline condition. The reason for this may lie in our use of the reverse fading feature. We did not expect the subjects, at least initially, to be able to maintain above-criterion response during fading when the non-preferred stimulus, the adult, was present. The reversing feature was included so that they would be able to regenerate erection to the child stimulus and·start fading forward again. We expected that this would permit the frequent pairing in time of high arousal with adult stimuli, eventually enabling the subjects to produce erection in the presence of the adult stimulus alone. This was apparently not a tenable assumption, at least within the limited context of this investigation. It may be that the reverse fading had the effect of continuously informing the subject that he was failing to maintain his erection to the adult. This experience of continuous failure in fading may possibly account for the subjects' inability to produce the response to the adult alone. In support of this interpretation, S1 reported that child to adult fading was actually destructive of his efforts to alter his responsiveness:

When the picture fades from a little girl to an adult woman, I am under pressure to find something sexually exciting about her before the fading reverses. . . . I believe this is reinforcing my feeling that adult women are not really rewarding and fulfilling sex partners, and further reinforces this by the picture fading back to a little girl that I see as . . . relaxed, rewarding, and fully enjoyable.

It is worth noting that the Barlow and Agras (1973) fading technique had a limit to which the subject could fade backward and did not permit this experience of failure. In their procedure, if the subject did not meet the criteria for forward fading, he was presented with 18 consecutive trials in an attempt to succeed before there was any change in the criterion for fading. Following fading, they were able to demonstrate increased responsiveness to a previously non-preferred stimulus presented alone.

However, when the present fading procedure was reversed (adult to child) and covert self-instructions added, both subjects were able to produce criterion erections to the adult in order to fade in the child, use self-instructions to fade the child out, then reproduce the response to the adult. McCrady (1973) also reported successfully altering responsiveness in a homosexual by fading an adult female into an adult male. He used a procedure similar to that of Barlow and Agras (1973) but did not require the emission of a criterion erection for fading to begin. Fading proceeded independent of the penile response, and the fading increment at which maximum erection occurred on that trial was recorded. McCrady's subject eventually produced erection to the female slide alone, and the responsiveness was shown to generalized to slides not used in treatment.

It must be emphasized that the adult to child fading procedure produced marked change in responsiveness *only* following the 70 percent criterion series. At T3, S1 showed 75 percent time above criterion, an increase of 52 percent above baseline level. When the criterion was raised to 80 percent for S1 he was able to produce only a single criterion erection, resulting in an 18 percent decrease below baseline level. At T3, S3 showed 65 percent time above criterion, an increase of 44 percent above baseline level. S3's response to adults following the 80 percent and 90 percent criterion series was not substantially different from that shown in the pretreatment baseline. No firm conclusions may be drawn from these results at the present time. The subjects had only a minimum of four and a maximum of six fading sessions prior to the responsiveness tests. Seventy percent is an easier criterion to meet than 80 percent or 90 percent, and the data reflect this. More extensive training at the higher criteria might well produce very different results.

The percentage of time above criterion is a somewhat deceptive measure in that it is only informative about arousal beyond an already high level. Relatively high but subcriterion arousal could be occurring throughout a test session and not be recorded. If we examine the average percentage of erection in the adult test sessions, we get a clearer picture of what happened in the tests following both fading procedures. The child to adult procedure did not produce overall heightened response to adults according to this measure. S1 showed an average percentage of erection to adults of 55 percent during baseline, 55 percent during T1, and 54 percent during T2. Similarly, S3 showed 46 percent during baseline, 43 percent during T1, and 47 percent during T2. When we examine the average percentage of erection in the adult tests following the adult to child fading, the picture is considerably different, but only for S. S1 showed an average percentage of erection of 78 percent during T3 and 29 percent during T4, which was consistent with the time above criterion measure. S3, on the other hand, showed an average percentage of erection of 72 percent during T3, 60 percent during T4, and 85 percent during T5. The time above criterion measure was reasonably consistent with the average percentage of erection at T3, but proved to be an underestimate of S3's general level of arousal at T4 and particularly at T5.

There was little change in the subjects' response to children presented alone following the child to adult fading sessions. This is not unexpected since the known responsiveness to children was used to trigger the fading. In addition, they were given no instructions to suppress their response to children other than to attempt to switch their fantasies to adults when the adult slide became visible.

Following the adult to child fading series, a decline in responsiveness to children in the test sessions was evident in both subjects although it was less pronounced in S3. The data in Fig. 3 and the response records in Fig. 4 clearly show that the subjects were altering their response to children during the fading sessions by the use of the covert self-instruction procedure. This albeit brief training apparently contributed to the lowered responsiveness to children presented alone in the test sessions. Verbal reports by the subjects suggest that this indeed was the case. S1 reported: "The need to lose my erection when the little girl comes on makes it impossible to think of her in any erotic way. . . . My thinking of the little girl as *not* a good sex partner causes me to realize her negative qualities and see her as just an immature girl." S3 reported: "I think your machine has done something to my head. I'm having more and more trouble getting it on with the boy."

The question remains as to how the subjects were able to produce criterion erections to adults in the adult to child series. Several interpretations can be offered, none of which is entirely adequate alone, but which in combination offer the best overall explanation. First, neither subject was totally unresponsive to adults as the average percentage of erections from baseline indicates (55% for S1, 46% for S3). Each had had sexual experience with adults, although S1 was dysfunctional due to his obsessive fantasies of children, and S3's adult homosexual contacts had been limited.

Second, there may have been a practice effect from the earlier child to adult fading sessions. The practice in pairing above-criterion arousal with adult fantasy may have facilitated the ability to produce erection in the adult to child sessions. The data from T1 and T2 argue strongly against this interpretation, however.

The third, and most persuasive explanation, is that the use of covert self-instructions enabled the subjects to interrupt sexual thought processes associated with children. The attendant loss of erection assisted them in separating sexual arousal from these stimuli. The resulting fading in of the adult and switching to positive thoughts of adults were experienced as a reinforcing and relaxing state that facilitated sexual responding to adult stimuli. Reports from the subjects support this interpretation. S1 stated: "I am not under pressure to achieve an erection, and I am able to look at the woman . . . and let my erection happen more naturally. The alternating off-on of the woman with corresponding off-on thinking sexually seems to build my erotic feeling for the woman." S3 stated: "I was told to think negative thoughts toward the boy after he faded in: 'This is why I'm here. . . . I want out of this bag, not deeper into it.' It has become an easier thought to the adult and an automatic negative thought to the kid."

Fourth, and finally, both subjects reported increased confidence in themselves and in their ability to socially interact with adults outside of the investigation. S1 entered a family treatment program at the hospital where he was required to deal realistically with his marital difficulties as well as interact on an extensive basis with female program personnel. S3 joined the homosexual club at the hospital. This meant that he was involved in therapeutic activities such as gay social skills training and gay consciousness raising with adult members of the homosexual community, and was in addition placed in contact with gay community service centers that could provide posthospitalization job finding, housing, counseling, religious, and social opportunities.

In summary, it is our belief that this pilot study of a new method produced several promising if tentative results. The child to adult fading did not "work" in the sense that we had intended. This could be due to the reverse fading feature discussed above, or it could be due to the small number of fading sessions. Further work should include much more extensive training before any responsiveness tests are attempted. Should extensive training not result in increased responsiveness in test sessions, we might fairly conclude that the reversing feature was indeed providing a built-in failure experience. Adult to child fading produced increased independent response to adults but only following the 70 percent criterion series. Again, more extensive training at the higher criteria is indicated. More importantly, however, the present study failed to demonstrate which procedure, the fading or the covert self-instructions, was responsible for the changes observed. Further work must not only increase the number of training sessions but also compare fading with and without covert self-instructions to clarify this confounding. Finally, this method must be tested with a more heterogeneous subject population. We worked with only two pedophiles, one heterosexual and one homosexual, both of whom had had sexual experience with adults. More data are required on subjects of this type, but especially on pedophiles with no adult sexual experience, before we can begin to make any conclusions regarding the efficacy of the technique.

The findings of this investigation add support to a growing body of evidence that positive rather than the typical aversive conditioning procedures can be used for the alteration of maladaptive sexual behavior. In a time of increasing suspicion about the means and ends of behavior modification, such procedures offer an inviting alternative deserving thorough exploration.

REFERENCES

Barlow, D.H., & Agras, W.S. Fading to increase heterosexual responsiveness in homosexuals. *Journal of Applied Behavior Analysis,* 1973, **6**, 355-366.

Barlow, D.H., Becker, R., Leintenberg, H., & Agras, W.S. A mechanical strain gauge for recording penile circumference change. *Journal of Applied Behavior Analysis,* 1970, **3**, 73-76.

Hartman, W.E., & Fithian, M. *The treatment of sexual dysfunction.* Long Beach, Calif.: Center for Marital and Sexual Studies, 1972.

Laws, D.R., & Pawlowski, A.V. A multi-purpose biofeedback device for penile plethysmography. *Jouranl of Behavior Therapy and Experimental Psychiatry,* 1973, **4**, 339-341.

Lazarus, A.A. *Behavior therapy and beyond.* New York: McGraw-Hill, 1971.

LoPiccolo, J., & Lobitz, W.C. The role of masturbation in the treatment of orgasmic dysfunction. *Archives of Sexual Behavior,* 1972, **2**, 163-171.

Marks, I.M., & Gelder, M.G. Transvestism and fetishism: Clinical and psychological changes during faradic aversion. *British Journal of Psychiatry,* 1967, **113**, 711-729.

Marquis, J.N. Orgasmic reconditioning: Changing sexual object choice through controlling masturbation fantasies. *Journal of Behavior Therapy and Experimental Psychiatry,* 1971, **1**, 263-271.

McCrady, R.E. A forward-fading technique for increasing heterosexual responsiveness in homosexuals. *Journal of Behavior Therapy and Experimental Psychiatry,* 1973, **4**, 257-261.

Rachman, S., & Teasdale, J. *Aversion therapy and behaviour disorders: An analysis.* Coral Gables, Fl.: University of Miami Press, 1969.

Serber, M. Videotaped feedback in the treatment of couples with sexual dysfunction. *Archives of Sexual Behavior,* 1974, **3**, 377-379.

Sado-Masochistic Behavior

Sado-masochistic behaviors generally involve two individuals whose sexual behaviors are mutually reinforcing: one whose sexual satisfaction is associated with inflicting pain ("sadism"), and the other whose sexual satisfaction is associated with having pain inflected upon him ("masochism"). Of course, such individuals may engage in sadistic or masochistic behaviors with others who have neither orientation, although those with such orientations usually seek out each other as consenting sexual partners (Katchadourian & Lunde, p. 352).

Much sadistic and masochistic behavior is limited to fantasies. Such fantasies are stimulated by reading sado-masochistic literature or looking at sado-masochistic photographs or drawings involving whippings, pain-inflicting devices and bondage and may accompany masturbation or other sexual activities.

Overt masochistic behavior is rarely reported to police since it usually poses no harm to others. However, overt sadistic behaviors may range from the common "love bites" during sexual intercourse to mutilation of sexual partners, rape and, occasionally, murder.

There have been few reported cases of the use of behavior therapy with sadistic or masochistic behavior. The first case is by Mees and describes "Sadistic Fantasies Modified by Aversive Conditioning and Substitution." The case describes the psychiatric hospitalization of a 19-year-old male diagnosed as a "paranoid schizophrenic," the diagnosis apparently having been developed because the client assaulted a woman with the intention of carrying out a sadistic fantasy. Although the client appears to have been receiving several forms of treatment and also developed a nonsadistic heterosexual relationship during the treatment (thereby confounding the results), apparently major decreases in sadistic fantasies and increases in nonsadistic fantasies came about following a combination of electric shock treatment for the sadistic fantasies and the development and strengthening of a "normal seduction fantasy." Interestingly, by about midtreatment, the client took over all aspects of the procedure including administration and data collection. Six months after the termination of treatment, the client was discharged from the hospital, apparently relatively free of sadistic fantasies.

In the second case, Davison reports on "Elimination of a Sadistic Fantasy by a Client-Controlled Counterconditioning Technique." In this case, involving an imaginative combination of techniques. Davison used client-controlled masturbation sessions in which strong sexual feelings were paired with pictures and images of females in nonsadistic contexts. This positive counterconditioning was supplemented by the use of aversive counterconditioning in the form of covert desensitization, in which an extremely disgusting scene was paired in imagination with a typical sadistic fantasy. Although there were several confounding variables (and in fact, a partial return to the use of sadistic fantasies for sexual stimulation some months after treatment), Davison believes that an additional important part of the treatment involved the client's reconstruction of his problem in conditioning terms, rather than in terms of mental illness and punative unconscious processes.

REFERENCES

Katchadourian, H. & Lunde, D. *Fundamentals of human sexuality*. (2nd Ed.) New York: Holt, Rinehart, and Winston, 1975.

63
Sadistic Fantasies Modified by Aversive Conditioning and Substitution: A Case Study

HAYDEN L. MEES

Treatment of the present clinical case was undertaken on the assumption that reducing the tendency to have sadistic fantasies would also reduce the probability of an overt sadistic act. Techniques to reduce the strength of sadistic fantasies while strengthening incompatible fantasies were developed. In the process of collecting the data, a number of fortuitous events occurred which provide evidence for some problems basic to behavior modification.

The patient, a 19-year-old male, was committed as mentally ill to a State Hospital. Two years earlier he had assaulted a women with the intention of carrying out a sadistic fantasy. Ensuing psychiatric examinations found him to be developing a paranoid schizophrenic reaction with little hope for recovery.

Before his assault, the patient was considered to be a "model child," a good student, and a religious church-goer with no apparent sexual interest or deviation. As the only child, he was very close to his mother but distant from his father. He did not socialize with girls and was not popular with boys, generally preferring the company of his mother.

From the age of 12, he had fantasies about binding and injuring women and about dressing as a woman and being injured. He occasionally dressed in women's underclothes and swim clothes. His fantasies were fed by wild, sadistic detective and pulp magazines and were reinforced by sexual stimulation and masturbation.

In the hospital he appeared young and naive, somewhat aloof, anxious and quiet but not an unattractive person. He was intellectually superior, had no outward signs of serious maladjustment, and got along well with other patients and staff.

During the first few months he lived on a ward with other adolescent boys and finished high school. He was then transferred to an intensive group treatment program for sex offenders (Di Furia & Mees, 1963). Both programs provided ample opportunity and encouragement for him to develop social relations with patients and staff of both sexes. He occasionally visited his home and seemed generally well adjusted. Nevertheless, he was unaggressive, dependent, socially withdrawn and continued his previous fantasy and sexual behavior.

Attempts by the therapy group to deal with his fantasies failed. Group members had

537

tried shaming him for them, ignoring them, substituting normal sex fantasies, arranging dates and dances, and an interested girl even tried to seduce him. None of these techniques had any apparent effect on his fantasies.

Before starting aversive conditioning, a technique for collecting baseline data was developed. The patient was eager to cooperate in this treatment, and was taught to keep records of his own fantasies, sexual behavior and feelings about his behavior. Each day he turned in a record of any fantasies that led to masturbation, where and when they occurred, their content, and his feelings afterward. He quickly became an apparently reliable self-observer.

By an odd administrative circumstance, the start of the program was delayed almost 6 months. Data were collected during this period, providing a stable measure of behavior and minimizing adventitious influences, such as the effects of data collecting of his behavior.

Figure 1 contains cumulative records of orgasm associated with all masturbatory behavior, sadistic fantasies, normal fantasies and heterosexual intercourse. Significant incidents are identified as they occurred during the period of data collection.

During the first 5 weeks of data collection, five normal sexual fantasies were reported. No great influence on total masturbation was noted until the 11th week (Point A) when he started associating with a slightly older, sexually experienced women. He abstained for 2 weeks during which he visited the woman at her home (B) and engaged in some preliminary lovemaking. During the 14th week (at C) he masturbated without any fantasy (this occurred again during the 25th week).

His first heterosexual experience occurred with this woman during the 16th week, and D starts his cumulative record of sexual intercourse. Six weeks later, at E, the patient broke off his sexual relationship with the woman. During this period his rate of

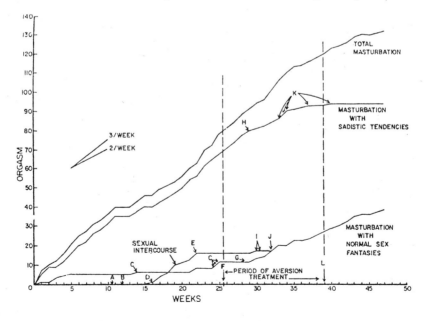

Fig. 1. Frequency of Sexual Behaviors per Week in Treatment.

masturbation with sadistic fantasies appeared relatively unchanged.

Halfway through the 26th week of data collection (F), the aversion treatment began. An ECT machine (Reiter Electrostimulator, Model CW47D) was used to deliver current to the dorsal surface of two alternate fingers above the nail. Voltage was set by the patient at a very uncomfortable but not sharply painful level.

The patient's task was to visualize selected parts of his fantasy as suggested by the therapist. When the image was clear, the patient signaled with his thumb and was briefly shocked. Regular sessions lasting 30-45 minutes were scheduled twice a day. Series of shocks were interspersed with brief interviews about his images and feelings. A week later after this treatment began, the patient was shocking himself and long sessions of over 2 hours without interruption were started. During these sessions, latencies ranged from 3 or 4 seconds to more than 2 minutes. The following week, sessions were again dropped to an hour or less on an irregular basis. At the 8th week, the patient took over his treatment completely, even keeping data and regulating the length of sessions (which lasted about an hour for 30-45 shocks). During the 14th week of treatment (at L), shocks were discontinued.

No change in the rate of either normal or sadistic fantasy masturbation was observed during the first 3½ weeks of aversive conditioning. Consequently, at G, the patient was instructed to develop and write a "normal seduction" fantasy, getting whatever help he needed from his friends. A few days later, at H, he had a fantasy with mixed content, but with a sadistic climax.

During the 30th week of data collection, he again saw his woman friend and had intercourse. He claimed this contact was the most satisfactory he had experienced. However, at I, he became impotent on two occasions while attempting intercourse. He decided he had to break off with her and concluded that he had been selfishly using her without accepting any responsibility for her feelings and plans. She wished to marry him, but he definitely asserted that he would not, and at J, she left the State.

Emotional reactions, which had appeared in mild form as anxiety and restlessness at the beginning of aversion treatment, seemed to reach a peak during this 30th week as well. The patient became verbally hostile toward the therapist and started having problems with temper-control in group therapy. Finally, he had an outburst on the ward, smashing his wristwatch and crying. Thereafter, temper-control was no longer a problem.

In the 8th week of aversion treatment, sadistic fantasies became more difficult to develop for masturbation. On five occasions (K), a sadistic fantasy broke up and a normal heterosexual fantasy occurred before climax. The last of these, following the end of the treatment, may have been a "last fling" spontaneous recovery. During the last 11 weeks of data collection, only two sadistic fantasies occurred, both abortive. The rate of masturbation declined somewhat, and normal fantasy seemed to be regularly accompanying masturbation during this time.

DISCUSSION

The aim of most behavior modification involves the generalization of results from the laboratory or therapist's office to the patient's life. In terms of classical conditioning, the UCS may be so powerful that generalization to all normal situations occurs. On occasion, overgeneralization occurs. Sanderson, et al. (1963), using a curarizing drug as a UCS, found one subject aversively conditioned to alcoholic beverages who could not put antifreeze into his auto and another who could not fill his lighter with fluid. Such powerful conditioning is rare, and in the case of modifying sexual behavior, undesirable.

Using a milder UCS, electric shock, McGuire and Vallance (1964) report that following ten sessions, lasting 20 to 30 minutes each, a patient with a problem of 10 years duration lost interest in his compulsive masturbation to masochistic and fetishistic fantasies. From the day of his first treatment, he never masturbated to these fantasies again. Wolpe (1965) reports that a physician with a drug addiction significantly reduced his "craving" with only nine "distinctly strong shocks" from a portable induction coil. By contrast, in the present case, the patient received more than 6000 shocks in 65 sessions over a 14-week period. Obviously there was no dramatic suppression of sadistic fantasies and substitution of normal fantasies. Rather, the progress was slow, tedious, and a gradual substitution of fantasies occurred.

Conceptualizing the behavior as a chain in which covert mediating events[1] are followed by an aversive, rather than reinforcing, consequence, the results of this study resemble other extinction curves in which an aversive consequence is involved (Ferster & Skinner, 1957; Wolf et al. 1964). Had the punishment been stronger, an immediate suppression of the fantasy might have occurred, at least in the laboratory situation. The data indicate, though, that the change from sadistic to normal fantasies were gradual with several mixed fantasies occurring, but only after the construction of a normal seduction fantasy. Neither the punishment nor overt heterosexual experiences influenced sadistic fantasies alone. It is not unusual in clinical practice to find that fantasy and overt sexual behavior do not coincide. During the period in which he was having sexual intercourse, the patient never had a fantasy about the woman involved.[2]

This patient did not have the typical adolescent sexual development in which a great amount of elaborate fantasy about sex occurs before overt sexual relationships occur. Kinsey et al. (1953) noted that most of his male sample had usually fantasized while masturbating. Such fantasies generally involved memories of previous sexual experiences, future hopes or wishes. In the present case, overt heterosexual behavior did not appear to influence fantasy. There was no evidence relative to the question of whether overt behavior would be influenced by fantasy modification.

Rachman (1965) has discussed the undesirable consequences of pain-elicited aggression in behavior therapy. In this case, however, the increased emotional tone was seen as a desirable alternative to his previously flat, somewhat aloof demeanor. Essentially, he became more assertive, using his aggressiveness constructively.

Six months following the terminaton of data collection, the patient was discharged from the hospital. During the intervening period, he had a few abortive sadistic fantasies, but did not use them for masturbation and did not fantasy actually hurting a woman. His woman friend reappeared and they renewed their sexual relationship satisfactorily.

Acknowledgments: Without the patient's complete cooperation and the active support of Dr. Giulio Di Furia, Superintendent of Western State Hospital, F. Steilacoom,

---

[1] Homme (1965) has coined the term *coverant* to identify mental events such as fantasies, since they are self-produced and covertly operate on the (phenomenological) environment of the organism.

[2] Sexual offenders often have a repetoire of sexual behavior which includes both "normal" and deviant sex acts, apparently under the control of different initiating and maintaining stimuli. A pedophile, exhibitionist or obscene telephone-caller may have a relatively independent sex life with his wife.

Washington, this study could not have been done. Dr. Terrence Fromong was a most valued colleague and assistant during the conduct of this experiment. Drs. Gerald Patterson and Richard Littman have presented me several valuable criticisms of this paper, for which I am grateful.

REFERENCES

Di Fura, G. & Mees, H.L. Intensive group psychotherapy with sexual offenders. *Proceedings of III International Congress in Group Psychotherapy.* Milano-Stressa, Italy, 1963.

Ferster, C.B. & Skinner, B.F. *Schedules of reinforcement.* New York: Appleton-Century-Crofts, 1957.

Homme, L.E. Perspectives in psychology: XXIV. Control of coverants, the operants of the mind. *Psychol. Rec.,* 1965, **15**, 501-511.

Kinsey, A.C., Pomeroy, W.B., Martin, C.E. & Gebhard, P.H. *Sexual behavior in the human female.* Philadelphia: Saunders, 1953.

McGuire, R.J. & Vallance, M. Aversion therapy by electric shock: A simple technique. *Br. Med. J.,* 1964, **1**, 151-153.

Rachman, S. Pain-elicited aggression and behaviour therapy. *Psychol. Rec.,* 1965, **15**, 465-467.

Sanderson, R.E., Campbell, D. & Laverty, S.G. An investigation of a new aversive conditioning treatment for alcoholism. *Quart. J. Stud. Alc.,* 1963, **24**, 261-275.

Wolf, M., Risley, T. & Mees, H. Application of operant conditioning procedures to the behaviour problems of an autistic child. *Behav. Res. & Therapy.* 1964, **1**, 305-312.

Wolpe, J. Conditioned inhibition of craving in drug addiction: A pilot experiment. *Behav. Res. & Therapy.* 1965, **2**, 285-288.

64

Elimination of a Sadistic Fantasy by a Client-Controlled Counterconditioning Technique: A Case Study*

GERALD C. DAVISON

The modification of deviant sexual behavior has been approached largely through the contiguous pairing of a primary aversive stimulus with a stimulus eliciting an undesirable response (the "symptom"), the goal being to endow the inappropriate stimulus with negative properties, or at least to eliminate the unwanted positive attributes. Many such cases have been reviewed by Bandura (in press), Feldman (1966), Grossberg (1964), Kalish (1965), Rachman (1961), and Ullmann and Krasner (1965). Therapy of fetishism, homosexuality and transvestism has tended to follow this counterconditioning model (e.g., Blakemore, Thorpe, Barker, Conway & Lavin, 1963; Davies & Morgenstern, 1960; Freund, 1960; Lavin, Thorpe, Barker, Blakemore & Conway, 1961; Raymond, 1956; Thorpe, Schmidt, Brown & Castell, 1964). In addition, several workers have introduced complementary procedures in attempts to endow suitable social stimuli with the positive attributes necessary to make less likely a reversion to the inappropriate goal-object. Thus, for example, Freund (1960) gave his male homosexuals not only aversion conditioning trials to pictures of men, but also exposures to pictures of nude women after injection of male hormones. Similar procedures have been employed by Thorpe, Schmidt and Castell (1963) and Feldman and MacCulloch (1965).

Of particular relevance to the present study is the work of Thorpe et al. (1963). These writers report therapeutic benefit following presumably counterconditioning sessions during which efforts were made to pair female pictures with orgasm from masturbation. It was assumed that this intensely pleasurable sexual response counterconditioned the aversion to females which appeared to play a crucial role in the behavior of the homosexuals. These authors recognized the importance of a person's fantasy life to his overt behavioral adjustment, and they assumed that beneficial generalization would occur from pictorial to the real-life situation, similar to the assumptions made for systematic desensitization (Davison, in press; Wolpe, 1958). Although the therapeutic

*This paper was written during a postdoctoral traineeship at the Veterans Administration Hospital, Palo Alto, California. For critical comments and helpful suggestions, the author thanks Walter Mischel, Arnold A. Lazarus, David Fisher, and Thomas J. D'Zurilla.

542

outcomes reported by Thorpe and his co-workers are equivocal in respect to actual sexual behavior, the procedures did have considerable effect on fantasies.

The possibility of extending this kind of work to an outpatient setting presented itself to the author during the course of his private practice. Various modifications of procedures used by Thorpe et al. (1963) were employed, apparently to good effect. In addition, other important issues became evident in the course of therapy, which required fewer than 5 consulting-room hours over a span of 10 weeks, and it is for these heuristic reasons that the following is reported.

CASE STUDY

The client was a 21-year-old unmarried white male college senior majoring in history. The university counseling center had received an anxious letter from his parents, requesting help for their son in treating his introversion, procrastination and "masochism." After working with the student for a few weeks on his tendency to wait until the last minute in his academic work, the psychologist at the center referred him to the author for help with his sexual difficulties.

Mr. M.'s statement of the problem was: "I'm a sadist." There followed a rather troubled account of a complete absence of "normal" sexual fantasies and activities since age 11. Masturbating about five times a week, the client's fantasies had been exclusively sadistic ones, specifically, inflicting tortures on women. He declared emphatically that he had never been sexually aroused by any other kind of image. Although generally uninterested in dating girls, he felt no aversion to them; on the contrary, he sometimes felt a "warm glow" when near them, but did not describe this at all in sexual terms. Because of his extreme concern over the content of his fantasies, however, he had dated very little and expressed no interest in the coeds at the college. He recalled having kissed only two girls in his life, with no sexual arousal accompanying these fleeting episodes. He had never engaged in any homosexual activities or fantasies. Although expressing no guilt about his problem, he was very much worried about it inasmuch as he felt it impossible to ever contemplate marriage. This concern had recently been markedly increased upon reading an account of a Freudian interpretation of "sado-masochism." He was especially perturbed about the poor prognosis for this "illness."

Because his concern over the gravity and implications of his problem seemed at least as disruptive as the problem itself, the therapist spent most of the first session raising arguments against a disease interpretation of unusual behavior. Psychoanalytic notions were critically reviewed, and attention was directed especially to the untestability of many Freudian concepts (Levy, 1963). Instances in the therapist's own clinical work were cited to illustrate the liberating effects observed in many people when they interpret their maladaptive behavior as determined by "normal" psychological processes rather than by insidious disease processes (Davison, 1966; Glasser, 1965; Maher, 1966; Mainord, 1962). Mr. M. frequently expressed relief at these ideas, and the therapist, indeed, took full advantage of his prestigious position to reinforce these notions.

At the end of the session, the counterconditioning orientation which would be followed was explained (Davison, in press; Guthrie, 1935; Wolpe, 1958), as well as the specific activities which he was to engage in during the coming week. When assured of privacy in his dormitory room (primarily on the weekend), he was first to obtain an erection by whatever means possible—undoubtedly with a sadistic fantasy, as he indicated. He was then to begin to masturbate while looking at a picture of a sexy, nude woman (the "target" sexual stimulus); *Playboy* magazine was suggested to him as a good source. If he began losing the erection, he was to switch back to his sadistic fantasy until he could begin masturbating effectively again. Concentrating again on the *Playboy* picture, he was to continue masturbating, using the fantasy only to regain erection. As orgasm was approaching, he was at all costs to focus on the *Playboy* picture, even if sadistic fantasies began to intrude. It was impressed on him that gains would ensue only when sexual arousal was associated with the picture, and that he need not worry about indulging in sadistic fantasies at this point. The client appeared enthusiastic and hopeful as he left the office. (Table 1 summarizes the client-controlled masturbation assignments following this and succeeding consulting-room sessions.)

Table 1 "Target" and "Back-Up" Sexual Stimuli for Client-Controlled Masturbation Sessions

Week	Target Stimulus	Back-up Stimulus
1	*Playboy*, real stimulus	Sadistic fantasy
2	Bathing-suit, real stimulus	*Playboy*, real stimulus
	Playboy, imaginal stimulus	Sadistic fantasy
3	Same as Week 2	Same as Week 2
4	Bathing suit, real stimulus	*Playboy*, real stimulus
	Playboy, imaginal stimulus	None

At the second session he reported success with the assignment: he had been able to masturbate effectively and enjoyably three times over a weekend to a particular picture from *Playboy* without once having to use a sadistic fantasy; however, it did take significantly longer to climax with the *Playboy* photograph than with the usual kind of sadistic fantasy. During the rest of the week, when he had not had enough privacy for real-life visual stimulation, he had "broken down" a few times and used his sadistic fantasies.

Much of this session was then spent in talking to him about some of the social-sexual games which most males play in our culture, especially the "mental undressing" of attractive women. The purpose was to engage him in the kind of "stud" conversation which he had never experienced and which, it was felt, would help to change his orientation toward girls. The therapist reassured him that the first direct contacts with girls are sometimes disappointing; he had to admit, however, that his extreme sensitivity about the sadistic fantasies had severely limited his experience.

During the coming week he was, first of all, to ask out on a coffee date any girl whom he felt he *might* find attractive, even for a sadistic fantasy. He was also to spend some time between classes just looking at some of the coeds and noting some of their more remarkable attributes. Finally, his masturbation sessions were to be structured as follows: The real-life pictorial stimuli were to be girls either in bathing suits or lingerie, used in the same way as the *Playboy* picture the preceding week; this latter stimulus was to be used as "back-up" stimulus, replacing the sadistic fantasies in the event that he was losing his erection. Attention was also to be directed to imaginal sexual stimuli, and when masturbating in this way he was to use the *Playboy* image, with a sadistic fantasy as back-up.

The third session lasted half an hour. He had procrastinated so long in asking for a date that the girls he contacted had already made other plans; the therapist expressed his disappointment quite openly and urged him even more strongly to follow through with this task. He had managed to spend some time looking at girls but did not note significant sexual arousal, except when a sadistic fantasy crept in occasionally. He had masturbated only once to real-life stimuli, using some bathing-suit pictures from a weekly national news magazine; this was successful, though it took longer even than when the *Playboy* material was used previously. When masturbating to imaginal sexual stimuli, he had relied almost exclusively on his sadistic fantasies rather than utilizing the *Playboy* picture in imagination as he had in real life 1 week earlier.

His reluctance to give up the sadistic fantasies prompted the use of the following procedure, the idea for which had been obtained from Lazarus (1958). With his eyes closed, he was instructed to imagine a typical sadistic scene, a pretty girl tied to stakes on the ground and struggling tearfully to extricate herself. While looking at the girl, he was told to imagine someone bringing a branding iron toward his eyes, ultimately searing his eyebrows. A second image was attempted when this proved abortive, namely, being kicked in the groin by a ferocious-looking karate expert. When he reported himself indifferent to this image as well, the therapist depicted to him a large bowl of "soup,' composed of steaming urine with reeking fecal boli bobbing around on top. His grimaces, contortions and groans indicated that an effective image had been found, and the following 5 minutes were spent portraying his drinking from the bowl, with accompanying nausea, at all times while peering over the floating debris at the struggling girl. After opening his eyes at the end of the imaginal ordeal, he reported spontaneously that he felt quite nauseated, and some time was spent in casual conversation in order to dispel the mood.

His assignments for masturbation during the coming week entailed increasing the frequency of his real-life masturbatory exposures to bathing-suit pictures, along with concerted efforts to use the *Playboy* stimuli in imagination as he had in real life 2 weeks earlier, resorting to sadistic fantasies if necessary.

The fourth session lasted only 15 minutes. He had managed to arrange a date for the coming weekend and found himself almost looking forward to it. Again, he had masturbated several times to a real-life picture of a bathing beauty. In fantasy he had managed to use the *Playboy* girl exclusively two out of five times, with no noticeable diminution in enjoyment.

He was to continue using the bathing-suit picture while masturbating to real-life stimuli, but to avoid sadistic fantasies altogether, the idea being that any frustration engendered by this deprivation would simply add to his general sexual arousal and thereby make it all the easier to use the *Playboy* stimuli in imagination.

The fifth session, also lasting only 15 minutes opened with Mr. M. animatedly praising the efficacy of the therapy. He had masturbated several times, mostly to real-life bathing-suit pictures, with no problems and, most importantly, had found himself *unable* to obtain an erection to a sadistic fantasy. In fact, he even had difficulty conjuring up an image. He had also spent considerable time with two girls, finding himself at one point having to resist an urge to hug one of them—a totally new experience for him. He enthusiastically spoke of how different he felt about "normal dating," and a 1-month period without interviews was decided upon to let him follow his new inclinations.

The sixth session, 1 month later, revealed that his sadistic fantasies had not reappeared, and that he had been masturbating effectively to both real-life and imaginal appropriate sexual stimuli. He had not, however, been dating, and some time was spent stressing the importance of seeking "normal" sexual outlets. He felt strongly, however, that the sexual problem had been successfully handled and requested that his procrastination problem be taken up. Two sessions were subsequently devoted to following the same general strategy that had been adopted, with some success, by the college counselor, that is, arranging for various rewards to be made contingent upon certain academic task-performances. Mr. M. did report doing "an enormous amount of work" during 1 week—out of fear of having to admit to the therapist that he had been loafing. Practical considerations, however, made it clear that this handling of the problem, even if it should prove effective, was not as realistic as his facing the reality that there was no "magic pill" to eliminate his procrastination. Therapy, therefore, was terminated, with no sadistic fantasies having occurred for over 1 month, and with the problem of procrastination left more or less untouched.

A follow-up of 1 month was obtained by telephone. Mr. M. reported that there was still no sign of sadistic fantasies and that, indeed, he was no longer even thinking about the issue. He had still not "gotten around" to asking any girl out on a date, and the therapist urged him in no uncertain terms to tackle this aspect of his procrastination problem with vigor that he had shown in regard to his studies (where significant improvement had been made). Extensive and persistent questioning failed to evoke any reported aversion to girls as the basis of his reluctance to ask them out.

DISCUSSION

As with every case study, one must necessarily speculate, to a large extent, on the "active ingredients." Hypotheses are not readily strengthened from such data. As a demonstration of various strategies, however, the present report does seem to be of heuristic value.

1. The first significant event in therapy was the author's general reaction to the client's statement of the problem: "I'm a sadist." After Mr. M. had recounted the horror with which he had read about his mysterious "illness" in Freudian terms, the therapist countered with a logical attack that made the hour take on more the characteristics of a graduate seminar than a psychotherapy session, except perhaps for the warmth, support and acceptance which were deliberately conveyed. A key factor in this initial phase was an attempt to change the client's general orientation to his problem. As this writer has usually found, the client had been regarding himself as "sick," qualitatively different from so-called "normals." Furthermore, the idea that much of his behavior was determined by forces working in devious ways in his "unconscious" was quite troubling, as was the poor prognosis. As reported in the case material, these issues were dealt with immediately, and significant relief was afforded the young man simply by reconstructing the problem for him in conditioning terms. It would, indeed have been interesting and valuable to attempt some sort of assessment of improvement at this very point.

2. Inextricably intertwined with the foregoing was the outlining of a therapeutic strategy: his sadistic fantasies were to be attacked by procedures aimed at counter-conditioning the maladaptive emotional reactions to specific kinds of stimuli. The client perceived the theoretical rationale as reasonable and was satisfied with the actual

techniques which would be employed. Furthermore, being able to buttress the plan with both clinical and experimental data added to its credibility. It must be emphasized that whether the data cited, or the explanation offered, are valid is an irrelevant question in the present situation. The important point is that the client's enthusiastic participation was enlisted in a therapeutic regime which, by all counts, was to be highly unconventional.

3. A third conceivably relevant variable was the "older brother" type of relationship which the therapist established in talking with Mr. M. about conventional sex. Clearly the client had missed this part of the average American male's upbringing and, as has been reported, much time was spent in deliberately provocative "locker-room talk," not as an end in itself, but rather as a means of exposing him to the kinds of heterosexual ideations which seemed to the author useful in promoting nonsadistic fantasies about girls.

4. It is likely that the two positive exposures to actual women contributed to therapeutic improvement. Mr. M., having been goaded into direct social contact with girls, was fortunately able to appreciate the enjoyment that can come from a satisfactory relationship with a woman, albeit on nonsexual terms. In addition, having felt a very strong urge to hug one of them, in a nonsadistic fashion, was reported by the client as a highly significant event and must surely have fostered some change in his concept of himself as a sexual misfit. Furthermore, aside from any alleged counterconditioning with respect to appropriate stimuli (*see* below), it is also suggested that a favorable change in self-concept developed as he saw himself able to respond sexually to imaginal and pictorial stimuli that had previously left him unaroused.

5. It is assumed that the most important variable in therapy was the masturbation sessions which the client carried out privately. As discussed by Thorpe et al. (1963), it was felt that more appropriate social-sexual behavior would probably follow upon a change in sexual fantasies; in the present case a focus on the fantasies seemed all the more reasonable in view of the fact that *they formed the basis of the referral.* According to the client, it was his fantasy life which had retarded his sexual development, and it was this that he was most worried about. It was assumed that generalization to real-life girls would be effected in a fashion similar to the generalization which has been reported for Wolpe's technique of systematic desensitization (Davison, in press; Lang & Lazovik, 1963; Lang, Lazovik & Reynolds, 1965; Lazarus, 1961; Paul, 1966; Paul & Shannon, 1966; Rachman, 1966; Schubot, 1966; Wolpin & Raines, 1966; Zeisset, 1966). Of course, whether Mr. M. would actually begin dating regularly, or at all, would seem to depend importantly on factors other than those dealt with in this brief therapy, for example, the client's physical attractiveness, his conversational and sexual techniques, the availability of women attractive to him and so forth. The generalization spoken of here, then, is best restricted to the thoughts and feelings which he had about women and about the prospects of relating to them nonsadistically; the case-study data contain ample verification for this.

The actual procedure followed was unique in that control of the pairing was vested entirely in the client, as is done in the use of differential relaxation with *in vivo* exposures to aversive stimuli (Davison, 1965; Wolpe & Lazarus, 1966). The sadistic fantasies were used initially to enable Mr. M. to obtain and maintain an erection. During this arousal, he looked at culture-appropriate sexual stimuli (a nude *Playboy* photo) and masturbated. The assumption is made (and must obviously be investigated experimentally) that the pairing of masturbatory arousal with the *Playboy* picture served to replace neutral emotional responses to the picture with intensely pleasurable sexual responses. In succeeding sessions the content of the new sexual stimuli was changed to less openly provocative female pictures (bathing-suit photographs), with the already established *Playboy* picture used as back-up. Then the stimuli were made solely imaginal in similar fashion. Obviously, if this procedure worked for counterconditioning reasons, the client exhibited considerable control over the content of his fantasies, switching back and forth as he had been directed. This control of imagery is a central issue in desensitization research as well (Davison, in press).

6. Probably very instrumental in changing the content of his fantasies was the intensive "imaginal aversive counterconditioning" (or "covert sensitization," viz, Cautela, 1966; Lazarus, 1958) conducted by the therapist, in which extreme feelings of disgust were generated by fantasy and then related to the sadistic image. One can fruitfully compare this technique with the "emotive imagery" procedure described by Lazarus and Abramovitz (1962), in which pleasant images were generated in fearful children and then related by the therapist to conditioned aversive stimuli. The procedure was resorted to in the present case because the client appeared unable to give up the sadistic fantasy solely on the basis of beginning to find the nonsadistic pictures and images effective in maintaining erection and leading to orgasm.

The assessment of therapeutic outcomes poses some difficulty here, as indeed it does for any therapy. Explicitly rejected as criteria of "cure" are the client's "self-actualization," "mental health," "ego strength," or other vague notions. While the intention is not simply to beg the question, it does seem more appropriate for the present case report to restrict judgment to the problem as presented by the client, namely, the sadistic fantasies and the attendant worry and doubt about suitability for normal human intercourse.

The clinical data on change in fantasy are self-reports, supplemented by the therapist's inference of the client's credibility. The orderliness of response to therapy, along with the enthusiasm which accompanied the progress reports, serves to bolster the conclusion that Mr. M. did, in fact, give up his sadistic fantasies of 10-years standing in favor of the kinds of fantasies which he felt were a sine qua non for appropriate sociosexual behavior. Both preceding and accompanying these changes was the radical difference in outlook. Simply stated, Mr. M. stopped worrying about himself as an "oddball," doomed to a solitary life, and did make some initial attempts to establish appropriate relationships with girls. That he has not yet done so (as of this writing) may, indeed, be due to a return of the original problem; however, this alternative seems less likely than that verbalized by the client, namely, that he has always had trouble doing what he knows he ought to do, and that, above all, being a so-called sexual deviate has ceased being an issue for him. Moreover, as mentioned above, variables other than the content of fantasies would seem to bear importantly on the matter of overt sexual behavior. Clearly, if usual dating habits were to be used as a criterion for outcome, the therapy must be considered a failure—although this would qualify many a young adult as "maladjusted" or "abnormal." Be that as it may, a relevant, well-established class of behaviors was modified, setting the stage for a social adjustment from which the client had initially seen himself utterly alienated.

SUPPLEMENTARY FOLLOW-UP DATA

A follow-up report was received by mail 16 months following termination. The client reported that, since the therapy had so readily eliminated the arousal from sadistic fantasies, and most importantly, had altered his outlook for "normal" sexual behavior, he allowed himself, "premeditatedly," to return to the use of the sadistic fantasies 6 months after termination, ". . . resolving to enjoy my fantasies until June 1, and then to reform once more. This I did. On June 1 [1967], right on schedule, I bought an issue of *Playboy* and proceeded to give myself the treatment again. Once again, it worked like a charm. In two weeks, I was back in my reformed state, where I am now [August 1967]. I have no need for sadistic fantasies. . . . I have [also] been pursuing a vigorous (well, vigorous for *me*) program of dating. In this way, I have gotten to know a lot of girls of whose existence I was previously only peripherally aware. As you probably know, I was very shy with girls before; well, now I am not one-fifth as shy as I used to be. In fact, by my old standards, I have become a regular rake!"

A telephone call was made to obtain more specific information about his return to the sadistic fantasies. He reported that the return was "fairly immediate," with a concomitant withdrawal of interest in conventional sexual stimuli. His self-administered therapy in June 1967 followed the gradual pattern of the original therapy, although progress was much faster. The author advised him not to make any more "premeditated" returns, rather to consolidate his gains in dating and other conventional heterosexual activities and interest. The client indicated that this plan could and would be readily implemented.

Of the past 16 months, then, the client has been free of the sadistic fantasies for 7 months, the other 9 months involving what he terms a willful return for sexual stimulation while masturbating. Constant throughout this follow-up period has been the relief which he derived from finding himself able to respond sexually to conventional sexual stimuli. Additional gains are his dating activities, which, it will be recalled, were not in evidence while the writer was in direct contact with him.

Still aware of the limitations of these case-study data, it does seem noteworthy and possibly quite important that the client's self-initiated partial "relapse" took place in a step-wise fashion, that is, without a *gradual* reorientation to the sadistic fantasies: he reported himself almost immediately excited by them once he had made the decision to become so. This sudden shift raises questions as to whether "aversive counter-conditioning" underlay the indifference to the fantasies which was effected during therapy. This surprising finding also underlines the probable importance of other-than-conditioning variables in the treatment.

REFERENCES

Bandura, A. *Principles of behavior modification.* New York: Holt, Rinehart & Winston, in press.

Blakemore, C.B., Thorpe, J.G., Barker, J.C., Conway, C.G. & Lavin, N.I. The application of faradic aversion conditioning in a case of transvestism. *Behaviour Research and Therapy,* 1963, **1**, 29-34.

Cautella, J.R. Treatment of compulsive behavior by covert sensitization. *The Psychological Record,* 1966, **16**, 33-41.

Davies, B. & Morgenstern, F. A case of cysticercois, temporal lobe epilepsy, and transvestism. *Journal of Neurological and Neurosurgical Psychiatry,* 1960, **23**, 247-249.

Davison, G.C. Relative contributions of differential relaxation and graded exposure to *in vivo* desensitization of a neurotic fear. *Proceedings of the 73rd annual convention of* the *American Psychological Association,* 1965, 209-210.

Davison, G.C. Differential relaxation and cognitive restructuring in therapy with a "paranoid schizophrenic" or "paranoid state." *Proceedings of the 74th annual convention of the American Psychological Association,* 1966, **2,** 177-178.

Davison, G.C. Systematic desensitization as a counterconditioning process. *Journal of Abnormal Psychology,* 1968; (in press).

Feldman, M.P. Aversion therapy for sexual deviations: A critical review. *Psychological Bulletin,* **1966, 65,** 65-79.

Feldman, M.P. & MacCulloch, M.J. The application of anticipatory avoidance learning to the treatment of homosexuality: I. Theory, technique and preliminary results. *Behaviour Research and Therapy,* 1965, **2,** 165-183.

Freund, K. Some problems in the treatment of homosexuality. In H.J. Eysenck (Ed.), *Behaviour therapy and the neurosis.* London: Pergamon, 1960, 312-326.

Glasser, W. *Reality therapy: A new approach to psychiatry.* New York: Harper & Row, 1965.

Grossberg, J.M. Behavior therapy: A review. *Psychological Bulletin,* 1964, **62,** 73-88.

Guthrie, E.R. *The psychology of learning.* New York: Harper, 1935.

Kalish, H.I. Behavior therapy. In B.B. Wolman (Ed.), *Handbook of clinical psychology.* New York: McGraw-Hill, 1965, 1230-1253.

Lang, P.J. & Lazovik, A.D. Experimental desensitization of a phobia. *Journal of Abnormal and Social Psychology,* 1963, **66,** 519-525.

Lang, P.J., Lazovik, A.D. & Reynolds, D.J. Desensitization, suggestibility and pseudotherapy. *Journal of Abnormal Psychology,* 1965, **70,** 395-402.

Lavin, N.I., Thorpe, J.G., Barker, J.C., Blakemore, C.B. & Conway, C.G. Behavior therapy in a case of transvestism. *Journal of Nervous and Mental Disease,* 1961, **133,** 346-353.

Lazarus, A.A. New methods in psychotherapy: A case study. *South African Medical Journal,* 1958, **33,** 660-663.

Lazarus, A.A. Group therapy of phobic disorders by systematic desensitization. *Journal of Abnormal and Social Psychology,* 1961, **63,** 504-510.

Lazarus, A.A., & Ambramovitz, A. The use of "emotive imagery" in the treatment of children's phobias. *Journal of Mental Science,* 1962, **108,** 191-195.

Levy, L.H. *Psychological interpretation.* New York: Holt, Rinehart & Winston, 1963.

Maher, B.A. *Principles of psychopathology: An experimental approach.* New York: McGraw-Hill, 1966.

Mainord, W.A. A therapy. *Research Bulletin,* Mental Health Research Institute, Ft. Steilacom, Washington, 1962, **5,** 85-92.

Paul, G.L. *Insight vs. desensitization in psychotherapy: An experiment in anxiety reduction.* Stanford: Stanford University Press, 1966.

Paul, G.L. & Shannon, D.T. Treatment of anxiety through systematic desensitization in therapy groups. *Journal of Abnormal Psychology,* 1966, **71,** 124-135.

Rachman, S. Sexual disorders and behaviour therapy. *American Journal of Psychiatry,* 1961, **118,** 235-240.

Rachman, S. Studies in desensitization—III: Speed of generalization. *Behaviour Research and Therapy,* 1966, **4,** 7-15.

Raymond, M.J. Case of fetishism treated by aversion therapy. *British Medical Journal,* 1956, **2,** 854-857.

Schubot, E. The influence of hypnotic and muscular relaxation in systematic desensitization of phobias. Unpublished doctoral dissertation, Stanford University, 1966.

Thorpe, J.G., Schmidt, E., Brown, P.T. & Castell, D. Aversion-relief therapy: A new method for general application. *Behaviour Research and Therapy,* 1964, **2,** 71-82.

Thorpe, J.G., Schmidt, E. & Castell, D. A comparison of positive and negative (aversive) conditioning in the treatment of homosexuality. *Behaviour Research and Therapy,* 1963, **1,** 357-362.

Ullmann, L. & Krasner, L.P. (Eds.) *Case studies in behavior modification.* New York: Holt, Rinehart & Winston, 1965.

Wolpe, J. *Psychotherapy by reciprocal inhibition.* Stanford: Stanford University Press, 1958.

Wolpe, J. & Lazarus, A.A. *Behavior therapy techniques.* New York: Pergamon, 1966.

Wolpin, M. & Raines, J. Visual imagery, expected roles and extinction as possible factors in reducing fear and avoidance behavior. *Behaviour Research and Therapy,* 1966, **4,** 25-37.

Zeisset, R.M. Desensitization and relaxation in the modification of psychiatric patients' interview behavior. Unpublished doctoral dissertation, University of Illinois, 1966.

Voyeuristic Behavior

Voyeuristic behavior involves the intense observation of a sexual object as a primary source of sexual stimulation. Again, such behavior is usually exhibited primarily by men. Most well-functioning individuals enjoy observing sexual stimuli, whether they be *Playboy* or *Playgirl* centerfolds or the unclothed body of their sexual partner. However, voyeurism usually involves the focusing of all sexual interest on secretly viewing undressed women or couples without their knowledge or consent. It is the secrecy and danger of the viewing which seems to enhance the sexual excitment associated with voyeuristic behavior. Masturbation usually accompanies voyeuristic activities.

Gebhard et al., (1965) found that 95 percent of those convicted of voyeurism were observing strangers. Those engaging in these behaviors tended to be unmarried young men with an average age of just under 24. Otherwise, they were a very heterogeneous group. Very few of them molested their victims, and, indeed, they were very careful not to be seen by those they were watching. Almost always they are "caught" by neighbors or passersby rather than the observed person.

The only two individual cases involving behavior therapy with voyeuristic behavior that could be located in the literature are reported here. The first, by Jackson, is a brief account of "A Case of Voyeurism Treated by Counterconditioning." The treatment involved the use of a technique similar to the one reported by Davison in the previous article. Simply stated, the client was told to masturbate in private to pornographic pictures every time he felt the desire to "peep." The masturbatory orgasm was gradually associated with sexual stimuli of decreasing similarity and arousal-potential from voyeuristic fantasies to the point where after eight sessions and a nine-month follow-up, the client reported an absence of voyeuristic behavior and fantasies, and more desirable and socially acceptable sexual behavior had taken its place.

The second article by Gaupp, Stern and Ratliff describes "The Use of Aversion-Relief Procedures in the Treatment of a Case of Voyeurism." In this case, electric shock was administered to the client in the presence of slides of words and phrases related to voyeuristic behavior (as opposed to the more typical use of pictorial or marginal stimuli), while the stimuli associated with the relief from shock were words or phrases related to the condition which led to sexual behaviors with the client's wife. Following 12 sessions, the client reported a "disinterest" in voyeuristic behavior and a more satisfying sexual relationship with his wife. These effects were maintained at an eight-month follow-up. An interesting feature of this report is the use of GSR and EKG to monitor the client during treatment and as additional support of its effects.

REFERENCES

Gebhard, P.H., Gagnon, J.H., Pomeroy, W.B. & Christenson, C.V. *Sex offenders.* New York: Harper and Row, 1965.

65
A Case of Voyeurism
Treated by Counterconditioning

B.T. JACKSON

The role of fantasy in maintaining sexual deviations has received considerable attention in recent publications (Evans, 1968, Davison, 1968, McGuire, Carlisle & Young, 1965, Lazarus, 1968). The essence of an hypothesis propounded by McGuire, Carlisle & Young (1965) is that the fantasy of the aberrant behavior is used during masturbation. Thus, the act (voyeurism, exhibitionism) has value primarily for providing later imaginal stimuli.

Davison (1968) reported the successful use of counterconditioning governed by the client in the elimination of a sadistic fantasy. This study reports a favorable outcome with a voyeur employing the same method as Davison (1968).

CASE STUDY

The S was a 20-year-old unmarried male who referred himself to a mental health clinic because of anxiety, irritability and depression. His anamnesis revealed a somewhat directionless life. He left school after Grade VIII and has held down sundry menial jobs, although he is reported to be above average potential.

During the third interview after much reluctance and balking, he admitted peeping in windows for the last 5 years without being caught. His voyeurism occurred about 5 times a week with his preferred object being a young nude female. Sporadically after the session of peeping he would masturbate, thus positively reinforcing the voyeurism on an intermittent schedule.

This behavior was interpreted to him in learning principles, and he manifested great relief and hope when told that this behavior could be extinguished. A survey of potentially exciting stimuli revealed that pornographic pictures had the maximum arousing properties after voyeurism. After that came pictures of nude females such as found in the centerfold of *Playboy*.

It was then suggested that the next time he felt the urge to peep, he would masturbate in the privacy of his bedroom to the most exciting pornographic picture he had in his collection. He was told to focus on the picture at the time of orgasm. This was done for the next 2 weeks, by the end of which he reported no desire to look in windows. The next step involved pairing his orgasm with a nude picture. If he found it necessary he could maintain an erection through imagining a pornographic picture but had to concentrate on the *Playboy* picture at the point of ejaculation. From this juncture, further progress was rapid, and he reported no urges to peep and actually experienced two satisfactory heterosexual relations. Treatment was terminated after 8 sessions. Nine months later, he stated that his desire for voyeurism had dissipated and his sexual energies were directed along more socially acceptable lines.

DISCUSSION

By associating his orgasm with sexual stimuli of decreasing similarity and arousal-potential from voyeuristic fantasy, a positive attraction was created to more acceptable objects. Consistent with the hypothesis propounded by McGuire, Carlisle and Young, in this case, the act served to supply fantasy material for subsequent masturbation. The reinforcing value of the voyeurism was maintained on a variable-ratio schedule. The rapidity with which the client reported a cessation of his desire to peep was quite unanticipated. It must be kept in mind that this lad's level of motivation was probably optimal to remove this behavior from his repertoire.

REFERENCES

Davison, G.C. Elimination of a sadistic fantasy by a client-controlled counterconditioning technique. *J. Abnorm. Psychol.*, 1968, **73**, 84-90.

Evans, D.R. Masturbatory fantasy and sexual deviation. *Behav. Res. & Therapy*, 1968, **6**, 17-19.

Lazarus, A.A. A case of pseudonecrophilia treated by behavior therapy. *J. Clin. Psychol.*, 1968, **24**, 113-115.

McGuire, R.J., Carlisle, J.M. & Young, B.G. Sexual deviations as conditioned behavior: A hypothesis. *Behav. Res. & Therapy*, 1965, **2**, 185-190.

66
The Use of Aversion-Relief Procedures in the Treatment of a Case of Voyeurism

LARRY A. GAUPP, ROBERT M. STERN, and RICHARD G. RATLIFF

Few cases of voyeurism treated by behavior modification techniques have appeared in print (Wolpe, 1958; McGuire, Carlisle & Young, 1965; Jackson, 1969). The present report describes the successful application of aversion-relief procedures to an individual exhibiting voyeuristic behavior.

CASE HISTORY

The client, a 24-year-old married graduate student, was self-referred to the Psychological Clinic. The client was apprehended for "peeping" and agreed to seek psychological assistance to avoid adjudication; the peeping behavior began when he was about 10 years old.

The client's desire to peep was situationally specific to the dormitories located on the university campus. His desire was also stimulus specific to the breasts of females of a comparable age. The desire usually arose when he was either bored or frustrated. This frustration was not sexual, however, since he reported having achieved a very satisfying sexual relationship with his wife (the client was not convincing in this regard). The client's behavior strongly suggested the presence of heterosexual anxiety—he was unable to confirm or discount the validity of this hypothesis.

While peeping, he never experienced sexual arousal per se (i.e., he never experienced an erection or attempted masturbation). Upon returning home, he either masturbated to fantasies associated with what he had seen (a pattern he had followed since the onset of his peeping behavior) or engaged in sexual intercourse with his wife while having fantasies about his peeping experience. If the opportunity to engage in peeping was not available, he would masturbate to *Playboy* centerfolds.

PROCEDURES

Prior to the initiation of the treatment procedures, the rationale underlying the treatment process was explained. The client was instructed to record the weekly

556

frequency of the desire to peep, the frequency of actual peeping, and to maintain similar records for the masturbation to the *Playboy* centerfolds.

The treatment procedures employed were similar to those of Gaupp, Stern and Galbraith (1971). The aversive stimuli consisted of 11 slides of words and phrases related directly to peeping (e.g., "peeping," "wasting time while peeping," "spying on strange girl's sexual privacy" and "masturbating to peeping fantasies"). The aversive stimuli were accompanied by an electric shock delivered to his right ankle 7 seconds after stimulus slide onset. All shocks were delivered for 0.3 seconds. Shock intensity ranged from 6.0 mA for the first four aversive stimuli, 6.5 mA for the next three, to a maximum of 7.0 mA for the last four aversive stimuli.

The relief stimuli consisted of 11 slides of words or phrases related directly to the conditions which led to sexual behaviors with the client's wife (W) and to peeping (e.g., "boredom," "frustration," "sexual excitement from W," "sexual intercourse with W"). Every session ended with the relief stimulus, "sexual intercourse with W." All stimuli were determined during the initial interview.

During each session the 22 stimuli were randomly presented. Each stimulus was presented for 15 seconds. Time intervals between stimulus presentations varied randomly from 15 to 45 seconds.

RESULTS AND DISCUSSION

The weekly occurrence of the urge to peep and actual peeping behavior are presented in Table 1, together with similar data for both the urge to masturbate and actual masturbation to *Playboy* centerfolds. The aversive stimulus, "masturbating to magazine photos of nude girls," was introduced during Session 2. At Session 3, the client reported the complete absence of both peeping and masturbatory behavior despite ideal conditions for peeping and the reading of *Playboy*.

Table 1 The Weekly Occurrence of the Urge to Peep, Actual Peeping, the Urge to Masturbate and Actual Masturbation to *Playboy* Centerfolds across Treatment Sessions

	Base				Term	Base							
	I	1	2	3	break	II	4	5	6-7	8	9	10	11-12
Urge to peep	6	5	1	0		5	6	2	0	3	1	1	0
Peeping	2	2	0	0		3	2	1	0	0	0	0	0
Urge to masturbate	2	3	6	0		0	0	0	0	0	0	0	0
Masturbation	1	0	1	0		0	0	0	0	0	0	0	0

Peeping behavior was reinstated following a successful midnight excursion during the academic recess. At this time, he was instructed to limit himself sexually to his wife but strictly to avoid engaging in any type of sexual behavior on those nights preceded by either the urge to peep or the actual peeping act itself. Treatment, reinstituted during Session 4, was followed by a marked reduction in the peeping behaviors by Session 5. During Session 8 a partial schedule of punishment was introduced in an attempt to heighten the anxiety-relief response pattern. With this schedule, an electric shock was presented concomitant with six of the 11 aversive stimuli.

By Session 10 the client was reporting that the feeling of "disinterest" in peeping was becoming both stronger and occurring almost immediately following the urge to peep. During the treatment sessions he found himself reacting immediately with a feeling of "uncomfortableness" and a feeling of "safety" to the presentation of the aversive and relief stimuli, respectively. It was also noted that this sexual relationship with his wife was reportedly more "interesting," "meaningful" and "satisfying."

At Sessions 11 and 12 the client reported the complete absence of all maladaptive sexual behaviors despite the presence of ideal conditions for these behaviors, i.e., he was not busy and was temporarily separated from his wife. Treatment was discontinued following Session 12. Because his wife was unaware of his deviance no independent assessment of behavior change was possible.

The GSR response data for the aversive and relief stimuli across blocks of treatment sessions are presented in Fig. 1. Visual examination of Fig. 1 suggests a large increment in GSR responding to the aversive stimuli and a concomitant decrement in GSR responding to the relief stimuli across blocks of treatment sessions.

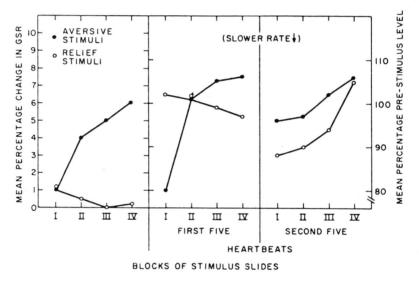

Fig. 1. Mean Percentage Change in GSR Responding and Mean Percentage of EKG Responding for the First and Second Five Heart-beats after Stimulus Onset to the Aversive and Relief Stimulus Slides across Blocks of Treatment Sessions.

The EKG response data for the aversive and relief stimuli across blocks of treatment sessions are also presented in Fig. 1. Visual examination suggests a large increment in EKG responding to the aversive stimuli for both the first and second five heart beats after slide onset across blocks of treatment sessions.

At a 6-month follow-up the client reported the continued absence of the maladaptive sexual behavior. Sex with W was reported to be "highly enjoyable." He also reported that he has become more assertive with and relaxed around women and that he no longer felt "inferior" to women. He recalled the hypothesized heterosexual anxiety and felt it was probably valid. At an 8-month follow-up treatment effects continued to be maintained.

The present results, while not qualifying as acceptable experimental data, do suggest several hypotheses pertinent to the experimental investigation of aversion therapy. First, that differential classical conditioning is the effective process operating in the aversion therapies. Second, that this process is important to the development of a more adaptative cognitive-sexual orientation. Third, that the nature of the CS, ie., written descriptions of behavior, acts more directly to bring about cognitive change than pictorial or imaginal stimuli. Fourth, that such written descriptions enhance extra-therapeutic generalization of treatment effects.

REFERENCES

Jackson, B.T. A case of voyeurism treated by counterconditioning. *Behaviour Research and Therapy*, 1969, 7, 133-134.

McGuire, R.J., Carlisle, J.M. & Young, B.G. Sexual deviations as conditioned behaviour: A hypothesis. *Behaviour Research and Therapy*, 1965, 2, 185-190.

Wolpe, J. *Psychotherapy by reciprocal inhibition.* Stanford: Stanford University Press, 1958.

Miscellaneous Behaviors

There is almost an infinite variety of undesired or maladaptive sexual behaviors exhibited by individuals which create problems either for them or those in their environment. These problems may be characterized by undesired objects as sexual stimuli, or by undesired responses to the sexual stimuli. These behaviors range from such relatively rare behaviors as sexual activities with corpses (labeled "necrophilia") to such common but vague problem behaviors as having sex too often (labeled "nymphomania") or with too many partners (labeled "promiscuity").

There are also a variety of sex-related problems experienced by individuals or those in their environment as a result of the individual being part of sexual problem-prone groups such as the aged (who may experience stress as a result of physiological changes, or as a result of the loss through death of a long-time sexual partner) or the retarded (whose judgment about sexual decisions—who to go to bed with and, under what circumstances—may be impaired).

The articles in this section describe several problematic sexual behaviors—and/or behavioral programs—that are not easily categorized in any of the previous sections.

In the first article, "A Case of Public Masturbation Treated by Operant Conditioning," Wagner describes the treatment of an 11-year-old girl reported by her teacher as masturbating publicly in the classroom as often as seven times per hour. As opposed to many attempts to decrease sexual responses through the use of aversive methods, the procedure employed by Wagner involved positive reinforcement, on first continuous and later intermittent schedules, of an incompatible response (non-masturbatory behavior). After 74 school days of treatment, the non-masturbatory response was established and persisted the remainder of the school year. This demonstration of the apparent effectiveness of this procedure with a behavior that appeared so strongly entrenched suggests the possibility of expanding the use of operant conditioning emphasizing positive reinforcement in the treatment of mal-adaptive sexual problems to a greater extent than previously has been the case.

The report by Lazarus involves "The Treatment of a Sexually Inadequate Man." The "sexual inadequacy" appeared largely to involve the client's inability to achieve an erection, even though he maintained a superb "social facade." The first part of the treatment involved an attempt to correct some of the client's misconceptions plus advice to masturbate to the point of orgasm only when he had a "reasonable" erection. The second part of the treatment involved systematic desensitization to four stimulus configura-tions: sexual, aggression to females, physical violence and rejection. These sessions apparently were extremely successful since follow-up found the client married to an ex-beauty queen and the father of a daughter.

In the next article, Anant demonstrates the use of "Verbal Aversion Therapy with a Promiscuous Girl." This technique was applied to a 20-year-old woman who was a resident of an institution for the retarded and who had been unable to function in job situations apparently because she would seduce the first man who came along. The technique involves training in relaxation, imagination of aversive scenes and "practice" of those scenes. After 10 sessions, the client showed substantial improvement in the therapy sessions, accepted a new job and, after eight months, reportedly was func-tioning well.

In the next article, Wickramasekera reports on "Desensitization, Re-sensitization and Desensitization Again." In this case, systematic desensitiza-tion was applied to a client's anxiety reactions to images of the theme of infidelity by his wife in an effort to decrease what Wickramasekera describes as "obsessive compulsive sexual behavior." Initially, the desensitization appeared to be having a positive effect in that the undesired forms of sexual behavior did decrease. In a possibly questionable, but successful, "reversal" experiment, the author then "re-sensitized" the client and undesirable behav-ior recurred. This was finally overcome by resuming the standard progression of scene presentations. An interesting feature of this study is a use of the type of charting procedure generally associated with operant methods. As this case demonstrates, however, such recording may be suitable also for use in association with nonoperant procedures, and it offers an important method for cross-validation of results.

The article by Lazarus presents the only available article in the literature of "A Case of Pseudonecrophilia Treated by Behavior Therapy." In this report, pseudonecrophilia (masturbatory fantasies focused on corpses), was treated first by providing reassurance of the fact that his fantasies were not "psychotic," and use of behavior rehearsal to help the client express his anger toward women. The second phase of treatment involved the use of systematic desensitization to desensitize him to varying degrees of wake-fulness and awareness in women while engaged in sex. The treatment worked even faster than anticipated, and 11 months after termination, the client reported that "all was well."

The next article, by Kraft, reports on "Treatment of the Housebound

Housewife Syndrome." In this case, a 30-year-old woman who had been "housebound" for six years was treated for several components of the problem. The first aspect, involving the client's inability to achieve satisfactory intercourse or orgasm, was successfully handled through systematic desensitization. The second aspect involved the housebound problem itself, and this too was successfully treated by desensitization. The final aspect of treatment involved decreasing the dependence on the therapist through the technique of thought-stopping. The total amount of treatment involved 73 one-hour sessions; a nine-month follow-up indicated all improvement had been maintained. Interestingly, in a letter to the editors (May, 1975), Kraft indicated that today, some 9 years after treatment was terminated, the client still had maintained her improvement.

The next article is Rosen's "Conditioning Appropriate Heterosexual Behavior in Mentally and Socially Handicapped Populations." This article, rather than presenting a case study, describes a program for sex education of handicapped individuals through use of behavioral procedures. Rosen points out that the treatment of undesired sexual responses and the teaching of desired sexual behavior represent two parts of the same problem. He notes that sex education programs for the mentally handicapped typically attempt to teach inhibition and control rather than to reinforce adequate sexual behavior. While behavior change should be the ultimate goal of such programs, the teaching of factual knowledge is rarely effective for that purpose. Rosen's program includes systematic desensitization, programmed heterosexual experience, role-playing, reinforcement for sex-related talk, suggestions to masturbate and aversive conditioning. The goals Rosen suggests involve extinguishing anxiety associated with desired sexual responses, making undesired responses more aversive and substituting more desired behaviors for them.

In addition to pointing to the likely necessity for use of multiple techniques combined into a program for the treatment of most sexual problems, Rosen's article is important because it emphasizes, often only implicitly, the need for preventive as well as remedial measures in the areas of sexual problems. Behavior therapy, with its assortment of procedures for both increasing and decreasing behaviors, is readily adaptable to efforts to use those procedures to teach the prevention as well as the treatment of sexual problems. Indeed, perhaps the surest indicator of the success of any field is that utopian point in time when the problems to which it is addressed no longer occur. While the treatment of problems that already have manifested themselves will probably always be a major preoccupation of clinicians, hopefully those who use behavioral procedures also will address at least part of their efforts—in work in schools, institutions, parent and family-life education and so on—to the broader arena involved in the prevention of maladaptive human behavior.

The brief report by Marshall, "Reducing Masturbatory Guilt," illustrates some of the difficulties that may be encountered when modifying sexual fantasies where guilt is associated with masturbation, and demonstrates one method for reducing such guilt. The therapist used a reinforcement pro-

cedure to successfully increase positive thoughts and feelings about masturbation so that orgasmic reconditioning was facilitated.

The final article in this volume is Carr's, "Behavior Therapy in a Case of
Multiple Sexual Disorders." The intervention program described involved
careful orchestration of a variety of behavioral techniques in order just to
differentiate the complex contingency relationships and then modify the
target behavior. Of particular interest in this case is first, that the procedures
by and large were carried out by the client himself so that the client was able
to learn self-management, and second, even with multiple sexual disorders, a
creative and flexible use of behavioral principles augers well for changing
positively problems long thought to be highly refractory to treatment.
Indeed, it is just such creative and flexible use of behavioral techniques that
augers well for successful intervention into a wide variety of dysfunctional
human circumstances, and promotes a justifiable optimism about the demonstrated and potential value of behavior therapy with sexual problems.

67

A Case of Public Masturbation Treated by Operant Conditioning*

MERVYN K. WAGNER

The treatment of "compulsive" masturbation has received scant attention in the literature except for a few highly theoretical articles within a psychoanalytic framework (Mertz, 1955; Hammerman, 1961). The behavior therapy approach had one of its earliest representatives in Dunlap (1960) who in 1932 reported success with the alleviation of compulsive masturbation through the use of negative practice. More recently McGuire and Vallance (1964) utilized an electric shock in three cases but their success with this aversive conditioning method was not reported. It is possible that other cases have been treated with behavior modification methods, but it is probable that, like most sexual symptoms, it has been treated with aversive conditioning (Rachman, 1961; Blakemore et al., 1963; Grossberg, 1964).[1]

The operant conditioning paradigm has been adapted to the modification of many classes of behavior by Skinner (1953) and his students, and its effectiveness has been well established. This case illustrates the use of primarily positive reinforcement within an operant conditioning framework to alleviate "compulsive" public masturbation in an 11-year-old girl. The behavior modification regime took place over a 7-month period, with the primary role of therapist being assumed by the subject's sixth-grade classroom teacher.

DESCRIPTION AND BACKGROUND

This girl was referred as an outpatient by a pediatrician upon the recommendation of her classroom teacher[2] who was concerned that the subject's almost constant

*Prepared within the framework of activities supported by the V.A. Psychiatric Programme Evaluation Staff.

[1] It is interesting that a survey of the literature in behavior modification methods suggests the possibility that we may be falling into the same 'morality' trap as other disciplines by punishing sexual behaviour which might be considered immoral or antisocial.

[2] This paper would not have been possible without having an excellent classroom teacher, Mrs. Robert Arey, serving as therapist.

masturbation in the classroom was a disturbance to others, and that it prevented her from accomplishing even minimal personal academic achievements. She primarily used the edge of her desk, rocking back and forth, but in addition she periodically used her hand or foot. The teacher estimated that this occurred as often as four or five times per hour in the morning, and six or seven times per hour in the afternoon. She frequently achieved orgasm, and the response was fairly obvious to her classmates and teacher.

The teacher inquired of the subject's previous teachers and found that the masturbatory behavior had been increasing in frequency since the first grade. Many methods had been attempted to eliminate this activity including the involvement of a number of different physicians. She had been spanked, scolded, rewarded, shamed and medicated, but all to no avail. At the time of the referral she was masturbating almost constantly in the classroom. Her present teacher discovered a method which was momentarily inhibiting—she would have the subject do something she especially enjoyed, such as painting or handing out papers. She had been with essentially the same classmates since entering school, and while it appeared that they ignored the sexual behavior, at the same time they ignored the subject, causing her to be a social isolate. The parents stated that, to their knowledge, the behavior had not taken place at home, and when a teacher two years earlier had discussed it with them they took the girl to a mental hygiene clinic. The clinic psychologist obtained a W.I.S.C. I.Q. of 90 and also believed that she was not disturbed enough emotionally to need treatment.

The primary focus of this paper will be the control of the masturbatory response, even though when this girl was first seen a number of other behavior problems were present, and some time was spent working with the parents in developing methods for dealing with these problems. She was grossly dependent upon her overprotective and critical mother, to the point where, for example, she needed help dressing in the mornings so as not to be late for school. She most effectively controlled her family by crying and whining. There was some possibility that she may have had encephalitis when she was approximately three years of age, even though this had never been diagnosed.

GENERAL PROCEDURE

The principal method used was operant conditioning, with the target response being nonmasturbation in the classroom. The program was begun with considerable trepidation since it was questionable that any reinforcement could compete with orgasm. The teacher was seen only once in the beginning to set up the program, and all other contacts were by telephone. The teacher was particularly competent and readily understood and was able to apply the reinforcement procedures. A time sampling technique was utilized to determine the initial level of the masturbatory activity. The reinforcement routine specified that when the subject desisted for even a few minutes she was to be given some special attention by the teacher in the form of a pat on the head or a positive comment, thus reinforcing the nonmasturbatory response. In the morning, if she went as long as an hour without masturbating she was to be rewarded with something she especially liked to do. In the afternoon, because of the increased frequency of its occurrence, only one-half hour of abstinence was necessary to earn a reward. No longer was she to be rewarded for the non-desired behavior, which was the previous practice. A list of many activities such as distributing other pupils' requirements, correcting papers and helping the teacher was compiled to use as rewards. When she was able to complete a full day without masturbation a note was to be written to her parents stating how well she had behaved on that particular day. The parents were instructed that these notes were to signify that something special needed to be done for her. We compiled a list of special things from which the parents could choose reinforcements, including such things as buying a "pop" record for her, letting her stay overnight with her grandmother and taking her bowling. The parents were interviewed nine times, but these sessions were related primarily to obtaining history and dealing with the home behavior problems mentioned earlier. Once the parents were called in for an interview when it was felt by the teacher that they were negatively reinforcing the subject when she *did not* bring home a note. When the subject was observed by the teacher to be masturbating in the classroom, the teacher spoke the subject's name aloud as a negative reinforcement.

The reinforcement schedule was intended to be as continuous as possible, with it later being changed to a fixed interval (FI) reinforcement schedule when notes were given for two consecutive days of non-masturbation. The schedule was finally changed to an aperiodic schedule in order to decrease the possibilities of quick extinction of the non-masturbatory response.

SPECIFIC PROCEDURES AND RESULTS

The data for this study are by necessity only gross estimates, as the teacher was able to keep only a rough record of the subject's behavior and changes in the procedure, concurrent with her usual program for the rest of her sixth-grade class.

From the beginning of school on August 30, 1966, until November 7, 1966, the teacher informally observed that the subject masturbated daily as often as four or five times per hour in the morning and six or seven times each hour in the afternoon. Orgasmic experience was frequent and obvious to the teacher and the class. It was noted that during her menstrual period she did not masturbate. During the week following November 8, a basal level was determined by having teacher observe the subject for a 5-minute period three times per day for four school days. For five of the eleven observations, she was masturbating. If this were generalized it could suggest that she masturbated as much as 45 percent of the time. A fifth day was lost since she began having her menstrual period, and one other observation was lost since she had gone to the library.

The schedule for the behavior modification procedure began on November 15, 1966 and proceeded as follows. The numbers in parentheses represent the actual number of school days after behavior modification procedures were initiated.

(1) Began behavior modification procedure. Since this program calls for the shaping of the non-masturbatory response, she began by getting some positive and negative reinforcements from the first day. The masturbatory activity began dropping out quickly for the morning period, but the afternoon was more restive.

(10) Masturbation had reduced to a few times in the afternoon only.

(12) The first note went home for having completed an entire day without observed masturbatory activity. Notes were sent home on the subsequent days (14) and (17).

(21) Went 5 days without masturbation, but this was during menstrual period.

(36-40) Moved the subject's desk to the middle of the room; masturbation increased to at least a few minutes each day. Moved her back to her previous seat in front of the room after 3 days.

(41-55) Undesired behavior decreasing with a few notes sent home.

(56-60) Three notes sent home this week.

(61-64) Notes every day.

(65) Switched to FI reinforcement schedule. Notes given for two days of non-masturbatory activity. Only occasional masturbation which was quickly stopped with a word or glance from the teacher.

(70-78) Very infrequent masturbation. Sometime during this period the response dropped out entirely.

(79) Began requiring two notes in order to obtain reinforcement from parents.

(109) Changed the subject's desk to the back of the room without reoccurrence of masturbatory response.

(113) Began aperiodic reinforcement schedule.

(129) School year over (May 26, 1967).

On October 13, 1967, the new school year has been in session for seven weeks, and the mother reports that her conference with the subject's new teacher indicates no resumption of public masturbatory behavior.

DISCUSSION

This practical demonstration of the effectiveness of this procedure with a behavior as typically recalcitrant as "compulsive" masturbation further generalizes the utility of the operant conditioning model. Since this positive approach is based on the strengthening of an incompatible response rather than the extinction or punishment of the undesirable response, it is less likely that the response will spontaneously recover. If school had continued, it would have been desirable to have lengthened the aperiodic reinforcement schedule and eventually to have discontinued it, thereby making the results more definite. Since starting school again after summer vacation, the masturbation has not resumed, and it appears to have extinguished. An additional important result was the effectiveness with which the teacher handled the operant conditioning method with only a modicum of training and supervision.

REFERENCES

Blakemore, C.B., Thorpe, J.G., Barker, J.C., Conway, C.G. & Lavin, N.T. The application of faradic aversion conditioning in a case of transvestism. *Behav. Res. Ther.*, 1963, **1**, 29-34.

Dunlap, K. Cited by Lehner, G.F.J. Negative practice as a psychotherapeutic technique. In *Behaviour Therapy and The Neuroses.* (Ed. by Eysenck, H.J.). London: Pergamon Press, 1960, 194.

Grossberg, J.M. Behavior therapy: A review. *Psychol. Bull.*, 1964, **62**, 77-88.

Hammerman, S. Masturbation and character. *F. Am. Psychoanal. Ass.*, 1961, **9**, 287-311.

McGuire, R.J. & Vallance, M. Aversion therapy technique by electric shock. In *Conditioning techniques in clinical practice and research.* (Ed. by Franks, C.M.). New York: Springer, 1964, 178-188.

Mertz, P. Therapeutic considerations in masturbation. *Am. F. Psychother.*, 1955, **9**, 630-639.

Rachman, S. Sexual disorders and behavior therapy. *Am. F. Psychiat.*, 1961, **46**, 57-70.

Skinner, B.F. *Science and human behavior.* London: Macmillan, 1953.

68
The Treatment of a Sexually Inadequate Man

ARNOLD A. LAZARUS

Where high degrees of anxiety produce an almost complete inhibition of sexual responsiveness, therapy must employ a broad range of anxiety-eliminating procedures. In the case outlined below the well-known virtues of a nonrejecting therapist furnished an interpersonal context in which several specific techniques were effectively administered.

Roy came for treatment at the beginning of May 1960. A 33-year-old engineer with a lucrative business of his own, this talented, charming, well-read individual was nonetheless profoundly inadequate. His social facade was impenetrable. His feelings of panic and withdrawal sheltered behind a guise of aloofness and independence. What he recognized as crippling inhibition within himself, his friends termed "slight reticence," and women found that his "boyish shyness" tended to stimulate real or imaginary maternal needs in them.

Roy brought his well-practiced social graces into the therapeutic relationship and concealed his basic problems behind his habitual defenses. "I have come to you," he said, "in order to prove to myself that our social values are depraved." The first three sessions were taken up with impersonal topics that nevertheless revealed a common thread. With extraordinary articulation, Roy embroidered the proposition that the females of our culture blossom into maidenhood with "warped," "twisted," "attenuated" and "truncated" personalities due to their complete preoccupation with "marriage and propagation." The emerging personalities of young girls, he maintained, were irrevocably stuned by emotional straitjackets. They were insidiously brainwashed until the potential virtues of proper male-female friendship and comradeship were complely annihilated. He labored the point that on innumerable occasions he had persistently endeavored to establish a "proper friendship" with a woman but that the repercussions had always been mutually disastrous. "Their crippled perceptions are only capable of whittling men into two categories—eligible or ineligible marriage partners or lovers."

Roy dexterously avoided all attempts at meaningful therapeutic communication. Apart from what could be inferred from the above account, his most personal remark was that his acute awareness of the need for social reform frequently made him feel profoundly depressed.

He telephoned before his fourth appointment to ask the therapist whether further sessions were necessary. Roy maintained that he had gained some clarity of thought from the discussions and that in his opinion "therapy" should be terminated. Thereafter the conversation continued along the following lines:

Therapist: But you haven't even come out with your real problem.
Roy: How do you mean?
Therapist: Why must you keep up this pretence?
Roy: What pretence?
Therapist: You know what I'm getting at.
Roy: You psychologists think everyone's insane.
Therapist: Things like anxiety and sexual problems have little, if anything, to do with insanity.
Roy: (After a long pause) All right! I'll come in and see you tomorrow.

The fourth session was totally different from the three preceding discussions. In an affectless tone, Roy stated that he was utterly inadequate sexually. His most successful sexual attempt had occured a year previously with a prostitute with whom he had managed to have an extra-vaginal orgasm and ejaculation with a completely flaccid penis. His life history revealed that his background provided a "breeding ground" for neurosis.

He was born in England and emigrated to South Africa with his parents and siblings after the outbreak of war. "I was an unwanted sixth child in an already overpopulated family consisting of two miscarriages and five daughters. My mother was a militant feminist and my father was an equally devout pacifist." Roy was expected to revere his sisters, to adore his mother and to tolerate his father. Actually, he feared his sisters, was terrified of his mother, and loved his father.

His attitude toward sex was obviously influenced by his mother's overzealous denunciations of promiscuity. An implicit belief in the virtues of chastity made the onus of protecting five daughters from the ravages of temptation a perpetual struggle. Roy and his sisters were constantly reminded that men inadvertently sought to undermine the moral fiber of the nation and that the women had to uphold the dignity of the human race, if there was to be hope for future generations. Roy was admonished to think of his sisters if ever faced with the temptation or opportunity to lead some misguided female astray.

Another influential factor in determining Roy's sexual inadequacies was a two-year period spent at a boarding-school between the ages of 15-17 years. A favorite pastime of the senior boys in his dormitory was suddenly to pull the bedclothes off some unsuspecting victim and to penalize him if he was found to have an erection. Consequently, Roy taught himself to masturbate *without an erection.*

Now 33 years of age, Roy could not remember when last he had had a complete erection. He masturbated almost daily, occasionally obtaining a transient erection. His fantasies during masturbation were exclusively heterosexual, usually involving "mature, persuasive and very seductive women." The reason for his complete refusal to reveal his sexual inadequacies when he first consulted the therapist was that he attributed his disabilities to his masturbatory indulgence, when he viewed with guilt and shame. (It was not out of character for his mother to have threatened him with insanity as the penality for what she regarded as "self-abuse.")

The first therapeutic objective was a concerted endeavour to correct Roy's misconceptions. His combination of genuine sophistication and worldiness was offset by remarkable areas of naivete and widespread misinformation. One direct consequence of his mother's pejorative teachings was his social submissiveness and masculine ineptitude. This hinged largely on his confused and contradictory attitudes toward women. His ambivalence was exemplified by his tendency to fawn over women at the overt behavior level while inwardly mocking them. Numerous illogicalities between his thoughts, feelings, and actions were pointed out to him. This provoked definite feelings of antagonism in Roy that tentatively led to open hostility toward the therapist. At first, any expression of his own antagonism made him contrite and apologetic, but with practice (which the therapist encouraged both in and out of the therapeutic situation) Roy became less afraid of his own aggressive impulses. Therapy at this stage consisted largely of coaxing him into more and more assertive action tendencies. Although he became less reticent socially, he was still somewhat uncomfortable in feminine company.

Roy had been advised to masturbate to the point of orgasm only when he had a reasonable erection. After three months he reported that he usually awoke in the morning with an erection (which he claimed had last been present when he first entered boarding school) but close physical proximity with women still failed to evoke any reassuring signs of potential sexual adequacy.

At this stage Roy had undergone more than 20 sessions spaced over approximately three-and-one-half months. He became increasingly despondent about his basic lack of progress. He began to express doubts about the therapist's competence on the grounds that other "behaviorists," often claimed to achieve dramatic results in less than twelve sessions. The therapist dealt with this impasse by accepting the patient's doubts while pointing out that they were largely based on subjective premises.

Apart from his specific sexual aberrations, Roy's chief failings centered around three dimensions: 1) An aversion to having personal altercations with women, typified by his complete inability to "stand up to" his mother or his sister; 2) a morbid dread of physical violence and 3) an exaggerated concern for public approval.

These areas together with Roy's sexual anxieties were concurrently treated by means of systematic desensitization. In essence, the desensitization procedure consisted of the following steps:

a. Training in progressive relaxation;
b. constructing anxiety hierarchies; (that is, graded lists of situations to which the patient responded with neurotic anxiety);
c. systematically presenting each item on the anxiety hierarchies to the imagination of the relaxed patient.

The four hierarchies constructed in Roy's case were as follows:

1. *A Sexual Hierarchy.* (There were eight items consisting of sexual situations requiring increasing initiative, that is, embracing, kissing, fondling, undressing. . . .)
2. *An Aggression-to-Females Hierarchy.* (There were twelve items such as expressing disapproval a) to a strange woman, b) to his sisters, c) to his mother; refusing to accede to an unreasonable demand made a) by his sisters, b) by his

mother; actually shouting at his sisters; and so forth.)
3. *A Physical Violence Hierarchy.* (There were six items ranging from a mild wrestling match between two young boys, to newspaper headlines dealing with violent riots in a foreign country.)
4. *A Rejection Hierarchy.* (There were six items consisting of the following type of situation: overhearing a mildly uncomplimentary remark passed about him; being called neurotic; a woman finds fault with his manners; and so on.)

Roy required 57 desensitization sessions spaced over approximately eight months before he was able to picture the most exacting scenes in each hierarchy with comparative equanimity. Throughout this period, fluctuating changes accrued to his personality in an almost imperceptible but nontheless discernible manner. Roy's attitude toward the therapist constantly vaciliated between antipathy and adulation.

About three months after the commencement of desensitization, Roy reported that he obtained an erection whenever he danced with a girl. After two months, he successfully allowed himself to be seduced by "a notorious nymphomaniac." A few weeks later, Roy reported that he was having regular sexual relations with a woman at work.

At the time of writing, Roy is the adequate husband of a 23-year-old former beauty queen and the father of a 2-month old daughter.

69
Verbal Aversion Therapy with A Promiscuous Girl: Case Report

SANTOKH S. ANANT

Although drugs and electric shocks have been widely used as aversive stimuli in the elimination of undesirable habits (e.g., alcoholism, drug addiction, homosexuality, smoking, etc.), relatively little work has been reported on the use of verbal aversion. Rachman (1965) mentioned the possibility of the use of unpleasant auditory stimulation and other forms of aversive techniques. During 1965-66, this author used a verbal aversion technique with alcoholics and drug addicts and with one case of homosexuality. My technique and results have been reported earlier (Anant, 1966, 1967). This report describes the successful application of this technique with a promiscuous girl. The fact that this girl was also mental defective, increases the significance of such an application of verbal aversion therapy.

The patient was a 20-year-old resident of an institution for the mentally retarded. Her Full Scale IQ on the WAIS administered in 1967, was 59. She had a long history of promiscuous behavior and had given birth to an illegitimate male child when she was 15. Whenever she was sent out to work on some job, in a cafeteria, etc., she would seduce the first available customer and disappear with him, with the result that no establishment was prepared to hire her any longer.

She was seen in 10 one-hour sessions over a period of 2 weeks. The program of treatment, viz., training in relaxation, imagination of aversive scenes and practice of these scenes, was outlined to her in the first session. In the same session, it was pointed out to her that such relations may lead to one or more of the following consequences: unwanted pregnancy, as there is no foolproof contraception, syphilis and other venereal diseases and murder at the hands of a "sex fiend." She was trained in relaxation, using combination of the modified Jacobsen technique (Wolpe, 1958) and breathing exercises. In the subsequent sessions, she was asked to imagine scenes based on the three situations listed above, i.e., scenes in which her indiscriminate sexual behavior would lead to pregnancy (with strong emphasis on the embarrassment to her, as she was asked to imagine that she was living in a respectable neighborhood), a venereal disease (syphilis was used as such a disease in almost all scenes in this category) and a strong possibility of being murdered by a sex criminal. A typical scene in the third category is described below.

Imagine that you meet a stranger in a bar where you are working. You agree to go out with him after your work. He drives you to a deserted place, far removed from the main road. There, he has sexual relations with you in a very aggressive way. You become a little bit scared. After the intercourse, he takes out a rope from the car and, before you realize what he is doing, he ties your hands and feet. Then he gags you and tells you that he would kill you. You are very much scared. You can't even scream for help. Now, he takes a knife out of his pocket and opens it. It is a very big, and shining knife. He approaches you with the knife. You are scared like hell, but are quite helpless. You start feeling sorry that you came with him. Imagine that the knife is just one inch away from your throat and you are already anticipating your death. Now, stop and relax again.

After each scene, the patient was asked to describe her fright on a percentile scale. If the fright level was below 50, the frightening elements of the subsequent scenes were increased, until her fright was close to 100 level. It took some time to explain to her the meaning of percentile scale and how to judge her fright on a dimension. She was also asked to practice these scenes at least twice a day, while she was in her room on the ward.

After 10 sessions, the level of her fright in all the situations had reached near 100. At about the same time, a job opportunity was presented to her. She was advised to accept the job, as the real test of the success of the treatment was to be her ability to exercise control in real life situations. She accepted the job and has been functioning fairly well since then (a period of 8 months). Her ability to hold a job successfully i.e., without being fired for undue interest in men, is considered a measure of adequate functioning. A telephone conversation with the superintendent of the institution on February 28, 1968, indicated that she was still working fairly well. The success of the verbal aversion therapy with this case indicates that use of this technique is not limited to alcoholics and drug addicts, but suggests application, with slight modification, to sexual behavior and with retarded persons.

REFERENCES

Anant, S.S. The treatment of alcoholics by a verbal aversion technique: A case report. *MANAS; A Journal of Scientific Psychology,* 1966, **13**, 79-86.

Anant, S.S. A note on the treatment of alcoholics by a verbal aversion technique. *Canadian Psychologist,* 1967, 8a, **1**, 19-22.

Rachman, S. Aversion therapy: Chemical or electrical. *Behav. Res. Ther.,* 1965, **2**, 289-299.

Wolpe, J. *Psychotherapy by reciprocal inhibition.* Stanford, Calif.: Stanford Univer. Press, 1958.

70
Desensitization, Re-sensitization and Desensitization Again: A Preliminary Study

IAN WICKRAMASEKERA

This paper describes the apparently successful desensitization, re-sensitization and repeat desensitization of a case of obsessive-compulsive sexual behavior. The typical procedure for isolating effective treatment variables is the group comparison. An alternative approach is to attempt an intra-subject replication. The intra-subject replication can provide a demonstration of the functional relationship between antecedent and consequent variables. Comparing the procedures Sidman (1960, p. 85) notes: "Intra-subject and to a lesser extent intra-group replication provides a unique demonstration of a technique's reliability."

BACKGROUND INFORMATION

The patient, Mr. C., a 41-year-old, white, married male, was referred to our clinic by his family doctor for the treatment of "obsessive thoughts of a sexual nature which are disturbing his marriage and which threaten his employment." The subject (S) had been married for 17 years and employed on the present job for 12 years.

S attributed the onset of his symptoms to the discovery (in the form of love letters) of his wife's infidelity, 6 months prior to his first contact with the present therapist. His symptoms had apparently not responded to various medications prescribed by physicians. The primary presenting symptoms were restlessness, insomnia, sporadic crying and extended outbursts of verbal abuse (bitch, whore, etc.) focused on his wife. In addition, he had lost weight (approximately 30 pounds), was demanding and attempting sexual intercourse with his wife several times a day (range 1-7) and was extremely suspicious of her. He appeared to have an "uncontrollable urge" to drop whatever he was doing several times a day and rush home to "check" on her, remind her of her infidelity and have intercourse. The frequency of these unscheduled visits home was such that his employer was threatening to discharge him.

The patient's wife admitted that she had been "unfaithful" (several sexual contacts with the same man in motels and in her own home) for a period of approximately 4 months, but insisted that after her husband had discovered her infidelity and "exploded," all contacts (verbal and nonverbal) with her lover had ceased. She claimed that her marriage had been in a "rut" and that she did not "really love" the man she had been involved with. She said that she was sorry for the pain she had cost her husband and had attempted unsuccessfully to make it up to him in the last 6 months. But she claimed that his sexual preoccupations, abuse of her, loss of weight and unauthorized absences from work had only increased. She stated that she believed he wanted to continued to punish her.

The patient stated that since the onset of his symptoms his wife had improved her housekeeping, quit work and was more attentive to him as a wife. *S* stated that he wanted to be hypnotized so that he could "forget" his wife's infidelity and no longer be "possessed" by it. He stated that thoughts of his wife in different "positions" and "places" with her lover were what was "driving him crazy."

METHOD

Formulation of Treatment Plan

"Psychodynamically" a sado-masochistic interaction between husband and wife seemed the central problem. The patient's compulsive sexuality and his wife's need to atone seemed to be reinforcing their complementary role enactments (Kelly, 1955).

The treatment plan was to desensitize the respondent consequences of the patient's obsessive thoughts (operants) and to guide his thoughts toward a rationale or "insight" for giving up his symptoms, no longer to leave him vulnerable to future recurrences of infidelity. An attempt was also made to help the patient find some "meaning" in his present suffering. Specifically, he was encouraged to see his present symptoms as having contributed to some degree to the revitalizing of his marriage.

Preliminary Procedures

The background information having been gathered in an intensive (2 hour) interview with *S* and his wife, separately and together, *S* was told that it would be 3 weeks before his next appointment. He was instructed to start keeping a careful record each Friday evening of his weight till treatment was terminated, and arrangements were made to weigh him on each visit to the clinic. In the course of a private interview with *S's* wife, she was instructed immediately to start observing and recording 2 types of information about her husband's behavior: 1) the frequency of all his visits home on working days between 8 a.m. and 5 p.m. (excluding the regular return home from work at the end of the working day). This class of observations would be an index of paranoid behaviors. 2) The frequency of his attempts at sexual intercourse (partial or total removal of his pants with statement of sexual interest) with her each week. Those observations would be an index of sexual behaviors. Careful observing and accurate recording were stressed and she was told to make every attempt to ensure that her husband did not know she was collecting these data. The decision was made to monitor these 2 areas (paranoid and sexual) of behavior in addition to his weight, because they seemed more amenable to objective

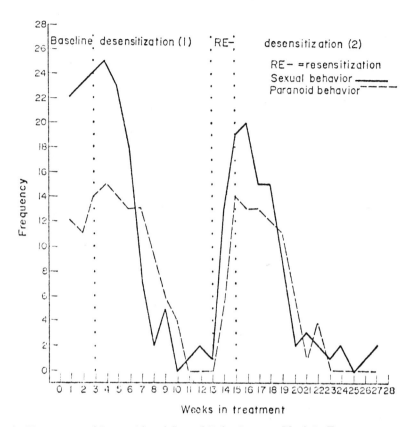

Fig. 1. **Frequency of Paranoid and Sexual Behaviors per Week in Treatment.**

specification than other symptoms and because they were very disruptive to his life.

In terms of Figs. 1 and 2, the initial intensive interview occurred at "0 weeks in treatment." After the 3 weeks baseline period, the Stanford Hypnotic Susceptibility Scale (SHSS) Form A, was administered to measure the S's current hypnotic susceptibility, since he had requested hypnotic treatment in the initial interview. His score on the SHSS was low (2), and the clinical impression was that he was resisting "induction." After the administration of the SHSS, the S was told that the present therapist suspected that his "resistance" to hypnosis was based on the fear that through hypnosis the memory of his wife's infidelity would be erased and that would leave him vulnerable to similar infidelities in the future. He was told that there was an "unpleasant" procedure involving sensory restriction (Wickramasekera, 1969, 1970) which might reduce his "resistance to hypnosis," but an alternative "pleasant" method called "desensitization" which did not involve hypnosis was also available for treating him. He was told that desensitization would "drain the pain out of his memories but leave them fresh and clear." The desensitization procedure was described briefly and presented as being "nonhypnotic." He was told to think about these alternatives (sensory restriction and hypnosis, or desensitization) and make a decision before the next session.

First Desensitization

In the next session ("4 weeks in treatment" according to Figs. 1 and 2) the patient requested the desensitization treatment and hierarchy construction and desensitization was begun. The total hierarchy consisted of 48 scenes. The least aversive scene (1) was seeing himself at home lying on the couch listening to his wife cooking in the kitchen. The most aversive was (48) seeing Mrs. C. indulging in an "unnatural act" of sex with her lover on *S*'s own bed.

Each scene was put on a separate note card (total 48 cards) and very infrequently changed in order or content during treatment. Relaxation training was given both in the office and by means of a taped set of relaxation instructions recorded on a cassette tape. The portable recorder and tape were rented to *S* for a sum of $10.00 per week (not included in regular fee per treatment session). The major purposes of the recorder rental procedure were to motivate speedy acquisition of the relaxation skill and to increase the probability of the practice of relaxation in the patient's natural habitat.

Sessions were one week apart. Each session was 55 to 60 minutes. The only departure from the standard desensitization procedure (Wolpe, 1969) was that during the entire treatment (desensitization and re-sensitization) the patient was told to keep his eyes open and concentrate on the empty white wall in front of him.

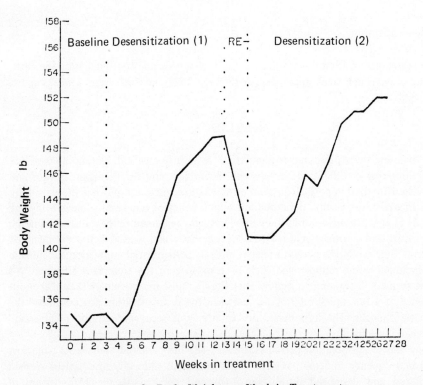

Fig. 2. Body Weight per Week in Treatment.

Re-sensitization

An attempt was made to re-sensitize the patient in the 13th and 14th session of treatment.

Wolpe (1958) observed and Wolpe (1969, p. 127) specifically states that "exposure and prolonged exposure in particular to a very disturbing scene can seriously increase phobic sensitivity." Though an "obsession" may be different in many respects from a phobia, the present treatment procedure was based on the assumption that they had similar "respondent" (excessive autonomic arousal) consequences. From an ethical point of view there appeared to be no problem, since there was no solid evidence that "re-sensitization" was even possible with the procedure to be described below.

Re-sensitization consisted of telling the patient that "a slightly different but improved method will be used today. Please signal any discomfort or anxiety you feel in the usual way, but continue to imagine the scene until I tell you to stop imagining it." When the desensitization procedure was terminated, there remained 30 scenes which had not been presented. All 30 of these scenes were presented in rapid succession during the attempted re-sensitization procedure (sessions 13 and 14). During re-sensitization whenever the patient signaled anxiety (with left forefinger) the presentation was continued for 1½ minutes from the time the signal was observed. The re-sensitization sessions were approximately equal in length (55-60 minutes) to the regular desensitization sessions.

Second Desensitization

Standard desensitization was resumed at the 15th session and continued until the 28th. Sessions were again one week apart, except that the 19th and 20th were 5 weeks apart.

RESULTS

The "baseline" was presented to the patient as a waiting period. During the base line there was no verbal or other contact between the subject and the therapist. Both S and his wife called in their reports to a secretary, who recorded and plotted the data they reported. Figure 1 shows that paranoid and sexual behavior increased somewhat during this period. Figure 2 indicates that the patient's weight remained fairly stable. During the first desensitization period (scenes 1-18) the paranoid and sexual behaviors declined steadily over time while the patient's weight increased. Associated impressionistic clinical features included good rapport and lack of resistance in the treatment situation. S's symptoms seemed to respond so rapidly that the therapist was genuinely skeptical about the existence of a functional relationship between the desensitization procedure and the symptomatic changes. The hypotheses of "spontaneous recovery" and/or a "placebo" effect seemed more likely.

During the re-sensitization period (scenes 19-48) the paranoid and sexual behaviors increased in frequency and the patient's weight declined. Clinically, the patient seemed more agitated and depressed during the 14th and particularly the 15th session of treatment. The therapist continued to try to maintain rapport by being sympathetic and attentive. Before the 15th session, the patient's wife called the clinic and insisted on speaking to the therapist. She seemed extremely agitated and insisted that he was getting worse. She stated he had come home intoxicated twice, was eating less and not sleeping (lying in bed awake and sporadically abusing her and demanding intercourse). The therapist tried to be sympathetic and stated that all he could do was to continue to try to "find out what was wrong with the patient." When the patient came in for the 15th session he seemed more agitated than ever before and was even "hostile." He spontaneously stated: "Doc, last time you threw too much at me, you hit me with a sledgehammer." The therapist's response was to accept the patient's "insight" and to suggest that we "slow down and back up" to the previous procedure.

In the 15th session systematic desensitization was restarted 10 scenes down from where it had been stopped in the first desensitization phase. It was subsequently continued to scene 48. During this phase of desensitization the patient's paranoid and sexual behaviors again declined in frequency and his weight began to increase steadily till termination. Clinically the patient also appeared to improve in terms of rapport and seemed more calm and optimistic about his future. Desensitization was completed in the 24th week in treatment.

Three additional sessions were spent mainly guiding the patient's thinking toward a rationale for his previous "suffering" and reinforcing the view that through his symptoms his marriage had been "enriched" and salvaged from the "rut it was in." An intensive follow-up with a structured interview with the wife and husband 6 months after termination indicated that there had been no reactivation of the previous symptoms nor had new symptoms developed.

DISCUSSION

Since the patient's obsessive thoughts were not directly observable (a covert symptom), three apparently correlated aspects of his problem were monitored. In the final analysis the relationship between the obsessive thoughts and his overt symptoms is only inferential. The two behavioral measures (paranoid and sexual) could be specified relatively objectively but the accuracy with which the patient's wife observed and recorded these behaviors is unknown. Diagnostically it appears that the patient's problem was of the "acute" type that is known often to "remit spontaneously." But the observation that the symptoms could be manipulated up and down suggests the attainment of a measure of stimulus control over these symptomatic responses. How many reversals are necessary with clinical problems of this type is a question which has both statistical and ethical implications. It seems that the results of "implosive therapy" (Stampfl and Levis, 1968), and practical considerations have discouraged previous attempts to determine if the "re-sensitization" could be produced in the manner implied by Wolpe (1969).

One may doubt the generality of the phenomena demonstrated in this case study. But as Sidman (1960) notes: "Once we find that repeated manipulation of a variable produces consistent inter-subject replication simply points the way to a more intensive functional investigation." Parametric studies of the variable in question should then be undertaken.

The re-sensitization procedure described in this paper seems relevant to what Eysenck (1968) has called the "Napalkov phenomenon" which he describes as "an increment in the CR over a period of time when the CS is applied once or a number of times, but without reinforcement." Normally this procedure would give rise to extinction. Eysenck suggests that his concept of incubation, "increments in the CR after several evocations of the unreinforced CS," is necessary to account for certain phenomena in the formation of neuroses and for the effects of "aversion therapy." From his formulation of "incubation," Eysenck derives two parameters. These are strength of the UCR and score elevation on "neuroticism-anxiety-emotionality inventories." It would be interesting to see the results of further studies of "re-sensitization" with better controls and outcome measures along the parametric dimensions suggested by Eysenck.

Clinicians have anecdotally reported that "*in vivo*" re-sensitization occurs, but there does not appear to be any previous empirical demonostration in the literature of specific re-sensitization with a non- "*in vivo*" or imagination-relaxation procedure. The use of a desensitization-re-sensitization-desensitization design appears to be a promising approach to the validation and more intensive study of "active process variables" in systematic desensitization.

REFERENCES

Eysenck, H.J. A theory of the incubation of anxiety/fear responses. *Behav. Res. & Therapy,* 1968, **6**, 309-321.

Kelly, G.A. *The psychology of personal constructs.* New York: W.W. Norton and Co., 1955.

Sidman, M. *Tactics of scientific research.* New York: Basic Books, 1960.

Stampfl, T.G. & Levis, D.J. Implosive therapy—a behavioral therapy. *Behav. Res. & Therapy,* 1968, **6**, 31-36.

Wolpe, J. *Psychotherapy by reciprocal inhibition.* Stanford: Stanford University Press, 1968.

Wolpe, J. *The practice of behavior therapy.* New York: Pergamon Press, 1969.

Wickramasekera, I. The effects of sensory restriction on susceptibility to hypnosis, a hypothesis and some preliminary data. *Int. J. of exp. Hypnos.,* 1969, **17**, 217-224.

Wickramasekera, I. The effects of sesnory restriction on susceptibility to hypnosis: a hypothesis and more preliminary data. *J. abnorm. Psychol.,* 1970, **75**, 68-72.

71
A Case of Pseudonecrophilia Treated by Behavior Therapy

ARNOLD A. LAZARUS

Morbid sexual attraction to corpses has been described in ancient as well as modern writings. Psychiatric literature has chiefly concerned itself with the possible causal and other psychodynamic factors. Reports reveal how (and supposedly why) individuals secured work as undertakers' assistants or frequented funeral parlors, cemetery chapels or hospital morgues for the purpose of having sexual contact with corpses. Pseudo-necrophilia (erotic fantasies and masturbation, but no actual contact with corpses) has also beeen described (Klaf & Brown, 1958).

The present report is unique in several respects: a) It is the only account of behavior therapy applied to this condition; b) it offers simple and benign etiological considerations; and c) it is one of the few accounts (if not the only account) of a successful therapeutic outcome in a pseudonecrophile.

One of the primary advantages of adopting an S-R approach to clinical problems is that complex disorders are thereby reducible to specific and discrete areas of tension, sensitivity, etc., and may thus be eliminated systematically and in piecemeal fashion. Perhaps the most illuminating feature of the following case is the demonstration that bizarre and complex deviation from societal norms was capable of so economical a resolution in terms of therapeutic time and effort.

CASE STUDY

The patient, an intelligent 23-year-old student, complained initially of concentration difficulties, anxiety and depression. He sought therapy chiefly because his emotional condition was interfering with his studies. He attempted to conceal the nature of his sexual practices and fantasies from the therapist. In fact, his glib and facile replies to routine sexual questions during history-taking immediately alerted the therapist to the likelihood of serious difficulty in this area. A nonmoralistic and deterministic discourse on all sexual matters prompted the patient reluctantly and hesitantly to begin describing his sexual fantasies.

His first knowledge of sex was derived from schoolmates at the age of 11 or 12 years. The details of sexual performance were apparently misrepresented as a form of assault to which women protestingly submitted. From time to time, his mother had allegedly made allusions to the utter contempt with which women viewed men's erotic needs. A specific formative incident concerned a female cousin with whom he was "fooling around" when they were both approximately 15 years of age. Upon discovering that he had obtained an erection, she taunted him and accused him of being evil-minded. "I felt deeply ashamed." His masturbatory fantasies then took the form of murdering his cousin and performing "fellatio" with her corpse. Over the years, his fantasies shifted from woman to woman—"always beautiful, always dead, usually murdered by someone else." The imagined sexual acts varied from "fellatio," to vaginal penetration, to masturbation while fondling the corpse's breasts.

The patient stated that he enjoyed female company and frequently went dancing and out on "dates." He engaged in kissing and petting, but claimed never to have proceeded further than this. He described himself as terrified of the prospect of engaging in genital contact with "a real live woman." He also reported never having had any homosexual contacts or inclinations.

His general mental and emotional status suggested no schizophrenic or other psychotic features. His over-all tension, anxiety and depression seemed related to the guilts and general misgivings arising out of his sexual fantasies (which he viewed as "more than potentially psychotic") and the objective fact that poor study habits had resulted in several failing grades, despite his intellectual abilities. There was also evidence that his inconsistent and overbearing mother, in conjunction with two older "vituperative female siblings," had created a passive-aggressive attitude to women. Significantly, although adequately assertive in his dealings with men, the patient was inclined to stifle the over expression of all negative feelings toward women. It seemed clear that this had emanated from punitive consequences when he opposed his mother's (and to some extent his sisters') wishes.

Due to the patient's initial reluctant to reveal the nature of his sexual difficulties, the information outlined above was obtained during the course of four or five weekly interviews. The next five or six sessions consisted of a) providing reassurance of nonpsychotic involvement and discussing various "taboo thoughts" in which many "normal" individuals engage, b) encouraging him, by means of behavior rehearsal (role-playing) to express legitimate anger and resentment toward his mother, sisters, and toward women in general, and c) outlining a regime of effective study habits employing principles such as "active participation" and "distributed practice."

The patient was willing and cooperative, and soon became enthusiastic about his new and different "modus vivendi." In fact, in overzealous moments he was inclined to overstep his assertive prerogatives and on two occasions, he actually came to blows with one of his sisters. The only change in his sexual outlook, however, was a new-found ability to masturbate to his usual fantasies without guilt.

At this stage, the main focus of therapy was to instigate normal heterosexual behavior. How was this to be achieved? One colleague suggested an aversion-relief program in which the patient would receive an electric shock while engaging in his usual masturbatory fantasies, the cessation of shock being paired with a normal heterosexual fantasy. However, since the writer is averse to the blind application of mechanistic procedures, a more detailed exploration of the patient's sexual functioning was first undertaken. An interesting trend emerged.

It will be recalled that he had come to believe that women regarded sexual arousal in men with scorn, derision and contempt. Intellectual reassurance to the contrary had no therapeutic effect. The most humiliating event of which he could conceive was that of a woman, and especially his mother, reacting with disgust at the sight of his erect penis and his own sexual excitement. (At this point certain theorists might speculate that his masturbatory fantasies were in part a defense against unresolved Oedipal wishes. The question would then arise whether insight into this and related areas would be a necessary or sufficient therapeutic goal.) Since shame-at-being-seen-with-an-erection was so clearly aversive, the case lent itself to systematic desensitization based on relaxation (Wolpe & Lazarus, 1966). After training the patient in the necessary relaxation procedures, he was asked, while deeply relaxed, first to imagine himself sexually aroused by and in front of a dead female and then by an unconscious female. Next, he was asked to picture himself having sexual contact with an anesthetized female, followed by a woman who had passed out after having had too much to drink. The next scene involved a semi-conscious female who would remember nothing when she regained consciousness. The following step on the hierarchy consisted of his imagining intercourse with a prostitute whose attention was diverted while he was engaging in sex.

His masturbatory fantasies kept pace with the desensitization items. In fact, after the second desensitization session, he reported that his former erotic fantasies were distinctly aversive and that he now concentrated exclusively on semi-conscious females. The intention was to desensitize him to varying degrees of wakefulness and awareness in women while engaged in sex, but this proved unnecessary. After the fifth desensitization session, he "took the plunge" and had sexual intercourse with a girl friend. Fortunately, the entire encounter was satisfactory. He reported his delight and astonishment at the fact the females also become sexually aroused, and he was particularly comforted to find that he had been praised and lauded for his sexual potency and ardor instead of receiving criticism and contempt. As Weitz (1964) points out, "no counselor should exclude luck from his essential bag of tricks."

During the course of the next few weeks he extended his range of "sexual conquests." Before terminating therapy, role-playing was again conducted to insure that he would be capable of dealing with possible ridicule or scorn from women either for too much or too little sexual ardor. The total duration of therapy was 17 sessions over a period of four-and-a-half months. A note from the patient read as follows: "When I look back a few months and realize what a wretched and confused human being I was, and when I now see myself as a member of the human race, I feel like someone who will soon wake out of a pleasant dream. I can't even believe that I can now study and concentrate with ease. When it comes to the other thing, well, words fail me." As the therapist went overseas shortly afterwards, a personal and systematic follow-up could not be obtained. Approximately 11 months after terminating therapy, the patient indicated in a letter that all was well.

SUMMARY

This is the first report of a relatively uncommon condition, pseudonecrophilia (masturbatory fantasies focused on corpses) treated by behavior therapy. While psychodynamic implications were rampant, the deliberate adoption of an S-R approach reduced the complex disorder to specific areas of interpersonal tension. The relatively piecemeal resolution of these unadaptive responses resulted in an economical and timesaving regime.

REFERENCES

Klaf, F.S. & Brown, W. Necrophilia, brief review and case report. *The Psychiatric Quarterly,* 1958, **32**, 645-652.
Weitz, H. *Behavior change through guidance.* New York: Wiley, 1964.
Wolpe, J. & Lazarus, A. A. *Behavior therapy techniques.* Oxford: Pergamon Press, 1966.

72
Treatment of the Housebound Housewife Syndrome

T. KRAFT

Although the housebound housewife syndrome is found relatively frequently in psychiatric practice, there seem few reports which deal specifically with this condition. Roberts' (1964) retrospective study of 41 married women admitted to St. George's Hospital, London, showed that only 23.7 percent recovered enough to be able to leave their homes unaccompanied. The treatment offered to these patients consisted of psychotherapy and firm encouragement to go out, at first accompanied, and later alone. It is important to note that half the patients in this series required further treatment at a later stage, and even in the "recovered" group, two of the patients had other symptoms.

In five cases of agoraphobia treated by behavior therapy, Meyer and Gelder (1963) report some improvement in three of the cases treated, but no patients made a complete recovery. They report that two of the patients became dependent on the hospital or on the therapist, but did not receive treatment for this dependence. In the present study, the patient's dependence was treated separately and became an essential part of the behavior therapy program.

A more promising approach, the "thiopentone sleep treatment," reported by King and Little (1959), uses the intravenous injection of a 2.5 percent solution of thiopentone. These authors reported that complete recovery was rare, but some of the patients who had been housebound for many years did resume a relatively normal life. In the present study, the author employed a weak solution of methohexitone sodium (Brietal), which is also a barbiturate.

In a group of twenty housebound housewives examined by the author, all appeared to be frigid. The present study was designed to investigate the possibility of completely curing a housebound housewife by concentrating first on the treatment of her frigidity, then dealing with the housebound aspects and finally resolving her dependence on the therapist. The report concerns a 30-year-old married woman, housebound for six years, who appears to have made a complete recovery after a course of behavior therapy.

CASE REPORT

A 30-year-old married woman was admitted as a day patient to St. Clement's Hospital, London. She had already received an eight-month course of psychotherapy at this hospital in 1961. When her earlier therapist told her that he was returning to Australia, her immediate concern was that she would not be able to follow him there. She had made some improvement during this course of therapy, but had relapsed when the doctor left the country. On the advice of her general practitioner, the patient returned to this hospital in 1966, with more intense symptoms which drove her to consider a course of treatment with the author.

On detailed history-taking, the patient describes her mother as an extremely anxious woman, who has always had difficulty in crossing roads. The patient is aware that her own difficulty in crossing roads may in some way be related to her mother's acute anxiety.

At the age of 19, she became engaged to her present husband, and they married a year later. Before meeting him, she had several boy friends and had enjoyed sexual intercourse with them, though she had never reached climax level at any time.

Shortly after becoming engaged, she was aware that she could not develop adequate sexual arousal in relation to her fiance. She had premarital intercourse, but enjoyed it only on the first two occasions; after this, she merely "put up with it." Detailed history-taking showed that the major source of anxiety revolved around her husband touching her body with his hands, and that she finds his caresses even more stressful then sexual intercourse. Her sexual difficulties have persisted throughout her married life, and she finds that sexual intercourse has become more distasteful since the birth of her second child in March, 1966.

The patient finds all sexual activity with her husband revolting, and whenever he makes sexual advances toward her, she has a strong desire to push him away. She has successfully concealed her feelings of disgust, by pretending to enjoy intercourse, not wishing to upset her husband, but on many occasions, she made the excuse that she was too tired. When the husband was interviewed, he appeared to be quite oblivious of the fact that she had always been frigid, and registered surprise when this was pointed out to him.

Her marriage has been punctuated by a series of lovers with each of whom she has had sexual intercourse, enjoying this rather more than with her husband, but never reaching a climax.

In 1961, she had her last important extramarital relationship, which lasted for seven months, and her phobic symptoms started in June, 1961, at a time when her lover was losing interest in her. It seems relevant that her husband does not know of any of her extramarital relationships.

On June 24th, 1961, her husband bought a new car, and on the following day she went out for a trip with her husband, sister and brother-in-law. She felt extremely anxious throughout the journey, and was terrified that they might meet with an accident. Four days later, when her husband traveled in the car and she remained at home, she suddenly became panic-stricken that he might be killed. Since that time, she has been very anxious whenever her husband arrives home late from work, fearing that he might have been involved in a serious accident. Because of this, a telephone was installed in their house, in 1962, and her husband always rings if he intends arriving late home from work.

When the extramarital affair came to an end in 1961, she found it very difficult to leave the house to go shopping, and, for a period of three weeks, remained indoors all day. Her husband did all the shopping at this time. Her mother then attempted to mobilize the patient by accompanying her and exerting some pressure that she increase the distance walked each day. Her efforts were not very successful, and the patient could not reach shops a hundred yards away from her home. The patient had great difficulty in describing the nature of her disturbance except to say that her legs felt like jelly, which prevented her from walking any further away from home. She recognized that her inability to continue walking was a psychiatric disturbance rather than a physical one.

In 1962, the situation improved in that she could go shopping when accompanied by her sister. She then tried visiting the shops on her own, but found it an exceedingly difficult task.

In 1963, during her first pregnancy, she improved considerably and felt much easier about leaving the house on her own. Her first therapist had recommended that she start a family as a therapeutic measure. When the baby girl was born, she found that she could leave the house by pushing the child out in her pram, but she was quite unable to leave the house on her own. Later, she also felt at ease when taking the child out in a push-chair.

From 1963 to 1966, her condition remained static, but after the birth of her second child, a son, she became considerably worse than in 1961: in addition to being completely housebound for a period of three weeks, she was also panic-stricken all day while alone in the house. It was for this reason that she called in her general practitioner, who suggested that she have a course of treatment at St. Clement's Hospital.

TREATMENT

The treatment was based on Wolpe's (1958) method of systematic desensitization and relaxation was induced by methohexitone sodium (Kraft, 1967; Kraft & Al-Issa, 1968). A 2.5 percent solution of methohexitone sodium was used in treatment, as recommended by Friedman (1966). A loading dose of 25 mg. was injected, and then, with the needle still in the vein, further quantities were injected at intervals to maintain a constant level of relaxation.

Methohexitone sodium, an ultra short acting barbiturate, appears to be safer than thiopentone (Pitts et al., 1965), and has the added advantage that the recovery time seems quicker (Jolly, 1960).

The first course of treatment consisted of a carefully graded stimulus hierarchy which was designed to combat her excessive anxiety associated with sexual contact with her husband. She required 31 treatment sessions for the first phase of treatment. In the first treatment session, she was asked to imagine undressing and being in bed with her husband, without any physical contact. Later, she was required to visualize her husband putting his hand on her shoulder, and gradually scenes of increasing intimacy were introduced, finally leading to sexual intercourse. She found it even more stressful to cope with her husband putting his arm around her when watching television, and this had to be treated at a later stage. Each scene had to be repeated a number of times before she was completely anxiety-free, and it was found necessary to introduce relief responses, such as eating strawberries or smelling roses, in order to reduce her anxiety level.

The second course of treatment, designed to mobilize the patient, consisted of 18 more treatment sessions. At first, she was asked to imagine going to the local shops with her children, and later, on her own. The main difficulty seemed to be in crossing roads, and particular attention had to be paid to the type of road, presence of vehicles, and distance from home. Later she was asked to imagine traveling to the hospital by bus, first with both children, then with the older child only, and finally, on her own. During the treatment sessions, the patient had to describe the journeys in great detail and each item was repeated until the patient was free from anxiety about it.

At this stage, the patient had developed a great dependence on the therapist, and a further treatment program was designed to counteract it. This phase of the treatment required a further 24 sessions. At first, the number of treatment sessions were reduced from 3 sessions per week to two, then to one session each week. The dependence on the therapist was treated by a process of "thought-stopping" (Wolpe, 1958). Whenever the patient spoke of the therapist during a treatment session, she was switched to something else, such as her favorite flowers, and calming suggestions were given until she was completely relaxed. She also required some reinforcement on sexual relations with her husband, as she was finding intercourse more difficult as the number of treatment sessions was reduced.

RESULTS

After the second treatment session for her frigidity, the patient found that she could undress in front of her husband without any anxiety, a new experience for her, and she could also enjoy being kissed by him. She commented that she derived a completely new satisfaction from physical contact with her husband. As treatment progressed, she found that she could manage more intimate contact without feeling anxious, but it was not until after the 23rd session that she could enjoy sexual intercourse with him. She was delighted with her new level of sexual excitation, and admitted that she could now reach climax level for the first time. After the 31st session, she was happy about her sexual adjustment to her husband, but complained that she still could not go out unaccompanied.

Attention was now focused on her housebound difficulties. Having made a graded list of all the roads she wished to cross, the patient was desensitized to each of these in turn. After the 5th session, she managed to cross a minor road without any anxiety, and a few days later, reported that she could now cross one of the major roads in the area. After the 11th session, she was surprised that, when accompanied by the children, she could travel to the hospital by bus, without experiencing any anxiety throughout the journey. After the 14th session, she traveled to the hospital with the older child only, finding this easier than traveling with both children, and gradually she learned to travel on her own. After the 18th session, she felt completely at ease when going out of doors, but remained highly dependent on her therapist. The remaining sessions were directed toward this dependence.

In the 4th session dealing with her dependence, the patient commented that, although delighted with her progress so far, she could not envisage the time when she would be able to manage without the therapist. She was given firm assurance that the dependence would eventually diminish, but remained unconvinced.

In the 6th session, she was happy to report that she could now take the older child to school, and that she could go out or stay indoors as she pleased. During the 8th session, she declared her intense desire for the therapist, who impressed upon her that the therapeutic relationship had to be different from her previous experiences and that a sexual relationship with the therapist would be a mere repetition of her previous sexual maladjustment. In her 24th and last treatment session for dependence, she reported visualizing sexual intercourse with the therapist, at which point the needle was immediately withdrawn. This acted as a severe aversive stimulus, and after this treatment session she stated that she wished to discontinued injections of methohexitone.

This was a turning point in her treatment, and she began to make a more adequate adjustment to her husband. At the end of her treatment, she wrote out the following for the therapist: "I can go to the hairdresser, go shopping in any shop by any route, go into big stores and supermarkets, travel by bus, go to parks and other public places, such as funfairs, take my little girl to and from school, go to restaurants, go dancing, visit friends, cross main roads with very little difficulty, stay at home on my own or without anyone nearby, relax in the evening in an armchair without having to get up for periods of time, go to the cinema.

"I am more placid, not aggressive any more, less self-conscious, not so self-centered, not bad-tempered, not moody, more realistic in my attitude toward life. I am happier than I can ever remember and my relationship with my husband is much better. I am able to communicate and discuss things with him and we are closer than we have ever been."

She has been followed up for a period of nine months, and her spontaneous comment is that she feels "disgustingly well." She has recovered from her housebound syndrome, and can tolerate intercourse with her husband, who is delighted with her recovery.

DISCUSSION

The author had noticed that several patients suffering from the housebound syndrome had tended to be frigid, and it was for this reason that this patient was given a treatment program in which her frigidity and her fear of traveling were separately treated. When the patient had been effectively treated for these two conditions, it was found that she had become highly dependent on the therapist, and the third phase of the treatment was designed to counteract it, by a process of "thought stopping." In her last treatment session, her therapist withdrew methohexitone sodium which had a breaking effect on her dependence on the therapist, and from then onward she was quite happy to continue with discussion sessions only.

On completing the three phases of treatment, she now enjoys great freedom of movement and is free from anxiety. This is a rare treatment result in the housebound housewife syndrome, and it is suggested that the initial treatment of her frigidity may have been an important contributory factor in her recovery. Although she has no further need for individual treatment sessions with the therapist, she would like to continue attendance at the Post Behavior Therapy Club (Kraft, 1967).

It is of interest that though no specific treatment was directed toward her fear of impending disaster on her husband arriving late home from work, this symptom has disappeared as her general condition improved.

The hypothesis might be put forward that, in keeping with Freudian theory (1949), the degree of improvement in her case may well be related to the strength of her transference to the therapist.

SUMMARY

This report concerns a 30-year-old married woman, housebound for six years, who appears to have made a complete recovery after a course of behavior therapy. The treatment was based on Wolpe's (1958) method of systematic desensitization, and relaxation was induced by intravenous injections of a 2.5 percent solution of methohexitone sodium.

The patient was treated initially for her frigidity, and later for her housebound troubles. When these had been effectively treated, it was found that the patient had become highly dependent on the therapist, and a further treatment program was needed to counteract it. The treatment was completed in nine months, and she received 73 one-hour sessions in all. A follow-up of nine months shows that the patient's improvement has been maintained.

Acknowledgments: The author wishes to thank Dr. John Denham, Medical Director, for his permission to publish this study. The author also wishes to thank Dorothy Clare-Yeldham, Clinical Psychologist, for her critical appraisal of the manuscript.

REFERENCES

Freud, S. *Collected works of Freud.* London: Hogarth Press, 1949.

Friedman, D. A new technique for the systematic desensitization of phobic symptoms. *Behav. Res. Ther.,* 1966, **4**, 139-140.

Jolly, C. Recovery time from methohexital anaesthesia. *Brit. J. Anaesth.* 1960, **32**, 576-579.

King, A. & Little, J.C. Thiopentone treatment of the phobic anxiety-depersonalization syndrome. A preliminary report. *Proc. Roy. Soc. Med.,* 1959, **52**, 595-596.

Kraft, T. The use of methohexitone sodium in behavior therapy. *Behav. Res. Ther.,* 1967a, **5**, 257.—A post-behavior therapy club. *Newsletter, Ass. Advancem. Behav. Ther.,* 1967b, **2**, 6-7.

Kraft, T. & Al-Issa, I. The use of methohexitone sodium in the systematic desensitization of premature ejaculation. *Brit. J. Psychiat.* (In press, 1968).

Meyer, V. & Gelder, M.G. Behavior therapy and phobic disorders. *Bri. J. Psychiat.,* 1963, **109**, 19-28.

Pitts, F.N., Desmarais, G.M., Stewart, W. & Schaberg, L. Induction of, anesthesia with methohexital and thiopental in electroconvulsive therapy. *New Engl. J. Med.,* 1965, **273**, 353-360.

Roberts, A.H. Housebound housewives—a follow-up study of a phobic anxiety state. *Brit. J. Psychiat.,* 1964, **110**, 191-197.

Wolpe, J. *Psychotherapy by reciprocal inhibition.* Stanford: Stanford University Press, 1958.

73
Conditioning Appropriate Heterosexual Behavior in Mentally and Socially Handicapped Populations

MARVIN ROSEN

Modern programs of social and vocational rehabilitation for the mentally retarded person now include educational curricula for teaching social skills and work behaviors needed for independent functioning in the community. However, surprisingly little attention is devoted to basic social learning deficits in the ability to deal with heterosexual relationships. For many retarded persons, particularly those living in institutions, there is little opportunity for the learning or practice of appropriate sexual responses. Fear, superstition and doubt cloud professional attitudes about sexual development of the retarded, resulting in a significant vacuum in the programming for their social development. This paper is intended to explore some new techniques for dealing with general social and sexual deficits and for specific sexual deviations, such as homosexual behavior in persons with mild or borderline intellectual limitations. The techniques which derive from strategies of behavior modification (Ullmann & Krasner, 1966), can be used in individual therapy in a way that should not threaten or disrupt the operation of the typical training facility.

RATIONALE

Programs for social learning in the area of heterosexual activities are applicable to all but the very lowest levels of mental retardation. However, the most predominant needs are those of educable, mildly retarded persons with potential for independent community functioning. These persons fall into two categories with regard to sexual adjustment: 1) those with social-learning deficits but no overt behavioral deviation; 2) those who also manifest perverted or inappropriate sexual behavior. Persons falling into the first category require programming for appropriate sexual response. Persons falling into the second category may also need to learn inhibitory responses for inappropriate behavior. Both conditions may result from the absence of opportunity for normal heterosexual learning experiences after years of sheltered institutional living or because of overly repressive or protective family situations. In both conditions the treatment plan is to promote a greater level of social competence through a structured hierarchy of social learning experiences.

Programming needs in this area have not gone unrecognized in the field of mental retardation, but the approach has typically emphasized control and inhibition rather than the reinforcement of appropriate behavior. A rehabilitation program for females developed at a Texas institution for the retarded (Dial, 1968) illustrates this point. Recognizing that many client failures in the community occurred because of heterosexual problems rather than vocational incompetence, the staff initiated a sex education program consisting of lectures, films and group discussion. A published description of this program suggests that it was geared to inform, correct misconceptions, and teach controls to the young adult, mildly retarded, female students. Venereal disease, pregnancy, "losing one's reputation" and other negative consequences were described as the results of sexual behavior. There was no indication that equivalent time was devoted to the type of social learning necessary for effecting satisfactory boy-girl relationships.

The basis for the lag in this fundamental social learning area seems to stem from the confusion of two problems that might better remain separated—sex education as opposed to marriage and childbearing for the retarded. Uncertainty about the inheritance of mental deficiency and doubts about the capacity of mentally subnormal parents to adequately care for their children (Bass, 1964) serve as deterrents to clear thinking about the psychological and physiological needs of mentally and socially deficient persons. Although the evidence is unclear that mentally retarded persons become inadequate parents, this issue seems only weakly related to the question of the advisability of sex education and sex training. Competence at sexual roles and competence as marriage partners or parents represent two different areas of social learning. It is possible that, with appropriate techniques, both sets of behavior can be taught. The desirability of providing marriage and childrearing training to the retarded is beyond the scope of this paper. The teaching of sexually appropriate behavior, however, is not only desirable, but necessary since the learning of sexually deviant behavior is a strong alternative when such teaching is not available. The most successful programs are likely to be those that undertake to teach new behaviors rather than those purporting to provide information, change attitudes, or uncover feelings. Maximum success will also accrue to those programs structured to undo rather than perpetuate anxiety and inhibition in relation to sexual responsiveness.

TECHNIQUES

1. Desensitization

The absence of opportunities for constructive learning experiences with members of the opposite sex often makes the prospect of heterosexual contacts extremely fearful. Consequently, techniques of systematic desensitization, described by Wolpe (1958) and evaluated in numerous studies (Geer, 1964; Lang & Lazovik, 1963; Paul, 1966), are often the method of choice for reducing anxiety and initiating approach responses. A graduated fear hierarchy is constructed beginning with experiences that are without fear-producing qualities for the client, and increasing in gradual steps to more frightening situations. The client is instructed and practiced in methods of deep muscle relaxation, and treatment proceeds by the presentation of structured fantasies representing each level of the fear hierarchy. Each subsequent step in the hierarchy is presented only after the client reports the absence of a fear reaction to the preceeding fantasy. In the area of heterosexual relationships, hierarchies can be started with group activity situation (dances, parties) before progressing to individual dating relationships. Depending upon the needs and experience, as well as the prospects for community placement of the individual, this hierarchy can progress to more mature relationships including sexual intercourse. The method reduces anxiety in the real situation and also, provides the client with information and suggestions for behavior.

2. Programmed Heterosexual Experience

Subsequent to successful completion of desensitization procedures, the individual can be practiced in actual experiences with members of the opposite sex. A procedure of gradually shaping responses to females was suggested by Ferster (1965). He argues that it is desirable to start with a response which is relatively likely to be reinforced, such as simply speaking to females, and then to proceed up the hierarchy of responses which are increasingly less likely to be reinforced, not advancing to the next item in the hierarchy until the preceding one has been well established. Feldman (1966) reports that it may take as long as six months before sexual approach responses to females are well learned, particularly in those persons who report no sexual attraction to females. We have found it useful to use female psychologists and teachers to structure a series of exercises for the male client with social deficits. The client is instructed to report his momentary tension using a simple five-point scale, and these reports determine the rate at which new tasks are presented. The female confederate serves as co-therapist and is practiced in a supportive, yet realistic feminine role with the client. Typical situations can progress from merely seeing a female at a distance, approaching and entering her office, maintaining eye contact, engaging in a pre-programmed conversation, spontaneous conversation, taking a walk with her and taking her to the coffee shop.

Once the limits of this technique are exhausted, the client is instructed to simulate the same graded series of behaviors in real situations. More freedom exists in halfway houses or outpatient settings than in institutions, but the technique is the same.

3. Role-playing

There is a great deal of clinical evidence that role-playing can be a powerful technique for initiating behavior for which there is a strong inhibitory response (Salter, 1949; Wolpe, 1958). The use of this technique involves the practice of behaviors that are low in the response repertoire of the client in a controlled and supportive manner. Wolpe and Lazarus (1967) have elaborated on the use of role-playing techniques, as well as encouragement and reinforcement for such behavior in the real situation as part of more general procedures of assertive training. In this context, their use is viewed as the overcoming of anxiety responses in interpersonal situations. "The counterconditioning of anxiety is thus intertwined on each occasion with the operant conditioning of the instrumental response (acts of assertion) and each facilitates the other." The role-playing of anxiety-evoking behaviors is sufficient to elicit timidity and defensive behavior resembling that which occurs in the actual situation, but repetition and practice can result in marked improvement, both in the imaginary and real situation. Modeling of the desired response is accomplished after demonstration by the therapist and reinforcement of the client's attempt at imitation. This is especially helpful when inhibition is severe, and is used in teaching conversation skills, telephone behavior, asking for a date, social etiquette, as well as general assertive behavior associated with the sexual role. Role-playing can be used in conjunction with programmed heterosexual experience.

4. Sex-related Talk

Davison (1968) has referred to the information value of sex-related "locker room" talk in adolescents. Although this activity is probably the source of misconceptions and distortions in the sex knowledge available to many adolescents, it may be the only source of information available. Within institutions, the lack of adequate sources of authoritative information or opportunities for self-correcting, validating experiences make sexual knowledge markedly deficient. Because of language deficits, even slang expressions for genitals and sex behavior are misunderstood or entirely absent from the verbal repertoire. Frank sexual talk with a therapist explaining the meaning of slang terms for genital organs, masturbation and intercourse serves to reduce anxiety related to those topics.

5. Suggestions to Masturbate

We have found among boys with deviant sexual behaviors a surprising absence of masturbatory activity. In three out of four cases of boys who were not masturbating, direct suggestion was sufficient to elicit this behavior. Assurances that such behavior was quite prevalent and generally healthy, when no other outlet is available, serve to dispel notions leading to guilt and fear. We have found it useful to provide clients with 3 x 5 index cards to make daily records of the frequency of successful masturbation and sexually inappropriate responses, such as homosexual contacts. Weekly graphs prepared by the therapist in the client's presence show progress in the substitution of masturbation for inappropriate behavior.

6. Aversive Conditioning

When clients have developed inappropriate, bizarre or perverted sexual behaviors, aversive conditioning techniques may also be useful in teaching inhibitory responses. Feldman (1966) has pointed out that most of the operant responses involved in homosexual behavior cannot be reproduced in a treatment setting and, so, are not available for manipulation. This also holds true for other forms of deviant sexual behavior. The majority of therapists using aversive procedures have therefore, utilized a classical conditioning model to associate fear or another strong negative emotion with the previously attractive sexual stimulus. There is some evidence (Cautela, 1966; Davison, 1968) that this association can also be accomplished in a fantasy situation. Davison successfully applied this method to a college student preoccupied with sadistic fantasies.

The initial phase of this treatment involved the counterconditioning of more appropriate sexual fantasies to sexual arousal. The client was instructed to use his sadistic fantasy to masturbate, but to interrupt this fantasy to stare at a photograph of a nude female as long as possible without losing his erection. As orgasm was approaching, he was "at all costs" to focus on the photograph. After the client began to report sexual arousal to images of nude females, an imaginal aversive conditioning ("covert sensitization") method was applied to the sadistic fantasy. An extremely disgusting scene was paired in imagination with the client's sadistic fantasy until the fantasy was no longer sexually arousing.

While case reports describing the use of imaginal aversive techniques are rare, the method holds promise because of its flexibility with regard to a wide variety of sexual stimuli and behaviors, and because of its ease of application in an office setting. Instructions to the client can be tape recorded and presented during repeated therapy sessions without loss of effectiveness.

CONCLUSION

The effects of social learning techniques for sexual responses are yet to be adequately demonstrated. Experimental studies are needed to evaluate specific types of behavioral intervention upon criteria of behavioral changes, object choices, and other pertinent indices of psychosexual adjustment. Long-term follow-up studies are essential to evaluate properly the procedures described earlier. Therapeutic efforts must be more closely linked to experimental research and theory than have previous rehabilitative efforts in other areas of training. Future studies may indicate that sexual deviations, occurring as a result of the absence of opportunity to learn appropriate behavior, as in institutional settings, are more amenable to change than similar behaviors derived from more complex family situations of personality dynamics. Our experience has been that significant change occurs with relatively minor effort when compared to the very severe aversive conditioning techniques (using electric shock and chemotherapy), which have been used with homosexuals and sexual fetishists. The most successful efforts will likely be those utilizing skillful learning techniques for teaching new behaviors rather than those relying upon aversive conditioning for deviant responses. Whether aversive techniques will still be needed when more sophisticated methods for teaching appropriate social behaviors become available is a question for future research. Whatever the methodology, it is clear that the time for fear and superstition, associated with social learning in sexual areas, has long passed and the problem deserves the rigor and enthusiasm of creative experimental approaches.

REFERENCES

Bass, M.S. Marriage for the mentally deficient. *Mental Retardation*, 1964, **2**, 198-202.

Cautela, J.R. Treatment of compulsive behavior by covert sensitization. *The Psychological Record*, 1966, **16**, 33-41.

Davison, G.C. Elimination of a sadistic fantasy by a client-controlled counterconditioning technique: A case study. *Journal of Abnormal Psychology*, 1968, **73**, 84-89.

Dial, K.B. A report of group work to increase social skills of females in a vocational rehabilitation program. *Mental Retardation,* 1968, **6**, 11-14.

Feldman, M.P. Aversion therapy for sexual deviations: A critical review. *Psychological Bulletin,* 1966, **65**, 65-79.

Ferster, C.B. Reinforcement and punishment in the control of homosexual behavior by social agencies. In H.J. Eysenck (Ed.). *Experiments in behavior therapy,* London: Pergamon, 1965, 189-207.

Geer, J.H. Phobia treated by reciprocal inhibition. *Journal of abnormal and social Psychology,* 1964, **69**, 642-645.

Lang, P.J. & Lazovik, A.D. Experimental desensitization of a phobia. *Journal of abnormal and social Psychology,* 1963, **66**, 519-525.

Paul, G.L. *Insight vs. desensitization in psychotherapy: An experiment in anxiety reduction.* Stanford: Stanford Univ. Press, 1966.

Salter, A. *Conditioned reflex therapy.* New York: Creative Age Press, 1949.

Ullmann, L.P. & Krasner, L. *Case studies in behavior modification.* New York: Holt, Rinehart & Winston, 1966.

Wolpe, J. *Psychotherapy by reciprocal inhibition.* Stanford: Stanford Univ. Press, 1958.

Wolpe, J. & Lazarus, A. A. *Behavior therapy techniques.* London: Pergamon, 1967.

74
Reducing Masturbatory Guilt

W. L. MARSHALL

The effective therapeutic use of masturbation to modify inappropriate sexual behavior has been described by Davison (1968), and subsequent reports have confirmed the value of such procedures (Marquis, 1970; Marshall, 1973, 1974). Marshall (1973) has suggested that an attempt to modify masturbatory fantasies be part of any overall treatment program aimed at altering unacceptable sexual behavior. However, it is not always simply a matter of instructing the patient in the appropriate methods for change. It is not uncommon for a patient with sexual problems to have quite inappropriate attitudes toward masturbation and for such attitudes to serve as cues for considerable guilt feelings. The use in therapy of a behavior that creates considerable guilt might cause serious difficulties. First, the patient may not carry out all instructions for a host of reasons, among which might be wanting to delay the onset of guilt and the attention—interfering effects of anticipated guilt. Furthermore, if masturbation functioned as a cue for guilt, the reinforcing effects of successfully changing the content of masturbatory fantasies might be markedly diminished. It is, therefore, necessary in any program utilizing orgasmic reconditioning (or any variant thereof) to minimize masturbatory guilt. The present case illustrates one possible way of achieving this end.

CASE STUDY

A 22-yr-old male complaining of persistent homosexual thoughts presented himself for treatment. He had no direct sexual experience of any kind and could not be persuaded that homosexuality was an acceptable form of behavior. His homosexual thoughts appeared throughout each day in various settings usually triggered by the sight of a "desirable" young man. These thoughts were persistent and the patient was unable to control them. He did occasionally have heterosexual fantasies and while these were rather idealized they were quite acceptable to him.

It was clear that sexual fantasies not only played an important role in this man's problem behavior, they in fact were his problem. Treatment was therefore aimed at changing the content of the fantasies. The method of choice seemed to be orgasmic reconditioning, but the patient claimed that he masturbated infrequently because such behavior was "wicked" and he always felt guilty immediately and for some hours afterwards. However, after considering the matter for a week he agreed to try orgasmic reconditioning.

In order to optimize his following instructions, and maximize the reinforcing effects of positive changes, an attempts was made to reduce masturbatory guilt before commencing orgasmic reconditioning. The patient was instructed to masturbate at least once a day over the next week. Immediately upon- completing masturbation he was to repeat to himself a statement from a prepared list of possible positive remarks about the value of masturbation. This list included such statements as "Masturbation is a sensible and normal way to reduce sexual tension," "Masturbation is a healthy enjoyable practice," "I really enjoyed that," "Boy I feel really great now." Immediately upon making this statement, the patient was to deliver himself a reinforcer. The reinforcers ranged from pleasant and enjoyable thoughts (e.g. daydreaming about happy childhood experiences) to the self-delivery of external events (e.g. listening to his favorite music, having a candy, going for a walk). All the reinforcers were chosen by the patient himself and rated by him as high in attractiveness. He was given no instruction at all at this time regarding the content of his masturbatory fantasies.

After 1 week the patient reported that he had masturbated once the first day and twice each day thereafter. On each occasion he had successfully followed the program. He reported that he now felt no guilt after masturbating, could think about it without any negative feelings, and in fact actually enjoyed it. He expressed amazement at the success and was told that the pleasurable experience of masturbation had probably enhanced the effectiveness of the reinforcement procedure. He was encouraged to continue with the reinforcement procedure for the rest of the treatment program.

Orgasmic reconditioning was begun and proved successful in changing masturbatory fantasies, but had no effect on sexual fantasies at other times. This observation agrees with the findings of an earlier case study (Marshall, 1974), and again self punishment procedures proved effective in eliminating these other fantasies.

REFERENCES

Davison, G.C. Elimination of a sadistic fantasy by a client-controlled counter conditioning technique: A case study, *J. abnorm. Psychol.* 1968, **73**, 84-89.

Marquis, J.N. Orgasmic reconditioning: changing sexual object choice through controlling masturbation fantasies, *J. Behav. Ther. & Exp. Psychiat,* 1970, **1**, 263-272.

Marshall, W.L. The modification of sexual fantasies: A combined treatment approach to the reduction of deviant sexual behavior, *Behav. Res. & Therapy,* 1973, **11** 557-564.

Marshall, W.L. A combined treatment approach to the reduction of multiple fetish-related behaviors, *J. Consult. Clin. Psychol.,* 1974, **42**, 613-616.

75
Behavior Therapy in a Case of Multiple Sexual Disorders

JOHN E. CARR

Behavior therapists are frequently confronted with cases with multiple sexual disorders. Behavioral analysis in such cases is complicated by the often complex interdependence of the behaviors and their respective antecedent and consequent conditions. Thus intervention requires a careful orchestration of a variety of techniques at different times in the treatment program in order to accomplish first a differentiation of the respective contingency relationships and then their successful modification (Wolpe, 1969; Agras, 1972). The following case report is offered as an example of how such a behavioral analysis and program formulation can be conducted.

CASE HISTORY

The patient was a 25-year-old, recently divorced white male referred for what was described as a "complex sexual disorder." At 13 the patient experienced a peak orgasmic response in the course of a self-administered enema. Shortly thereafter he discovered, apparently through a fortuitous association, that the response could be augmented first by the presence and then the actual wearing of women's underclothing before and during the enema. Within a year the cross-dressing response had so generalized that the patient was wearing women's underwear whenever possible, the frequency varying from week to week according to the availability of opportunities.

In high school the patient did well academically but was socially withdrawn. Gradually, at college, he acquired some social confidence, dated, and had a few heterosexual experiences, one with a girl whom he eventually married. The marital adjustment was initially satisfactory and he reported many happy moments in the marriage.

While the patient had apparently been successful in hiding his cross-dressing and autoerogenous activities throughout his public school and college years his marriage was thrown into crisis by the wife's discovery of his cache of feminine underwear and enema bag. Following an initial confrontation and his confession with full particulars, the wife reluctantly agreed *not* to seek a divorce if he agreed to seek professional help. The couple met with a marriage counselor who urged the wife to be "understanding" but unfortunately offered little encouragement to her regarding the prognosis, citing the notorious refractoriness of such disorders to treatment. To promote "understanding" she encouraged the patient to talk about his sexual urges and reluctantly assured him that it really didn't bother her all that much. When no significant change appeared after 9 months, the couple decided to terminate the therapy. Soon thereafter the wife precipitously announced she was leaving, and shortly filed for divorce. She ruled out reconciliation. Distressed by her action, and panicked by the implied devastating consequences of his behavior, he sought treatment for the purpose of "eliminating the sexual problems" once and for all.

Treatment

During the initial interview the patient was instructed to review in detail the history of the disorder beginning with the conditions surrounding the origin. Particular attention was given to the time and place of each occurrence, and the events that preceded and followed. Finally, a detailed description of relevant contingent events (e.g. wife's behavior) up to the divorce was obtained. No attempt was made to obtain detailed information regarding the patient's family or early childhood at this time, and indeed, the patient was discouraged from delving into such topics unless the information had direct relevance to the history of the behaviors in question.

A preliminary behavioral analysis of the patient's retrospective history data indicated:

(1)   The sexualization of the enema dated from age 13 when the patient masturbated and achieved orgasm while giving himself an enema.

(2)   The patient has repeated this original association up to the present time, i.e. simultaneous enema and masturbation followed by orgasm.

(3)   The patient occasionally gave himself an enema, but did not masturbate, and over the years observed a gradually increasing ratio of successful to unsuccessful orgasm in response to the enema alone. It was noted that the total number of enemas without masturbation did not vary.

(4)   The original cross-dressing behavior was obviously fortuitous and similarly reinforced by the orgasm.

(5)   This original association had also continued and generalized, i.e. the patient now put on underwear early in the morning (under other clothes) which heightened his sexual anticipation over the day, leading to the enema and orgasm at the end of the day. The cross-dressing, however, was insufficient by itself to induce orgasm, and the patient occasionally did not cross-dress because he was "bored with it." Thus the cross-dressing behavior seemed relatively weak in the repertoire, related to if not dependent upon the enema-giving behavior, and therefore likely to drop in response to a reduction of the enema behavior.

(6)   Enemas were administered almost always in evenings on weekdays or late afternoon on weekends. They were commonest on Tuesday and Friday nights. He always had some activity on Monday nights, e.g. a meeting, and on weekends, and *never* gave himself an enema on those days. Frequency was heightened when he felt "*lonely, bored, or depressed.*"

(7)   The frequency of enema and cross-dressing behaviors had decreased from about five per week to two per week with his marriage, apparently because there was less opportunity for enemas, and because sexual intercourse with wife (1-4 times/week) provided some alternative satisfaction. The wife almost always achieved orgasm and could "really turn on" the patient, at least early in the marriage. Intercourse was pleasurable and he reported no significant erectile problems.

(8)   Following the wife's discovery of the enema bag, the frequency of enemas gradually increased, apparently as a function of the increasing permissiveness of his wife who made herself noticeably scarce during peak risk times, and of the reinforcing effect of the wife's inquiries ("We had to have something to talk about and she seemed intrigued by it . . . ").

Two treatment goals were agreed upon, (1) to decrease enema and cross-dressing behavior, and (2) to increase social contacts and heterosexual behavior. Based on the above information, the following program for attaining these goals were developed.

(1)   Decreasing the opportunities for enema and cross-dressing behaviors by scheduling competing reinforcing activities at peak risk times (e.g. movies, out to dinner, meeting with friends, sports events). This was easily instituted since it involved essentially a re-arranging of existing activities.

(2)   Increasing opportunities for socially rewarding contacts with sexual potential. The patient was intelligent, good-looking with social skills. He had opportunities at work and in his apartment house to take girls whom he found attractive to lunch and out on dates, to go to parties where the probability of potential contacts was high, and to do one *new* and unusual social activity every week to extend his social repertoire—opera, horse racing, sailing, skin diving, art shows, riding the ferry, mountain climbing, hiking, beach-combing.

(3)   Differentiating and removing sources of reinforcement for the enema behavior, by progressively increasing the latency between the enema and the masturbation-induced orgasm.

Behavioral analysis indicated the ability of the enema to produce orgasm without masturbation was maintained by frequent trials involving masturbation. By increasing the latency period so that the enema was never closely followed by masturbating to orgasm—would lead to the extinction of the enema response.

(4)   Reducing the fear and heightening the probability of success of heterosexual activities. He was instructed initially to date girls who demonstrated an obvious sexual interest, to engage *only* in sexual behavior when *highly* motivated (thereby increasing the probability of maximum positive reinforcement) and once the opportunity for sex arose and the drive was high, not to delay intercourse too long. He had reported that occasionally intercourse was not successful, especially if there had been a long (sometimes 2 hours) foreplay period.

(5)   Reducing the anticipatory enema response. He had reported that he would try to avoid thought of the enema during the day. Extinction of the anticipatory enema response could be aided by "cognitive replay" two times daily at low risk times (e.g. at office) where no reinforcement was possible.

The patient was instructed to keep a detailed daily log noting the time of all events, who was present, what preceded and what followed, his affective state at the time (pleasurable or not), and any other information deemed relevant. He was told especially to attend to and record

a. enemas
b. cross-dressing
c. dates, specifics of event, place and time, e.g. dinner, dance, watch TV show
d. coitus. In addition, the patient was asked to relate the degree of satisfaction or pleasure accompanying enemas, cross-dressing, and heterosexual behavior along a subjective scale from very unpleasant to very pleasant.

In 3 weeks cross-dressing behavior had reduced from its initial level of five per week to zero. By the thirteenth week, enema behavior had gone down from four per week to zero. No recurrence of either behavior was reported at follow up 5 months later.

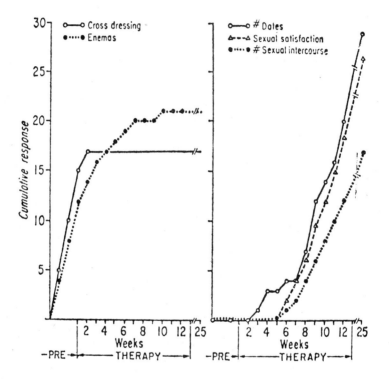

Fig. 1. Cumulative number of behaviors as a function of time in treatment.

Dating increased from an initial zero per week to five per week by the end of the thirteenth week. Frequency of sexual intercourse increased from zero to two per week, with the qualitative rating shifting from an initial "mildly unpleasant" to "very pleasant" by the thirteenth week.

Concurrent with these changes was the patient's expressed increased feelings of confidence and self-worth.

Certain advantages of this program should be noted. First, all procedures were carried out by the patient himself. He thus not only obtained therapeutic benefit, but learned self-management. Second the specific programming of alternative behaviors, positively reinforcing and therefore self-sustaining, provided some degree of insurance against spontaneous recovery of the original undesirable behaviors.

While previously considered to be "notoriously refractory to any form of treatment"

(Yates, 1970) and therefore judged to be treatable only by the relatively more severe aversive methods, sexually deviant behaviors would appear to be readily modifiable in response to other behavioral management techniques when administered in such a fashion as to maximize their effects.

REFERENCES

Agras, W.S. *Behavior Modification: Principles and Clinical Applications,* Boston: Little, Brown, 1972.
Wolpe, J. *The Practice of Behavior Therapy,* New York, Pergamon, 1969.
Yates, A.J. *Behavior Therapy.* New York, 1970.

Additional Selected Readings

Bentler, P.M. A note on the treatment of adolescent sex problems." *Journal of Child Psychology and Psychiatry,* 1968, **9,** 125-219.

D'Zurilla, T.J. Reducing Heterosexual Anxiety. In Krumboltz, J.D. and Thoresen, C.E. (Eds.), *Behavioral counseling: Cases and techniques.* New York: Holt, Rinehart and Winston, 1969, 442-453.

Geisinger, D.L. Controlling Sexual and Interpersonal Anxieties. In Krumbolts, J.D. and Thoresen, C.E. (Eds.), *Behavioral counseling: Cases and techniques.* New York: Holt, Rinehart and Winston, 1969, 454-469.

Ince, L.P. Behavior modification of sexual disorders. *American Journal of Psychotherapy* 1973, **XVII** No. III, 446-451.

Olson, K.A., & Kelley, W.R. Reduction of compulsive masturbation by electrical-aversive conditioning to verbal cues: A case report. *Canadian Psychiatry Association Journal,* 1969, **14,** 303-305.

Quinsey, V.L., Steinman, C.M., Bergersen, S.G., & Holmes, T.F. Penile circumference, skin conductance, and ranking responses of child molesters and "normals" to sexual and nonsexual visual stimuli. *Behavior Therapy,* 1975, **6,** 213-219.

Sharp, R., & Meyer, V. Modification of cognitive sexual pain by the spouse under supervision. *Behavior Therapy,* 1973, **4,** 285-287.

Name Index

This index includes authors referred to in both Volumes I and II of this Handbook. Volume I includes names on pages i to liii and 1-258. Volume II includes names on pages i to xxvi and 259-604. Roman numerals in bold type refer to Volume II.

Subject Index

This index includes subjects discussed in both Volumes I and II of this Handbook. Volume I includes subjects discussed on pages i to liii and pages 1-258. Volume II includes subjects discussed on pages i to xxvi and pages 259-604. Roman numerals in bold type refer to Volume II.